Tantra, Ritual Performance, and Politics in Nepal and Kerala

Numen Book Series

STUDIES IN THE HISTORY OF RELIGIONS

Series Editors

Steven Engler (*Mount Royal University, Calgary, Canada*)
Richard King (*University of Kent, UK*)
Kocku von Stuckrad (*University of Groningen, The Netherlands*)
Gerard Wiegers (*University of Amsterdam, The Netherlands*)

VOLUME 166

The titles published in this series are listed at *brill.com/nus*

Tantra, Ritual Performance, and Politics in Nepal and Kerala

Embodying the Goddess-Clan

By

Matthew Martin

BRILL

LEIDEN | BOSTON

Cover illustration: A Navadurgā ritual performance in Bhaktapur, Nepal. Photograph by author.

Library of Congress Cataloging-in-Publication Data

Names: Martin, Matthew, 1991- author.
Title: Tantra, ritual performance, and politics in Nepal and Kerala : embodying the goddess-clan / by Matthew Martin.
Description: Leiden ; Boston : Brill, [2020] | Series: Numen book series. Studies in the history of religions, 0169-8834 ; volume 166 | Revision of author's PhD dissertation. | Includes bibliographical references and index.
Identifiers: LCCN 2020029408 (print) | LCCN 2020029409 (ebook) | ISBN 9789004438996 (hardback) | ISBN 9789004439023 (ebook)
Subjects: LCSH: Shaktism–Rituals. | Durgā (Hindu deity)–Cult–Nepal–Bhaktapur. | Theyyam (Dance)–India–Kerala. | Durgā-pūjā (Hindu festival)–Nepal–Bhaktapur. | Religious dance–India–Kerala. | Religious dance–Nepal–Bhaktapur. | Mediums–Religious aspects–Shaktism. | Religion and politics–India–Kerala. | Religion and politics–Nepal–Bhaktapur.
Classification: LCC BL1282.255 .M37 2020 (print) | LCC BL1282.255 (ebook) | DDC 294.5/38–dc23
LC record available at https://lccn.loc.gov/2020029408
LC ebook record available at https://lccn.loc.gov/2020029409

Typeface for the Latin, Greek, and Cyrillic scripts: "Brill". See and download: brill.com/brill-typeface.

ISSN 0169-8834
ISBN 978-90-04-43899-6 (hardback)
ISBN 978-90-04-43902-3 (e-book)

This book is printed on acid-free paper and produced in a sustainable manner.

Contents

Acknowledgements IX
List of Figures X
Abbreviations XI
Style, Format, and Interview Transcriptions XII

Introduction: Methodology and Context 1
1 Folk Śākta Performances: Sovereignty, Goddesses, and Macro-Clans 3
2 Teyyāṭṭam and Navadurgā Compared: The Research Process 6
3 Methodological Orientations 7
3.1 *Anthropologically Informed Religious Studies* 8
3.2 *Methodological Node 1: Ethnographic Fieldwork* 9
3.3 *Methodological Nodes 2 and 3: Triangulating Secondary Sources and Neo-Durkheimian Theory* 11
4 Fieldwork Locations & Informant Introductions 12
4.1 *Bhaktapur, Kathmandu Valley, Nepal (February–December 2016)* 12
4.2 *Kannur, Northern Malabar, Kerala (September–December 2015 & February 2017)* 16
4.3 *Folk Śākta Performances as Spiraling Web-Like Ritual Networks* 18
4.4 *First Level: Societal* 18
4.5 *Theoretical Interlude* 19
4.6 *Second & Third Levels: Metaphysical and Political* 22
5 Contextual Background 24
5.1 *Mapping the Historical Trajectory of Indic Religion: Vedic, Brahmanical, and Tantric Systems* 24
5.2 *Political Structure in Tantric Malabar (North Kerala) and Bhaktapur: Vertical Caste Purity, Horizontal Political Kingdom, or Both?* 43
5.3 *Transregional-Regional Tantra: Teyyāṭṭam and Navadurgā in Bricolage Webs of Ritual Knowledge* 46
5.4 *'Deity Possession' as a Category: Folk Possession, Śākta Deity Embodiment, or Both?* 49
5.5 *Folk Śākta Mediums: Ancestral Divinities* 53
5.6 *Structure of the Book* 56

PART 1: CASE STUDIES

1 **Introducing the Southern Case Study—Teyyāṭṭam, Northern Malabar, Kerala** 59
1 Ancestors, Land, and Divinities (*Teyyam*) in Northern Kerala 60
2 Lineages, Clans, and Ritual Kinship 65
2.1 *Matrilineages in Kerala* 65
2.2 *A Dancer-Medium Lineage in Kannur: Pre-ritual Purification* 66
2.3 *A Teyyāṭṭam Performance in Six Stages* 67
2.4 *Stages (1) and (2): Preparations* 68
2.5 *Stages (3) and (4): Deity Embodiment* 73
3 Blood Sacrifices, Offerings, and Swords 75
3.1 *Stages (5) and (6): Sacrifice and Blessings* 77
4 Cosmology, Metaphysics, and Textual History 79
4.1 *Historical Communities in Kerala: Mappilas* 80
4.2 *Teyyāṭṭam: Hegemony, Ritual, Resistance* 85
5 Caste Identities, Politics, and Performance in North Malabar 89
5.1 *Teyyāṭṭam: Political Movements and Definition—Art, or Ritual?* 90

2 **Introducing the Northern Case Study—Navadurgā, Bhaktapur, Nepal** 93
1 Hindu-Buddhist Tantra in Newar Society: The Case of Bhaktapur 94
2 Bhaktapur City: Blood Symbols, Goddess-Clan, Space, and Society 96
3 Monsoon, Power, and the Goddess-Clan: Banmala Dancer-Mediums during the Ritual Cycle 98
3.1 *Stage (1): Gotamangal, Navadurgā God-Masks, and the Buffalo* 102
4 Blood Sacrifice, Mohani, and the Navadurgā Cycle 104
4.1 *Stage (2): Autumnal Festival of Mohani and Goddess-Clan Reanimation* 104
4.2 *Mohani: First Day* 105
4.3 *Mohani: Ninth Day* 105
4.4 *Stage (3): The Navadurgā Ritual Cycle (October–June)* 106
5 Cosmology, Tantric Texts, and Newar Hinduism in Bhaktapur 110
6 Politics and Caste Structures in Bhaktapur 113
6.1 *Newar Social Structure: Kinship, Caste, and Guṭhi in Bhaktapur* 115
6.2 *Politics in Bhaktapur: NWPP Communism* 117

PART 2: THEMES

3 **Dancer-Medium Communities and Ritual Kinship** 123
1 Introduction 123
2 Dancer-Medium Communities: Teyyāṭṭam and Navadurgā 123
3 Teyyāṭṭam 125
3.1 *Communities in North Kerala* 125
3.2 *Kōlakkaran among Three Communities* 134
3.3 *Processes of Teyyam Embodiment: Rites, Narratives, and Power* 139
4 Navadurgā 144
4.1 *Bhaktapur's Navadurgā Troupe: A Family of* ujāju 144
4.2 *Preparing To Be a Banmala Medium: The Career of a Troupe Member* 148
4.3 *Banmala Bodies: Masks, Ritual Cycles, and Tantric Power* 153
5 Conclusion 161

4 **History and Assimilation in Tantric Cosmology** 163
1 Introduction 163
2 Teyyāṭṭam 165
2.1 *Tantric Texts, Temples, and Kingship in Northern Kerala* 165
2.2 *Interactions between Tantric Texts, Teyyāṭṭam Rituals, and Sacerdotal Communities in Kerala* 174
2.3 *Multivalence in the Cosmology of Teyyāṭṭam* 180
3 Navadurgā 184
3.1 *Newar Tantra, Texts, and Local Deities in Bhaktapur* 184
3.2 *The Autumnal Festival of Mohani: Transactions between Navadurgā, Taleju, and Kingship in Bhaktapur* 190
3.3 *Navadurgā Performances, Banmala Mediums, and Somatic Texts* 195
4 Conclusion 200

5 **Sacrifice, Earth Cycles, and Self-Reflexive Affect** 202
1 Introduction 202
2 Teyyāṭṭam 204
2.1 *Chicken Sacrifice at the Northern Altars: Terrestrial Goddesses, Warfare, and Communion* 204
2.2 *Sacrifice as Self-Reflexive Affect: Narratives on Sacrifice and Emotion in Malabar* 214

3 Navadurgā 217
3.1 *Sacrifice in Newar Bhaktapur: Lineage Deities, Goats, and Buffaloes* 217
3.2 *Sacrifice to Navadurgā Dancer-Mediums: Five-Animal Sacrifice (pañcābali), the 'Shivers' (jhinjhan minjan) and Self-reflexive Affect* 225
4 Conclusion 228

6 Politics, Ritual Performance, and Caste 229
1 Introduction 229
2 Marxist-Influenced Politics and Ritual Performance in Postcolonial South Asia 230
3 Teyyāṭṭam 233
3.1 *Kerala Revolutionaries: The Historical Emergence of CPI(M) Politics* 233
3.2 *'What Is Pure and What Is Impure, Please Tell Us!': Teyyam Narratives, Lower-Caste Resistance, and Existential Politics* 241
4 Navadurgā 245
4.1 *The Historical Emergence of NWPP in Bhaktapur: 1964 Land Reform, Caste Subservience, and Newar Farmers* 245
4.2 *Religious-Communism 'Interpellated': Navadurgā, Folk Performance, and "Marxism"* 252
5 Conclusion 258

Conclusion 260
1 Teyyāṭṭam and Navadurgā Compared: Revisited 261
2 Dancer-Medium Communities and Ritual Kinship 263
3 History and Metaphysical Underlays of Folk Śākta Ritual 264
4 Blood Sacrifice and Self-Reflexive Affect 264
5 Politics and Caste Structure 265

Glossary of Key Terms 267
Bibliography 274
Index 290

Acknowledgements

First and foremost, I wish to thank several interlocutors I had the honour of meeting during my fieldwork in South Asia. In Kerala, I thank the dancer-medium troupes, especially 'Akash' and his family, for their generosity, time, and explanations. The gracious assistance of my home-stay hosts, Nazeer and Roshanara, was also very much appreciated. In Nepal, I am grateful to Kailash for providing useful contacts at the fieldwork's early stages. Special thanks go to the Banmalas—particularly 'Ujesh', 'Krishna', 'Dinesh', and 'Babita'—for their hospitality, patience, and tutelage: *Banmala pariwaar lai ek dam dherai dhanyabaad.*

This research would not have been possible without the financial support provided by the Arts and Humanities Research Council (AHRC), Pembroke College, and the Spalding Trust, and I express gratitude to all these organizations. I also thank my supervisors at Oxford, Gavin Flood and Sondra Hausner, for their continued support; their rigorous erudition is also an inspiration. At Universität Heidelberg, Laxmi Nath convened a comprehensive Summer School in Nepali Language (Summer 2015), and I am thankful to Laxmi ji for his tuition. During the doctorate, Graham Ward, Justin Jones, Jessica Frazier, and David Gellner provided constructive feedback on earlier versions of this work, for which I am grateful. Bjarne Wernicke-Olesen and Roland Hardenberg examined this work, and I thank them for their guidance.

At Brill, I thank Tessa Schild and Laura Morris for their help during the manuscript's submission. I also thank the two anonymous reviewers for their detailed comments on the monograph.

Most importantly, I extend love and gratitude to my family, who continually encourage my efforts. And, at Ysgol Gyfun Ystalyfera, I thank the Religious Studies department ('Astudiaethau Crefyddol')—Mrs Gibbs, Mrs Richards, and Mrs Roberts. Their engaging enthusiasm for Religious Studies inspired my journey to this point; *estynaf ddiolch arbennig i chi.*

Figures

1 Goddess *Cāmuṇḍi* in performance (Kannur, Kerala). Photograph by author 61
2 Early morning Teyyāṭṭam performance (Kannur, Kerala). Photograph by author 64
3 Pre-ritual preparations in the make-up hut (Kannur, Kerala). Photograph by author 69
4 Offerings to an enshrined deity (Kannur, Kerala). Photograph by author 72
5 A god distributing blessings. Photograph by author 78
6 A Teyyam goddess. Photograph by author 87
7 Navadurgā Performance. Photograph by author 103
8 Portable shrine of goddess Mahālakṣṃī. Photograph by author 107
9 *Māviliya Gandharvan Kāvu,* (Kannur, Kerala), 17th November 2015. Photograph by author 130
10 Female priestess, 17th November 2015. Photograph by author 132
11 Shrine of Gulikkan (god of time). Photograph by author 140
12 Tripartite oil-wicks holder. Photograph by author 141
13 Annotated floor plan of *dyo bokegu,* Navadurgā Temple (outside entranceway), (Gacchen Twā, Bhaktapur). Illustration by author 158
14 Offerings (*dyo bokegu*) to the Navadurgā, (Dhulikel, Nepal). Photograph by author 159
15 Śri Andalur Kāvu, Thalassery, Kerala. Photograph by author 175
16 Maṇipravālam manual. Photograph by author 180
17 *Kaḷam*. Photograph by author 207
18 Wayanād Kuḻīvan. Photograph by author 211
19 Goat sacrifice, (Kamalpokharī, Bhaktapur). Photograph by author 219
20 Communist monument outside Parasinikkadavu Muttappan temple, (Kannur, Kerala). Photograph by author 237

Abbreviations

BJP	Bharatiya Janata Party
CE	Common Era
CPI(M)	Communist Party of India (Marxist)
CSP	Congress Socialist Party
CUP	Cambridge University Press
Inf.	Informant
Lit.	Literally
Maly.	Malayalam
MM	Matthew Martin
Nepa.	Nepali
Newa.	Newari—Bhaktapurian dialect
NWPP	Nepal's Workers and Peasants Party
NSA	Nityāṣodaśikārṇava
OUP	Oxford University Press
RSS	Rashtriya Swayamsevak Sangh (Party)
SA	Śeṣasamuccaya
Skt.	Sanskrit
TS	Tantrasamuccaya
VS	Vikram-Sambat (Hindu lunar calendar)
§	Section sign used in the text to denote a sub-section or chapter

Style, Format, and Interview Transcriptions

Each case study in this book—Teyyāṭṭam, Kerala, and Navadurgā, Bhaktapur, Nepal—is grounded in a differing locale and is based on distinct languages. For Teyyāṭṭam these are Malayalam and Sanskrit, while for Navadurgā, its languages are Nepali, a Bhaktapurian dialect of Newari, and Sanskrit. All words and phrases transliterated from these languages will be italicized in the text and noted using standard diacritical marks (*jātrā, kalaripayāṭṭu* etc.).

Names of specific informants ('Ujesh', 'Krishna', 'Akaś' etc.) are pseudonyms. Any public political figures mentioned in Chapter 6 are their actual names elicited from readings and newspaper articles.

Certain quoted information and interview sections have been abridged to condense this material for the reader; in these instances, abridged material will be noted with a '[...]'. Extracts from interview material will adhere to the following format:

> [MM:] ...
> [Inf.] ...

Introduction: Methodology and Context

Across mid-medieval South Asia, two petty kingdoms—one Southern and another Northern—bestowed an honorary obligation upon certain subaltern lineages. On grounds of sovereign loyalty, these lineages were conferred as the land's dancer-mediums, whose task was to embody ancestor deities, commanded by the king's goddess-clan ('Nine Durgās'[1] in Bhaktapur or 'Seven Mothers'[2] in Kerala), who flanked that kingdom's political perimeters. In rotational ritual performances—scheduled by agricultural cycles and military deployment—male mediums donned god-masks or headdresses to mobilize sword-wielding divinities into their bodies. Such performances continue into the present, and, as dancing deities, mediums sacrifice animals to appease them, and, in Kerala, they sing narratives recounting their histories. As a result, mediums can summon a deity's power from royal shrines and lineage temples to induce many awe-inspiring feats. Medium-troupes are also bestowers of material well-being; devout votaries—from lower castes—might also seek their services as tantric healers, fertility enhancers, and prophesying diviners. The "Tantric" techniques of mediumship applied in these ritual performances—what I label Folk Śākta performances—maintain an unshakable presence today throughout the subcontinent, but this study is limited to two regional case studies: Teyyāṭṭam (lit. 'dance of the deity') in Northern Malabar, Kerala, and Navadurgā *pyākhan̩* (lit. 'the dance of the Nine Durgās') among the Newars of Bhaktapur, Nepal.

Typologically, Folk Śākta performances are collective festivals designated as "Tantric" (lit. 'to weave', 'web', or 'vein-network'[3]). Among Indologists and anthropologists alike, "Tantra" is a particularly contentious category: in its broadest sense, it denotes a mélange of extra-Vedic, ritual-focused cultic schools composed of various interlapping ideas about body and cosmos that span centuries across the Indian subcontinent. These schools arose around the 5th century CE until they reached their developmental apex circa. 11th–13th centuries CE. By 'extra-vedic', I mean the ways Tantric cults developed

1 The 'Nine Durgās' (*Navadurgā*) are a clan of related goddesses, whose names are: Brahmāṇī, Indrāṇī, Maheśvarī, Mahākālī, Bhadrākālī, Kumārī, Varāhī, Tripurasundarī, and Mahālakṣmī.

2 The 'Seven Mothers' (*Saptamātṛkā*) are also a goddess-clan, whose goddesses are: Brahmāṇī, Maheśvari, Kumārī, Vaiṣṇavi, Varāhi, Indrāṇī, and Cāmuṇḍi.

3 'Tantra' in *A Sanskrit-English Dictionary*, by M.A. Monier-Williams, (Oxford: Clarendon Press, 1872).

 DOI:10.1163/9789004439023_002

as ruptured traditions from an already pre-existing Vedic ideology. (Although, as Brooks contends, Tantra is often pigeonholed as an esoteric heterodoxy (*rahasya*) which emerged in opposition to the orthodoxy of Vedism that predated it[4]). Emic descriptions, collated during my fieldwork, show how "Tantra"—in Newari and Keralan society—expresses a mode of collective worship characterized by its use of pollutive substances, like blood sacrifice and alcohol, which is aimed at accruing material power for a polity or medieval kingdom. These offerings—whether blood-based or grown in the earth—placate a fierce, but tutelary, divinity (be that a goddess-clan, Bhairava, Gaṇeśa, or a deified ancestor). This placation, in effect, releases a circuit of worldly energy (*śakti*) conglomerated across the civic body's castes, family acreages, and Tantric lineages in the guise of lineage divinities, whom lower-caste mediums incarnate.[5] The god-troupes who embody these local deities must be initiated into distinctively low-birth lineages: interestingly, all these lineages—despite their low-caste status on society's peripheries—are linked totemically to a sovereign goddess-clan, and within performance, they radiate this power to heterogenous participants sojourned there. To this day, god-troupes circumambulate a kingdom's boundary and, in civic or temple spaces, they are worshipped in communion with their devotees. During a festival season, these peripatetic performances are conducted annually in nine-monthly cycles timed by tillage patterns, which uproots corporeal power into bodies. Flood describes how, for most Śākta traditions, 'ritual cycles [...] are closely associated with seasonal changes and worship of the Goddess, identified with the earth'.[6]

These goddess-oriented Tantric performances—focused on kings, territory, and ancestors—are, I suggest, particular to Northern Kerala and the Kathmandu Valley. Outside these areas—in North India's Gangetic plateau (Bengal and Kashmir)—Tantric schools were alternatively organized as esoteric cults dedicated to specific deities who have no public veneer.[7] For their initiated neophytes, these cults were, and are, clandestine lineages (*gotra*) aimed at soteriological goals of world liberation. By contrast, Folk Śākta performances

4 Douglas Brooks, *The Secret of the Three Cities*, (Chicago: University of Chicago Press, 1990), pp. 17–18.

5 Sax calls this Indic view, 'distributive agency', that is, a deity is "built up, as it were, from subordinate forms of agency distributed amongst individuals, families, clans [etc.]". See William Sax, 'Agency' in *Theorizing Rituals: Issues, Topics, Approaches*, ed. By Jan Kreinath et al., (Leiden: Brill, 2008), p. 481.

6 Gavin Flood, *An Introduction to Hinduism* (Cambridge: CUP, 1996), p. 196.

7 Alexis Sanderson, 'Śaivism and the Tantric Traditions' in *The World's Religions*, ed. by Stewart Sutherland et al., (London: Routledge, 1988), p. 661.

are formulated as **public** Tantric festivals sponsored by the state (previously the king), during which worldly divinities are reanimated within the bodies of dancer-mediums attached hereditarily to a low-birth clan.

1 Folk Śākta Performances: Sovereignty, Goddesses, and Macro-Clans

For folk Śākta performances—either Navadurgā or Teyyāṭṭam—local gods and goddesses are ceremonially awakened within dancer-mediums, priests, and worshippers who join forces as intimate *ritual kin* to glorify them. Here, 'ritual kinship' refers to a distinct form of inter-group coherence created in ritual that unifies a territory's heterogeneous families as a **macro-clan**[8] via the communal worship of a royal pantheon which, in our context, manifests as a clan of goddesses bestriding animal vehicles (*vahana*). (Throughout this book, ritual kinship is also described as a state of *affective kin-like intentionality*).

All Folk Śākta deities—terrestrially enshrined—are kindred to this regal goddess-clan as ancestral revenants of a polity's territory. Outside a Folk Śākta performance, these deities are 'family gods' (Skt: *kul daiva*) installed near land-tracts of proletarian kin groups ('lineages') on the margins of a former medieval kingdom: but, in ritual performance, these gods—whether fierce goddesses or ancestral warriors—are pooled and reconceptualized as ritual kin, that is, mothers, uncles, or sisters of the body politic, who, together, invigorate the civic order. Such ritual kinship is assembled among circumscribed lineages through flows of pollutive gifts (blood sacrifices, food etc.) with enclave deities rendered intravenously in low-caste mediums. These gifts are not commodities[9] as such, but extensions of subterranean feminine energy, fructified by monsoon rains, that props a polity's all-pervading power (*śakti*).

In a similar fashion, among the goddess dancers[10] (*devadāsī*) of Jagannātha temple (Odisha), Marglin explains how food, and, conceptually, menstrual

8 By a 'macro-clan', I mean a territory-wide cohesion of usually segregated or endogamous kin groups.

9 Capital profit-making defines a 'commodity', unlike the sociality of gifts. See Arjun Appadurai, ed., *The Social Life of Things: Commodities in Cultural Perspective*, (Cambridge: CUP, 1986), pp. 11–12.

10 'Devadāsīs' are royal female dancers who perform outside Odisha's Jagannātha temple; their status as nonmarried or unchaste ritualists is enounced in their designation as fertile 'prostitutes or courtesans'. See Frédérique A. Marglin, *Wives of the God-King: The Rituals of the Devadasis of Puri*, (Oxford: OUP, 1985), p. 98.

blood are biodegradable 'leftovers [...] which return to the earth'[11] that, in ritual, are distributed to unify the kingdom's life-force (*śakti*) to increase its fecundity. Marglin explains:

> The king's function of bringing good rains [...] depends on a specifically female life force concretely manifested in female sexual fluid. This female life force can be conceptualized as the female aspect of sovereignty, and the *devadasis* represent it in the world [...] The sharing of sovereignty [...] crosscuts caste ranking [...] Auspiciousness, unlike purity, does not speak of status ranking, but a nonhierarchical state of general well-being.[12]

In Odisha, *devadāsī* dances—with their focus on 'female life force'—dissolve caste to strengthen an entire (ex-)kingdom's auspiciousness (*maṅgala*). Contrary to Hocart's understanding of liturgical ritual as the origin of caste society,[13] *devadāsī* rituals, rather, dismantle caste in place of the territory's worldly auspiciousness, albeit ad interim. In Bhaktapur's Navadurgā temple—dedicated to their Malla kings—aspects of 'auspiciousness' also feature, since the Sanskrit term for auspiciousness, *maṅgala*, is inscribed in a *mantra* on a wooden beam in its ceremonial space.[14]

Although, unlike Odishan *devadāsīs*, Folk Śākta performances differ, for they circulate *śakti*, as gift exchanges, between a locale's moiety structure—the segregation of caste 'purity' and the togetherness of lineage 'impurity'—that form *spiral* formations across them. By spiraling a society's moiety order, the group is ritually transformed into a synthetic *web-like ritual network* to effectuate the ritual's auspicious ends. To summarize: 'web-like ritual networks' are sequences of ritual cohesion—portrayed aesthetically in cosmic diagrams (*maṇḍalas*)—that interconnect an (ex-)kingdom's lineages and castes with gods and ancestors as a macro-clan, by attuning them, through blood sacrifice, with agrarian cycles symbolized by a goddess-clan's menstrual synchrony. By calling on combined ancestral power in this way, Folk Śākta performances—as *web-like ritual networks*—strengthen collective agency to boost crops, induce bravery, or criticize societal oppression. Within ritual performance, social togetherness—

11 Frédérique A. Marglin, 'Refining the Body: Transformative Emotion in Ritual Dance', in *Divine Passions: The Social Construction of Emotion in India*, ed. by Owen Lynch, (Berkeley: University of California Press, 1990), p. 215.

12 Ibid., p. 216.

13 Maurice Hocart, *Caste: A Comparative Study* (London: Metheuen, 1950).

14 For a transcription of this mantra (known as the *argala strotra*), see § 3.4.3.

bodies and land in sync, past and present—is the auspicious ground of ancestral vitality (*śakti*) which male mediums, of low birth, evoke.

Folk Śākta performances, then, are collective spectacles, wherein sets of dichotomies—e.g. human/divine, pure/impure—converge as ritual kin in *web-like ritual networks*. Socially adhesive rituals like these magnify empowerment and public proximity in a platial[15] group, as against private endogamy-enclosed worship. Indeed, when a natural disaster strikes, these rituals' aptitude for communal cohesion becomes spotlighted in the extreme, and, on 25th April 2015, a devastating earthquake hit Nepal's Kathmandu Valley:[16] a year later, after the tremors subsided, most of my informants affirmed that devotion to the Navadurgā-clan—their terrifyingly powerful 'mothers'—had deepened.

∴

Informed, in part, by ethnographic fieldwork, this book will compare two Folk Śākta Performances with the aim of shining new theoretical light on Śākta traditions. Catalyzed by the project's empirical depth, this fresh perspective will incorporate classical theory on ritual performance—inaugurated in Durkheim's scholarly lineage—into a contextual network of emic theories and understandings. As a starting point, the study's initial research questions will be posed as follows: (1) Can culturally *Keralan* (Teyyāṭṭam) and *Newari* (Navadurgā) performances be compared as historically related phenomena? Did these distant cultures partake in overlapping, but distinct, pan-South Asian Tantric traditions stemming from the medieval era? To be sure, both performances self-identify—both textually and in praxis—as lower-caste Śākta Tantric or 'goddess-oriented' traditions; (2) Assuming (1) is the case, did Navadurgā and Teyyāṭṭam inherit any structural-multifunctional resemblances? Their teleologies, for example, are associated with transforming an individual's or group's worldly experience and aspirations in ritual by putting communal power to good use; and (3) What implications can this study illuminate for Durkheim's position on ritual performances as *collective effervescence*? Can this comparative study bring to light some overlooked debates in Durkheimian Studies, such as the role of historical process, political movements, and doctrinal or textual formation in collective ritual? By echoing the goddess-clan, perhaps we can network Durkheim's academic lineage with Weber's and Marx's to, potentially, uncover his quiescent nuances.

---

15 'Platial' is the adjectival form of 'place', just as 'space' is adjectivally 'spatial'.

16 For Newars, earthquakes are caused by immorality, demons, or lack of devotion to the deities.

2 Teyyāṭṭam and Navadurgā Compared: The Research Process

Before I started research on this book, my interest in ritual performance—particularly subaltern ones where mediums channeled their ancestors—meant I had read widely on styles of Tantric possession and mediumship in Kerala. With some further investigation, I realized that these Folk Śākta phenomena were not insular to Kerala alone; Newars in the Kathmandu Valley also had a tradition of dancer-mediums that appeared sometime before the 16th Century CE. In identifying such parallels between Kerala and the Newars, it transpired that my initial observations were not unfounded ones. Axel Michaels, for example, presents a series of relations—cultural, mythological, and commercial—that existed between Nepal and South India (specifically Kerala) around the 12th–13th Century.[17] In addition, the compendia of D.R. Regmi provides lucid historical data which, again, draws parallels between Kerala and the Newars.[18] In these sources, three points of evidence are specifically resonant for this study: (1) the well-known legend that the Newars may be ethnically originated from the Nāyars of Malabar; (2) how pagoda-style architecture, definitive of Newar civilization, is replicated in some regions of Southern Kerala; and (3) how Brahman priests from South India migrated to Nepal's Valley to worship at Paśupatināth, a temple complex—dedicated to Śiva—in Kathmandu.[19]

In Chapter 4, I claim these cultural resonances were actualized through the circulation of Tantric literature between Northern and Southern South Asia. Throughout the mid-medieval period, this transmigration of ideas was possible through the teachings of householder ascetics (*Nāth*), who navigated the subcontinent's pilgrimage sites equipped with their Tantric literature.[20] One such corpora was the Nityāṣodśikārṇava [NSA], a Tantric text that formed the cult of Tripurasundarī, which is extant in Nepal and Malabar. In both regions, Lidke and Freeman confirm that cosmic diagrams associated with NSA—the *Śrīcakra maṇḍalas*—are used regionally in royal Tantric temple-worship.[21] Moreover,

17 Axel Michaels, 'On 12th–13th Century Relations between Nepal and South India', *Journal of the Nepal Research Centre*, 7 (1985), pp. 69–73.

18 D.R. Regmi, *Medieval Nepal Vols. I & II* (Kolkata: Rupa & Co., 1965b).

19 Michaels, 'On 12th–13th Century Relations between Nepal and South India', pp. 69–73.

20 James Mallinson, 'Nāth Sampradaya', in *Brill's Encyclopedia of Hinduism*, ed. by Knut Jamison et al., (Leiden: Brill, 2011) for a detailed summary of Nāth traditions.

21 Jeffrey S. Lidke, 'The Resounding Field of Visualised Self-awareness', *Journal of Hindu Studies*, 4 (2011), p. 249 & John R. Freeman, 'Śāktism, polity, and society in Medieval Malabar', in *Goddess Traditions in Tantric Hinduism: History, Practice, and Doctrine*, (London: Routledge, 2016), p. 156.

Śākta song literature—in Newari and Malayalam—also reflects Śākta intertextuality; Sanjukta Gupta verifies how each locality participated in contiguous Śākta-style *mantra* praxes.[22] Several contemporary resonances exist, too, between Bhaktapur and Northern Malabar that are equally engaging: both areas practice Tantric religion as dominant paradigms of public religiosity; and both regions became bastions of Marxist-influenced ideology with the advent of mid-20th Century postcolonialism. (Though Nepal was never colonized by the British). Newars and Northern Keralans, then, share a Śākta Tantric worldview and a political allegiance to communism grounded in culturally particular manifestations; the two cultures are distinct yet congruous, set like interlocking spirals.

To date, no academic work has directly juxtaposed Northern and Southern, or Newari and Keralan Tantra for comparative analysis. In scholarly circles, comparative perspectives on Śākta religion receive scant scholarly attention. By coordinating fieldwork with historico-cultural study, this book offers new insights which advance our understanding of Folk Śākta performances (including how intertextuality mobilized the development of this Śākta practice between Nepal and South India). Until now, most ethnographic accounts of modern Tantric groups are critiqued **either** for overlooking issues of Tantric textuality, **or** for comprehending subaltern practices from the purview of elite informants.[23] In a timely shift towards textually-aligned ethnography, Freeman's *oeuvre* on Teyyāṭṭam succeeds in integrating various ethno-historical perspectives, particularly from dancer-mediums themselves. In that light, this book will consolidate the voices of dancer-mediums—gathered in conversation and informal interviews—as tantamount to a *counter-narrative*.[24]

3 Methodological Orientations

Widely conceived, this book is situated at the intersection of social science and humanities viz. the human sciences. As such, its approach is set within

22 Teun Goudriaan & Sanjukta Gupta., ed., *Hindu Tantric and Śākta Literature* (Wiesbaden: Otto Harrassowitz, 1981), p. 177.

23 Todd Lewis, 'Review of *Mesocosm: Hinduism and the Organization of a Traditional Hindu Newar City in Bhaktapur* by Robert I. Levy', *Himalayan Research Bulletin* [*Himalaya*], 14.1 (1994), pp. 53–55.

24 'Counter-narratives' are "the stories which people tell and live which offer resistance, either implicitly or explicitly, to dominant cultural narratives" in Michael Bamberg & Molly Andrews, ed., *Considering Counter-Narratives: Narrating, Resisting, Making Sense* (Amsterdam: John Benjamins Publishing, 2004) p. 1.

the boundaries of Religious Studies, which triangulates, neutrally, between secondary sources, fieldwork observations, and social theory. As indicated by Ninian Smart,[25] Religious Studies is a 'methodologically agnostic' discipline that takes the object of study—**religion**—as entry point into potential methodological perspectives that display religion's polyvalence as a social phenomenon. In line with the Durkheimian tradition, I agree with Clifford Geertz here: culture, with religion, co-influence social complexity.[26]

Throughout the book, I define 'culture' as a ground of multi-individual connectivity—geographically proximate or dispersed—that establishes a sense of belonging through common cosmologies, praxes, histories, genealogies, and concepts vis-à-vis embodied or in-the-world existence. As a category of group belonging, 'religion', too, displays many of these elements, except that 'religion', throughout the centuries, has been (re-)constructed through various power-structures from differing discursive vantage points, whether hegemonic, subaltern, or institutional. This stance—a postmodernist one, endorsed famously by Talal Asad—asserts that the category of 'religion', as we perceive it today (namely as an axiomatic reality), was compounded during the colonial age: under colonialism's control, the religio-cultural worlds of colonized peoples were modified into bounded 'religions' commensurate with Protestant, not indigenous, ideals of 'religion' which, Asad argues, enabled colonial dominion (i.e. over a colony's socio-economic resources in particular).[27]

3.1 *Anthropologically Informed Religious Studies*

Analyzing 'religion' as a human construct—whichever locale or timeframe we may encounter it—can be interpreted through diverse methodological lenses. For the human sciences, contemporary 'religion' is tended, most efficaciously, via an **anthropological** approach that examines 'religion' manifested in culturally specific contexts. Looking exclusively to the past, **historians of religions** sift through documented or archival accounts of 'religion', *in situ*, across delineated periods of time. In this book, however, I seek to fuse elements of the two as a self-confected method of *anthropologically informed religious studies*, that is, an emic-focused approach that shifts systematically between three methodological nodes—'anthropological', secondary 'historical', and 'theoretical'—through an analysis of ritual's core dimensions, which

---

25 Ninian Smart, *The Phenomenon of Religion* (London & Basingstoke: Macmillan Press, 1973).

26 Clifford Geertz, *The Interpretation of Cultures*, (New York: Basic Books, 1973), p. 119.

27 Talal Asad, *Genealogies of Religion: Discipline and Reasons of Power in Christianity and Islam* (Baltimore: The John Hopkins University Press, 1993).

are: history, social structure, sacrifice, and politics. In this way, I am influenced by Richard King's approach to Religious Studies: for King, scholars of religion—unlike theologians—eschew 'truth-claims' in their studies of 'religion', by, instead, applying an unbiased, objective (or anthropology-esque) position as developed in cultural studies.[28]

The first node of my research model—'anthropology'—encompassed modern-day interactions with dancer-medium communities through ethnographic fieldwork (or 'participant-observation'), which entailed spending time—culturally immersed—among these groups. The duration of my field-study lasted some twelve months altogether and was undertaken in two separate field-sites: Bhaktapur, Nepal and Kannur, Kerala. (Admittedly, however, my fieldwork was not always unfettered—largely in Kerala—where issues of community access caused periodic delays). During this time, I observed some fifty Teyyāṭṭam and Navadurgā performances, as well as other aspects of religio-cultural life that were obliquely connected to these performances, such as autumnal festivals and ritualized healing. For a large part of the research, I conducted a series of semi-structured interviews with a range of informants, some of which were voice-recorded with consent. I also enjoyed speaking with people in colloquial exchanges too: these valuable interactions occurred during pertinent gaps between ritual performances, when interlocutors were most dynamized in responding to my questions. In Part 2, all these ethnographic descriptions will be presented as reflexive accounts set within a broader discussion of scholarly literature. Below, I discuss each methodological node—ethnographic fieldwork, secondary historical literature, and theory—in turn.

3.2 *Methodological Node 1: Ethnographic Fieldwork*

In his magnum opus, *The Interpretation of Cultures*, Clifford Geertz promulgated 'thick descriptions' as definitive of anthropological writing. In line with anthropologists who preceded him, he endorsed participant-observation—cultural immersion within social groups—and qualitative interviewing as pivotal to an ethnographic field-study. For socio-cultural anthropologists, the output of fieldwork forms an ethnography or 'thick description', which constitutes a text, or report, detailing a community's cultural milieu as experienced during cultural immersion. Geertz states: 'Anthropologists don't study villages (tribes, towns, neighborhoods …); they study in villages'.[29] As Davies shows, ethnography should also coalesce postmodernist stances—an 'archaeology of knowl-

28 Richard King, *Orientalism and Religion*, (London: Routledge, 1999).

29 Clifford Geertz, *The Interpretation of Cultures* (New York: Basic Books, 1973), p. 21.

edge'[30] as Foucault called it—by acknowledging the ways knowledge is produced and re-produced through structures of power (colonial or otherwise). She notes:

> [...] ethnographers must seek to utilize creatively the insights of those postmodernist perspectives—[...] incorporation of varying standpoints [etc.] The research is a conduit that allows interpretations and influences to pass in both directions [between ethnographer and informants].[31]

In this spirit, my research—as an ethno-historical investigation—was sensitive to these crucial epistemic matters.

Out in the field, I adhered to anthropology's reflexive approach, defined here as deep communicative engagement with interlocutors in their shared cultural environments that dissolves the analyst-study (or subject-object) boundary. The ethnographer's course of action—viz. co-habiting with a group to co-experience their sociocultural life—establishes a genuine connection with fellow informants: certainly, among my host family in Bhaktapur, I was accepted as the family's fictive relative, their *videśī dāju* (lit. 'foreign brother'). Through social connectivity, experience and analysis mutually reinforce a *multi-layered translation* of that community's culture, which the analyst interweaves with first-hand observations and life-stories he or she accrues in reciprocal dialogue: materiality, subjectivity, and body language texture cultural worlds, as do words, concepts, or texts. By embracing participant-observation, the analyst secures an accurate representation of the cultural situation, which later forms the 'thick description'.

Participant-observation, then, constitutes a panoptic immersion in the lives of one's informants, which generates a *multi-layered translation* of the cultural situation. By 'multi-layered translation' I mean the collation of data and knowledge—in all forms—that extracts a series of non-linguistic subtleties otherwise excluded from non-anthropological analyses (e.g. narratives, dispositions, and material objects). On rare occasions during fieldwork, I noticed how responses from certain informants seemed somewhat contrived, as if they had recapitulated an official or formulaic ideology. To counter this impediment, I began observing nonverbal cues—body language and material culture usage—whilst also documenting multiple narratives from diverse individuals. Only by observing attentively can anthropologists, or ethno-religionists,

---

30 Michel Foucault, *The Archaeology of Knowledge* (London: Routledge Classics, 2002 [1969]).

31 Charlotte Davies, *Reflexive Ethnography: A guide to researching selves and others* (London: Routledge, 1999), pp. 5–6.

produce stronger interpretations of the cultural context(s). Yet, logistically, attaining thoroughgoing ethnographic consistency cannot always be achieved, especially if one's task is to examine two field-sites, as this book does. Multi-sited fieldwork does not adhere to the long-term cultural immersion that the discipline advocates. Indeed, at the best of times, human behaviour can be idiosyncratic and arbitrary; not every person or group a researcher encounters on fieldwork—in two field-sites—will be wholeheartedly cooperative, and understandably so. Gaining the trust of one's interlocutors and vice versa, in whatever field, requires years of fieldwork engagement. Luckily, in Kerala and Bhaktapur, my interlocutors were always collaborative and communicative in relaying their cultural life-worlds, either in interviews or informal exchanges.

By and large, multi-sited fieldwork requires sedulous cross-checking of data sources, which, in this book, is derived largely from previous anthropological literature. The secondary literature in this study will serve as an empirical foundation that contextualizes the sites for the researcher. It is to a discussion of secondary literature that I now turn.

3.3 *Methodological Nodes 2 and 3: Triangulating Secondary Sources and Neo-Durkheimian Theory*

To solve the logistical issues many multi-sited fieldworkers face, researchers of contemporary religion or culture must rigorously contextualize their research by cross-checking literature or informant samples that reinforces their data. This model—also known as 'triangulating research designs'—is advised by LeCompte and Goetz; this framework was formulated from their critique of participant-observation as a method in isolation. They argue that ethnography—mainly multi-sited fieldwork—can pose certain problems regarding the overall validity of informant data. As an alternative, triangulating between data sources requires: '[using] a variety of strategies, including listing, Q-sorting, and constant cross-checking in discussion with informants. Triangulating many data sources formalizes the meanings [...] to ensure that interpretation[s] [...] are examined rather than assumed'.[32]

This book's method—*anthropologically informed religious studies*—brings my own fieldwork data—from Nepal and Kerala—into comparative conversation with social history and ethnographic literature. My fieldwork descriptions, then, will add to scholarly debates insofar as they update the literature: indeed, many ethnographies of Newari and Keralan societies were conducted in the

32 Margaret D. LeCompte & Judith P. Goetz, 'Problems of Reliability and Validity in Ethnographic Research', *Review of Educational Research*, 52.1 (1982), p. 53.

1980s–2000s, and undoubtably, these communities have undergone considerable change in recent years. For instance, in this work, I have included details of socio-political events or disasters—in Nepal and Kerala—that occurred there, i.e. the effects of the 2015 earthquake in Bhaktapur: these contemporary issues were inevitable points of discussion for my interlocutors, which I sought to ascertain in conversation with them.

For the Teyyāṭṭam case study, my field observations are placed in dialogue with the following literature: (1) anthropologists Freeman, Gabriel, Tarabout, and Vadakinnyil on Teyyāṭṭam; (2) Gough, Freeman, Fuller, and Osella on Keralan history and society; and (3) political scientists Menon, Jeffrey, and Chaturvedi on Kerala's politics. And, for the Navadurgā case study, I discuss: (1) Levy, Parish, Toffin, Gellner, Teilhet, Vergati and Grieve on Bhaktapurian and Newari culture; and (2) Hacchettu and Gibson on Bhaktapur's politics.

Throughout this study, the method's theoretical node will network Durkheim, Weber, Marx, and their descendants—Mauss, Bloch, Geertz etc.—whose discussions on exchange, kinship, *assemblage*, history, and politics enhanced their ancestors' ground-breaking studies on society, religion, and ritual. The fusion of Durkheimian thought on religion—traced in the *Elementary Forms of Religious Life*—alongside the work of Marx, Weber, and their descendants I call Neo-Durkheimian. This Neo-Durkheimian stance on ritual will complement the four dimensions examined in Chapters 3–6: community; history; sacrifice; and politics. All the concepts listed here feature prominently in Neo-Durkheimian approaches to ritual, **and** in studies of South Asian Tantric ritual.

4 Fieldwork Locations & Informant[33] Introductions

4.1 *Bhaktapur, Kathmandu Valley, Nepal (February–December 2016)*

In Nepal, Bhaktapur is known as the 'city of devotees' situated some 10 km east of Kathmandu. Within the Kathmandu Valley's basin, the cities of Kathmandu, Bhaktapur, and Lalitpur—originally three medieval kingdoms ruled by Newar dynasties—are administrative loci for the settlements (villages and towns) surrounding them. Bhaktapur's position on the eastern side of the basin means it was a hub of trade with neighbouring Tibet and China; Bhaktapur was proclaimed for its commercial trade of precious metals. These metals—bronze and silver—were sold to other cities of the Valley to decorate their temple com-

33 To note, I use the terms 'interlocutor' and 'informant' interchangeably, and detailed biographies of all interlocutors are provided in Chapter 3.

plexes: the interior of Lalitpur's temples, for instance, are metallic, whereas Bhaktapur's are wood-carved. The location of Bhaktapur city—elevated on a hill above the Valley basin—is also atypical, and until recently, many Bhaktapurians, most of them farmers, remained insular, with older generations, including my informants' grandparents, speaking exclusively in Bhaktapur's Newari dialect. It is fair to say that Bhaktapur, though a thoroughfare for foreign trade, is (and has always been) a hermit kingdom in its own right.

Having arrived in Nepal, I decided to live in Bhaktapur City itself—which was most productive—and for the first trip (February–May 2016), I lived at a home stay in Durbar Square. At first, I proceeded fieldwork by orienting myself with the city's geography, which meant re-adjusting my routine to the daily rhythms of its Newar citizens. Most mornings, after sunrise, I watched local worshippers—mostly elderly men and women—awakening the deities at shrines or *śakti-pīṭhas* that lined the winding red-bricked streets. Several of these shrines had suffered considerable damage after the earthquake of 2015, but they remained active sites of worship because their cores—the sacred stone of the residing deity—endured intact.

To this day, I recall the moment when I entered the city's main gates: I was stunned by its architectural beauty. Bhaktapur is a city famed for its temples and landmarks, which are situated in and around its three temple squares: *Durbar, Dattatraya*, and *Taumadhi*. These central squares are connected by a bazaar forming red-brick paths lined on each side by four-story red-bricked houses, public porches, and temple shrines. Shrines are tended by local Bhaktapurians on a regular basis, sometimes daily since they house ancestral or clan divinities. Communal feasting and blood sacrifices are common practices at temple-shrines, especially during Bhaktapur's festival season. In this regard, Gellner cites a famous Newar proverb which is prominent among Newar communities: "the nawab (alternatively, Parbaitya or Chettri) ruins himself with luxury, the Newars by feasting".[34]

With Navadurgā performances aside, I witnessed many other collective festivities within the city walls, including the chariot festival of Bisket jātra, the autumnal festival of Mohani (known as Navarātra elsewhere in South Asia), and the Newari festival of Tihar. All these celebrations were, in some way, linked to the Tantric deities of Navadurgā whose shrines delineated the civic territory: without a doubt, Bhaktapur's annual festivals are high points for the local population. These various festivities—which last several days—unify the city's

---

34 David Gellner, 'Language, caste, religion, and territory: Newar identity ancient and modern', *Archives Européennes de Sociologie*, 27.1 (1986), p. 113.

precincts in social events characterized by communal sharing, feasting, and dancing: for example, my closest interlocutor, Ujesh Banmala, often expressed sadness at a festival's conclusive rite. For Ujesh, these events were occasions of Newar comradery, during which the population were socially cooperative and powerful, re-enlivened by the presence of the deities they worshipped.

Before I began my work with Navadurgā performers, I had obtained locations of initial Navadurgā rituals from local Newars I had met at a homestay; the first was at Nasamāna, and the second at Gāhiti twa (Taumadhi). At these rituals, I tried to spark conversation with Navadurgā performers I had seen there, to no avail. The preliminary stage of any participant-observation is tricky; potential interlocutors will be naturally cautious of foreigners. It was at the third performance on 9th March 2016—a *nya lakegu* at Durbar square—that I met the most helpful of my interlocutors, Ujesh Banmala, a man in his early-thirties. Ujesh was born into a lineage of Navadurgā dancer-mediums, who, with his family's support, decided to pursue a different career as a MA student at NATHM ('Nepal Academy of Tourism and Hotel Management'). In our initial talks, I clarified the reasons for my visit: I was a doctoral student interested in Newar religiosity and ritual performance for a comparative study. Ujesh complied with enthusiasm, and he was eager to acquaint me with his relatives in the days that followed; I was making some fortuitous progress. I also told Ujesh of my plans to return to Bhaktapur to observe the autumnal festivals. Upon further discussion, the family offered me a room at their home for this second trip (October–December 2016), which I gladly accepted. During my stay at the Banmala household, I experienced many aspects of Newar religion, which included a healing ritual administered by the family healer (*vaidya*).

With all formalities settled, I achieved a sense of camaraderie with the elders of the Navadurgā ensemble. At first, I was amusingly dubbed the unconventional tourist; my disinterest in photography and strained attempts at speaking Nepali must have seemed unconventional. In time, however, this designation waned due to my limited familiarity with Newari language. My exiguous use of Newari was attributed to the efforts of Ujesh's mother, who patiently introduced vocabulary to my already deficient lexicon: while preparing morning tea (*chiya*), we often laughed as I pronouced (or rather, mispronounced) Newari words with unabating determination! Ujesh's mother was the family's only vegetarian, though, oft-times, she'd prepare family meals, all meat-based, from donated sacrificial animals.

I spent countless hours in the company of Ujesh's family, including his brother, Dinesh, who, in his mid-twenties, was also a university student. Occasionally, he invited me to join him at a gathering of fellow Newars—farmers and mediums—in a tea shop (*chiya pasal*) near his home. With his friends,

Dinesh (like Ujesh) participated in an active 'cultural group': among Newars, networking across groups in this way to plan festivals is not uncustomary. In Newar society, any 'cultural group' is twinned with *guṭhi* as its modern corollary, where fictive siblinghoods, of all ages, gather to promote upcoming Newari festivals; sure enough, the Banmalas would champion Navadurgā performances as displays of their clan's might in mediumship.

My most immediate interloctor was Ujesh's father, Krishna, who was a Navadurgā troupe veteran: I repected his dedication to the Navadurgā ritual, and after dinner, accompanied by his family, we spoke, often at length, in his home's communal room. In these conversations, he described his life-experiences as a dancer-medium, and, being a well-established virtuoso, he clarified some complex ritual processes associated with the Navadurgā dance; much of this material informs Part 2. And when the time came to leave Bhaktapur, Krishna and his wife—my fictive father and mother—blessed my departure with ritual offerings, and, as our eyes met for the final time, my own welled with tears—such is the effectiveness of ritual kinship, and participant-observation as a method.

In personality and kinesics, the Banmala mediums were also astonishingly charismatic, so much so that I suspected charisma was a clan-inherited trait. It appears the Banmalas had bequeathed charisma—a "superhuman" aura, in Weber's words—from their extrasensory, or totemic alliance with the gods. Theoretically, in Parsons' introduction to Weber's study, charismatic authority—of all kinds, from political leaders to religious specialists—showcases a virtuoso's "superhuman" facets, which, Parsons believes, coincides with the energy generated from their followers' collective fervor (in Durkheimian argot, this energy is *collective effervescence*).[35] In all certainty, most deity-mediums I met in Nepal and South India were truly charismatic.

Apart from the Banmalas, I also interviewed seven other interlocutors in fourteen separate meetings. I met these individuals—in their homes and offices—on two separate occasions and, for brevity, I list their respective backgrounds here: (1) an octogenarian social scientist, (2) two historians (one lived near Lalitpur and another in Bhaktapur), (3) a Karmācārya priest, (4) a septuagenarian householder (and former *yogī*), (5) an architectural preservationist, and (6) a NWPP activist. Most of these interviews were organized through Ujesh's social connections: however, in the social scientist's case, his interviews were arranged via a local home-stay host, who knew him well. All interlocutors asked that their responses be anonymized in the text.

---

35 Talcott Parsons, 'Introduction', in *The Theory of Social and Economic Organization* by Max Weber, (New York: The Free Press, 1947), pp. 75–76.

4.2 *Kannur, Northern Malabar, Kerala* (*September–December 2015 & February 2017*)

Situated on India's south-west coast at the tip of the subcontinent, Kerala's tropical climate between the hills of the Western ghats and the shorelines of the Arabian sea enabled various trades, including spice growing and trawling to prosper, for which Malayālis—a term for speakers of Malayalam—are esteemed. Most residents in Kerala engage in one or several of these vocations, though, among millennial Malayālis, business-minded individuals tend to migrate to the Gulf seeking further employment. During the medieval period, much of the population lived in the mid-lands working rice-paddies and coconut groves under a system of feudalism.

During my fieldwork, I stayed in Kannur, a town in Northern Malabar, that became a central base from where I could navigate the region's temple groves. Kannur is a relatively small city, known locally as the 'city of looms and lores', bordered by numerous beaches, anchored among coconut groves, and housed by laterite red-brick buildings. Vestiges of Kerala's colonial past—by Dutch, Portuguese, and, later, British forces—are also evident in certain monuments throughout the city, for instance, at the 16th Century Portuguese fort of St Angelo.

Most days, I travelled to the city on the local bus, which drove through villages to get there. Interestingly, though a heartland of Marxist politics, Kannur's neighbourhoods are distinguished by banners that display each territory's political loyalty, situated around saffron Hindu temples, red Marxist meeting houses, or green Islamic Mosques. Even the train station houses its own divinity, Railway Muttappan, who is worshipped weekly in ritual performance. Notwithstanding its varied identity politics, I was told that Kannur city is known for its religious plurality, thanks to the uniqueness of its matrilineal mores and to its idiosyncratic, if sometimes paradoxical, communist history. Certainly, several of my interlocutors described Kerala as a land of contradictions: as a case in point, Kerala's official slogan, "God's own country" seems inconsistent with the state's political allegiance that is driven, largely, by Marxist-influenced ideology. And yet, in a traditional Keralan rendering, 'God' is not understood in a theistic sense, since, as per materialism, local deities—or *Teyyam*—constitute the ancestors, whose presence reanimate the material world.

In recalling my initial fieldwork encounters in Kannur, it appears my research did not begin as felicitously as I anticipated. In these earlier stages, I encountered some setbacks that fortunately improved. Unlike my participant-observation in Nepal, establishing contact with Teyyāṭṭam lineages in Northern Malabar proved somewhat problematic. I suspect this initial stalemate was due, in part, to the dispersed distribution of Teyyam communities—hundreds of Teyyam groves are disbanded across a vast region that stretch over four districts (Nileśvaram, Kasaragod, Payyanur, and Kannur).

There was also a sense that these communities had become uncertain about the intentions of foreign researchers; I was told Keralan authorities were stern about visas with more security checks in response to political tensions with Pakistan. Before my arrival on the Malabar coast around late September 2015, I had not contacted any local Malayālis beforehand, nor could I speak Malayalam. Gradually, these earlier fieldwork anxieties subsided when I began attending Teyyāṭṭam performances at differing Teyyam groves across the region.

Throughout Northern Kerala, Teyyam groves are found on most hillsides, or neighbourhoods, and many of them are owned by a local clan, or household. For eleven months of the Malayalam calendar, Teyyam temple groves are nonfunctioning, aside from regular oil-wick lighting, by low-birth priests, in honour of the shrine's family ancestors. However, it is during annual Teyyam festivals that groves become hives of ritual activity and social gathering. Across Malabar, each Teyyam space is different: however, in general, each grove contains a set of laterite-bricked shrines, a canopy, a coconut grove, and a family home nearby. I came to know when a Teyyam performance was scheduled in a locale, because most families ignite fireworks to announce—to the entire neighbourhood—that a performance is imminent. Most of these Teyyāṭṭam performances occurred before sunrise, and, for that reason, I arose at 2am to attend them; at such an hour, only a pre-booked auto rickshaw could drive to these remote temple sites. Once I arrived at a performance, opportunities to converse in edifying discussion with potential interlocutors became recurrent (throughout my stay in Malabar, I conversed with many devotees, which forms much of my data).

Luckily enough, more providence arose in the form of my gracious homestay hosts, who offered their assistance: for one, they supplied locations of some twenty-five Teyyāṭṭam which I later attended, and, most importantly, they interpreted during an interview I had organized with two dancer-medium families. (However, in the second family—also from Kannur—the family's English-speaking mediums genially guided these interactions). In Kannur, the first family I interviewed was a lineage of dancer-mediums, led, throughout the meeting, by Akash, their lineage elder (Maly: *Kārṇavan*). Akash was a wise and well-informed man who, in conversation, was consistently forthcoming when he explained his community's intricate culture. When I spoke with Akash, other mediums and priests gathered to join our conversation, and their contributions also pepper this book.

When I returned to Kannur in February 2017, I continued to meet with Teyyam mediums and their worshippers. During this second trip, I also visited the region's 'folklore academy' in the town of Chirakkal, a museum which is dedicated to the conservation of Teyyāṭṭam regalia. The academy is located near a lake which is believed to be the original site of King Kōlattiri's medieval palace. Whilst visiting there, I read some literature, in translation, about Teyyam narratives (compiled in Trikaripur's *Mooring Mirror*) and, in passing, I spoke with the museum's academic director.

4.3 *Folk Śākta Performances as Spiraling Web-Like Ritual Networks*

This book's core premise advances how Folk Śākta performances operate as collective sites of ritual action that synthesize dichotomies into web-networks at three levels: *societal*, *metaphysical*, and *political*.[36]

4.4 *First Level: Societal*

At the first level, I suggest that Folk Śākta performances negotiate a binary in a Tantric society's ontological network of being. By 'ontological', I mean cultural categories of being (whether human, deity, or animal) that populate a regional worldview grouped in territorial social structures. This societal dialectic is bifurcated as follows: (1) the vertical structure of caste-based distance pollution ('Brahmanical' idealism) and (2) the horizontal structures of proximate bodily connection within familial life, that are, consanguineal and/or affinal relations ('Tantric' materialism). In Indic societies, 'horizontal' structures are patterned according to Tantric lineages or autochthonous moiety organization. For Kerala, this indigenous social configuration is evidenced in matrilineal joint families, and for Bhaktapur, within inter-caste organizations (Newa: *guṭhi*).

During Teyyam and Navadurgā performances, a vertical-horizontal dialectic is redressed via ritual kin connections—produced through impure gift-giving—between these two structures, which synthesizes them as a *web-like ritual network*. In the main, a ritual web-network, led by lower-caste mediums, entwines bygone ancestors, kings, gods, animals, castes, and families by reigniting the shared carnal vigour (*śakti*) that unites them as a civic territory. This idea became clear to me when I visited the home of an octogenarian social scien-

36 This structure aligns with the Kashmir Śaiva (Trika) concept of a threefold goddess as a lotus-trident emerging from a cosmic centre (*triśūlābjamaṇḍala*) (Sanderson, 'Śaivism and the Tantric Traditions', p. 674). Also, it corresponds both to the Kāpālika understanding of Bhairava's trident and, additionally, a Kāpālika ascetic's use of ash, drawn as three lines on their forehead, as a marker of their identity. See David N. Lorenzen, *The Kāpālikas and Kālāmukhas: Two Lost Śaivite Sects* (Los Angeles: University of California Press, 1972).

tist in Bhaktapur: at one stage in our meeting, he pointed at a set of miniature Navadurgā masks framed on his parlour wall and imparted "[T]hese gods are representations [*citraharu*] of our own energy [*śakti*]".

A ritual web-network—epitomized by this goddess-clan's civic power (*śakti*)—clusters lower-caste lineages as ritual relatives—or rather, a macro-clan—of a shared province scheduled by the land's reproductive cycle of material energy. I argue that consubstantial commensality and blood sacrifice across lineage divides recirculates the earthly life-force of a polity such that, in a spiral, caste **purity** (or distance pollution) is infringed via Tantric lineage **impurity** (or bodily proximity) by recasting the populace into connections of ritual kinship—founded on the goddess-clan (*kula*)—as *affective kin-like intentionality*. Pradhan reinforces how the word for a 'gift', or 'gift-giving' in Newari, that is, *bicā* 'from *vichār yāyegu* [lit.] 'to think [or] be concerned about'',[37] precisely resonates with the inter-human solidarity formed during the ritual. Folk Śākta performances, in this way, conjoin the body politic in web-like ritual networks bonded by defiling blood sacrifice; an exsanguinating animal represents the social bonds ritually flowing there.

4.5 *Theoretical Interlude*

4.5.1 Ritual Kinship and Fictive Kinship: Are They Related?

In any genealogy of anthropological thought, definitional issues surrounding 'kinship' are universal. For any ethnographer, capturing what is meant by 'kinship' can be a knotty endeavour; the term is a particularly loaded category that can encompass a multitude of human, and animal, assemblies, ranging from families, lineages, clans, support groups, fraternities, and so on. I believe Sahlins accurately encases what the term 'kinship' conveys in its widest possible signification, that is, 'a manifold of intersubjective participants, which is also to say, a network of *mutualities of being*'.[38] Janet Carsten's *After Kinship* also developed her own slant on kinship studies with her focus on 'relatedness', which brings emotionality or subjectivity into the study of kinship structures.[39]

However, for this book, I argue that Carsten's 'relatedness' and Sahlins' 'mutuality of being' are too wide-ranging in scope; a ritual's interpersonal connections are contained only to the duration of its performance. On the contrary, I suggest Folk Śākta 'ritual kinship' or 'affective kin-like intentionality'

---

37 Rajendra Pradhan, 'Sacrifice, Regeneration, and Gifts: Mortuary Rites among Hindu Newars of Kathmandu', *Contributions to Nepalese Studies*, 23.1 (1996), p. 169.

38 Marshall Sahlins, *What kinship is-and is not?* (Chicago: University of Chicago Press, 2013), p. 20.

39 Janet Carsten, *After Kinship* (Cambridge: CUP, 2004).

is a ritually-confined **fictive** or non-affinal/non-consanguineal network forged across multileveled realities (humans, deities, kings, and animals) through acts of sacrificial blood-spilling which bind groups in non-stratified bonds with the earth or goddess. In this ritual space, then, dancing deity-mediums become their devotees' short-term godmothers, godfathers, god-siblings, or god-uncles.

According to Qirko, such ritual dynamics appear most frequently in politically- and/or religiously motivated fictive kin groups. These fictive kin groups, he argues, are 'modelled on siblingship, created and cemented by common experience and the sharing of blood, food, or other substances. Examples include age-grade transitions to adulthood through rites of passage, gangs, "brothers in arms" in military organizations and sororities'.[40] In a sense, Folk Śākta performances produce ritually contained networks of fictive kinship, where donations are distributed to the lower-caste mediums performing there; in non-ritual environments, I claim these inter-personal processes operate hierarchically in caste-organized or endogamous stratification. (Yet, relationships within a ritual's macro-clan are not, themselves, wholly egalitarian because certain members—seniors or lower-caste mediums—are prioritized). The ritual's distribution of capital and land-based assets is redistributive, such that funds and food are given to those at the lower end of a revenue scale. In the spirit of kindling closeness, a Folk Śākta ritual blurs any ontological demarcation dividing actors (individual-collective-sacrifice-material-territorial; self-other-worldview-object), bleeding together.

4.5.2 Folk Śākta Performances: Societal Centre-to-Periphery Spirals

Later, I unpack, in symbolic terms, how the sanguineal nature of Folk Śākta performances is constitutive of **menstrual synchrony** generated amid lineages through food distribution or blood offerings. By 'menstrual synchrony', I refer to the biological process whereby groups of cohabiting women attune somatically (or unconsciously) by bleeding together in menstrual unison; during Folk Śākta ritual, lineages 'bleed' together in sacrificial communion. This understanding runs somewhat counter to Raheja's interpretation of gift-exchange: for Raheja, inter-caste prestation upholds the 'centrality' of land-holding castes by shifting inauspiciousness (*nāśubh*) to 'peripheral' caste groups.[41] In Nepal, this ritual dynamic also unfolds at Dolakha district's Devikot-jātrā festival: Shnei-

40 Hector N. Qirko, 'Fictive Kinship and Induced Altruism', in *The Oxford Handbook of Evolutionary Family Psychology*, ed. by Todd K. Shackleford & Catherine A. Salmon, (Oxford: OUP, 2011), pp. 310–311.

41 Gloria G. Raheja, *The Poison in the Gift: Ritual, Prestation, and the Dominant Caste in a North Indian Village* (Chicago: University of Chicago Press, 1988), pp. 248–250.

derman describes how, during this Newar festival, subordinate Thangmi *nari* ('shamans') drink blood from a buffalo—equated with Mahiśaṣura, a demon-incarnate—to protect the Newar community from malevolent forces.[42] Yet, from the *nari*'s perspective, their status of marginality **is** strength. For a Nari shaman, the festival demonstrates how Raheja's order spirals across the centre-periphery divide, as Shneiderman's informant conveys: "We [the *nari*] may look like demons, but if we don't, the Newars can't have their ritual, and that is our power".[43]

As with Bakhtin's notion of carnivalesque,[44] states of ritual marginality—imposed on low-birth mediums—can be empowering, such that societal oppression and physical pain fan the flames of their phoenix-like reemergence. To illustrate, Dyczkowski cites the biography of *Gayapati*, a Newar Brahmin priest, who learned prodigious spells from 'untouchable' priests socially marginalized from the central institution.[45] In fact, shrines to fierce goddess-clans—*central* to the regal cult—are installed on territorial borders—the abode of low-castes inhabitants in Bhaktapur **and** North Kerala—to guard the population from external invasion or demonic infiltration.

While instances of spiraling reversals—from regal hub to subaltern margins, and vice versa—are operative in most cases, Freeman shows how, in Kerala, a central-periphery hierarchy is maintained during occasions where higher-castes patrons sponsor Teyyam rites: by transferring a sacred flame from high-caste temples into Teyyam groves, Freeman noticed how 'the social hierarchy is mirrored in the divine energy of the gods flowing down a chain of authority, from the temple gods to the teyyam shrine through the medium of the flame'.[46] Even so, at another Teyyāṭṭam performance, Freeman observed how subaltern lineage deities can curse affluent Nāyar lineages by 'seiz[ing] the spirit of the [cursed] deceased, merging it into itself'[47] as an inimical display of redistribu-

42 Sara Shneiderman, *Rituals of Ethnicity: Thangmi Identities between India and Nepal* (Philadelphia: University of Pennsylvania Press, 2015), p. 236.

43 Ibid., p. 238.

44 Mikhail Bakhtin describes 'carnivalesque' as a reversal of hierarchy experienced in festivals which challenges a society's tradition order. See Mikhail Bakhtin, *Rabelais and his world*, trans. by Helene Iswolsky (Bloomington: Indiana University Press, 1984 [1965]).

45 Mark Dyczkowski, *The Cult of the Goddess Kubjika: A Preliminary Comparative Textual and Anthropological Survey of a Secret Newar Goddess* (Stuttgart: Franz Steiner Werlag, 2001), p. 3.

46 John R. Freeman, 'The Teyyam Tradition of Kerala', in *The Blackwell Companion to Hinduism*, ed. by Gavin Flood, (London: Blackwell, 2003), p. 313.

47 John R. Freeman, 'Purity and Violence: Sacred Worship in the Teyyam Worship of Malabar', (Ph.D. diss., University of Pennsylvania, 1991), p. 311.

tive justice. In these cases, ritual macro-clans do not demonstrate egalitarian lineage-conglomeration, for these performances are embedded within volatile, material worlds, where possibilities of harm and healing also spiral. Thus, in this ritual, I argue that central-peripheral bifurcations are not static but **spiraling** betwixt them: by deifying low-caste virtuosi, the hierarchy is adopted, dismantled, and rebuilt anew within a performance's spiraling web.

As acknowledged above, Folk Śākta performances form spirals that reconstruct the social norms of 'purity' (as caste) and 'impurity' (as lineages) into *web-like ritual networks*. By 'spiraling', I refer to an experiential shift between sets of existential norms—in a group or within an individual—from one to another, and vice versa; Sondra Hausner would call this process an 'oscillation' between dyadic structures.[48] Certainly, during ritual performance, this dynamic is set in motion when male mediums become female goddesses, or when they harness their ancestors' power. In short, 'spiraling', here, describes perpetual shifts between vertical purity and horizontal impurity at the central radix of a polity's power, from which a kingdom's webbed macro-clan emanates in synthesis. Yet, within this macro-clan, social relations are not wholly non-hierarchical, since statuses of seniority—teachers, ancestors, or lineage elders—are valued above all else. True to Weberian sociology, elder exaltation is culturally ingrained, in such a way that it also finds expression in political spheres, too; in Bhaktapur, teachers and elders are leaders of the city's governing party, the NWPP.

As I explain later, the spiraling cores of Folk Śākta ritual are symbolized by kings, warrior gods (e.g. Bhairava), and goddess-clans, whose personalities also spiral between states of **impure** violence and **pure** protection. Indeed, caste purity must be marked in this ritual to transgress its dominance with a defiling antithesis—a Tantric lineage. In other words, Brahmanical hierarchy creates somatic distance between caste groups, while a Tantric lineage creates bodily proximity borne from vertical hierarchy as its transgressive converse. As a pivoting matrix, a Folk Śākta performance concentrates its kingdom's population into a macro-clan, which arises from a moiety spiral that spins caste distance into lineage proximity, and vice versa.

4.6 *Second & Third Levels: Metaphysical and Political*

Further to the ontological level, I argue web-like ritual networks affected Folk Śākta tradition on two further levels: metaphysical and political. By metaphys-

48 Sondra Hausner, *The Spirits of Crossbones Graveyard: Time, Ritual, and Sexual Commerce in London* (Bloomington: Indiana University Press, 2016).

ical, I mean the doctrinal grounds—notions about the cosmos or human existence in textual corpora or oral folklore—that are essential to the workings of a cultural worldview. By spiraling across Brahmanical and Tantric religiosity, a Folk Śākta worldview incorporates Folk, Tantric, Vedic, Brahmanical, and, in Nepal, Newar Buddhist (Vajrayāna) systems as ritual kin modelled on its spiraling web-like structure. As I expound in Chapter 4, Folk Śākta cosmologies merge a series of connexions among related Tantric texts—performed through a virtuoso's body—to incrementally re-generate itself as a *bricolage web of ritual knowledge*. My use of this term combines Lévi-Strauss' bricolage,[49] that is, a pastiche of multiple sources, with Deleuze & Guattari's slant on bricolage as an affective, intersubjective assemblage.[50] Padoux elaborates on Tantra's metaphysical complexity, as a *bricolage web of ritual knowledge*, here:

> Tantric traditions [...] can coexist with the outward respect of brahmanical norms. [Tantra] differ[s] from the ancient, solemn Vedic cults [...] a return sometimes [...] promoted by an Indian reactionary political ideology. (In such Vedic reconstructions [...] elements of Tantric origin are anachronistically included) Apart from such cases, *vaidika* and [*Vajrayāna, Jaina, Śaiva, and Śākta*] *tāntrika* elements run alongside one another or combine variously to different degrees.[51]

In this extract, Padoux emphasizes how elements of Vedic religion can be re-envisioned, politicized, and romanticized to fortify a certain 'Indian reactionary political ideology'. In the same way, I argue that Tantric performances in Kerala and Bhaktapur promote a spirit of revolution: the ritual's idiosyncratic reframing of caste via ancestor worship supports an anti-caste stance, which, in contrast to right-wing Vedism, is consistent with a uniquely territory-conscious Marxist ideology. Politically, *spiraling web-like ritual networks* foster class consciousness, insofar as verticality ('pure' segregation) is recognized to enable its dismantlement at certain phases of ritual through 'pollutive' macro-clan proximity. At first sight, the synchroneity of ancestor worship with a progressive political ideology may seem divergent and tendentious. However, in postcolonial Kerala and Bhaktapur, Marxist-influenced parties spiral across conservatism and radicalism as coextensive with Folk Śākta performances. In

49 Claude Lévi-Strauss, *The Savage Mind* (Hertford: The Garden City Press, 1966 [1962]), pp. 19–21.

50 Gilles Deleuze & Felix Guattari, *A Thousand Plateaus: Capitalism and Schizophrenia* (London: Continuum, 1988), p. 25.

51 Andre Padoux, *The Hindu Tantric World: An Overview* (Oxford: OUP, 2017), p. 9.

these areas, Folk Śākta performances—as nascent displays of group-identity or macro-clan worship—paved the way for political parties that advocate an intra-state revolutionary ideology ('Marxist'-influenced).[52] This politicization is not atypical in Nepal; for example, Ghimire explains that many of East Nepal's Maoist supporters were worshippers of a local goddess.[53]

5 Contextual Background

5.1 *Mapping the Historical Trajectory of Indic[54] Religion: Vedic, Brahmanical, and Tantric Systems*

5.1.1 Vedic Traditions

Most analyses of early-medieval literature—in Sanskrit and regional languages—tend to delineate two ideological systems that emerged in the textual record: a Vedic (*vaidika*) and a Tantric (*tāntrika*) order. To begin, the core features of the Vedic order can be parsed as follows: First, the Vedic school was an 'orthopraxic' (*āstik*) order, which initiated twice-born priests into an elite priesthood through a rite of passage known as *Upanayana* (i.e. the receival of the sacred thread). In this order, daily life was concerned with upholding ritual purity and appeasing the deities in a sacrificial rite (*yajña*) performed beyond the temple walls. During ritual sacrifice, the oblation was an animal scapegoat, which was offered to a pantheon of meteorological divinities headed by Indra and Prajāpati. In later adaptations of Vedic practice, animal slaughter was rescinded and substituted with vegetative libations offered into a fire (*homa*).[55]

Secondly, maintaining a caste system—however this may have looked in Vedic times—was a social ideal. Briefly, caste or *varṇa* was a hierarchy that divided social groups according to occupation and birth; in Vedic myth, this social stratum finds its conceptual origin in the *Puruṣasukta* hymn (lit. 'the primordial man').[56] Doniger shows how 'sacrifice is central to many concepts of

---

52 Hugh Urban, *Tantra: Sex, Secrecy, Politics, and Power* (Los Angeles: University of California Press, 2003), pp. 199–201 for Tantra and politics.

53 Pustak Ghimire, 'Living Goddesses Everywhere? On the possession of women by the goddess Bhagavati in some mountain villages in Eastern Nepal', in *Religion, Secularism, and Ethnicity in Contemporary Nepal*, ed. by David Gellner et al., (Oxford: OUP, 2016), p. 185.

54 'Indic' is used to classify regions that share religio-cultural characteristics (Bali, Nepal, etc.) stemming from the subcontinent.

55 Flood, *Introduction to Hinduism*, pp. 40–41.

56 Ṛg Veda 10.90 in Wendy Doniger, *The Rig Veda: An Anthology* (London: Penguin Classics, 1981), p. 23.

[social] creation',[57] which, in the Vedic context, consists of a caste system and the terrestrial division between the forest (*jangal*) and the village (*grāma*). Abiding by this caste hierarchy required strict adherence to rules of distance pollution among differing caste groups, which consolidated ritual purity.

Third, divine revelation or salvation is attained through one's soul (*ātman*), which is identical to the transcendent cosmic principle, *brahman*. For later *vaidikas*, material existence (*prakṛti*) was considered transient and illusory, so ritual observance was prescribed early on to maintain the soul's purity. And fourth, all divine revelations (*śruti*) about the absolute (*brahman*) were integrated in Vedic literature—the hymns (*Vedas*), commentaries (*Brāhmaṇas*) and philosophical texts (*Upaniṣads*)—compiled by *ṛṣis* (lit. seers) and other sages.

In later Indic society, such Vedic norms (which include ritual purity) were socially implemented: within this social order, all persons were grouped in insular caste groupings (*varṇa*). As per this system, a caste group could not share food or bodily proximity with persons from other castes because food and bodies, grouped at lower strata, were pollutive. In an essay on caste, Marriott and Inden emphasize how a person, in this Brahmanical framework, is composed of '[…] structured flow[s] of coded substances'[58] that make up a fluid 'dividual': in other words, a person's body is comprised and re-shaped by flows of organic substances and moral qualities (*guṇa*) linked to one's *varṇāśramadharma* (i.e. one's life-cycle in relation to one's social duty) which are inseparable from their engagements with matter and bodies. As Marriott famously encapsulates, a Hindu person is affected by a monistic worldview, whereby exchanges of material substances between persons determine each respective individual's moral configuration.[59] Such cultural principles, then, prescribe that individuals from, say, a Brahmin caste can **only** share food and bodily proximity with individuals of that caste group, because substances accepted by a lower-caste person (say, a *kṣatriya*) precipitates a defiling effect on the receiver, which detrimentally alters that person's moral (*karma*) or social (*dharma*) condition. For instance, a section of Bṛhadāryaṇyaka Upaniṣad 6.4.13 provides a list of prohibitions for menstruating women, i.e. they should avert all contact with lower-caste persons, and they should not use metal cups to drink.[60]

---

57 Ibid.

58 McKim Marriott & Ronald Inden, 'Toward an ethnosociology of South Asian caste systems', in *The New Wind: Changing Identities in South Asia*, (The Hague: Moulton, 1977), p. 236.

59 McKim Marriott, ed., *India through Hindu Categories* (New Delhi: SAGE Publications, 1990).

60 *Upaniṣads*, trans. by Patrick Olivelle, (Oxford: OUP, 1996), p. 90.

As we shall see, such restrictions are intentionally contravened in a Tantric context: impurity, in Tantric thought, holds much material vitality, which can be 'magically' transformed by Tantric practitioners to recast matters of worldly existence (*laukika*), what is described by Sunthar Visuvalingam as 'transgressive sacrality'. As a term, 'transgressive sacrality' refers to '[…] bundling together (seemingly) disparate phenomena that directly or indirectly violate the founding rules of a given religious tradition but for the same reason are held to be all the more sacred'.[61] Any act of defilement—be it blood sacrifice or alcohol consumption—constitute the energy-enhancing 'transgressive sacrality' that Tantric religion embraces. In spite of that, many sacrificial rites originated in early Vedic ritual, and I claim a specific Vedic sacrifice—the *Aśvamedha* or horse sacrifice in particular—provided an early template for Tantric sacrifices, especially those that consecrated the royal cult.

5.1.1.1 *Vedic Rituals*

Broadly speaking, all Vedic sacrifices—outlined in Vedic and Brāhmaṇa literature (approx. 1500 BCE–500 BCE)—can be systematized into three distinct branches: (1) public sacrifices (*śrauta-yajña*), (2) domestic sacrifices (*gṛhya-yajña*), and (3) great sacrifices (*mahā-yajña*) which combine elements of both public and domestic rites.[62] Among these rituals, a votive act—known as *homa*—was routinized for all public and great sacrifices: during a *homa*, an animal sacrifice was offered into a fire (*vedi*)—personified as Agni, a fire deity—that was surrounded by a hearth (*āhavanīya*) tended by *ādhvarya* priests. The smoke emitted from the charred flesh ascended to the heavens through the winds of deity Vāyu to gratify Indra, the god of fertility.[63] Each stage of the sacrifice was followed by meticulous rites of purification that ensured ritual enclosures were free from contamination. Ritual purification averted somatic pollution, which affected the bodies of priests gathered there.[64]

Frits Staal—who recorded the last vestiges of Vedic sacrifice among Brahmins in Kerala—postulates that Vedic sacrifice served to present an asymmetrical offering to distant, celestial divinities. To the eyes of unaccustomed householders, a sacrificial ceremony was far removed from the temporal practicalities of communal customs. A Vedic sacrifice, then, was soteriological not social religion: in different terms, a Vedic rite was an 'activity of purity' devoid

61 Sunthar Visuvalingam, 'Transgressive Sacrality in the Hindu Tradition', in *Antonio de Nicolas: Poet of Eternal Return* (Ahmedabad: Sriyogi Publishers, 2014).

62 'yajña' in *The Oxford Dictionary of Hinduism*, ed. by Will Johnson, (Oxford: OUP, 2009).

63 Doniger, *Rig Veda*.

64 Flood, *Introduction to Hinduism*, pp. 40–41.

of any tangible goal bar actualizing ritual regulations (what Staal calls 'ritual syntax') that governed the maintenance of the sacrificial fires (*vedī*).[65]

The *Aśvamedha*, or 'horse sacrifice', on the other hand, was a public (*śrauta*) ritual of royal investiture which was, at its core, a 'transference of power' drawn from divine pantheon into mundane king. Indeed, as a rite of political legitimation, aspects of Aśvamedha may have functioned as nascent progenitors to medieval Tantric sacrifice. Charles Malamoud notes how the Aśvamedha was a consecratory rite where a feral horse roamed the wilderness (*araṇya*) of the kingdom, before being re-captured, tied to a sacrificial post (*yūpa*), slaughtered, and its remains apportioned to several divinities.[66] Sacrifices of smaller animals (or 'village animals' (*grāma paśu*)) coincided with the horse's immolation, which presents a clear dichotomy in Vedic religion between the untamed power of the wilderness and the civilized limits of the *grāma* ('village').[67] Malmoud highlights that the word '*grāma*' has etymological connections with the noun 'troop' or 'battle', which may resonate with Folk Śākta divinities as entrenched in iconography of militia, which shields their citizens from 'wild' intrusion. Malamoud continues:

> The stability of the grāma depends more upon the cohesion of its constituitive group than it does upon the space that it occupies.[68]

In his essay on the horse sacrifice, Zaroff shows how a marked 'socio-political element' underscored *aśvamedha*, which manifested through the transference of seed (*bīja*) via a series of 'power copulation' symbols enacted in the ritual.[69] Zaroff adds:

> [...] the kingdom is viewed as a micro-Universe, and proper performance of the ritual assures not only the stability and continuity of the state, but also maintains the cosmic order.[70]

As Doniger and Smith have argued, whenever a connection (*bandhu*) is formed between Vedic ritual and social processes, then the rite is efficacious in terms

---

65 Frits Staal, 'The Meaninglessness of Ritual', *Numen*, 26.1 (1979), p. 3.

66 Charles Malamoud, *Cooking the World: Ritual and Thought in Ancient India* (Delhi: OUP, 1996), pp. 74–75.

67 Malmoud, *Cooking the World*, pp. 74–75.

68 Malmoud, *Cooking the World*, p. 75.

69 Roman Zaroff, 'Aśvamedha—A Vedic Horse Sacrifice', *Studia Mythologica Slavica*, 8 (2005), p. 77.

70 Ibid., p. 78.

of substantializing worldly power, since it 'work[s] simultaneously and sympathetically on natural, supernatural, and social analogues'.[71] The same could be posited for Vedic *Śrāddha* or ancestor-feeding rites. In these rites, food-morsels and rice-balls (*piṇḍas*) are fed to crows, who incarnate a lineage ancestor's ethereal body (*bhoga-deha*). Nicholas states how an inadequately fed ancestor could chasten his/her neglectful descendants by returning as a rancorous ghost (*preta*). By feeding an ancestor, one can 'sustain [...] relationships with those one loves after death'.[72] To be sure, ancestors also make a segue into Folk Śākta performances, guised as heroic warriors, oppressed females, territorial goddesses, or medieval kings.

5.1.2 From Pre-Gupta Vedism to Gupta Smārta Brahmanism

Throughout the subcontinent, a process of second urbanization (240–590 CE) gave rise to significant changes in Vedic society, which were conditioned by larger political alterations with the efflorescence of Gupta-empire imperialism. These socio-political shifts heralded a process of Vedic amalgamation, whereby Vedic schools fused with later philosophical (Upaniṣadic) and legal (Dharmaśātric) codices to create Smārta Brahmanism. (Smārta Hindu tradition was validated by Gupta rulers, over Buddhist and Jaina traditions—known collectively as *śramaṇa* traditions—that disseminated after the fall of the Mauryan empire[73]).

As a reinstated Brahmanical ideology—labelled 'Classical Hinduism' by Axel Michaels[74]—Smārta religion was enhanced with the addition of *Purāṇic* canons. In short, the Purāṇas were encyclopedic digests based on reconceived Sanskritic deities, whether Śaiva (Śiva-oriented), Vaiṣṇava (Viṣṇu-oriented), or Śākta (goddess-oriented).[75] In addition, the sweeping vernacularizing of Prākrit and elitization of Sanskrit also accompanied the rise of Gupta Smārta culture. Moreover, this new Sanskritic pantheon was hegemonized as Gupta-ratified religion, which subverted (though not entirely) indigenous deities. Under monarch Samudragupta, this religious and provincial homogenization

---

71 Brian K. Smith & Wendy Doniger, 'Sacrifice and Substitution: Ritual Mystification and Mythical Demystification', *Numen*, 36.2 (1989), p. 196.

72 Ralph W. Nicholas, 'Śrāddha, Impurity, and the Relations between the Living and the Dead', *Contributions to Indian Sociology*, 15.2 (1981), p. 377.

73 Naomi Appleton, *Shared Characters in Jain, Buddhist, and Hindu Narrative: Gods, Kings, and Other Heroes* (London: Routledge, 2017), pp. 4–5.

74 Axel Michaels, *Hinduism: Past and Present* (Princeton: Princeton University Press, 2004), p. 39.

75 For details of this history, see Thomas Hopkins, *The Hindu Religious Tradition* (Belmont: Dickenson, 1971), pp. 52–63.

reached its apogee into, what John Keay labels, the 'golden' age of Sanskritic civilization. (Albeit sans South Indian rulers—Kadamba, Pandya, and Pallava dynasties—and the Newar kingdoms, who remained unseized as autonomous polities). Keay's historical account notes how:

> Tributary *rajas*, or kings, were essential as validating and magnifying agents. In the same way as local cults and lesser deities were harnessed to the personae of Lords Vishnu or Shiva, so lesser rulers were inducted into an enhancing relationship with the 'world-ruler'. Precedence and paramountcy were what mattered, not governance or integration.[76]

At this time, Vedic rituals were also re-rendered into Brahmanical ones, influenced, no doubt, by the world-renouncing ideology of *śramaṇa* traditions: as Flood tells us, animal sacrifice became symbolic through its 'internalization' into the self as individual conduct.[77] In this context, 'sacrifice internalization' refers to the way Vedic ritual had been reclaimed as a set of **internal** or **individualized** actions construed disparately by householder (*gṛhastha*) and ascetic (*sannyāsī*) social factions. For householders, sacrifice became a metaphor for a person's adherence to moral and ritual duties according to *Varnāśramadharma* which protected his/her inner divine essence (*ātman*).

Meanwhile, ascetic (*sādhu*) communities conceptualized sacrifice as symbolically constitutive of their role as world-renouncers:[78] an ascetic's body, according to Hausner, incarnates the fires (*dhūni*) of sacrificial power to immolate his/her householder ties.[79] Flood expounds further: '[...] the true sacrifice becomes the fire oblation on the breath (*prāṇāgnihotra*), a sacrifice to the self within the self'.[80] The 'internalisation' of sacrifice, then, re-framed Vedic praxes, into what Heesterman calls *second-order ritualism*:

> Second-order ritualism ... deals with the invisible ... [and] was strangely impervious to the world around it. It was exactly ... a mechanistic construct, purposely at right angles to lived-in reality that enabled the endurance of Vedic ritualism in a changing world.[81]

---

76 John Keay, *India: A History* (London: Harper Collins Publishers, 2000), p. 140.

77 Flood, *Introduction to Hinduism*, pp. 83–85.

78 Sondra Hausner, *Wandering with Sadhus: Ascetics in the Hindu Himalayas* (Bloomington: Indiana University Press, 2007), p. 185.

79 Hausner, *Wandering with Sadhus*, p. 121.

80 Flood, *Introduction to Hinduism*, p. 84.

81 Jan C. Heesterman, *The Broken World of Sacrifice: An Essay in Ancient Indian Ritual* (Chicago: University of Chicago Press, 1993), pp. 77–79.

As per this model, second-order rituals developed from first-order rituals, which, contrastingly, '... derive[d] directly from the transposition of worldly tension and strife to the sacrificial arena'.[82] Thus, a second-order ritual (the 'internal' sacrifice of Brahmanism) became theoretically disparate from the first-order's worldly (*laukika*) concerns, because the second-order asserted a new metaphysical dualism between matter and spirit. As such, any second-order ritual was: (1) preoccupied with an individual's or collective's engagement with the illusory world of matter and bodies, charted by cosmic cycles of soul-reincarnation, which was centred on; (2) the soul's (*ātman*) identification with the absolute or *nirguṇa brahman* (lit. divine principle 'without qualities').

In Bṛhadāryaṇyaka Upaniṣad 4.4.13, the body is alluded as a 'dense jumble' where a thumb-sized *ātman*—'immortal' and 'spotless'—resides in the heart.[83] This outlook apprehends sentient entities as individual souls propelled in an illusory, and pollutive, material plane, where commitment to duty-based schemas (deontology) has repercussions on that entity's moral constitution. In this way, being, morality, and physical interaction are interdependent as a form of 'monistic idealism', or an explanatory model of the human condition comprehended from the stance of transcendent space-time cyclicality (*saṃsāra*). First-order ritual—and Folk Śākta Tantric cosmology—is its inverse: a complex lifeworld oriented toward materialism[84] symbolized by ancestral gods/goddesses, political sovereignty, insignia, and visceral life-energy (*śakti*). However, unlike the fully-fledged materialism of the Cārvāka school, Folk Śākta tāntrikas are not *de facto* materialist atheists.

Second-order idealism was stimulated by changing theological views about the 'absolute' (*brahman*), which were conditioned by the development of philosophical ideas in the Upaniṣads viz. *brahman-ātman* homology, a notion where the soul co-corresponds with the absolute. Quoting Hanns-Peter Schmidt, Heesterman claims that second-order ritual became the 'ritual theory of *ahiṃsā*'.[85] In essence, the sacrificial first-order ritual, like *Aśvamedha*, (which, I argue, distantly preceded Tantric notions of sacrifice) were attached to the world in horizontal networks of corporeal interactions, while, in the second-order, these first-order interpretations become *symbolic*, that is, as analogies of

82 Ibid., p. 77.

83 *Upanisads*, p. 66.

84 Marawaha's article discusses Tantra's 'proto-materialism' as 'liberation only in terms of the development and culture of the body'. See Sonali B. Marwaha, 'Roots of Indian Materialism in Tantra', *Asian Philosophy*, 23.2 (2013), p. 196.

85 Heesterman, *Broken World of Sacrifice*, p. 82.

personal "sacrifice". The meaning of first-order ritual became lost in second-order ritual because it had '[...] cut the links and ligatures that tied sacrifice to the organic world'.[86] Therefore, a sacrificial rite of blood (first-order ritual) differed from later understandings of sacrifice in Brahmanical or Smārta ritual (second-order ritual).[87] In second-order ritual, sacrifice had become interiorized within the body as a 'sacrificial contest ... with the "enemy within" one's own self'.[88] Heesterman explains:

> The ritualism of the Veda [...] dissolved the sacrality of sacrifice and remolded the dismembered pieces of the sacrificial cycle into the fully reflected mechanistic system of their transcendent ritual. Transcendence cast sacrality into the shade.[89]

5.1.3 Tantric Traditions

In South Asia, Tāntrika systems evolved in response to these Smārta conventions, approximately at the turn of the early medieval era (5th Century CE). Generally, Tantric initiates observed a system of 'heteropraxy' (*nāstik*) led by virtuosi from a multitude of caste groups. Their liturgies were designed to deliberately violate Vedic rules of ritual purity and ethical rectitude upheld in those communities. By doing so, Tantric adepts worked to access the hypogeal depths of immanent energy populated by fearsome, blood-accepting divinities, which is set in theoretical opposition to the transcendent world of Brahman.

To access worldly power, Tantric ideas systematized the body as a vehicle susceptible to ritualized discipline, which may involve extreme austerities or spiritual techniques. Years of training enhances a Tantric practitioner's constitution with the wider aim of attuning his body to corporeal powers (*śakti*) lodged in the material plane. To receive this knowledge, adepts must undergo initiation (*dīkṣā*) into an esoteric lineage which, according to Sanderson, is meant to:

> [...] destroy the rebirth-generating power of the individual's past actions (*karma*) in the sphere of Vedic-determined values, and to consubstantiate him with the deity in a transforming interfusion of divine power.[90]

86 Ibid., p. 78.
87 Ibid., p. 76.
88 Ibid., p. 82.
89 Ibid., p. 83.
90 Sanderson, 'Śaivism and the Tantric Traditions', p. 660.

Once initiated, *tāntrikas* learn to harness this divine strength (*śakti*) via specific ritual observances (*vidyā*) inculcated within their lineage. The power of *śakti*—unlike *ātman*—is a physical energy anthropomorphized as a feminine principle (or goddess) that vitalizes the material plane. (Samuel would draw a similarity here with alchemical notion of *qi* in Chinese cosmology[91]). Tantric logic stipulates that practitioners adopt routines of embodied gestures and verbal formulae (*mantra*) that vivify this omnipresent *śakti*. These practices work by stimulating the adept's subtle body—composed of various etheric nodes (*nādī*) and life-breaths (*prāṇa*)—from which the essence of ancestral divinities, as *śakti*, can appear within them. Since the medieval period, these power-enhancing rituals have enabled Tantric initiates to conjur magic (*siddhi*) or to manipulate matter (practices known as *tantra-mantra* in Nepal).

Tantric cults also demonstrate social plurality; members can be descendants from diverse caste backgrounds who are inducted as initiates of a common esoteric lineage headed by a teacher (*guru*). A Tantric syndicate is given momentum by a common Tantric god/goddess—either Bhairava (lit. 'the terrific one', the ferocious manifestation of god, Śiva) or a fierce (*ugra*) goddess—who inculcates his/her secret teachings via Tantric texts or *Āgamas* to his/her adepts. In Padoux's analysis, affiliations between adept and deity are frequently enounced as familial alliances, insofar as a Tantric lineage constitutes that deity's family (*kula*).[92]

While Gupta expansionism institutionalized Smārta Brahmanism, post-Gupta expropriation encouraged sweeping socio-religious change with the resurrection of parochial dynasties. Copper-plate charter documents (*sasana*) record how kings would adopt specific tactics to assure the security of their domain, specifically by indemnifying severe penalties.[93] Michaels describes how the Gupta empire's dismantlement into chiefdoms encouraged the growth of new regional cults (*deśī*), that diffused Tantric ideas from the Gupta heartland (the Gangetic plains); after the empire's disintegration, the dissemination of Tantric cults integrated them with regional divinities, that formed the royal cult of *deśī* polities.[94] Politically, such polities were re-structured as petty kingdoms ruled by rejuvenated royal lineages. To assure their protection, a regal lineage would sponsor a Tantric goddess-cult; for instance, among Newars, the Malla kings integrated warrior goddess, Taleju, into their court as an emblem

91 Geoffrey Samuel, *The Origins of Yoga and Tantra: Indic Religions to the Thirteenth Century* (Cambridge: CUP, 2008), pp. 278–279.

92 Padoux, *Hindu Tantric World*, p. 9.

93 Keay, *India*, p. 157.

94 Michaels, *Hinduism Past and Present*, p. 42.

of political sovereignty: Her iconic presence—in variegated manifestations—was enshrined in royal temple sanctums. According to Sarkar, a royal goddess' vitality—distributed among her 'sisters' as a goddess-clan—was renewed during an 'investiture' festival in autumn (Skt: *Navārātra*; Newa: *Mohani*; Nepa: *Daśain*), which secured the legitimacy of post-Gupta sovereign lineages.[95]

In these kingdoms, all ultra-transgressive rites, which included any power-inducing rite linked with death, eroticism, and bodily fluids, were identified with 'left-handed'[96] Tantric practice. Indeed, for today's Tantric initiands, the use of blood, alcohol offerings, and, in some cases, cremation-ground dwelling during ritual is commonplace. Less extreme praxes, or 'right-handed' rites (*dakṣinācārya*), are differentiated from 'left-handed' conduct (*vāmācāra*), though sometimes left- and right-handed were amalgamated.[97] Sanderson tracks the origins of such right-handed traditions to the 5th Century CE Śaiva ('Śiva worshipping') Saiddhantika (dualist) orders, who stemmed from an overarching Mantramārga tradition ('path of mantra'). On the other hand, left-handed customs can be traced to a lineage of Kashmiri non-Saiddhantika schools, that in Kerala and Nepal, combined nascent Śākta traditions (*kula-mārga*) with Kāpālika ideas (which preceded the Nāth tradition, and whose practitioners later dispersed these Śākta concepts).[98] This division between the left- and right-hand also appears within the Śākta textual transmissions, which, together, form the left-handed cults of Kālī (*kālīkula*), and right-handed cults of benign Tripurasundarī (*Śrīkula*),[99] the latter of which informed the Tantra of Kerala's Nambutiri Brahmins. Broadly, I argue Folk Śākta performances spiral and, therefore, synthesize Śaiva- and Śākta-cults in *bricolage webs of ritual knowledge*.

5.1.3.1 *What about Tantric Buddhism? Dākinīs, Bhairava, and the Power of Emotion*

Though Indian Buddhism emerged to counter Brahmanical religion, it too gradually splintered into sects of its own, and of these sects, Tantric Buddhism developed from earlier Mahāyāna ideas. According to Samuel, Tantric Buddhism's worldview also melded with Śaiva-Śākta culture—e.g. its pan-

95 Bihani Sarkar, *Heroic Shaktism: The Cult of Durga in Ancient India Kingship* (Oxford: OUP, 2017).

96 In South Asia, the left-hand is considered pollutive.

97 For a Durkheimian discussion on the left- and right-hand, see Robert Hertz, *Death and the Right Hand* (London: Routledge, 2013 [1909]).

98 Sanderson, 'Śaivism and the Tantric Traditions'.

99 Ibid.

theon linked nature spirits with *bodhisattvas* and wrathful divinities—as it sprang across the Indic subcontinent via the Indo-China trade route. Textually, Sanderson adds that mid-medieval Buddhist Tantra may have reciprocally interchanged elements from Śaiva Tantra.[100] To illustrate: the iconography of Śaiva god, Bhairava and his Buddhist counterpart, Mahākāla (Dharmapāla) merged, in such a way that Bhairava and Mahākāla—wielding ignorance-scything swords—drew upon material existence as a way of representing the Tantric path towards enlightenment.[101] (This pantheon-sharing—here, Śaiva-Buddhist—is particularly prominent among Newar communities, especially in Kathmandu's temples). In addition, fierce goddesses, too, were appropriated by Tantric Buddhism, namely, the *dākinīs*, who, like Śākta goddesses, are aggressively powerful. As Shaw highlights: "[Dākinī] is a radical departure from the neutrality of Mahāyāna nondualism and clearly derives from the Śākta view of women as possessors of a special spiritual potency and as vessels and channels of energy (*śakti*) that gives rise to life and well-being on all levels".[102]

Unlike Theravāda Buddhism—whose traditions describe enlightenment as ultra-transcendence (*parinirvāṇa*)—Tantric Buddhism was influenced by the idea that enlightenment was immanent in the world, according to Nagarjuna's concept of 'Buddha-nature'. For Nagarjuna, the world (or cyclical-worldly existence) (*saṃsāra*) and enlightenment (*nirvāṇa*) are cognate by nature, in such a way that one is percolatively encased in the other. As in Folk Śākta ritual, materiality—with its array of emotions derived from material transience—is the source of body-accelerating energy. In the *Mūlamadhyamakakārikā*, Nagarjuna articulates his view like so:

> There is not the slightest difference
> Between cyclic existence and nirvāṇa.
> There is not the slightest difference
> Between nirvāṇa and cyclic existence.
> Whatever is the limit of nirvāṇa,
> That is the limit of cyclic existence.[103]

---

100 Alexis Sanderson quoted by Bjarne Wernicke-Olesen, 'Introduction', in *Goddess Tradition in Tantric Hinduism: History, Practice, and Doctrine*, (London: Routledge, 2016), p. 6.

101 Samuel, *The Origins of Yoga*, p. 266.

102 Miranda Shaw, *Passionate Enlightenment: Women in Tantric Buddhism* (Princeton: Princeton University Press, 1994), p. 44.

103 Mūlamadhyamakakārikā, XXV: 19–20, trans. by Jay L. Garfield, *The Fundamental Wisdom of the Middle Way: Nagarjuna's* Mūlamadhyamakakārikā, (Oxford: OUP, 1995), p. 75.

The Tantric Buddhists—whose adherents comprised unconventionally transgressive *mahāsiddhas*—built upon Nagarjuna's Mahāyānist stance; for them, all beings-in-the-world can transform negative emotions (desire or ignorance) into a source of extranormal power. For example, Lewis claims that mahāsiddhas—a 'countercultural' group that defied Theravāda Buddhist and Vedic norms—would harness defiling emotions and abnormal behaviour to extirpate them;[104] as we commonly say, "like heals another like". As Samuel clarifies, all material existence—the pollution of rivers and natural diseases—are as much an embodiment of Buddha-nature than 'pure', unspoiled phenomena.[105] We can see how this shared cosmology—emphasizing impurity's potentiality—brought Tantric Hindu and Buddhist conceptions together, as we have seen in Newar societies, contra Brahmanical or Vedic ritual purity.

Be that as it may, higher-caste Brahmans have perpetually been initiated into Tantric lineages since their inception, insinuating that Smārta Brahmanism and Tantra were not altogether incommensurable. Certainly, hints at proto-Tantric ideas, such as yogic physiology, are listed in traditional Brahmanical canons. The Kaṭha Upaniṣad 6.10.13 reads:

> One hundred and one, the veins of the heart.
> One of them runs up to the crown of the head.
> Going up to it, he reaches the immortal.
> The rest, in their ascent, spread out in all directions.[106]

As Sanderson summarizes, Brahmin priests sometimes employed ritualized methods from a range of cultic systems to conduct their religious life, such that '[a Tantric practitioner can be] internally a Kaula, externally a Saiva, while remaining Vedic in one's social practice'.[107] In Kerala, for example, contemporary Nambūtiri Brahmans practice 'right-handed' Tantra in public worship. Teyyāṭṭam and Tantric temples otherwise adopt 'left-handed' practices (Brahman castes do **not** attend Teyyam performances because their rites utilize styles of transgressive *left-handed* conduct). In Teyyāṭṭam and Navadurgā tra-

104 Todd Lewis, 'Tantra: The Diamond Vehicle', in *Buddhism: An Illustrated Guide*, ed. by Kevin Trainor (London: Duncan Baird Publishers, 2001), p. 162.

105 Geoffrey Samuel, 'Paganism and Tibetan Buddhism: Contemporary Western Religions and the Question of Nature', in *Nature Religion Today: Paganism in the Modern World*, (Edinburgh: Edinburgh University Press, 1998), p. 134.

106 *Upaniṣads*, p. 246.

107 Alexis Sanderson, 'Purity and Power among the Brahmins of Kashmir', in *The Category of the Person: Anthropology, Philosophy, History*, ed. by Michael Carrithers et al., (Cambridge: CUP, 1985), p. 205.

ditions, exchanges of impure substances transcend the concerns of Brahmanical purity; the reciprocal sharing of contaminating substances across inter-caste groups within a political boundary harnesses the civic state's omnipotent energy. Said differently, it is worldly, political power of the king that primarily interested a circle of Tantric dancer-mediums, not the virtue of one's transcendental essence (*Brahman*).

If worshippers of Teyyam and Navadurgā are not initiated into a Tantric lineage, then by what means can non-initiated lineages participate in their ritual performances? Here, a certain description of medieval Śākta cults, presented by André Padoux, may help us historically. He claims that a more or less totemic link between the families of deity-mediums and their lineage goddesses—also attached to the royal cult—can expand outwards across the territory within a collective ceremony. He states:

> Yoginīs ... were wild, blood-drinking deities radiating out from the heart of a main deity as an all-pervasive network of power (*yoginījāla*). They are often described as hordes (*gaṇa*) organized in families, clans (*kula*), or lineages (*gotra*), usually considered as grouped in eight families presided over by a "Mother" (Mātṛ), who is often a very powerful deity. Yoginīs concentrate in power seats (*pīṭha*) where they are worshipped, while also possessing women and their dev.[108]

A Folk Śākta performance—as a collective space—forges 'an all-pervasive network of power' between different lineages and castes so that vibrations of power, mobilized by a medium-troupe's esoteric link to the goddess-clan, can affect the bodies of those uninitiated devotees. During the ritual, a series of symmetrical gift-exchanges and blessings between mediums and partisans affords this aptitude of **exotericising**—or making public—esoteric energies. In short, Folk Śākta performances made public the techniques of medieval Tantric virtuosi, whose mastery was previously confined to esoteric lineages. As such, the genesis of Folk Śākta performances chronologically succeeded the esoteric cultus. In both locales, this point of transition from esoteric liturgy to exoteric performance can be tracked circa 11th–16th Century CE. The exotericisation of a Śākta Tantric cosmology in ritual performance was ordered by sovereign decree: in Malabar, Kōlattiri-dynastic kings (11th Century CE) endorsed Teyyāṭṭam, and in Bhaktapur, King Suvarna (16th Century CE, Malla dynasty) consecrated Navadurgā.

108 Padoux, *Hindu Tantric World*, p. 49.

5.1.4 Folk Śākta Tantric Cosmology: The Goddesses, Gaṇeśa, and Bhairava

As a corporeal fount of earthly divinities, Tantric cosmologies are concentrated on terrestrial forces (*śakti*), which, in turn, produce worlds that are magically efficacious, capricious, and transitory. In these worlds, the focal point of the divine pantheon is its spiraling **centre**—a centre figureheaded by two divine beings who embody the worldly power of a kingdom's polity: usually, the centre represents a male-female unity of Bhairava (manifested as the polity's King[109]) with Durgā, his consort, the royal goddess (also known as Bhagavatī in Kerala, or Taleju in Bhaktapur). Folk Śākta pantheons tend to accentuate the female aspect of divinity represented by a goddess-clan—also known as Yoginīs or Mātṛs (lit. 'mothers')—centred on Durgā with Bhairava and Gaṇeśa, who, taken together, concretize state power.

From a historical perspective, Sarkar's monograph on Durgā traces her mythological beginnings—in Sanskrit literature—as Nidrā-kālarātri, an early Vaiṣṇava goddess (3rd Century–5th Century CE).[110] In Nidrā-kālarātri's mythology—narrated in the Harivaṃśa—she is known as the goddess of time, dreaming, and the monsoon, and a section of that narrative reads: 'the goddess of death/time in embodied form entered surrounded by clouds of the end'.[111] Nidrā-kālarātri's nature, then, is linked to the plane of unconscious, bodily, and material processes (fertility, menstruation, dreaming, life-blood, and death), unlike the transcendence of Viṣṇu, her 'pure' consort. Sarkar notes:

> So while Viṣṇu is connected to consciousness and mental processes, she is connected to his activity of creation unfolding covertly in beings while they are unconscious through her power [in] thought, dreaming, and sleep [...] In this way, Nidrā is hallucinatory power, a divine trickster, seizing the consciousness of beings.[112]

Indeed, for an Indic king, political decisions pertaining to his kingdom were indirectly influenced by regal goddesses who could guide him in visionary dreams.[113] Dream-like visions also feature in Teyyāṭṭam songs; Teyyam medi-

---

109 Astrid Zotter, 'State rituals in a secular state?', in *Religion and Secularism in Contemporary Nepal*, ed. by David Gellner et al., (Oxford: OUP, 2016), p. 267.

110 Sarkar, *Heroic Shāktism*.

111 Ibid., p. 50.

112 Ibid., p. 46.

113 Don Handelman, *One God, Two Goddesses, Three Studies of South Indian Cosmology* (Leiden: Brill, 2014), p. 126.

ums are well-known for their ability to contact ancestral gods and goddesses in their dreams.[114] By the early medieval period, Nidrā's paradoxical power—life-affirming and life-destroying like the monsoon she personifies—intertwined with a culture of body-based, unconscious-enhancing practices that produced a medieval Śākta cosmology: this cosmos—epitomized by Durgā, her goddess-clan, and the regal cult—is characteristically potent, volatile, and bio-spheric. Under Durgā's guardianship, the goddess-clan encompasses a polity's material power.

Drawing on an emic schema, Dyczkowski systematizes the goddess-clan as a set of seven, eight, or nine goddesses who correspond to aspects of body, space, and speech, expressed as a triad: (1) body physiology, (2) verbal formulae, and (3) directions of the compass.[115] In the Kathmandu Valley, Gaṇeśa and Bhairava also form octad clans—Aṣṭa-bhairava and Aṣṭa-Gaṇeśa—mapping Tantric-oriented polities.[116] Additionally, local ancestors and heroic warriors become genealogically affiliated with goddess-clans, for they are deified in regional shrines (*śakti-piṭhas*) that embed their macro-clan territory.

Among Śākta worshippers, Gaṇeśa, the protean mediator, is also celebrated for his notably protective reputation; he is, of course, the goddess' fictive son and second-generation deity:[117] as offspring to Śiva and Parvātī, Gaṇeśa is a cosmic gatekeeper and 'remover of obstacles' who was born from Parvāti's bodily residue—pollution—to guard her quarters.[118] Folk Śākta polities venerate Gaṇeśa to ensure that he, as a remover of obstacles, can stabilize the circuit of material power channelled during ritual ceremonies.

Here, I suggest that Gaṇeśa, like other Tantric deities, represents a spiraling wild-tame power-binary; put differently, he is a visual theology of Tantric sacrifice who embodies the goddess-clan's web-like ritual cosmos: by combining the wild head of elephant-demon Gajāsura and tamed body of a man, Gaṇeśa manifests the ambivalent power of this threshold. It is Gaṇeśa's ambiguous status as a therianthropic demon-deity sacrificed and reanimated by his father that places him at the boundaries between unruly, but bountiful, wilderness and the kingdom's tamed power. In Bhaktapur, as in Varanasi, Gaṇeśa and mother-

114 Dilip Menon, 'The Moral Community of the Teyyattam: Popular Culture in Late Colonial Malabar', *Studies in History*, 9.2 (1993), p. 204.

115 Mark Dyczkowski, *The Doctrine of Vibration: An Analysis of the Doctrine and Practices of Kashmir Shaivism* (Delhi: Motilal Barnarsidass, 1981), p. 199.

116 Gerard Toffin, *Newar Society: City, Village, and Periphery* (Nepal: Himal Books, 2007), p. 334 f. 23.

117 Philip Lutgendorf, 'Monkey in the Middle: The Status of Hanuman in Popular Hinduism', *Religion*, 27.4 (1997), p. 319.

118 Paul Courtright, *Gaṇeśa: Lord of Obstacles, Lord of Beginnings* (Oxford: OUP, 1985).

goddess shrines surround the margins of the polity: Tantric divinities—by integrating wilderness **and** civility—protect civilians from 'wild' incursions or demons. In keeping with Paul Courtright, I argue that Ganeśa externalizes the protean nature of Folk Śākta cosmology. With his severed head, Gaṇeśa is a therianthropic icon of blood sacrifice who intercalates cosmic dualities of wild/tame, impure/pure, and divine/human as one synthetic being. Courtright elaborates how '[Gaṇeśa is] the emblem of the cosmos itself, containing all dichotomies within his more than ample form'.[119] Gaṇeśa—like Bhairava, the King, and the goddess-clan—represents a web's centre that *spirals* between two oppositions on three levels: nature, form, and personality.

5.1.4.1 *Folk Śākta Material Worlds: Demons, Deities, and Animals*

Within Folk Śākta worlds, material power attracts the (unwelcome) agency of wild beings—demons (*daitya*), spirits, or avenging ancestors (*pitṛ*)—who can intervene in the life of a cursed individual or social group. One of the goals of the annual ritual cycle is to ensure that the surplus of worldly power *and* overall stability is sustained. A Teyyam or Navadurgā performance counterbalances these divergent poles—power and stability—to restrain the eruption of demonic forces into the civic state. These malevolent forces have veritable effects on the population; by infesting families and territories, demons can redirect a person's fate or a clan's material success to cause malfortune.

By rebalancing corporeal energies, Folk Śākta performances enable social healing; although, since a Tantric cosmos is continually changing, this redress is ephemeral. Deity-mediums exercise this caliber in consultations of traditional healing—collective, familial or individual—intended for clientele inflicted with 'spiritual' diseases. In Kerala, individuals inflicted by social ostracization—female or male—are deified in death as martyrs; all apotheosized ancestors become enshrined in a family's temple or grove. Dogs and crows are also considered ancestral messengers,[120] so a canine is Bhairava's, and in Kerala, Muttappan's vehicle (*vahana*). In this cosmos, then, deities, humans, animals, ancestors, and demons are subject to shifting metamorphosis; material success, demise, and death are all contingent possibilities. In a sense, Folk Śākta Tantra is a worldview populated by multiple agents entangled in existential interconnections charged with streams of visceral energies.[121]

---

119 Ibid., pp. 30–31.

120 Pradhan, 'Sacrifice', p. 169.

121 From the philosophical standpoint, this cosmology resonates with the Kashmir Śaiva tradition of *Spanda* ('vibration'). See Dyczkowski, *Doctrine of Vibration*, p. 29 for a succinct summary of Spanda.

5.1.4.2 *Folk Śākta Performances: Webbed Power as Menstrual Maṇḍalas*

By drawing on a 'web' to analogize the ritual's inner workings, I seek to present a partially emic position, i.e. 'Tantra' lit. translates as 'web'. In this light, I am influenced by McKim Marriott's ethno-sociology, which attempts to resolve an East-West divide by re-inserting indigenous categories into Indic-informed theorization.[122] As a *spiraling web-like ritual network*, a Folk Śākta performance integrates multivalent categories of being (not merely social affiliations, but also divinities, metaphysical doctrines, and historical realities) and lineages into a *macro-clan* through combined ritual action.

In South Asian Tantric ritual, web-like ritual networks are illustrated in a *maṇḍala* (also *yantra*), that is, a geometric space-time representation. These cosmic diagrams are composed of concentric circles surrounding a central point (*bindu*)—represented as a group of deities or a king—from which these outer circles emanate in symbiosis: deities, human bodies, societies, polities, and ritual performances reflect this spatial pattern. As affirmed in Tambiah's work on Thai society, maṇḍalic structures map the organization of medieval polities, what he conveniently coins 'galactic polity models'. Tambiah writes:

> [a] mandala (Thai: monthon), stand[s] for an arrangement of a center and its surrounding satellites and employed in multiple contexts to describe, for example: the structure of a pantheon of gods; the deployment spatially of a capital region and its provinces; the arrangement socially of a ruler, princes, nobles, and their respective retinues; and the devolution of graduated power on a scale of decreasing autonomies.[123]

In Tantric lineages, *maṇḍalic* circles represent deity clans (Skt: *gotra*); in this way, ritual connections of kinship bind distinct circles to their originating centre. As such, a *maṇḍala* conveys a unified cosmic reality, wherein individual, social, political, divine, material, and platial worlds are porous. White also summarizes a *maṇḍala's* nature: for him, a *maṇḍala* is an intersubjective, affective space that permeates beings at bodily and social levels; individual bodies, deities, and social processes co-produce a *maṇḍala*. He states:

> These often took the form of mystic diagrams (*maṇḍalas*), in which clans (*kula*) of the divinities [...] of Hindu Tantrism were set forth systematically. Such *maṇḍalas* or *yantras* were at once divine and human genealo-

122 Marriott's volume, *India through Hindu Categories*, capsulizes his position.
123 Stanley Tambiah, 'The galactic polity in Southeast Asia', *HAU: Journal of Ethnographic Theory*, 3.3 (2013), p. 508.

> gies, ritual and meditational supports, and models of and models for microcosmic, mesocosmic, and microcosmic reality, in which color, number, direction, divine name, vital breath [...] were so simultaneous proofs for the coherence of the world system they charted: structure and function were congruent.[124]

My interlocutors also routinely delineated Folk Śākta performances as *maṇḍala* spaces. Geoffrey Samuel alternatively calls *maṇḍala*-modelled rituals, "multimodal states", which, he claims, structure schemes of Aboriginal Australian dreamtime too.[125] In doing so, Samuel identifies Tantric ritual as affecting individual minds, bodies, land, and social being, all at once.[126] Outside "multimodal states", the sharing of food across caste groups is purity-related and, therefore, taboo; but, in ritual performance, this purity-based segregation is fleetingly disrupted through pollutive obeisance of *blood*.

In Folk Śākta cosmology, Tantric goddess-clans are literally uterine or menstrual constructs. (Grahn coins the term 'metaformic' for any cultural construction founded on menstruation[127]). On fieldwork, I discovered that uterine processes of **menstrual synchrony** co-produce the collective arrangement of ritual performances in Folk Śākta traditions, flowing within lineages as ritual kinship. In performance, social groups become 'metaformically' or 'menstrually' synchronous, in such a way that lineages from discrete castes fictively bleed as a macro-clan. It is through the sharing of food or sacrifice—proximity, in other words—that the goddess-clan's metaformic identity is emulated in a societal ritual. In Kerala, Caldwell argues that food-distribution and menstruation are organically linked since, in cultural terms, 'it is natural and obvious to associate [...] the *bijam* or reproductive blood-seed of the female with actual food'.[128] Flood also notes that a Śākta ritual connects the goddess, her community, and political territory through the practice of blood sacrifice. Flood states:

124 David G. White, *The Alchemical Body: Siddha Traditions in Medieval India* (Chicago: University of Chicago Press, 1996), p. 78.

125 Geoffrey Samuel, *Mind, Body, and Culture: Anthropology and the Biological Interfaces* (Cambridge: CUP, 1990), p. 70.

126 Geoffrey Samuel, 'The effectiveness of goddesses, or, how ritual works', *Anthropological Forum*, 11.1 (2001), p. 76.

127 Judith Grahn, 'Are goddesses metaformic constructs? An application of metaformic theory to menarche celebrations and goddess rituals of Kerala', (Ph.D. diss., California Institute of Integral Studies, 1999).

128 Sarah Caldwell, 'Oh Terrifying Mother: The Mudiyettu Ritual Drama of Kerala, South India' (Ph.D. diss., University of California, Berkeley, 1995), p. 295.

> Because the Goddess is all-giving and fecund, she must also be renewed with blood, the power of life, if her bounty is to continue. This renewing blood can be related to the Goddess' menstrual cycle, but is particularly the blood of sacrificial victims which can be seen as substituting for the devotee [or family lineage] him or herself.[129]

Contrary to expectations, however, sacerdotal representatives of the goddess remain largely male, while female priests are discouraged. When menstruating, a female's body is pollutive, which means women are excluded from roles of religious responsibility, even if, in Tantric societies, menstruation serves as a meta-symbol of ritual cohesion. (But, for Newar society, the practice of menstrual seclusion is not customary[130]). However, in Kerala and Bhaktapur, I witnessed two women functioning as para-priests for ritual performance, which may reflect changing attitudes toward women. For sure, recent events in Kerala indicate emerging female resistance against menstrual prohibition.

On 2nd January 2019 at Sabarimala temple—a famous pilgrimage site in Southern Kerala—two women of menstrual age disobeyed temple regulations by worshipping in its inner sanctum, which provoked pro-right BJP disapproval. Conservative Hindus claim that reproductive women contaminate the celibacy of Ayyappan, a god enshrined at the site.[131] Despite Kerala's legal stance in condemning menstruation-based restrictions,[132] disagreements among the Hindu right, worshippers, and the CPI(M)-governed state transpired into a public furore. Throughout Kerala, the influence of the BJP—patriarchal in its ideology—is intensified at Hindu sites like Sabarimala. In these environments, BJP dominance exacerbates female marginalization, even if Kerala state policy supports female tolerance vis-à-vis religious acceptance. In response, thousands of Malayali women gathered in protest, forming a 620 km 'Women's wall', arm-in-arm, as a statement of menstrual solidarity.[133] As I demonstrate in Chapters 1 and 4, there has, since the mid-medieval period, been a marked friction

129 Flood, *Introduction to Hinduism*, pp. 183–184.

130 For Newars, women of menstrual age must perform a menarche rite of seclusion known as *bārhā tayegu*. Afterwards, they are no longer subject to menstrual seclusion. See David Gellner, 'Initiation as a site of cultural conflict among the Newars', in Astrid & Christof Zotter, ed., *Hindu and Buddhist Initiations in Nepal and India* (Wiesbaden: Harrassowitz Verlag, 2010), pp. 175–176.

131 Caroline & Fillippo Osella, "Ayyappan saranam: Masculinity and the Sabarimala pilgrimage in Kerala", *JRAI*, 9.4 (2003).

132 'Sabarimala Case: How the deification of man affected woman', *Qrius*. August 28th, 2018.

133 'Two women below 50 claim they entered Kerala's Sabarimala temple', *The Times of India*. January 2nd, 2019.

between State and Brahmanical power in Northern Kerala: Kerala's postcolonial loyalty to communist politics—and its reputation as the only beef-eating state in India—distinguishes it as a devolved region that deviates from the communalist heartland of North India's 'Hindi belt'.

5.2 *Political Structure in Tantric Malabar (North Kerala) and Bhaktapur: Vertical Caste Purity, Horizontal Political Kingdom, or Both?*

For South Asianists, the relationship that supposedly divides political sovereignty from religious Brahmanical priesthood is a salient quandary: both Heesterman[134] and Dumont[135] postulate that a dichotomous conflict between politics:religion :: King:Brahmin pervaded South Asian polities universally. In medieval Malabar, apparent disputes between poligar kings and Nambutiris Brahmans are well documented (though, it seems, political rulership had ultimate authority over state affairs).[136] Bayly's account of medieval Southern Kerala shows how, before European colonialism (Dutch, Portuguese, and British), regnant authority—renewed in sacrificial ritual—was all-encompassing; Brahmins were contained under regnant rulership. She writes:

> The shedding of blood [sacrifice] was seen as a means by which to transfer or assert the warrior dynast's claims of dominion and to associate the power of the aspiring king with the supernatural domain of the region's warrior gods and power divinities.[137]

For Northern Kerala (Malabar), Mailaparambil demonstrates how political authority in Kōlattanādu kingdom was distributed among chieftain lineages (*kovilakam*), such that medieval 'power was not embodied in a raja, but manifested in its collective form—the *swarupam*',[138] and as such, 'rajaship [was] a ritual façade'.[139] In Kerala's medieval mythology, a 'Kōlattiri raja' is often lauded:

134 Jan C. Heesterman, *The Inner Conflict of Tradition: Essays in Indian Ritual, Kingship, and Society* (Chicago: University of Chicago Press, 1985).

135 Louis Dumont, *Homo Hierarchicus: The Caste System and its Implications* (Chicago, University of Chicago Press, 1966).

136 Freeman, 'Purity and Violence'.

137 Susan Bayly, 'Saints' Cults and Warrior Kingdoms in South India', in *Shamanism, History, and the State*, ed. by Nicholas Thomas & Caroline Humphrey, (Michigan: University of Michigan Press, 1996), p. 123.

138 Binu J. Mailaparambil, *Lords of the Sea: The Ali Rajas of Cannanore and the Political Economy of Malabar (1663–1723)* (Leiden: Brill, 2011), p. 37.

139 Ibid., p. 33.

Kōlattiri, in Malabar, refers to an early-medieval epithet which denotes a symbolic king, not a historical figure; it is a namesake which conveys a royal clan *en bloc*. Mailaparambil explains how the Kōlattiri clan was '*tampuram*—a common term [...] designat[ing] both local gods and [rulers] from the same cosmic category of the regional cosmos'.[140] Across South India, sovereign domains were essentially theocracies, where a king's popularity was amplified by his 'divine' role as a redistributor of land among local chieftains. As an example, Dirks describes the Tamil kingdom of *Pudukkoṭṭai*, which revered its King as a 'divinity' who was 'the symbolic head of the system of [chieftain] redistribution'.[141] Whereas Dumont viewed caste hierarchy as an Indic society's predominant 'transcendent' structure—where Brahmins dominated at the purest echelon of religio-political power—Dirks' interpretation upturns Dumont's understanding. About *Pudukkoṭṭai's* political arrangement, Dirks writes:

> The king himself is simply a Kallar [warrior], but by virtue of his connection to the entire kingdom—not just caste transcendence—he is also the *transcendent overlord* [and] by virtue of the [chieftains'] connection to the king, they do also 'transcend' their own community.[142]

In another study of Tamilnadu, Hart adds further detail: poligar kings, he explains, adopted Āgamic (Tantric) religion, not Brahmanical religion, because, among lower-castes, Āgamic influences had far-reaching appeal; in reality, no lower-caste citizen could worship within a Brahmanical temple. By embracing the religion of the masses, the king guaranteed his authority.[143] Naturally, lower-castes revered their king as the supreme deity, since the lion's share of civilians were barred from entering Brahmin temples: low-caste drummers (*kiṇai*) were contracted by their sovereign to sing eulogies praising him as a 'victorious' custodian of the domain. One such song (Puṟam 399) reads:

> '[Drummers:] I'll sing your victorious chariot in the courts of others, so your enemies tremble every time they hear, just as with every [hit of the drum] its subtle sound sharp, brought down on the eye, quivers'.[144]

140 Mailaparambil, *Lords of the Sea*, p. 38.

141 Nicholas B. Dirks, 'The structure and meaning of political relations in a South Indian little kingdom', *Contributions to Indian Sociology*, 13.2 (1979), p. 177.

142 Nicholas B. Dirks, "The Original Caste: power, history, and hierarchy in South India", *Contributions to Indian Sociology*, 23.1 (1989), p. 73.

143 George Hart, 'Early Evidence for Caste in South India', in *Dimensions of Social Life: Essays in honor of David B. Mandelbaum* (Berlin: DeGruyter, 1987).

144 Ibid., p. 471.

Similarly, in Bhaktapur, Ujesh's maternal cousin—a dancer-medium in his twenties—recited certain traditional Newari song to me on one occasion. All these songs were linked to the Navadurgā ritual, and all of them extolled the miraculous feats of Bhaktapur's foregone Malla kings.

It seems the Newars of Bhaktapur also favoured monarchical rulership; medieval Malla sovereignty, they claim, could overrule the authority of Brahman priests. Greenwold reports how his interlocutors also viewed kingship as the prevailing structure:

> [According to Greenwold's informant:] 'So you can see caste is really a matter of the king. The king can make untouchables clean and people of clean castes untouchable' [...] The priest is not omnipotent. Religious power depends in part upon the ruler's military and political power.[145]

Lichhavi and Malla dynasties actively sponsored Brahmin priesthoods, which meant that Brahmins were dependent on the crown's financial backing: this is a distinctly anti-Dumontian stance. To put it in Hocart's terms, a king would deploy Brahmanical purity as a way of legitimizing his supreme sovereignty at the apex of power. Like Dirks, Hocart goes further, with Weber in mind, insisting that medieval Indic polities integrated religious ideology and political kingship as commensurable.[146] Along these lines, Declan Quigley notes how Indic 'rule[rs] [the king] must be pur[ified]';[147] the king is emblematic of ambivalent god, Bhairava, equated with the body politic—an impure 'abomination'—which Brahmin priests must seek to purify through ritual.[148] For Bhaktapur, Quigley suggests that 'the transmission of his [king's] inauspicious qualities along with gifts of some kind [...] puts the Rajapadhyaya Brahmin [...] in something of a perilious position'.[149] Urban similarly attests that the king, like Tantra, had an ambivalent relationship with Brahmanical religion. This relationship, he says, was a 'complex negotiation between *brāḥmaṇic* traditions and the indigenous kings'[150] that, in turn, produced the Folk Śākta traditions. This hazy tension—of Tantric kingship (or, for Kerala, a decentralized ruler-

145 Stephen Greenwold, 'Kingship and Caste', *European Journal of Sociology*, 16.1 (1975), pp. 69–72.

146 Hocart, *Caste*, p. 67.

147 Declan Quigley, *The Interpretation of Caste* (Oxford: Clarendon Press, 1993), p. 169.

148 Declan Quigley, 'Kingship and 'contrapriests'', *International Journal of Hindu Studies*, 1.3 (1997), p. 578.

149 Ibid., p. 579.

150 Hugh Urban, 'The Womb of Tantra: Goddesses, Tribals, and Kings in Assam', *Journal of Hindu Studies*, 4.3 (2011), pp. 245–246.

ship) with Brahmanism—co-exist in Folk Śākta society since both traditions are autonomous, but connected, in spiraling web-networks which keeps them synchronous even in separation.

In contemporary Bhaktapur, I realized that any talk of caste among my interlocutors resorted to an awareness of status (i.e. 'so-and-so is of a lower-caste'), and yet they greeted their 'caste inferiors' as fictive brothers or sisters. From a Bhaktapurian perspective, everyone whose ancestors reside in Bhaktapur share deep senses of ethno-territorial belonging as Newar Bhaktapurians. I was told this mono-ethnic ancestral unity becomes intensified at every Navadurgā performance, and indeed, during all festivals in Bhaktapur.

5.3 *Transregional-Regional Tantra: Teyyāṭṭam and Navadurgā in Bricolage Webs of Ritual Knowledge*

Although Tantric religiosity was pan-Indic in distribution, Tantric elements acclimatized with regional or indigenous ordinances which naturally interlaced, like a web, across South Asia's kaleidoscopic milieu. It is fair to say that Newar and Keralan folk Śākta performances are eclectic and idiosyncratic among South Asia's performative traditions: Teyyāṭṭam and Navadurgā merge traditions that are pan-Indic in scope but autochthonous in form.

Tantric schools in South Asia did not develop in isolation: orders of Tantric lineages were given momentum by post-Gupta kings, who adopted their characteristically fierce divinities to represent royal religion, while Vedic traditions were governed primarily by Brahmin priests under monarchical aegis. In the early medieval period, this process of 'localising' transregional Tantric traditions, or *Tantricization*, was likely in operation throughout Indic kingdoms circa 11th–13th Centuries CE. Influenced by Srivinas' 'Sanskritization', the term *Tantricization* refers to the diffusion of Śaiva-Śākta cosmologies across the kingdoms of post-Gupta Indic territories, which were assimilated to invigorate new regal lineages and political territories. This process is discussed in Alexis Sanderson's famous article, *The Śaiva Age*.[151]

In Chapter 4, I argue these transregional Tantric systems co-networked—across South Asia—via migratory patterns of mendicant ascetic groups, particularly, the Nāth Siddha tradition (Skt. *sampradāya*), who charted pilgrimage routes. According to Padoux, the Nāth *sampradāya* are an ascetic community whose involvement with householder life is characteristically striking (as compared to other socially reclusive ascetic regiments (*ākhāṛa*)).[152] Further, Loren-

151 Alexis Sanderson, 'The Śaiva Age: The Rise and Dominance of Śaivism during the Early Medieval Period', in *The Genesis and Development of Tantrism*, ed. by Shingo Einoo, (University of Tokyo: Institute of Oriental Culture, 2009).

152 Padoux, *Hindu Tantric World*, p. 157.

zen claims the Nāth emerged from the ascetic regiments of Śaiva Kāpālikā and Kālāmukha groups, who focused on the worship of Ugra-Bhairava (whom, I argue further, is related both to the Newar exaltation of Bhairava, and to Kerala's deified untouchable, Pōṭṭan).[153] In Kerala and Nepal, Nāth yogis settled as householders, and formed their own caste groups; their status as domesticated yogis meant they were not hermetically sealed from society. Many Nāth specialists later disseminated their Śaiva-Śākta (and Sufi Islamic) Tantric knowledge to lower-caste virtuosi who surrounded their social circles. Being householders, Nāth siddhas were active in royal religion and politics as the state's 'warrior ascetics' (as Pinch calls them).[154] Within the Kerala context, ancestral warriors are regionally commonplace in the martial art of Kalaripayyāṭṭu: the Nāth siddhas' own warrior culture—brought by their migrations to Malabar—seems not inconsistent with native Kalaripayyāṭṭu (which, in later centuries, acquired Tantric paradigms of goddess worship practiced among Nāth groups). Padoux notes how contemporary Nāth communities:

> organize yearly festivals, traveling in groups to a main gathering point, always carrying with them their sacred fire, the *dhuni*. In Nepal, they have an important monastery at Caughera (in Dang province, near the Indian frontier), which is very prosperous and active. Surprisingly, even though the Nāthas are theoretically not Śākta, each year this monastery—dedicated to Gorakhnāth and to Bhairava—organizes a pilgrimage to a neighboring temple of the Goddess. Also unexpected is that the heads of the monastery are called pīr, a Muslim title. And there are roving Nātha yogis. But today, there are only a few thousand Nātha yogis. In Nepal, there is a particular Nātha group, the Kusle-Yogis, who are not renouncers but householders that form a caste (this also in Rajasthan). I alluded previously to the links between Nāths and Sufism.[155]

Nāth yogīs are worshippers of Bhairava, a god eminent in Śākta and Vajrayāna cosmology. Sax describes how Nāth yogīs spread the cult of Bhairava to and from the Himalayas, stating that: 'the cult of Bhairav [...] is connected with the tradition of the "eighty-four siddhas" which [...] is closely associated with Tibet as well as [...] the Kanphata yogi tradition'.[156]

---

153 Lorenzen, *Kāpālikas*, p. 35.

154 William R. Pinch, *Warrior Ascetics and Indian Empires* (Cambridge: CUP, 2006).

155 Padoux, *Hindu Tantric World*, p. 157.

156 William Sax, *God of Justice: Ritual Healing and Social Justice in the Central Himalayas* (Oxford: OUP, 2009), p. 37.

As per Parmenides' insistence that the mechanisms of existential being and metaphysical thought interface,[157] I advance the hypothesis that, from the 8th Century CE, Brahmanical, Vajrayāna Buddhist, and, in Kerala, Sufi Islamic systems reflect web-like connectedness in Folk Śākta performances, quite unlike the exclusivism of Vedic praxis. In this model, local religious systems—indigenous fertility cults and aniconic goddesses—were piecemeal subsumed into the 'web'-lineages of Śākta Tantra that spanned the Indic kingdoms.

Indeed, the assimilation of transregional Tantra with local cults could be ascribed to a broader 'Sanskritization' dynamic, as Srivinas describes.[158] 'Sanskritization' describes a process in which local gods/goddesses are appropriated in terms of high-caste Brahmanical religion, thereby imposing a preferred, if hegemonic, cultural interpretation (i.e. high-caste ideology onto lower-caste practices). Nevertheless, I tend to think 'Sanskritization' was more complex for Folk Śākta Tantra than Srivinas would assume. Throughout their history, sets of cultic interpretations—whether Śaiva, Śākta, Vaiṣṇava etc.—have gradually infused Folk Śākta performances; Dupuche articulates this understanding perfectly: "She [the goddess] appropriates all because she is all".[159] However, to deduce that South Asian religious identities display unremitting egalitarianism presumes a credulous idealism. According to Sax, identity politics and doctrinal rifts materialize on the ground:

> After all, adherents of the various traditions within Indian religion (Vaiṣṇava, Śākta, Jain, Sikh, Muslim, Christian, Ultilitarian etc.) do manage to communicate among themselves; so they must share at least some assumptions [...] If two traditions disagree about something—say, the meaning of a text—then the very fact of disagreement shows not only that they are operating in similar semantic and political fields but also that both sides perceive that there is something worth fighting for.[160]

157 Leonardo Tarán, *Parmenides: A Text with Translation, Commentary, and Critical Essays* (Princeton: Princeton University Press, 1964), p. 41.

158 M.N. Srivinas, 'A Note on Sanskritization and Westernization', *The Far Eastern Quarterly*, 15.4 (1956).

159 Dupuche, John, 'Appropriating the Inappropriate', in *Conceiving the Goddess: Transformation and Appropriation in Indic Religions*, ed. By Jayant Bapal & Ian Mabbett, (Melbourne: Monash University Press, 2017), p. 124.

160 William Sax, *Mountain Goddess: Gender and Politics in a Himalayan Pilgrimage* (Oxford: OUP, 1991), p. 9.

Regardless of this discrepancy, Folk Śākta performances seem preoccupied with collective praxis as opposed to doctrinal intricacies. Multiple interpretations on doctrinal matters are permissible in ritual performance; Folk Śākta Tantra's tenets form *bricolage webs of ritual knowledge*, which mirror the web-like connections created in ritual amidst lineages and bodies.

5.4 *'Deity Possession' as a Category: Folk Possession, Śākta Deity Embodiment, or Both?*

Since these rituals are (a) galvanized by warrior goddesses, (b) led by subaltern practitioners, and (c) narrated through local folklore, I use the typology of 'Folk Śākta Tantra' to classify them. In this way, I seek to differentiate Folk Śākta performances from other goddess dance-drama (be it Mudiyettu in Kerala or Devī dances in Bhaktapur) to avoid their conflation; the latter is not transformative ritual, but a theatrical rendition of myth. Padoux also stressed that goddess-oriented worship or 'Śāktism' can indeed be Tantric in orientation, but that many popular goddess cults do not explicitly display Tantric components, because the 'boundary line ... between what is popular and what might be considered popularly Tantric is difficult to draw'.[161] On the other hand, he adds that living goddess worship (typified in Navadurgā and Teyyāṭṭam) evince specificities that delineate them as Tantric in pedigree. In many ways, Navadurgā and Teyyāṭṭam are, essentially, rituals of 'possession', whereby a deity possesses an initiate's body (*āveśa*), which has Tantric resonances. In short, Folk Śākta rituals have many Tantric features that include: (1) deity possession in bodies, (2) blurring of caste distinctions through impure gift-giving, and (3) use of martial weapons. Padoux elaborates:

> Goddesses also appear as living goddesses (*jīvan mātājī*), embodied in women of the Charan caste, a caste of bards and shepherds. This tradition's rites are still very much alive today; it is an essential social cohesive element [showing] its more Tantric traits.[162]

By deploying 'Folk Śākta Tantric performances' as a typology, I seek to combine Padoux's description with June McDaniel's threefold model of Śākta Tantric traditions. McDaniel claims that Śākta Tantra displays three identifiable strands that are interlinked, but not necessarily coterminous: (1) the 'folk-tribal strand', related to local goddesses, fertility, and healing; (2) the 'yogic

161 Padoux, *Hindu Tantric World*, p. 158.

162 Padoux, *Hindu Tantric World*, pp. 158–159.

strand', which is based on Vedantic dualism—illusory world and transcendental soul—depicted iconographically in copulation imagery (*yab-yum*); and (3) the 'devotional-bhakti strand' associated with kinship relations between mother goddesses and their initiands.[163] These strands can be included or excluded from Tantric cults to varying degrees like 'strands of a rope',[164] and I suggest that Navadurgā's and Teyyāṭṭam's centrality on land, kingship, and goddess veneration means it is a conglomeration of **mostly** '*folk*' and '*devotional*' Śākta Tantra (it does not, however, eclipse the *yogic* strand). According to McDaniel, folk Śākta Tantra 'tend[s] to be the healing of disease or discord in the group, fertility (for plants, animals, or people), protection from danger, and the ability to prophesy and to exorcize spirits and ancestors.'[165] It seems Teyyāṭṭam and Navadurgā focus on ancestors, goddesses, and healing corroborates well with McDaniel's designation. And it is to the category of 'deity possession' that I now turn.

Many Indologists—informed by textual compilations—would bracket Folk Śākta performances as cases of 'possession'[166] (*āveśa*); the deity-mediums are 'possessed' by the deities (although, at first sight, the dancer-mediums may *appear* externally possessed). Indeed, what is really at issue is whether dancer-mediums experience 'deity possession' (*samāveśa*) **or** are embodying the deities (as outlined above, Tantric deities are both immanent and transcendent in nature). The taxonomy of 'possession' can imply that the subject has been spontaneously invaded by the force of an external agent, rather than premeditatedly induced. Dancer-mediums' own parlance for their experiences seemed closer to the latter; in their accounts, I heard no deity-medium using Newari or Malayalam derivatives of *samāveśa.*

In relation to the dynamics of possession, Platvoet broadly categorized four main elemental constituents which marks a state of possession. She labels them (1) *dissociation* from the 'normal' mundane world, (2) *hyperkinesis* or accelerated or total loss of muscular movement, (3) character alteration and (4) *post-possession amnesia* where activities performed during the trance-like state cannot be recalled, nay remembered.[167] Possession trance displays a sense

163 June McDaniel, *Offering Flowers, Feeding Skulls: Popular Goddess Worship in West Bengal* (New York: OUP, 2014), p. 6.

164 Ibid., p. 8.

165 Ibid., p. 8.

166 For an in-depth exploration of *āveśa* in Indic texts, see Frederick Smith, *The Self Possessed: Deity and Spirit Possession in South Asian Literature and Culture* (New York: Columbia University Press, 2006).

167 Jan Platvoet, 'Rattray's Request: Spirit Possession among the Bono of West Africa', in *Indigenous Religions: A Companion*, ed. By Graham Harvey, (London: Cassell, 2000), p. 82.

that an individual has been replaced by the agency of a deity/spirit, thereby rendering passive the identity of that person. Antithetically, within the Keralan and Newari contexts, 'personhood' and 'body' are portrayed as fluid and porous modalities, containing: (1) 'gross' elements such as physicality, one's socially-defined affiliation etc., and (2) 'subtle' elements or invisible vitality '[...] up to a claimed identity with the luminous essence of divinity itself'.[168] This divine luminosity (*śakti*) is universally-bound within all beings. According to Freeman, *śakti* hazes the ontological demarcations amid human and divine to such an extent that Keralans saw no distinction between them:

> [According to Freeman's informant]: 'In my house, there is no difference at all. Everyone is god's person. This fellow standing here is Gulikan's [a teyyam deity's] man'.[169]

Body, consciousness, and semantics, therefore, intertwine to create a 'multiple self' here: in Folk Śākta societies, two entities exist disparately, yet not without possibility of interaction, within one person. In a rejection of 'possession' as a category, Malik postulates *transformative embodiment* as a finer alternative. 'Transformative embodiment' refers here to intra-somatic shifts between body and consciousness that transforms a person—from human to deity—in ritual.[170]

Using Macann's notion of 'genetic ontology', Malik says this movement from body and consciousness operates like a rite de passage. These three internal phases he decodes like so: (1) pre-deity embodiment, where a person's 'body' and 'consciousness' are amalgamated in their mind-body complex; (2) once a medium incarnates a deity, there is a fissure of the 'body' and 'consciousness' and a heightened perception of the body is achieved; and (3) when a medium returns to his human state, 'body' and 'consciousness' reunite through a '[...] process of reflection'.[171]

Heightened embodied or subjective shifts in emotion were (broadly) the responses I received in both locales. Following Malik[172] above, I utilize the term

---

168 Terms 'gross' and 'subtle' here are used by John R. Freeman, 'Untouchable Bodies of Knowledge in the Spirit Possession of Malabar', in *The body in India: Ritual, transgression, performativity*, ed. by Axel Michaels & Christophe Wulf, (Paragrana: Akad-Verlag, 2009), p. 139.

169 Freeman, 'Purity and Violence', pp. 107–108.

170 Aditya Malik, 'Is possession really possible? Towards a hermeneutics of transformative embodiment in South Asia', in *Health and Religious Rituals in South Asia: Disease, Possession and Healing*, ed. by Fabrizio Ferrari, (London: Routledge, 2011), pp. 22–24.

171 Ibid., p. 24.

172 Aditya Malik, *Tales of Justice and Rituals of Divine Embodiment: Oral Narratives from the Central Himalayas* (Oxford: OUP, 2016), pp. 168–170.

'divine embodiment' over 'possession' because the latter conjectures dualism, where one external agent forcibly eclipses the passive human agent (These traditions are not *āveśa*).

Broadly speaking, I.M. Lewis characterizes two modes of 'possession-like ritual complexes' that persist in pre-modern societies cross-culturally: (1) 'spirit possession', performed by peripheral or marginally oppressed groups (women, lower-castes etc.), where their subaltern frustrations are expressed through being possessed by 'lower' spiritual beings. And (2) shamanic healing directed by priesthoods who channel a pantheon of 'higher' spirits or deities. In contrast to 'lowly' spirit possession, shamanism dominates as a central system of ritual practice at the highest rungs of that society.[173] As Raheja's ethnography also notes,[174] a central-peripheral distinction concretizes a hierarchization of auspicious 'central' and inauspicious 'peripheral' castes; possession is the subordinate religious system that keeps marginalized persons in their position, allowing no hope of mobilization. However, in Teyyāṭṭam and Navadurgā performances, the power of the god/goddess is transferred from central state-owned Tantric temples to lower-caste mediums in a shared ritual at the annual cycle's inauguration. In the manner of Bakhtin's carnivalesque,[175] central power (*śakti*) is channeled and spirals into lower-caste dancer-mediums, thereby precipitating a transient reversal of hierarchical structure into a territorial macro-clan.

In this shift to ritual web-networks, a performance becomes a potential site for hierarchical maintenance **and** transformation. Indeed, both *central* and *peripheral* cults of Tantra in Kerala and Bhaktapur conveyed human-to-divine transformation in similar ways i.e. accessing *śakti* through the subtle body's five energy portals (*nāḍī*). The fact that *central* (Tantric temple) and *peripheral* (Teyyāṭṭam and Navadurgā performances) cults emulated each other was also evident in accounts by subaltern dancer-mediums. I was told bodies were multi-agent beings or, in Marriott's theoretical language, "dividuals": human and divine beings are (theoretically) *nondual*. Put another way, divinity and humanity are internally related ontologies or worlds of being (transcendence within immanence, god within material bodies, etc). Folk Śākta gods are not extramundane and transcendent, but worldly and immanent. Amid deity and virtuoso, bodily connectedness, solidified in ritual through lineage bonds, binds them totemically. One of Freeman's interlocutors encapsulated

173 Ioan M. Lewis, *Ecstatic Religion: A Study of Shamanism and Spirit Possession* (London: Routledge, 2002 [1971]).

174 Raheja, *Poison in the Gift*.

175 Bakhtin, *Rabelais*.

this view: 'When it comes about that two selves are brought into a state of witnessing each other as one, in that place a divine power is created'.[176]

5.5 *Folk Śākta Mediums: Ancestral Divinities*

In positing this argument—Navadurgā and Teyyāṭṭam divinities as ancestral kin—I regard Folk Śākta deities as structural symbols of human relationships **and** as processual persons with their own agencies, life-biographies, and relationships. Divinities are structural **and** processual agents because they represent and constitute the society's many relations (their mothers, fathers, uncles and so on). In his article on Tamil possession worship, Moreno analyses deity possession as a way of exchanging power with divine realities. He writes:

> This personalistic view is crucial to an understanding of established patterns of worship [...] At both levels we can observe the dynamics of mutually rewarding reciprocity between divine and human persons, carried out by exchanges of substances which are thought to be restorative and life-enhancing.[177]

In *Śaivism and the Tantric Traditions*, Sanderson stresses that Yoginī nondual (*Kaula*) tantric tradition forged lineage relations between Tantric adepts and deities:

> [which] established a link between him [adept] and the incarnate Yoginīs, for these families of the eight mothers were also theirs. On days of the lunar fortnight sacred to his mother the initiate was to seek out a Yoginī of his family. By worshipping her he aspired to attain supernatural powers and occult knowledge.[178]

Some studies on Śākta Tantra tend to present a flagrant Orientalist romanticism that reduces Tantra's purview to mystic 'eroticism' (imagery of Śiva and Śakti in cosmic sexual union etc.). I think this does some disservice to the rubric of 'Tantra' and its complex pluri-typologies. As McDaniel's typologies details, 'Folk', 'devotional', and 'yogic' Śāktism make up a Tantric system. Navadurgā and

---

176 John R. Freeman, 'Performing Possession: Ritual and Consciousness in the Teyyam Complex of Northern Kerala', in *Flags of Fame: Studies in South Asian Folk Culture*, ed. by Heidrum Brückner & Lothar Lutzer, (Manohar: South Asia Books, 1993), p. 126.

177 Manuel Moreno, 'God's Forceful Call: Possession as a Divine Strategy', in *Gods of Flesh, Gods of Stone: The Embodiment of Divinity in India*, ed. by Joanne Waghorne & Norman Cutler, (Chambersberg: Anima Books 1996), p. 104.

178 Sanderson, 'Śaivism and the Tantric Traditions', p. 672.

Teyyam rituals fuse *mostly* tribal and devotional Śaktism in a principally nondual Śākta metaphysics. Tantra's erotic dimension constitutes the *yogic* strand of Śāktism in this framework, which is based upon the dualist philosophy of advaita vedānta. As described later in this section, dualism—symbolized as ritualized sexuality and visions of goddesses as pure consciousness—*can* be incorporated into Teyyāṭṭam and Navadurgā's nondual universe, but to a lesser degree. In forwarding this claim, I agree with Hugh Urban, who argues that references to sexuality in Śākta Tantra constitutes only one aggregate in the system's 'sexo-religious-political power':[179] Folk Śāktism's power (*śakti*)—stemming from the monsoon—links warrior goddesses, politics, land, and royal legitimation as a unique configuration of material reproduction. In Folk Śākta performance, these elements become co-constitutive through idioms of the body, as was explained to me by a Bhaktpurian social scientist as follows:

> [Inf.]: Śakti ['power' of the goddess-clan] not only resides in a weapon or sword, it is in the body. Without the body, how can we use the sword's power?

During Newar rites, Ujesh explained that goddesses can warn their votaries of impending problems by sweating or bleeding from their image (*mūrti*); the *mūrti* is their body too. In Folk Śākta traditions, bodies are not considered illusory impediments for harnessing the goddess-clan's power. On the contrary, bodies are themselves deified vehicles because, metaphorically, blood relations between a mother goddess and her initiates flow through them; for instance, in Brahmayāmala 46: 107–109,[180] goddess and adept are described as fictive mother and son.

The differentiation between these two nondualisms lies in advaita vedānta's later adoption of a material-spirit or *prakṛti-puruṣa* divide; transcendence becomes immanent through consciousness alone, and not its container, the *body*. Like Nidrā-kālarātri, all Tantric goddesses embody unconscious power, and not consciousness per se. From the perspective of morality, then, Newars claim that the internal goddess-within (Nepa. *bhagvān bhitramā*) guides their moral action in-the-world; any behaviour that is detrimental to the macro-clan is the work of a demon who, in ritual performance, is annihilated by the goddess-clan.

179 Hugh Urban, *The Power of Tantra: Religion, Sexuality, and Politics in the Study of Religion* (London: I.B. Taurus, 2010), p. 22.

180 Shaman Hatley, 'The Brahmayāmalatantra and the Early Śaiva Cults of Yoginīs', (Ph.D. diss., University of Pennsylvania, 2007).

I argue nondualism is not the same as unified 'monism' from this perspective; monism situates the macrocosm (deities) and microcosm (human/society) in all phenomena as identical within beings as consciousness, whereas nondualism recognizes them as inextricably interconnected, immanent within bodies, but not necessarily identical in form;[181] Navadurgā deities were often described as both transcendent (in external shrines) and immanent in all bodies as *bhagavān bhitramā* (Nepa: 'god-within'). Quoting the *Gorakṣa-siddhānta-saṃgraha*, Lorenzen states how Nāth-influenced or Folk Śākta worldviews are, clearly, "above dualism and monism (*dvaitādvaita-vivarjita*)".[182] Dualist logic, then, can be attached to Teyyam and Navadurgā performances: for example, 'lower-class' Teyyam deities were sometimes identified as Sanskritic deities, like Śiva or Durgā. Alexis Sanderson argues that this is true in the Śaiva textual record. In an exegesis of a Śaiva text, the *Mālinīvijayottaratantra*, he writes:

> [...] nondualism, being the transcendence of dualism, can accommodate the latter as a lower or provisional view, whereas dualism can only exclude nondualism as its antithesis.[183]

Nondualism permits a bricolage of plural interpretations to be interlaced, like a web-network, into Folk Śākta's metaphysical bedrock. In Kerala, a nondual cosmology recognizes Sufism, as Zarrilli puts it: 'Among Sufi Kalaripayyattu practitioners, importance is given to [...] actualizing higher states of [...] power'.[184]

In the field, a dancer-medium in Kannur wondered why I spoke about different religious traditions ('Tantric', 'Vedic' etc.) when I asked him about Teyyāṭṭam. He clarified that "anyone can go to a Teyyam grove, all you have to do is remove your shoes ... Not everyone can go into a [Brahmin] Temple". The same could be applied to Newari thinking, too, since their Tantric religion also shifts between Hindu and Buddhist modes of praxis. As such, Folk Śākta deities are polyvalent by nature: to illustrate, one worshipper at a Navadurgā performance in Nāla—a town located some 10 kilometers east of Bhaktapur city—stated: "here, [in Nala], Dūma is also known as Bhimsen and Simā as Draupati from the Mahābhārata". And yet, from the perspective of a social scientist in Bhaktapur: "Simā and Dūma are unlike the other Navadurgā, because they are not

181 Brooks labels Śākta Tantra as a 'type of theistic nondualism'. See Brooks, *Three Cities*, p. 87.

182 Lorenzen, *Kāpālikas*, p. 35.

183 Alexis Sanderson, 'The Doctrine of the Mālinīvijayottaratantra', in *Ritual and Speculation in Early Tantrism: Studies in honor of Andre Padoux* (Albany: SUNY Press, 1992), p. 282.

184 Phillip Zarrilli, *When the body becomes all eyes: Paradigms, Discourses, and Practices of Power in Kalaripayyattu* (New Delhi: OUP, 1998), pp. 150–151.

deities [*uniharulai devāta hoinan*], but vehicles". I propose this metaphysical eclecticism arises from a *bricolage web of knowledge* that grounds each ritual performance—local deities can be identified with their pan-Hindu counterparts, which reflects a Tantric polity's plurality.

5.6 *Structure of the Book*

In Chapters 1 and 2, this study will proceed with an introduction to each case study, the first, Teyyāṭṭam and the second, Navadurgā. From this, Chapters 3–6 will compare each case study through four shared themes, set out as follows: Chapter 3—kinship and dancer-medium communities; Chapter 4—history of Śākta Tantric Cosmology; Chapter 5—sacrifice; and Chapter 6—politics and caste structures. The conclusion will culminate by merging all these themes in neat collation.

PART 1

Case Studies

CHAPTER 1

Introducing the Southern Case Study—Teyyāṭṭam, Northern Malabar, Kerala

In a Teyyam temple-grove (*kāvu*), some ten kilometers from Kannur town, local families gathered to worship a series of Teyyam deity-mediums. Such temple-groves are diffused across Northern Kerala: specifically, a Teyyam grove is an open-air space, adjoined by coconut-tree glades, and demarcated on all sides by laterite-bricked shrines that house that region's divinities. These temple-groves—within which Teyyāṭṭam are enacted—are promulgated, regionally, as sacred spaces described, in Malayalam, as cosmic geometries (*maṇḍalam*). These groves are owned and overseen by parochial lineages (*illam*) or, in more latter-day groves, multi-caste administrative committees. Throughout Northern Malabar, *kāvu* are platial residences of enshrined ancestors and a territory's goddess-clan.

As devotees gather for a grove's ritual performance, deity-mediums proceed by harnessing the ancestral divinities and goddesses housed there. A deity's essence or power (*śakti* or *kalivụ*) originates from his or her presence within the landscape, or the woodlands that surround the grove. Having been enshrined, a divinity's power is conducted into regalia—swords, torches, or flames—which a medium later embodies in performance. Throughout the year, these shrines are tended by priests (*kōmamram*) who light oil-wicks, which preserves their ancestors' presence there.

To the rhythm of drums (*ceṇda*) and wind-instruments (*kuḻal*), deity-mediums dance by whirling swords, and hurling handfuls of rice, in all directions. Every medium's dance is unique to the deity he embodies, as is also conveyed by each medium's distinctive aesthetic appearance; deity-mediums wear costumes and headdresses which distinguish the deities they evoke. To assure this aptitude, adorned mediums—as ancestral divinities—must peer at their transformation in handheld mirrors (*vālkaṇṇati*): in that moment, they jump from their perched positions on stools (*pīṭham*) to cavort fervidly amid amassing devotees. At this stage, local worshippers stated that a dancer-medium's body had been consumed by his host divinity's inner power.

The hyperkinesia expressed in the medium's ecstatic performance—signaling his full transformation into a deity—is succeeded by an array of offerings and chicken sacrifices that pacify the deity's cantankerous nature. Certainly, deity-mediums harness forceful deities like Kandanar Kēlan—an

 | DOI:10.1163/9789004439023_003

ostracized nonconformist who perished in a forest fire, before reemerging from the flames an incandescent god.

As testament to their might, they may walk barefoot across cinders, leap over pyres, or demonstrate their skills with Kalaripayyāṭṭu weaponry; normally, deity mediums brandish double-edged swords called *uṟumi*. Calming these fierce gods requires a transference of their divine energy into sacrificial victims, usually chickens or coconuts (*teṅṅā*). Once this display draws to a close, mediums sit near a divinity's shrine, where they listen to their worshippers' concerns and allay their worries with blessings. Placated by blood or rice or any fruits of the land, the power of ancestor deities safeguards the lineage, village, and polity from external dangers, including from their own deities: curing in one moment, and cursing in the next, these gods are, themselves, invariably unpredictable.

1 Ancestors, Land, and Divinities (*Teyyam*) in Northern Kerala

Throughout North Kerala, Teyyāṭṭam are wide-spread ritual performances conducted over nine months between Tulām and Mēṭam (which, in the Gregorian calendar, equates with October–June).[1] The performances' links to traditional lineages (*illam*) and ancestors means they have become symbols of the region's cultural landscape, with many performances being celebrated across Kannur, Kasaragod, and Nileśvaram districts of Northern Kerala.[2] A plethora of sacred temple-groves are interspersed throughout these regions: centered around red brick quads, each grove have lineage deities and regal goddesses preserved in shrines (*tāṟa*), who, during annual Teyyam performances, make an appearance in embodied form as 'possessed' dancer-mediums. In some cases, *kāvu* groves are affixed to the lineal homes of patrons or families affiliated with dancer-mediums. Shrines connected with Teyyāṭṭam performances are scattered across Northern Malabar. The deities enshrined in a grove are apprehended as clan ancestors who are, at once, socially immanent and externally personified; a god's essence is embodied in the clan **and** enshrined in a familial plot. If, and when, a lineage re-locates, so too do their ancestors, and to accom-

1 These dates accord with agrarian cycles between the autumnal equinox and the monsoon season. This nine-month period was also utilised to time military deployment by the medieval Malabari royal lineages (Kōlattiri dynasty).

2 Such festivities are traditionally anchored in Malabar, Northern Kerala. Nevertheless, *teyyam* is a ritual phenomenon confined not only to the Kannur region. Rather it is a uniquely Northern Malayali tradition, evident across many districts (with similar *bhuta* rituals found in neighbouring Karnataka—although, as one of my informants made clear, *bhuta* in Karnataka are not as pervasive as Teyyāṭṭam is in North Kerala).

FIGURE 1 Goddess *Cāmuṇḍi* in performance (Kannur, Kerala)
PHOTOGRAPH BY AUTHOR

modate this, new Teyyam groves are built, multiplying across the region. When transported, *kōmamram* priests are called upon to resettle family ancestors in brand-new groves. As Malabar progresses into the future, Teyyam groves—and Teyyam liturgies—are not diminishing; quite the opposite, seeing that Teyyam divinities—with their familial descendants—dynamically migrate and resettle, albeit confined to Kerala.[3] All Keralan groves also contain shrines to a royal

3 Wayne Ashley & Regina Holloman, 'Teyyam', in *Indian Theatre: Traditions of Performance* (Honolulu: University of Hawaii Press, 1990), p. 133.

goddess that links them, mythically, to the former glory of medieval Kōlattiri kingship (dated c. 11th–17th centuries CE). This dynasty governed a decentralized, poligar polity in Northern Malabar, known collectively as Kōlattanādu.

Teyyam groves are superintended by lower-caste priests (*kōmamram*) and are linked to Tantric-influenced royal temples (like Mādāyi Kāvu), who were sanctioned by the monarchy in the medieval period: worshipping at these shrines capacitates deity embodiment within dancer-mediums during ritual performances. In general, Teyyam temple-groves are dissociated from higher-caste (*suvarṇa*) Nambūtiri Brahmans, since Teyyam's focus on blood sacrifice and antinomian divinities is theoretically inconsistent with a Brahmanical cosmology of maintaining bodily purity. King-allied religion and Brahmanism in Malabar were not originally homogenous, although gradual convergences between certain specialists of these disparate communities arose. Teyyāṭṭam, then, evolved as a popular ritual event for the lower castes (*avarṇa*) sponsored by patrons with the support of sovereign guardianship. Although, as Freeman suggests, higher-castes would, infrequently, sponsor Teyyam performances by lighting Teyyam torches from a flame of higher-caste temples.[4] However, in most cases, Teyyam performances were rituals where low-birth clans (*avarṇa*) could show allegiance to the Kōlattanādu kingdom by deploying their ancestors' power to protect their families, poligar chieftains, and agricultural yield, which, in the end, served the needs of those who cultivated the land.

To note, Teyyāṭṭam performances—of Northern Kerala—are grouped in stark differentiation to other deity performances famous across Southern Kerala, like Kathakālī. Though seemingly ritualistic, I was told Kathakālī is a theatrical rendition of local mythology, since it is based upon the principles of aesthetic (*rāsa*) theory, that is, a *techne* without *telos* (apart from entertaining an audience). In the state's southern provinces, the closest corollary to Teyyāṭṭam is a Mūtiyeṭṭu performance. In short, Mūtiyeṭṭu is a ritual performance staged by goddess-mediums who embody Bhadrakālī—Kerala's patron goddess. However, as compared to Teyyāṭṭam's subalternity, Mūtiyeṭṭu is restricted purely to participants of Nambutiri Brahmin or Nāyar provenance.[5] Teyyāṭṭam, by contrast, is a formalized tradition of collective worship whereby exchanges between low-caste devotees and their embodied ancestors bring about transformative effects and affects societally **and** politically. Teyyam, then, has multiple *telos* beyond its entertainment value, and is, therefore, multifunctional.

4 Freeman, 'The Teyyam Traditions', p. 313.
5 Caldwell, 'Oh Terrifying Mother'.

In Malayalam, *Teyyam* is a term which parallels the Sanskrit noun *deva/daiva* (meaning 'god'). Broadly, the term *Teyyam* refers both to ancestral deities—as individual agents or an entire pantheon—and, more informally, to the ritual *in toto*. Although, in local usage, 'Teyyāṭṭam' or 'Kaliyāṭṭam' more accurately describes the central rite of worshipping 'possessed', or closer still 'embodied', deity-mediums. By nature, Teyyam beings are definitively fierce forebears—controllable only by sacrificial libations that propitiate them—who are installed in hundreds of regional sacred groves, from which their superhuman essences derive. In appearance, Teyyam mediums are dressed in elaborate red costumes, headdresses, and weaponry unique to each deity: the blood-red colour they wear represents their deity's thunderous revival from their primordial pyres, and the dancer-medium's bulging eyes confirm this reawakening.

Ostensibly, Teyyam gods were formulated, early on, as animistic, or better, ancestral beings; though, in time, Teyyam gods were reworked as polyvalent beings: in other words, Teyyam pantheons amassed immortalized ancestors, pan-Hindu gods/goddesses[6] and localized spirits as co-equals enmeshed in terrestrial territory, who, in ritual performance, inhabit the bodies of predetermined dancer-mediums. Calculating who, within a Teyyam ensemble, will be delegated a 'deity-medium' within one or multiple temple-groves is determined astrologically through oracular consultation (*varaccu̧ vakkal*) with an associated priest (*kōmamram*). In Kerala, an oracle's concern is not only the stars, but the earth, and their techniques are closer to that of a water diviner, and not a cosmologist. In any event, oracular readings, within a temple-grove, *do* confirm calendrical timings of their annual Teyyāṭṭam performance. If oracular consultations are unavailable, then a grove's organization committee—its panel of patrons—settle whom, in a dancer-medium troupe, is delegated which Teyyam divinity enshrined at their grove.

Arguably, in Keralan culture, bodies, selfhood, terrestrial territory, and ancestral power are porous as co-constitutive elements within the world. For Osella, these corporeal elements 'flow' and 'connect', such that they resemble Kerala's natural network of backwaters and river confluences.[7] The source of divine power, then, is the material plane channeled through bodies, in opposition to Brahmanical transcendence, wherein, as Waghorne & Cutler suggest, the divine 'implodes' the illusory world as a hologram.[8] All ancestral

---

6 Goddesses are numerically dominant over male gods in Teyyāttam.

7 For more on Kerala notions of territory and bodies, see Caroline & Filippo Osella, 'Vital Exchanges: Land and Persons in Kerala', in *Territory, Soil, and Society in South Asia*, ed. by Daniela Berti & Giles Tarabout, (New Delhi: Manohar Publishers, 2009), pp. 232–233.

8 Waghorne & Cutler, *Gods of Flesh*, p. 163.

FIGURE 2 Early morning Teyyāṭṭam performance (Kannur, Kerala)
PHOTOGRAPH BY AUTHOR

divinities in Kerala—whether honourable warriors or oppressed women—are not distant entities, since their access-point is already embedded within familial territory. For sure, among Keralites, this notion of terrestrial divinity is reflected in funerary norms: cremation remains are not scattered in ever-flowing rivers, but buried in lineage plots as memorials.[9] Osella explains how "the soul (*jīvātmāvu*) may well stay on the land, fixed into a *kuryāla* (ancestral shrine) [with] part of their subtle matter and possibly also their spirits ... continu[ing] to be re-cycled".[10] Keralan cosmology, then, generally runs counter to Brahmanical dualism, a system that valorizes extramundane, masculine spirit (observable in the eternal ideal of male volunteer regiments or *sewa samiti*) over the passivity of feminine materiality (the ephemeral world symbolized by Mother India). In Kerala, a land-tract—infused with the essence and cremains of one's ancestors—is **not** illusory, insofar as all natural and somatic processes—considered subordinate to divine spirit in North India—are equally as pure as divine transcendence itself.[11] With these initial remarks in mind, I now turn to the Teyyāṭṭam's communities—their ritual clans and endogamous kinship patterns, matrilineal and patrilineal.

2 Lineages, Clans, and Ritual Kinship

2.1 *Matrilineages in Kerala*

Until its abolition by the State of Kerala (under the Kerala Joint Family (Abolition) Act of 1975), matrilineal kinship (*morūmakkathīyam*) was prominent on the Malabar coast as early as the medieval period. Though in decline, remnants of matrilineality still persist, especially among lower-caste village communities. In this arrangement, a *tarvād* or household is headed by a male *Kārṇavan* (elder) who is married to a female via a *sambandham* exogamous conjugal marriage. The couple return to the matrilocal household after the marriage ceremony. Even if a *Kārṇavan* is the household's financial provider, it is the female elder who owns the communal home (*taravād*). In addition, transmission of descent and inheritance adheres to the female bloodline, with each attached to a land-tract, an ancestral Teyyam grove, and a family deity (*kula daivam*). Matrilineal marriages also con-joined miscellaneous lineages through polyandrous unions; many lineage descendants were related through a common ancestress. Trautmann's seminal work on Dravidian kinship shows how

9 Osella, 'Vital Exchanges', p. 223.
10 Ibid., p. 230.
11 Ibid. p. 229.

South Indian practices of cross-cousin alliances, through affinity, intertwine lineages, which, for reasons of shared inheritance, amalgamated matrilines as matrilocal joint-families.[12]

In the scriptural record, Dharmaśāstra literature generally favours patrilineal marriage; a wife must leave her locality to resettle at her husband's household (Skt. *ghār*) to obey him like a deity. For Kerala's population, patrilineal and matrilineal customs co-exist; regardless of status—whether twice-born (*suvarṇa*) or untouchable (*avarṇa*)—certain clans (or castes) are patrilineal and others matrilineal. Despite the dominance of matrilineality, not all Teyyam communities were matrilineal: the Malayān—a clan of healers and exorcists—are organized as patrilineal in descent. Still, matrilineality is unique to Kerala, and matrilineal norms granted some domestic independence, albeit not unreservedly, to women. Fuller writes:

> In matrilineal communities such as the Nayars of Kerala, a woman enjoys greater rights, but matriliny is the custom of only a small minority of Hindus.[13]

With matrilineality notwithstanding, attitudes toward women in Kerala remain inflexibly unprogressive; at Teyyam performances, the segregation of males and females, especially menstruating women, is acceded. Rather than liberating women from their domestic roles, I argue that matriliny serve another socio-economic purpose: a matrilineal joint-family capacitates purpose-built lineage alliances for Keralans, which are reprocessed, in Teyyāṭṭam ritual, as a territorial macro-clan cast via food-sharing across inter-caste individuals. Further, it became apparent to me that Teyyāṭṭam's focus on hero worship, deified warriors, and sacerdotal males frames the phenomenon as incontestably hypermasculine.

2.2 *A Dancer-Medium Lineage in Kannur: Pre-ritual Purification*

Before a Teyyāṭṭam performance begins in earnest, all deity-mediums (*kōlakkaran*), typically male, must undertake an obligatory three-day purification rite. This stringent phase—requiring discipline—ensures the bodies of deity-mediums are cleansed for the ritual, wherein ancestral deities—sometimes their own—will be conjured within them. To prompt this cleansing, mediums

12 Thomas R. Trautmann, *Dravidian Kinship* (Cambridge: CUP), 1981.

13 Chris Fuller, *The Camphor Flame: Popular Hinduism and Society in India*, 2nd Ed., (Princeton: Princeton University Press, 2004), p. 20.

must renounce pollutive activities—meat consumption and sexual encounters—which, actually, re-attunes their constitutions prior to the ritual's intended surge of defilement; for all intents and purposes, blood-rites and alcohol propel terrene energy into bodies.[14] Not unlike the ablution practices of Hindu initiation (*upanayana*), groups of dancer-mediums must detach themselves in states of self-enhancing social seclusion (*vṛata*).[15] Crucially, the conditions facilitated by *vṛata* facilitate a sense of focus in the troupe, be it for self-meditation or choreographic improvement.

At one event, in Kannur, I witnessed a family of deity-mediums—belonging to the same clan—engrossed in an unusually communal state of *vṛata*. For one, the troupe members were **not** sequestered from public view. Instead, the group rehearsed martial movements as an interacting collective: at one point, the mediums—guided by their elder—directed one another's techniques, with each wielding a deity's weaponry, their regalia. (For the purposes of *vṛata*, wood-carved mock weapons were used, since the gods' *bona fide* swords are stored in temple-groves). I was also told that knowledge of Teyyāṭṭam (and Kalaripayāṭṭu) is transmitted communally, too, according to conventions of matrilineal descent. Medium tutelage, then, is implemented strictly within the clan, either from father-to-son or maternal uncle-to-nephew.

According to this family's elder, every movement or swing of the sword generates divine energy and thus commands exacting accuracy. The choreographed steps of Teyyāṭṭam are adapted from Kalaripayāṭṭu, Kerala's indigenous martial art, which is practiced in *Kalari* or gymnasia. Throughout medieval Kerala, *kalari* were centres for military training where regal warriors were primed for battle. Many *kalari* also contain shrines to Bhadrākālī, the royal goddess, and deity obeisance, itself intrinsic to Kalaripayāṭṭu praxis, is actively encouraged.

2.3 *A Teyyāṭṭam Performance in Six Stages*

Across North Kerala, any Teyyāṭṭam performance is brought into being by a sequence that I itemize here in six stages: (1) *tuttaṅṅal* or preliminary rites: at this stage, a series of tantric-inspired blessings are enacted to bless the temple-grove and to summon the stipulated divinities through specific invocatory callings, drumming, make-up and the receiving of banana-leaf and wicks offerings; (2) *tōṟṟam* (lit. 'creation'/'evocation'/'feeling'), which consists of nar-

14 Fuller, *Camphor Flame*, p. 147.

15 Balan Nambiar, 'Tāi Paradēvata: Ritual Impersonation in the Teyyam Tradition of Kerala', in *Flags of Fame: Studies in South Asian Folk Culture*, ed. by Heidrum Brückner & Lothar Lutze, (Manohar: South Asia Books, 1993), pp. 146–147.

rative recitations of specific Teyyam deities during adornment in the make-up hut; (3) *the mirror-gazing rite*, where the deity becomes embodied within the dancer; (4) *sacrificial dance*, during which the embodied deity-medium dances as the deity, which also includes a sacrifice (chicken or vegetative); (5) *communal worship*, where an interaction between gathering devotees and dancing deities is formed through co-operative donations and blessings between them; (6) *disembodiment*, a final rite where the headdress is removed and the sacred sword is returned to the shrine, which marks the ritual's end.[16] (Please note that, in the remainder of this chapter, I henceforth refer to these performative stages as 'stage (1)', 'stage (2)' and so on). In general, stages (2) and (3)—the recital phases (*tōṟṟam*)—are considered pivotal to the performance's overall efficacy, since recital accuracy—in the body—shifts the ancestral power of the deity from land into dancer-medium, what Freeman labels 'heightened state[s] of consciousness'.[17] In this state, the body of the *kōlakkaran* experiences "[...] shifts in the balance of his own consciousness blending with that of the deity".[18]

2.4 *Stages (1) and (2): Preparations*

To set the stage, a Teyyāṭṭam's preliminary stages (stages (1) and (2)) are orchestrated in a hut (*pati*) on a grove's peripheries, from where the ritual proceedings will unfold. From there, dancer-mediums—clustered by clan—huddle around a dancer-medium who is scheduled to perform as a god. Shoulder to shoulder, as confederated ritual relatives, they chant their deity's song, recited either as *mantra* or sung as *tōṟṟam* (which, in Sanskrit, are called *dhyāna-ślokas*). Accoutrements belonging to the medium's clan—headdresses, anklets, and costumes—are pendent within the hut, not to mention the deity's sacred sword, which, above all, conveys divine power from shrine to medium, and back again. As already addressed, mediums must be ceremonially purified, and, in the temple-grove, their location also, momentarily, reproduces rules of distance pollution; to be sure, dancer-mediums, from divergent families, are still partitioned in accordance with caste affiliations: Dancers belonging to, say, Vaṇṇān or Malayān castes congregate in one hut, and Vēlan dancers—of even lower status—are set apart in a hut at the grove's remotest end. Incidentally,

16 This is a logical sequence (see also Gabriel, *Playing God*, p. 140) of Teyyāṭṭam's liturgical stages.

17 Term used frequently by Freeman 1993; 1999 to describe the transformative process that the performer undergoes.

18 John R. Freeman, 'Dynamics of the Person in the Worship and Sorcery of Malabar', in *La possession en Asie du Sud: parole, corps, territoire*, (Éditions de l'École des hautes en sciences sociales, 1999b), p. 157.

FIGURE 3 Pre-ritual preparations in the make-up hut (Kannur, Kerala)
PHOTOGRAPH BY AUTHOR

these initial segregations do not last long, for soon after a god's manifestation—whereby ancestral vitality is re-energized via substantive gifts—then the group is ritually communalized as a macro-clan.[19]

The temple space must also be ritually sanctified, and as Freeman postulates, these purification rites are definitively Tantric modes of preparing shrines for image worship, which include: (1) meditating on specific Teyyam gods through *dhyāna* (visualization meditation); (2) singing *mantras*; (3) bathing the 'image'

19 Freeman, 'Purity and Violence', p. 182.

(*abhiśēkham*) or, in our case, a divinity's sword (*nāndakam*) housed at an aniconic shrine; (4) offerings of food and flowers (*naivēdyam*) to a god-shrine; and (5) waving a flame (*arti*) before the god-image or weapon.[20] By and large, *arti* flames are transported from local Tantric temples, a movement which, supposedly, bridges higher and lower castes, or Sanskritic and Malayali forms of religious life (though, as I mentioned earlier, this dynamic is more or less infrequent). Preceding the performance, at piecemeal intervals, the shrine-activation rites mentioned above are implemented by *kōmamram* priests to guarantee a performance's success.[21]

With pre-ritual purification nearing its end, the mediums advance, barefoot, to their respective Teyyam shrines to engage in a *puja* as a mark of reverence to the gods. In this act of worship—also *tutaṅṅal* (meaning 'beginning')—the priest smears sandalwood paste and sprinkles water on areas of a medium's body. (These bodily areas are analogous with *nādī* in Tantric cosmology. In these circumstances, *nādī* are portals in the flesh that can access terrestrial energy[22]). With that done, the mediums, now semi-adorned, chant the following verse. To summarize, the verse addresses the flock, and invites them to behold the stipulated divinity as transformed in his human configuration. He announces:

> *Varika niūvica karyavum viryavum*
> *Sadhaichu ñān chollum tottathe*
> *Kettu gunadhoshangal uṟiyaṭṭu*
> *Pirinjukolavan eẕunnalli*
> *Varika varika varika*
>
> Come and accomplish the matter and heroism intended.
> Arrive in pomp and hear the songs of praise I utter and
> Speak good and bad and then [I—*teyyam* deity will] depart.[23]

Once pronounced, the god-troupe—medium by medium—circumambulates the shrine.[24] At the altar, the priest presents a banana-leaf filled with an assortment of symbolic vegetative items—grains of rice, five lit oil-wicks, and a

20 See also Freeman, 'Purity and Violence', pp. 181–182.
21 Ibid., p. 181.
22 Freeman, 'The Teyyam Traditions', p. 314.
23 Translation from Theodore Gabriel, *Playing God: Belief and Ritual in the Muttappan cult of North Malabar*, (London: Equinox, 2010), p. 31.
24 Freeman, 'Purity and Violence', p. 216.

bundle of betel leaves—to a medium, who immediately showers the divinity's shrine with the rice grains, declaring (as one of Freeman's informants signalled): "may you [the deity] grace me with all your blessings".[25] At this point, the priest intercedes, by feeding the medium with the rice grains, and gesturing with the flame of the oil wicks.[26] Here, the medium literally ingests terrestrial *śakti*, epitomized by the blessed grains.

The use of rice is crucial to Teyyāṭṭam due to its association with ancestral land, the burial ground of ancestral cremains.[27] Any symbol of cultivation—be it rice, swords, coconuts, or blood sacrifice—shared during ritual attune lineages, land, ancestors, and goddess-clans together in web-like networks activated by the land's ancestral forces (*śakti*). Use of these symbols signals the taming of multivalent powers—terrestrial, royal, and cosmic—which are filtered into a medium's body—in the persona of an ancestral deity—whose material power can be transferred, in food or bodily markings of vermillion powder, to other lineages who flock there. This model of symbolic marking as a way of unifying bodies in groups I reorder from Fuller's analysis of *puja* offerings (*prasad*):

> the normal temporariness of the state of identity is aptly marked by the impermanence of almost all the materials used. Liquids used in bathing rituals drain away; flowers on the decorated images quickly fade and lose their scent [...] foodstuff is consumed; and the [...] powder smeared or sprinkled on the person at the end rapidly rub off. Taking *prasada* does not prolong the identity of the divine and the human for very long.[28]

Marking bodies with red vermillion powder (*kuṟi*) in Tantric ritual—unlike higher-caste puja as set out in Fuller's analysis—mark bodies across hierarchies as menstrually synchronous ritual kin. This interpretation throws into light the motivation for receiving *kuṟi* and rice during Teyyāṭṭam: by smudging red paste on a partisan's forehead, an ancestor's essence is transferred into his or her body through a sacred node (*nāḍī*) reposed between the eyes.

Once all food stuffs are distributed to the congregation, other food stuffs—enclosed in a banana leaf—are arranged at the altar in preparation for the rite's next juncture, the first singing phase (*tōṟṟam*). At this stage, the mediums must return to their tents for further adornment. For the purposes of this singing phase (*tōṟṟam*), the dancer-mediums don a simpler *tala-pāli* garment: a red

25 Ibid., pp. 187–188.
26 Ibid., pp. 187–188.
27 Ibid., p. 240 also makes this link.
28 Fuller, *Camphor Flame*, p. 75.

FIGURE 4 Offerings to an enshrined deity (Kannur, Kerala)
PHOTOGRAPH BY AUTHOR

cloth—emblazoned with 21 silver snake charms (an ode to local *nāga* or snake spirits)—is tied to the medium's forehead. In this attire, a medium must place a stool (*pītham*) next to his deity's shrine.[29] Just as before, rice and betel leaves—the fruits of the land—feature here; they are thrown in the direction of the stool

29 Freeman, 'Purity and Violence', pp. 188–189.

to activate its power. A chief priest (*antitiriyan*) blesses the stool to the sound of drumming, while the priests break out into two songs: the first is 'eulogistic',[30] praising all elders, social castes, and Teyyam deities in attendance.[31] The second is a rehearsed narrative (*varanvili*) which aims to evoke the personality of a stipulated deity.[32] These songs are biographical in tone, and document minutiae details which include, primarily: (a) the birth and mythological origins of the deity; (b) the mytho-geographical territory of the deity; and (c) the outward characteristics or façade of the deity.[33]

2.5 *Stages (3) and (4): Deity Embodiment*

At the song's climax, a final handful of rice is hurled (*uḻiyuka*), the mediums bow in each cardinal direction, before untying a red bow from their brow. For his final embellishment, a dancer continues to recite his deity's songs. The verbal recitation of deity songs is crucial at this final stage, for it summons a god or goddess completely from the grove's terrestrial boundaries. Freeman notes:

> As part of the logic of possession, this territory which instantiates the god's power is symbolically mapped into the dancer's mind ... Finally, in the recitation of the god's physical form, the possession song indexes and recapitulates the entire ritual process which the dancer has actually been undergoing through the costuming, and fixes the constructed form and its significance in the dancer's mind.[34]

At this juncture, the body, mind, territorial power, and biographical narrative internally synergize within him. And it is this concourse of body, territory, and mythological narrative which enables the Teyyam deity to become fully affixed in the medium's body. Now in full costume, the dancer is led to the stool (*pītham*) facing the eastern shrine. The appropriate headdress (*talappāli*) is affixed and the priests pass him a bronze mirror; the medium then proceeds by gazing at his reflection as a transformed Teyyam.[35] Upon seeing his reflection, the embodied dancer begins to tremble as he realizes that he has become the divinity. He announces this transformation verbally, in a shift from third-person ('she is the goddess') to second- ('you are the goddess') and finally to first-person

---

30 A term used by Nambiar, 'Tai Paradevata', p. 149 for this initial song.
31 Freeman, 'Puirty and Violence', pp. 189–190.
32 Ibid., pp. 188–189.
33 Freeman, J.R., 'Performing Possession', p. 124.
34 Ibid., p. 125.
35 Nambiar, 'Tai Paradevata', p. 153.

('I am the goddess'). This indexical shift, according to Freeman, precipitates 'a manner of the self witnessing itself ... when it comes about that two selves are brought together in a state of witnessing each other as one, in that place a divine power is created'.[36] This gesture of literal self-reflection on one's ancestral deity, I argue, actualizes the full transformation; the body, mind, insignia, territory, and *śakti* blend, thus triggering this transient state of hyperkinesia, in contrast to conventional embodied experience. In this state, the medium is harnessing a long-gone territorial deity, which he conjures into his body through ritualized gestures.[37]

Gabriel would disagree with Freeman's interpretation of this aspect of the rite.[38] He claims—no doubt influenced by Durkheim—that the whole community, as well as the dancer-medium, undergoes a homologous shift in consciousness. As a polity's ancestral deity, the deity-medium is, essentially, an agential projection of the communal group, reconceived in bonds of *affective ritual kinship*.[39] This is an intriguing point, and I alternatively claim that Freeman's and Gabriel's explanations are possible here: for one, narrative recitation, in any ritual, plays the role of collective consciousness (or *śakti/kalivu̧* in emic terms) because mythological narratives are culturally verified productions spawned from the cultural imagination of the social form over time: the biographical narrative of a lineages' ancestors—their essence verbalized—is equated with their *śakti*.

Sax adopts a similar position in his works on Uttarakhandi oracular rites, where he argues 'collective intentionality' (coined in Tuomela's thinking,[40] that is, a social group's intention for a metaphysical end that enhances social solidarity) is projected onto a 'complex agent',[41] who expresses this intentionality via the trained medium to the social group.[42] In this book, I develop this notion further, arguing that kin-like bonds—flowing in divine, virtuoso, and social bodies—are rejuvenated within ritual, in what I call *affective kin-like intentionality*. In brief, *affective kin-like intentionality* is synonymous with a mode

36 Freeman, 'Performing Possession', p. 126.

37 Ibid., pp. 125–126.

38 Gabriel, *Playing God*, p. 24.

39 Ibid., pp. 24–26.

40 Raimo Tuomela, *Social Ontology: Collective Intentionality and Group Agents* (Oxford: OUP, 2013).

41 The notion of a collective agent (i.e. council or assemblies) that is not limited to an individual person. See Ronald Inden, *Imagining India*, (London: Hurst & Co, 1990), pp. 267–268.

42 William Sax, *Dancing the Self: Personhood and Performance in the Paṇḍāv Līlā of Garwhal* (New York: OUP, 2001), pp. 159–161.

of ritual kinship, which, in South Asia, describes a state of collective strength dynamized by polity-unifying ritual relations.

In Kerala's matrilineal joint-families, fictive kinship—or colloquially, 'one's brother from another mother'—is a common form of relatedness. These relations are created between members of a household who are not consanguineally related in ritual bonds known, locally, as *pulasambandam*. Kottakkhunnummal describes how a matrilineal Mappilla-Muslim *taravād* form exogamous households '[...] held together by relations of real or fictive kinship [...] *Pulasambandam* implied the observance of common rituals [...] The kin bound through *pulasambandam* are [...] heirs'.[43] This suggests, however, that fictive kin are confined to an intra-caste as opposed to inter-caste contact in non-domestic settings. But, from my own experiences in Malabar, there were innumerable instances where cross-caste individuals engaged and met with each other for the purposes of conjoined celebration. This idiosyncratic kinship—as shaped in ritual settings—is common across Kerala (and Bhaktapur).

3 Blood Sacrifices, Offerings, and Swords

At stage (4), dancer-mediums—recognizing themselves as deities in the mirror—enter states of bodily elation by jumping from their seats (*pītham*). As if to declare this hyperactivity, fireworks are ignited, during which the mediums encircle their god's shrine, in all directions.[44] Stopping for a moment, the dancers walk to the priests (*kōmamram*), who hand-over each deity's weapon, that have been pre-blessed with sprinklings of rice.[45] The giving of a sword further accelerates the medium's movements, to an extent that Gabriel writes that a sword—in local belief—"vibrates by itself and signifies its possession by the divinity".[46] These swords are, in Freeman's adage, 'indexical icons' that represent unseen power[47] and evoke historical phases when Teyyam gods were warriors, swiddening pastoralists, or hunters. To illustrate: the goddess, Tāi Paradēvata—wielding a sword in her grip—gestures it in the direction of the assembled audience, which endows them with a spiritual stream of grace.[48] At

43 Manaf Kottakkunnummal, 'Indigneous Customs and Colonial Law: Contestations in Religion, Gender, and Family among Mappila Muslims in Colonial Malabar, Kerala, c.1910–1928', *SAGE Open*, January–March (2014), p. 2.

44 Nambiar, 'Tai Paradevata', p. 153.

45 Ibid., p. 153.

46 Gabriel, *Playing God*, p. 40.

47 Freeman, 'Purity and Violence', p. 246.

48 Nambiar, 'Tai Paradevata', p. 158.

that moment, the *kalaśakkāran* is summoned with a toddy pot blessed with a wave of the *teyyam's* sword. The *kalaśakkāran* proceeds by circling the shrine complex, splashing the toddy—an impure substance—on the ground; sometimes a *kalaśakkāran* shares this alcohol with male devotees.[49] Through the distribution of impurity—here, alcohol, and later, blood—the spatial purification so punctiliously implemented in Stage (1) has been reversed; a deity's material embodiment demands blood and alcohol to desecrate spatial purity, and vigorously so! Dancer-mediums fulfil their ancestor's demands by imbibing toddy and sacrificing a chicken in their honour. To accord territorial prosperity, grains of rice are stuffed in the chicken's beak, so that this divine favour exsanguinates back onto—or better, into—the land. The chicken's bloodied body is also dipped in a bowl of blood-water substitute (*guruti*), which is spilled near a dancing medium's feet. As the liquid is emptied forth, a benedictory phrase (translated by Freeman) is uttered: "May a great blessing come to the sacrificer, his patron, his cattle, children, his crops and produce"[50] to which the Teyyam dancer replies, "I am happy—very happy' ".[51] Overall, this benediction hints at sacrifice's purpose: blood-spilling necessitates togetherness, so that the web-nodes of agriculture, fertility, and lineages—bodies, land, and ancestors—can re-flow.

Blood sacrifice and alcohol swigging—impurity crushing the grove's opening purity—marks that moment when divine, human, material, and social worlds converge, and express one another; sacrifice is a communion from which impurity blurs the boundaries between bodies, unleashed in the ritual's spiraling space. In Durkheimian terms, blood, in general, is a binding *collective representation*; sacrifice is, thus, coterminous with the emotional charge of *collective effervescence*. It is blood that binds a ritual group to their ancestors, which overflows into the ground beneath them, electrified by familial emotion. As a collective representation, exsanguinating blood **represents** the connections created in the ritual. I suggest the unifying nature of blood sacrifice is also applicable in Newar society, primarily for Navadurgā rituals (see § 2.4). Ethnographic details in Freeman's later works note that sacrifice in Kerala is linked with divine power, in that:

> there is almost certainly some such idea in teyyāṭṭam as to why the breaths or elements of the mundane body are laid out as an offering

49 Nambiar, 'Tai Paradevata', p. 154.
50 Freeman, 'Purity and Violence', p. 284.
51 Ibid., p. 284.

where blood-sacrifices are performed; they must be destroyed before being replaced with their divine counterparts.[52]

With the main sacrificial libations completed, and all modalities connected as ritual kin, the now-propitiated Teyyam can communicate blessings to participants in need of them. These blessings, in tandem with the de-crowning of the deity, are the penultimate stages before the ritual concludes.

3.1 *Stages (5) and (6): Sacrifice and Blessings*

For these stages, deity-mediums—still embodying their ancestors' divine status—are, for the remainder of the rite, quite literally placed on a pedestal, and from this seated position, people gather around them requesting blessings. These blessings are given in exchange for multiple gifts and donations, ranging from coconuts, rice grains and, depending on urgency, more sacrificial chickens. I was told these reciprocal donations (Maly: *anugraham*[53] or *Viśēsikkal*[54])—a gift for a blessing—were pivotal in Teyyāṭṭam, with some worshippers coming to the ritual only to receive a divinity's grace. An exchange of gifts constructs physical communication with deities, of course, but also—as a webbed network—reciprocity becomes a support mechanism for groups or individuals to allay ill-will they may habour amongst themselves. The god-as-medium—an embodiment of the polity's integrality—operates as an advisory mediator in these disputes to inspire 'social healing'. According to Freeman, "sometimes there are even quarrels between parties, or between the performing troupe and the sponsors, which the dancer as deity may be called upon to settle".[55]

Blessings are not reserved for the lucky few who found themselves at the front of the queue, however. Aided by the assistance of priests (*kōmamram*), a system of placing *kuri* (a mark of sandalwood paste or another substance) upon participants who request it—or *praśādam*—is a commonplace feature at Teyyāṭṭam. As discussed earlier, one could argue that the red markings of *kuri* is the synchronous power of the goddess-clan, yoking individuals and lineages 'menstrually'. In some circumstances, Teyyam graces conclude with a procession around the land abutting the shrine, in which the embodied dancer (along with his assistants and the audience) visits the ritual's sponsors. De Maaker's

52 John R. Freeman, 'Possession Rites and the Tantric Temple: A Case-Study from Northern Kerala', *Diskus*, 2.2 (1994).

53 Freeman, 'Performing Possession', p. 128.

54 Term alternatively used by Gabriel, *Playing God*, p. 36.

55 Freeman, 'Performing Possession', p. 129.

FIGURE 5 A god distributing blessings
PHOTOGRAPH BY AUTHOR

ethnographic film depicts this quite clearly: the lower-caste dancing Teyyam grabs the arm of a higher-caste men at one stage (which would, without question, be socially unacceptable in diurnal contexts beyond the ritual frame).[56]

56 *Teyyam, The Annual Visit of the God Vishnumurti*, dir. by Eric De Maaker, (Leiden University: Department of Visual Ethnography, 1998).

And to ensure another successful season of Teyyāṭṭam festivals, some local male villagers cut down a coconut tree, as an act of cultivating—and, thereby, regenerating—the tellurian agency of their gods and ancestors.[57] In the grove, coconuts are also smashed against a sacrificial stone in a substitute ceremony named *Kalloppikkal*, which, again, re-engages local energies.[58] With such divinatory matters completed, the entire congregation return to the sacred grove, where uncrowning each medium's headdress signals the return of their gods to the shrines.

Near the grove's shrines, the deity-medium—with the head priest (*antitiriyan*)—felicitously acknowledges the presence of all who gathered there. In doing so, the god bestows upon them all future contentment, and, in the process, thanks all who sponsored the performance.[59] Turning to the medium, the priests remove his headdress (assisted by other priests, as this weighty headdress is an awkwardly monolithic garment). Doffing the headdress proclaims that the Teyyam divinity has departed the dancer-medium and has gone back to the shrine. Now human again, the dancer bows toward the equipment one last time, and he, with his assistants, re-enters the make-up room. The final ritual deed is done.[60]

4 Cosmology, Metaphysics, and Textual History

As most Keralans would testify, Teyyāṭṭam is a space that temporarily subverts the hegemony of status, caste, and purity by unifying multifarious attendees, all born in the locality. For Chandra, Teyyāṭṭam is congenitally inclusive, 'function[ing] as a social thread intertwining the different castes [...] and individuals into a single whole'.[61] However, one could ask: how is it possible that differing religions, perspectives, and statuses coexist at a ritual phenomenon like Teyyāṭṭam? How is ritual unification permissible within a society whose dominant worldview sustains caste segregation? Since the mid-medieval era in Kerala, I suggest that popular rituals—regulated under sovereign aegis by principles of Tantric heterodoxy—have stood in antithetical polarity to Brahmanical ideology. It is clear that Teyyāṭṭam's wide-ranging influences—from medieval

57 Ibid.
58 Gabriel, *Playing God*, p. 36.
59 Ibid., pp. 37–38.
60 Gabriel, *Playing God*, p. 38.
61 T.V. Chandra, *Ritual as Ideology: Text and Context in Teyyam* (New Delhi: Indira Gandhi National Centre for the Arts, 2006), p. 5.

times—pieced together a complex bricolage cosmology; Teyyāṭṭam, it seems, absorbed the cultural components of 'Vedic' (or 'Sanskritic') and 'Tantric' sects into a vernacular paradigm—a Malayali or 'Dravidian' cosmos. The cosmologies of popular rituals in Kerala were, and are, multi-valent. Payyanad summarises this point here:

> Both these [Tantra and indigenous Kerala ideologies] are forms of expression of different worldviews, which are contradictory in nature, and still in cohesion denote that the cult of Teyyam at present is a multilinear discourse as a result of assimilation of different systems of religions.[62]

As such, Malabar's cultural milieu has at its core several related cultural systems—Hindu tantra and indigenous forms of Kerala religion—that comprise the ritual performance's metaphysical foundation. Just like Teyyāṭṭam's web—networked in nodes of ritual kinship—doctrinal bloodlines, too, formed genealogical ties over time; all interpretations contained in this cultural web reflects the range of participants that build the ritual's macro-clan. In conversation with a friend I knew at a home stay in Kannur, he emphasised how, in Malabar society, several worldviews are articulated through Teyyāṭṭam rituals:

> [Inf.]: *Teyyam* predated 'Hinduism'. This [Hinduism] is just a label used by Westerners for 'people of the Indus'. Some Christians and Muslims go to *Teyyam*. This isn't particularly noted or mainstream, but Muslims go to *Teyyam* to give offerings [*nivedyam*] and get blessings to return to their communities. This is Keralan cultural history. If there could be a Maulafi [priest of a *masjid*] *teyyam* [deity], there would be.

4.1 *Historical Communities in Kerala: Mappilas*

Centuries before any Mughal invasion occurred in Northern South Asia (16th Century CE), Māppilya, or Muslim, lineages existed in Kerala. As early as the 8th Century CE, Malabari kings established trading agreements with Arabia; masses of Muslim—and Jewish—settlers emigrated to the Malabar coast across the Arabian sea.[63] Some Teyyam deities evoke this history, like *Mokripokker*, a deified Muslim boatman.[64] Ritual performances of Muslim deities also

62 Raghavan Payyanad, 'Religion—native and alien: Interaction, assimilation, and annihilation—a study based on worldview', in *Folklore as Discourse*, ed. by M.D. Muthukumarasaswamy, (Chennai: University of Madras, 2006), pp. 207–208.

63 For more details about Mappila history, see Mailaparambil, *Lords of the Sea*.

64 Chandra, *Ritual as Ideology*, p. 4.

attract non-Hindu devotees from local Māppilya communities. In Kerala, the multilayered nature of divine agency is also noticed by Freeman:

> I received answers which ranged from those treating teyyams as deceased ancestors and heroes, echoing themes of the earliest strata of Tamil literature, to those which posited them as lofty [Hindu] divinities.[65]

As a ritual performance, Teyyāṭṭam coalesces and combines at least three systems of religious thought prevalent in Kerala: (1) Tantric (Śaiva/Śākta nondualism), (2) Dravidian (indigenous), and most latterly, (3) Sanskritic (Purāṅic/Smārta) and Māppiya (Muslim) elements.[66] By 'Dravidian' or Malayāli, I mean a worldview and principles about the human condition indigenous to Northern Malabar, and includes South Indian culture—from Kannada-, Tuḷu-, and Tamil-regions—in its widest sense. Freeman's textual analysis of the Līlātilakam, a Maṇipravāḷam (medieval Malayalam) text, hints at the emic use of the term 'Dravidian'; in short, 'Dravidian' is a non-essentialized designation for describing elements of South Indian culture linked to poligar polities, regal goddesses, and fertility cults:

> The Līlātilakam's textual characterization of "Dravidian" identity as interweaving royal political culture with religious affiliation, parallels the merger of political and religious criteria which one actually encounters in the ranked instituitional offices (sthānams) of the temple- and shrine-complexes, even at the micro- or village-level.[67]

Deceased heroic ancestors, for example, pivot more towards Dravidian provenance, because these gods are apotheosized warriors or swidden pastoralists; in Kerala, divine immanence is both Dravidian **and** Tantric in tone. Freeman relates this cosmological rationale to a doctrinal crossroads that links the *purānic* principle of *avatāra* with the warrior-deification as espoused in the Dravidian substrate.[68] From the perspective of higher-caste Brahmins, these perspectives are hierarchized as 'ideologies of power' in tension, which can be distinguished as three ideal typologies ('brahmanical', 'warrior', and 'sorcerer' complexes). Each stratum is hierarchically ranked according to values of purity (not auspiciousness), just as divisions of the caste system are. In Freeman's ren-

65 Freeman, 'Purity and Violence', p. 123.
66 Ibid., p. 82.
67 Ibid., p. 34.
68 Ibid., p. 127.

dering, these are: (1) the Nambūtiri Brahmin ('Brahmanical'), (2) Nāyar ('Warrior') and (3) lower non-Brahmin castes ('Sorcerer'). All these interpretations of divine power are discrepantly valorized strata. According to this formulation, 'Brahmanical' values are exalted above native 'Warrior' ones for they are purer, though 'Warrior' and 'Sorcerer' practices generate more auspiciousness for regnant purposes, like battle.

Contrastingly, from my own fieldwork experiences, these ideological perspectives—Brahamanical, Warrior, or Sorcerer complexes—were coordinated and complementary, which was reflected in the ritual's eclecticism. In historical terms—that is, since the mid-medieval period—non-Brahmanical or Dravidian ideas (that include warrior worship and Śākta nondualism) were supported under the aegis of royal sovereignty and prevailed in Teyyam temple-groves. Heterdoxic by design, these traditions—supported by a king, **not** the Brahmin priests—accept every-*body* in the realm, from across caste divides. Indeed, anyone can enter a Teyyam grove, in contrast with Nambūtiri or Brahmanical temples (*kṣetram*), where access is restricted to Nambūtiri Brahamins. Indeed, in Teyyāṭṭam logic, Sanskritic (Purāṇic) or Brahmanical (Vedic) interpretations are in tension with its own because the former propounds dualism between the transcendent/immanent, purity/pollution, material/spirit, which divides people vertically in hierarchical formation. With the recent dissemination of Hindu right politics (BJP) into South India, Sanskritic or Brahmanical ideologies have infiltrated indigenous Teyyāṭṭam worship. In this regard, one of my interlocutors stated: 'Teyyam kāvu are now being built with signs that say the Sanskrit 'Kshetram' and not 'Kāvu'. This is happening a lot here recently'.

Returning to Teyyāṭṭam's polyvalent metaphysics, I maintain that the theological notion of *śakti*—an immanent divine power also known as *kalivụ* in the Malayalam vernacular—enables the marrying of several meta-cosmological systems extant in Malabar. *Śakti* is often described as an intimately bound somatic energy—linked to territory—that engenders the synchronization of Tantric, Dravidian, Sanskritic, and Mappila-Muslim logics. As an all-pervasive, binding essence, Śakti provides an existential nexus between Hindu deity, humans, ancestors, spirits, swords, and headdresses.[69] Thus, these Teyyam deities are multi-layered agents. According to Freeman, the gods are "[…] constellations of such immanent powers [Maly: *kalivụ* or Skt: *śakti*] externalized and personified".[70]

69 Gabriel, *Playing God*, pp. 38–40.
70 Ibid., p. 125.

From a gnoseological standpoint, a medium's heightened state of divine embodiment—as a god or goddess in ritual—is attributed to the activation of *śakti* immanent within corporeal bodies (which adheres more closely, I suggest, to Tantric/Kashmir Śaiva/Śākta discourse). Chapter 4.2.1 delineates, in greater detail, the historical influence of Kashmir Śaiva ideas—from textual corpora—into Northern Kerala: briefly, Freeman describes how a wide-spread transmigration of ideas—brought by householder ascetics or Nāth Siddhas—into South India. Perhaps this cultural motion was sparked following the collapse of Gupta empire in the North. These migrations, or rather, pan-Indic intellectual circuits also included the movement of Tantric cosmologies—mostly of Kashmir Śaiva-Śākta origin—that gradually bled into Malabar culture.

As I discuss in § 3.3.3, this cosmology is composed of four existential spheres: the highest Śākta (or *śakti*) suffuses the three levels of the material plane, described as Māyīya, Prākrta, and Pārthiva. This worldview is illustrated in the texts of Kashmir polymath, Abhinavagupta, whose manuscripts were discovered among Malabari Tantric priesthoods.[71] The mechanism of this metaphysical vision is described here: as we proceed from higher consciousnesses (namely the all-pervading source of Siva consciousness, which penetrates all ontologies, however distant they are from the source itself) to the lower consciousnesses of Māyīya, Prākrta and Pārthiva, the *tattvas* or ontological boundaries (i.e. person, consciousness, bodies etc.) become ever-more particularized and limited.[72] However, as we ascend further, perception becomes more widely universalized, and, at this level, body, cosmos, and world—like a performance's threefold *spiraling web-like network*—becomes inter-amalgamated as a collective wholeness. By visualizing a maṇḍala, one can access this *śakti* embodied as a trident of goddesses: *Parā* (cosmic body in a manifested form), *Parāparā* (collective body) and *Āparā* (individual body)).

During a Folk Śākta performance, the visualization of these threefold *maṇḍalic* goddesses is summoned by the dancer-medium; it is in this process that he dispels the 'I'-ness of his identity so that a deity's persona can inhabit him. Through this visualization, a medium conceives himself as encompassing all the 'I's'; the cosmic, collective, and individual body within one existential bodily receptacle—a de-individualized "I". This ontological motion from a dancer-medium's mundane self to the divine self (from human to Teyyam divinity)

71 Freeman, 'Untouchable Bodies', p. 160.

72 Gavin Flood, *Body and Cosmology in Kashmir Shaivism*, (San Francisco: Mellen Research University Press, 1993).

is documented in the *tōṟṟam* (Maly: 'creation/feeling/evocation') narratives, which are sung by priests in tandem with his rite of transformation. A verbal deictic shift from third, second, to first person in the narrative—whilst gazing at his aesthetic metamorphosis in a mirror—signals the complete embodiment of the divine agent in the dancer-medium's body.

Among scholars and anthropologists of the region, whether a *kōlakkāran's* inner-cognitive state (as himself) comes into play during his performance as a 'transformed deity' is contentious.[73] Indeed, one experienced dancer-turned-teacher told Ashley & Holloman:

> I see *teyyam* as an art not as a belief [...] I am a good performer. But I never tell anyone that I don't believe.[74]

However, this limited view of *'teyyam* as art' is not consistently adhered by every performer; a dancer-medium I interviewed (see §3.3.2.3) claimed the antithesis: the mantric power of biographical recitations induced a spiritual connection with the *bona fide* deity, which accelerated his performative capabilities.

Remaining loyal to methodological agnosticism on this matter, I suggest that *both* cases are viable in line with the *bricolage webs of ritual knowledge* that underlie Kerala Teyyāṭṭam rationale. The first understanding of embodiment—what I label *somatic textuality*—is induced by charting the personality of the Teyyam temporarily unto the performer's cognition. This process of superimposing the consciousness of divine agents onto revered dancer-mediums requires a **collectively** validated collection of biographical songs (*tōṟṟam*) that are sung by the medium to facilitate the embodiment. In this way, the narratives become **ritualized**, that is, the verbalization of mantra formulae as a bodily praxis that transforms the body (Catherine Bell would call ritual language as 'ritualization'[75]). In Indic-influenced nondualist philosophies, 'conventional language and verbalization' (*vikalpa*)—unlike a ritual mantra—has

---

73 Gavin Flood, 'Ritual Dance in Kerala: Performance, Possession, and the Formation of Culture', in *Indian Insights: Buddhism, Brahmanism, and Bhakti*, (London: Luzac Oriental, 1997), p. 173 argues that the internal state of the performer is not vital, rather the social performance itself.

74 Ashley & Holloman, 'Teyyam', p. 137.

75 Catherine Bell, *Ritual Theory, Ritual Practice* (Oxford: OUP, 1992) argues that 'ritualization' is a state of embodiment that distinguishes transformative 'ritual' practice and language from 'non-ritual' or conventional practice and language.

limitations since it reflects static, dualistic thinking (between mind-body, self-world, and divine-human). Muller-Ortega summarises this distinction from Abhinavagupta's perspective:

> Language, however, can also be used to free a person from bondage. In this usage, language is primarily an explanatory inducement towards the liberating experience. Perhaps even more importantly, it constitutes part of practice, in the form of "unconventional" mantric language, which leads to the *avikalpa* [*'non-verbal'*] transcendence of both duality and language itself.[76]

As one dancer-medium explained to me, mantra and biographical narrative are usually read from palm-leaf manuscripts by *kōlakkaran* in edifying preparation for upcoming ritual performances.

The second explanation of embodiment (which supports the 'performative-artistic' in the philosophy of nondualism)—also a mode of 'somatic textuality'—describes the internal dynamizing of immanent *śakti*, which engenders the agency of the ancestor within the medium. These highly Tantric processes conceive bodies as vehicles for expressing web-like power as a divinity, because in Śākta traditions, adepts and deities are intimately connected through lineage (*gotra*) relations. In short, a dancer-medium's body becomes an affective embodiment of his/her assigned lineage deity with his/her biographical histories. Given that understanding, a medium is himself a *somatic text*, which offsets the use of textual manuals (*paddhati*) in esoteric Tantric cults (see § 4.2.2.1).

4.2 *Teyyāṭṭam: Hegemony, Ritual, Resistance*

The content of the biographical songs (*tōṟṟam*) retell mythological narratives that hark back to the socio-political settings of the early-medieval realms of the Kōlattiri kingdom. (Dated to approximately 14th Century CE, the administrative centre of the kingdom—also Kōlatthanādu—was Māṭāyi Kāvu, located near Pazangadi, Kannur district). Generally, these narratives recount unjust cases of oppression inflicted upon lower-caste individuals, as well as glorifying the heroic zeal displayed by a warrior divinity in battle. In these biographical tales, then, a lineage's forebearer—before their deification—endured an unpropi-

76 Paul E. Muller-Ortega, *The Triadic Heart of Śiva: Kaula Tantricism of Kashmir Shaivism in the Nondual Shaivism of Kashmir* (New York: SUNY Press, 2010), p. 15.

tious and untimely demise, which assured their apotheosis as a deified local deity (*teyyam*), family/ancestral god (*kulivīran*), or a vengeful mother goddess (*bhagavati*). A deified individual became installed in a *samādhi* (memorial) of specific Teyyam groves by being enshrined in *tāṟa* (shrines) therein. These divinities are commemorated annually in ritual performances through the conduit of a dancer-medium's body.

On the peripheries of Kannur (November 2015), I once observed a Teyyāṭṭam performance, in which a medium was embodying a wild goddess (*bhagavati*). The performance was a raucous one; the goddess was being taunted by local men, children, and adolescents (see Figure 6), and some worshippers backed away cautiously, perturbed by the goddess' unrestrained sword-whirling. According to those I spoke with at the event, this provoking display was a performative re-enactment of the myth associated with this *bhagavati*. The goddess was once a woman who—unbalanced after the death of her husband—became a figure of unjust torment for local villagers. Humiliated, she threw herself into the flames of a local pyre in a tragic act of self-immolation.[77]

Such mythological narratives, I argue, bring critiques of hegemony—by resurrecting, and giving voice to, oppressed ancestors—for deployment in 21st Century performances. In fact, as Schröder's analysis of South Indian *charak pūja* (hook-swinging rituals) indicates,[78] Teyyāṭṭam, too, is refracted as a space of critical agency against persecution, whether colonial imperialism or gender inequality. In Teyyam narratives, imperialist subjugations include the medieval Sanskritization of folk religion by emigrating Brahmins led by Śaṇkara into Kerala (5th–7th Century CE) and, to some extent, 20th Century western imperial rule. Teyyāṭṭam utilises medieval folk narratives—linked with social justice and monarchical power—as iconoclastic opprobrium re-emanating within contemporary cultural consciousness. This is accomplished in Teyyāṭṭam through (1) its deconstruction of caste distinctions; and (2) by incorporating exclusivist cultural categories as related, which disobeys the hegemony of Sanskritic purity-hierarchies

By contrast, J.R. Freeman compellingly hypothesizes that Teyyāṭṭam was too chronologically early to be affected by the conditions of 20th Century colonization:

77 In Hindu traditions, this practice is known as *satī*.

78 Ulrike Schröder, 'Hook-swinging in South India: Negotiating the subaltern space within colonial society', in *Negotiating Rites*, ed. by Ute Hüske & Frank Neubert, (Oxford: OUP, 2011).

FIGURE 6 A Teyyam goddess
PHOTOGRAPH BY AUTHOR

> The political powers which teyyam worship itself describes and recognizes as having deep ideological significance are not located in the colonial or modern periods, but that of the traditional kingdoms of medieval Malabar. These kingdoms were largely dismantled by the close of the 18th Century, so it seems reasonable to conclude that teyyattam was developed in its current form and flourished at some point prior to this dismantling.[79]

Although very accurate, I would add the following: one impetus of Teyyāṭṭam *is* to expose hegemony's putative nature. Ideology, in a Tantric society, is deemed ephemerally ever-changing, like the cosmology on which it is based. By elaborating metaphors of body and blood, Teyyam performances elevate and ratify proximate bodily connectedness—ritual kinship—that unites all corporeal things and worlds. These ritual kin dynamics—shaped by ancestral regeneration—facilitates a redistribution of divine power and agency to **all** engaged in this territorial ritual, regardless of external social status. As I argue in Chapter 3, Teyyam dances create an evanescent flattening of all deities and bodies, because persons are consolidated within the polity's macroclan.

The songs dedicated to deity Pōṭṭan, for example, tells of a drunken untouchable—guised as Śiva in human form—who challenges Śaṅkarācārya's knowledge and, in some versions, the authority of local Nāyar agricultural landlords; 'the same blood flows [through our veins]' since we are all related to the deities and can access their power in our bodies. According to Lorenzen, this narrative is linked to the tale of Ugra-Bhairava in the Kāpālika tradition, who challenges Śaṅkara by '[…] turn[ing] [his] own Vedāntic doctrines against him'.[80]

Teyyam gods, and their mythological narratives, also recognize the traumatic repercussions of hierarchical oppression on Malabari cultural memory (which constitutes oppression in all its forms—either historical colonizations, imperializations, or imposed caste hierarchy). Bayly adds that British colonial rule altered the political establishment on the Malabar coast; kingship and poligar chieftains were suppressed in exchange for caste hierarchies derived from scriptural ideals (a "Protestant" system of religion was imposed). She states:

79 Freeman, 'Purity and Violence', p. 39.
80 Lorenzen, *Kāpālikas*, p. 33.

> With the suppression of the poligar chiefs at the beginning of the nineteenth century, the balance between temple-centered high Hinduism and the religion of blood-taking cult divinities [like Teyyam] shifted in favour of an artificially Brahmanized religious culture.[81]

In Chapters 3 and 6, I will re-examine this changing political climate on the Malabar coast between the medieval Kōlattiri and the 19th Century colonial period. But, for reasons of brevity here, I suggest that, to this day, Teyyāṭṭam are comprehended as group-empowering performances federated with *political* kingship, just as they were in medieval song literature. (In reality, the religious authority of the Brahmins was subordinate to the state). When the colonists arrived, Teyyāṭṭam responded with appropriate resilience; ironically, their liturgies remained undisturbed. The influences of European suzerainty could not halt these practices, and later on, the state's evolution into a Marxist province attests to its spirit of resistance.

5 Caste Identities, Politics, and Performance in North Malabar

Socially categorized lower castes[82] regulate Teyyam *kāvu*, since Nambūtiri Brahmans do not wholly recognize such festivities.[83] Several variations on Teyyāṭṭam rites are performed, either urban or rural, which all abide by a ritual uniformity, in style and structure. As listed on Kerala's public relations website,[84] a 2011 census records population density—within rural and urban settlements—of Kannur and Kasaragod districts, each of which is 225,1727 and 130,7375. No matter the settlement, caste rankings divaricate communal ménages. Below, I catalogue this caste hierarchy in descending order, ranked **only** by castes pertaining to Teyyāṭṭam. Nevertheless, a Kerala caste system—whatsoever the settlement—makes a general distinction between *Brahmin* (*suvarṇa*) and *Non-Brahmin* (*avarṇa*):

81 Bayly, 'Saints Cults', p. 129.

82 Avarna classes that perform *teyyam* consist of: (1) Nāyar, (2) Vāṇṇn [who constitute 60% of all *teyyam*, according to Nambiar, 1993, p. 141], (3) Malayān, (5) Vēlans, (6) Koppalan, (7) Pulayār.

83 Although, Brahmins are present during Teyyam organized by some higher-caste groups. See Freeman, 1991, p. 173.

84 http://kannur.nic.in/population.html [accessed: 02/06/2017].

Main group/ caste performers (kōlakkaran)	Associated groups (priests—kōmamram or sometimes performers)
Malāyan	*Nāyar*
Vāṇṇan	*Nambiār*
Vēlan	
Pulayār	
Mavilan	
Chiṅathān	
Kōpalan	
Anjutan	
Muṇṇutan	
Pulluvan	

The caste designations listed here are distinctively Northern Keralan. Indeed, linguistically and culturally, the culture and language of Kannur is its own vernacular, differing, however minute, from the districts further south. The six groups italicized in the table denote castes from which most of my interlocutors—native to Kannur—were members. Outside the Teyyam season—at the monsoon's height in summer—dancer-mediums assume non-ritual vocations; agricultural and manual labour seemed most prudent modes of employment for mediums.

5.1 *Teyyāṭṭam: Political Movements and Definition—Art, or Ritual?*

Despite its status as a subaltern phenomenon—described by religion-denying Marxists as a 'cultural art form', or BJP-supporting Hindus as a 'folkloric dance'—Teyyāṭṭam is not limited to Malabar's peripheral fringes. Most groups in Northern Kerala are **not** *suvarṇa* Brahmins or Nāyars (who can attend both Teyyāṭṭam or some Brahmin ceremonies); Teyyam groves **and** royal temples are places of worship where any group—their statuses aside—can pay homage to a local pantheon of deities. The temples of high-caste Brahmins, on the other hand, are out-of-bounds for most of the population. As already established, Teyyāṭṭam does not dismiss caste lock, stock, and barrel; purity-based norms—a byproduct of caste—stake out group subdivisions, until an ancestor's visitation ruptures the separative order. The Sanskritic rationale—on which caste is based—is preoccupied with gradations of bodily purity, whereas subaltern Teyyāṭṭam—in alliance with regnant poligars—perceived **all** human bodies—

warriors, farmers, and untouchables—as potential conduits for conjuring divine and political power. In spite of this Brahmanical/Political rupture, contemporary worshippers of Teyyam condense them in verbally evoking their deities; an indigenous, Dravidian goddess is commonly identified with a pan-Hindu (Purāṇic) one. As previously discussed in this chapter, a recent climate of 'Hinduization'—linked to the expansionism of BJP politics—may have influenced this trend, even if Kerala's sovereignty is ruled by a majority-communist government.

Attendees from various *avarna* groups participate in and support their local Teyyam performances; interlocutors often explained that these events reconnected long-lost relatives who may have returned from the UAE, purely, to glorify their primogenitors. Teyyāṭṭam turns back the clock, if only for a short time, to resuscitate familial-like sociality; the charisma of ancestral presence heals us, socially, against the tide of distance. Gabriel concurs, when he writes:

> A feeling of ecstasy and divine power is communicated to the congregation. This is why these rituals draw substantial crowds to their performances, often at very early or late hours, men and women alike.[85]

For Kerala's denizens, the magnetizing appeal of Teyyāṭṭam lies in its capacity to re-energize and, thereby, transfigure social cohesion. Indeed, by reconfirming members as kindred heirs of the land, Teyyāṭṭam amplifies (and makes visible) shared cultural worlds, wherein land-bound ancestors, warriors, and goddess-clans percolate bodies and lineages. And yet, for scholars of Theatre studies[86]—those who elucidate Teyyāṭṭam as 'theatre'—the ritual's complexity is an *art* form, and to suggest otherwise is to describe an extinct, medieval practice: in their view, calling Teyyāṭṭam a ritual is erroneous, considering that capital culture overrides cultural heritage among Kerala's millennials.

On one level, I agree: Teyyāṭṭam is resplendently aesthetic, which, we must recognize, is instrumental in triggering its superhuman blessings. In trying to disentangle this contentious debate, Vadakkinyil has made some progress: he highlights that Teyyāṭṭam, performed in the affluent urban areas, has become deeply *politicized* by BJP or Marxist divides—an art form whose *telos* the state has now compressed to endorse a Marxist agenda, or, conversely, a platform for the Hindu right (BJP) to trumpet Sanskritic values (in their reworkings, Teyyam

85 Gabriel, *Playing God*, p. 24.

86 Particularly: Ashley & Holloman, 'Teyyam'.

gods are conflated with pan-Indic gods and goddesses like Viṣṇu or Śiva).[87] Undoubtably, Teyyāṭṭam's unique choreography and creativity produces great advertisements that capture the imaginations of tourists, far and wide.

Supporting Vadakkinyil, I agree that construing Teyyam practice as mere 'art' undoes its broad-ranging appeal; for Kannur's local populace, Teyyāṭṭam is adduced as efficacious and powerful, reengaging Keralans with their genealogical pasts. Vadakkinyil writes:

> Reducing *teyyam* solely to art is making it empty and part of the structure of the state … In this re-presentation, we can see the paradox of *teyyam*: it has the potential to resist powers of the state, yet at the same time it has been co-opted within the state's structure.[88]

Whether a politically sanctioned art cranking up regional pride, or a ritual aimed at connecting participants with their ancestors, Teyyāṭṭam becomes (in both cases) an intensely emotive tool that shapes, tests, and re-shapes Keralan identity structures. In the next chapter I move north-ward to the Kathmandu Valley, to introduce the second case study: the Navadurgā ritual of Bhaktapur.

87 Dinesan Vadakkintyil, 'Images of Transgression: Teyyam in Malabar', *Social Analysis*, 54.2 (2010), p. 131.

88 Ibid., p. 131.

CHAPTER 2

Introducing the Northern Case Study—Navadurgā, Bhaktapur, Nepal

Nestled on a river confluence—some 13.5 km east of Kathmandu—Bhaktapur[1] is a small-scale but densely populated urban settlement. Of the Valley's three cities, Bhaktapur was, originally, Nepal's capital, famed for its elaborate architecture. It also retains a unique set of Newari customs (*sanskriti*) and festivals (*jātrā*)—of medieval provenance—which are celebrated with the same avidity. Since Robert Levy's fieldwork in Bhaktapur during the 1980s, the city's population has soared exponentially, from 40,000 to 81,748[2] in 2011; 21st century Bhaktapur is now a municipality. For Levy, Bhaktapur differed from other Newar cities, because its socio-cultural cityscape was, for him, definitively "ancient", "axial" but ritually "sophisticated", in opposition to the "modernity" or Western influence of other Nepali cityscapes, like Kathmandu.[3]

In his book, *Mesocosm*, Levy discerns Bhaktapur as a predominately Hindu city modelled on medieval Indic kingdoms; this observation accords with Sylvain Lévi's famous dictum, *'Népal est l'Inde qui ce fait'*.[4] In this medieval kingdom, Bhaktapurian ritual life was, for Levy, a 'civic ballet' of 'embedded symbols' (linked to everyday purity) coalescing with 'marked symbols' (linked to blood-rites and extramundane power).[5] While I sympathize with Levy's exhaustive analysis, Grieve, Gibson, and Hachettu have argued that his analysis precludes movements of social change—communism, ISKCON, Theravāda Buddhism, and Christianity—which have re-shaped this Newar city's traditionalism.

As a socio-ethnic group in Nepal, Newars self-identify as: (1) urbanized; (2) Kathmandu-Valley originated; (3) Newari-speaking, and (4) caste-organized people. Since the Lichhavi period (5th–8th Centuries CE), the Valley (Newa: *Nepāḷamaṇḍala*) was comprised of three sovereign city states—Kathmandu,

1 Also known as Khwōpa in Newari, or Bhadgāon in Nepali.

2 *National Population and Housing Census 2011: Bhaktapur*, Government of Nepal, Central Bureau of Statistics, Kathmandu, Nepal (published: March 2014), p. 16. Source: http://cbs.gov.np/wp-content/uploads/2014/04/26%20Bhaktapur_VDCLevelReport.pdf [accessed: 1/4/2015].

3 Robert I. Levy, *Mesocosm: Hinduism and the Organization of a Traditional Newar City in Bhaktapur Vol. 1* (Berkeley: University of California Press, 1990).

4 Sylvain Lévi, *Le Népal: étude historique d'un royaume hindou* (Paris: Ernest Leroux, 1905).

5 Levy, *Mesocosm*, p. 16.

 | DOI:10.1163/9789004439023_004

Bhaktapur, and Lalitpur—each surrounded by allied territories and towns. In the 21st Century, the Valley's Newar communities coexist within a multi-ethnic nation-state that forms Nepali society more broadly: these groups include Tamang, Chettri, Thāru, Magar, and Thangmi ethnicities. But in Bhaktapur, Newar inhabitants dominate demographically, and thus, culturally.

1 Hindu-Buddhist Tantra in Newar Society: The Case of Bhaktapur

Most, if not all, of Bhaktapur's native denizens ethnically identify as 'Newars': according to census statistics, some 99% of Bhaktapur citizens were Newar in the 1980s,[6] but now, this has decreased to 80%, as other ethnic groups—from Kathmandu and beyond—live and work in the city. Many indigenous Bhaktapurians are also bilingual in Nepali and Newari though, by and large, Bhaktapur's *lingua franca* is Newari.

From Lalitpur's villages to Bhaktapur's urban centre, Newari religious life encompasses Hindu Tantric **and** Vajrayāna Buddhist praxes; in certain shrines, a pan-Hindu goddess and a Vajrayāna *bodhisattva* share an interchangeable presence, but, in Bhaktapur—the "city of symbols"[7]—Hindu gods outnumber Buddhist ones. In contrast to Northern Malabar, Muslim communities—whatever their sect—are not recognized in Newar religion, even if, on Bhaktapur's urban margins, several Mosques serve its minority Muslim population. As described by Gellner, Newars designate Muslims as 'upside down' practitioners, whose religion is irreconcilable with Newari norms.[8] As we have gathered, only Hindu and Buddhist expressions—together forming Newar Tantric religion—are innately Newar: all in all, Lalitpurians and Kathmanduians pivot between Hindu and Buddhist Tantra, while Bhaktapur is largely Hindu Tantra (or, we could argue, Folk Śākta).

According to Hausner's and Gellner's work with Nepalis in diaspora, religious practice—outside the Nepal valley—is also non-exclusivist, what they call 'multiple belonging'.[9] For Hausner and Gellner, 'multiple belonging' surpasses the stasis of Judeo-Christian categories of religion; in Newar contexts,

6 Levy, *Mesocosm*, p. 59.
7 Ibid.
8 David Gellner, 'Hinduism, Tribalism, and the Position of Women: The Problem of Newar Identity', *Man*, 26.1 (1991), p. 105.
9 Sondra Hausner & David Gellner, 'Category and Practice as Two Aspects of Religion: The Case of Nepalis in Britain', *JAAR*, 80.4 (2012).

Western categories of religion cannot and do not apply.[10] And yet, on the ground, a semantic distinction between 'Śiva-margi' ('Hindu') and 'Buddha-margi' ('Buddhist') is made, but, in ritual, these tenets interconnect as a doctrinal network (what I call a *bricolage web of ritual knowledge*): in the present case, Bhaktapur's Banmala groups—whom ascribe, predominantly, as *Śiva-margi*—went to Buddhist temples near Lalitpur to worship Karuṇāmaya,[11] the Newar equivalent, I was told, of bodhisattva *Avalokiteśvara*, or *Matsyendranāth*. For Newars, Matsyendranāth has a dual identity: he is, at once, the founder of the Nāth Siddhas, and, from the Buddhist perspective, he is Karuṇamāyā, a *bodhisattva* of compassion.

In Bhaktapur, Buddhist festivals are also annually commemorated. Ujesh showed me a collection of photographs of Bhaktapur's Five-Buddha festival (*Pañcadān*)—concentrated on Dipaṅkara Buddha—which occurs sometime in January.[12] Within the Bhaktapurian calendar, another Buddhist celebration, the festival of *Vaisakh Purnimā*—which marks the birth of Buddha Śākyamuni—is also popular. During this festival, blood sacrifice is provisionally revoked to respect the historical Buddha's ideal of non-violence; although, the Newars of Patan—who are Tantric Buddhists—perform regular ritual sacrifices. However, throughout settlements of Bhaktapur's Municipality, Ujesh reminded me that Hindu goddesses always receive prioritization: in Banepa, near Bhaktapur, a goddess festival known as *Caṇḍeśwori jātrā* is celebrated, which decussates with the Buddhist celebration of *Vaisakh Purnimā*. Conventionally, Banepa citizens tend to sideline Buddhist festivities to venerate their regional goddess with blood sacrifices.

Despite the traditional inclusivity of Newar religion—its 'multiple belonging', as Gellner puts it—Bhaktapur is the exception, insofar as a Hindu Tantric worldview dominates.[13] Hindu pantheons and practices are also widespread in towns governed by Bhaktapur municipality—Banepa, Nala, and Panauti—which were, in the past, settlements of Bhaktapur's medieval kingdom. Only very few Buddhist monasteries (*vihāra*) survive in Bhaktapur city itself; when I lived there, a monastery near *Inācho twā*—a precinct close to Dattātraya temple—was one Buddhist centre I knew of. It is clear only a small minor-

10 Ibid.

11 This deity is also responsible for the harvest for Lalitpurians.

12 Toffin, *Newar Society*, pp. 39–40.

13 David Gellner, 'Does Symbolism Construct an Urban Mesocosm? Robert Levy's *Mesocosm* and the Question of Value Consensus in Bhaktapur' in *The Anthropology of Hinduism and Buddhism: Weberian Themes* by David Gellner, (Oxford: OUP, 2001), p. 301.

ity of Bhaktapurians belong to the Buddhist castes (Vajrācāryas and Śākyas).[14] In fact, all of Bhaktapur's deity-shrines—including Taleju (also Durgā), the eight mother goddesses (*mātrīkā*), nine Durgās (Navadurgā), Gaṇeśa, and Bhairava—form a Hindu Tantric pantheon that border the city's edges. These Tantric divinities—as members of a royal goddess-clan—protect the city by guarding its geographical boundaries.[15]

2 Bhaktapur City: Blood Symbols, Goddess-Clan, Space, and Society

Topographically, Bhaktapur's geopolitical parameters are charted by numerous boundary shrines (*śakti-pīṭh*), each containing a deity's power. The power generated from these shrines bleed into intra-city god-houses (*dyo-cheṇ*), which suffuse the city's differing neighbourhoods (Newa: *twā*, Nepa: *tol*). Paralleling an urban *maṇḍala* (Newa: *pauba*), these boundary deities safeguard Bhaktapur's interior from unwelcome exterior forces, be that foreign armies, meteorological disasters, or malevolent beings.

Bhaktapur's cityscape is thus an interconnected nexus of streets, temple squares, and 21 precincts (Newa: *twa*; Nep: *tol*) that all lead to the royal palace (*lāyaku*) at its heart. In a likewise arrangement, caste stratification is also spatially organized: central precincts closer to the palatial core comprise higher-caste householders, while at the peripheries, lower-caste households predominate.

One morning during my first fieldtrip to Bhaktapur, I was introduced to a local Karmācārya priest, who later became one of my interlocutors. In our conversation, he described the layout of Bhaktapur as a conch (*śankhā*), a regalia wielded by Narāyān, god of preservation. (Among Newars, Narāyān is a popular epithet for Viṣṇu). Indeed, *Purānic* myths exalt Narāyāṇ's conch as a tool used by kings for prophetic purposes.

With Bhaktapur's arrangement resembling an oval-shaped lineament, my interlocutor's interpretation seemed highly plausible to me. However, as my field-studies progressed, other informants—especially Ujesh and his relatives—were resolute in describing Bhaktapur's topography as a *khaḍgā* (i.e. a sword wielded by Mahākāli which annihilates demons (*daitya*)) or, even a *yoni* (i.e. a female reproductive organ). They said Sānkhu—also in the Kathmandu Valley—was Nepal's 'conch-shaped' town. Whether a sword or a reproductive

14 Ibid.

15 Jehanne H. Teilhet, 'The Tradition of Nava Durga in Bhaktapur, Nepal', *Kailash*, 2.6 (1978), p. 82.

organ, both are blood symbols—exsanguinating or menstrual—which allude to the connective flows that unite Bhaktapurian bodies—human and divine—within their territory.

Regarding the supposed provenance of Bhaktapur's god-shrines, a monograph by Shresta, *Bhaktapur ko Navadurgā gaṇa*, is a useful resource. Drawing on evidence from epigraphic inscriptions and chronicles, Shrestha claims Bhaktapur's 'incorporeal' goddess-clan—the eight mothers (*aṣṭamātrīkā*)—were first installed during the Lichhavi period, under monarch Amsuvarna Malla approx. 7th century CE. Later, in the 12th Century CE, goddess Tripurasundari was adopted into the clan through King Ānanda Malla. And in the 14th Century CE, Bhaktapur's patron goddess, Taleju, is said to have been imported to the Valley by Harisimhadeva, a king who was exiled from his throne at Simrangaud. His dynastic lineage stemmed from an antecedent royal lineage in Maithilā, known as the Karṇāta dynasty.[16]

Steadily, the kingdom's goddess-clan changed, and so too did her constellation in Bhaktapur's shrines: with the addition of Tripurasundari and Taleju, Bhaktapur's goddess-clan, and her terrestrial shrines, were definitively set in place.[17] According to Ujesh, the masked ritual of Nine Durgas (Navadurgā) was a later maturation, which coincided with Suvarna Malla's rule (16th Century CE).

Around the 16th Century CE, in Bhaktapur's Gacchen precinct, a temple to the Navadurgā clan was established by King Suvarna Malla, as was their ritual. In Banmala accounts, the Navadurgā ritual was inaugurated by the crown to alleviate a severe drought: during its initial performance, the goddess-clan's power, embodied in masked mediums (Newa: *ujāju*), ameliorated the harvest. In tune with post-monsoon agricultural cycles, every Navadurgā performance thereafter re-circulated the goddess-clan's energy across Bhaktapur's territories, which continues to this day. At these rituals, mediums dispense the goddess-clan's blessings as necklaces of five colours (Newa: *pāsuka*) in exchange for foodstuffs offered by their devotees. The god-masks worn by the mediums are also offered obeisance; they, too, channel the goddess-clan's *śakti*.

In Bhaktapur, a distinction is made between Navadurgā rituals and Devī dance-dramas, both of which use god-masks in performance. The latter, performed in the summer months, is designed for entertainment purposes only. Unlike Navadurgā's ritual practices (*siddhi*), Devī dances have *no* transformative effects on the population.

16 See also Sarkar, *Heroic Shāktism*.

17 Purusthottam L. Shrestha, *Bhaktapur ko Navadurga Gana*, (private copy, 2003).

As detailed in the Navadurgā myth, the goddess-clan acquired their power from the forest (*jangal*) they once occupied; having been tamed into shrines by a Tantric master, they were worshipped as guardians of Bhaktapur and its agricultural *terra firma*. By nature, the goddesses of the clan are, at once, wild (*ugra*) **and** tame (*saumya*), inside **and** outside, which is key to their apotropaic power: they are sanguinary goddesses who nurture the land by embracing imagery of militia; like warrior mothers, they shield their 'kin' (read, 'civilians') by defending them against exogenous hostile forces. During present-day Navadurgā rituals, dancer-mediums continue to disperse terrestrial energy to denizens, as per a ritual cycle, which rotates annually throughout lands that once formed a petty kingdom.

In the history of Tantric traditions, such intersecting of royal power, goddesses, and state rituals is commonplace. As early as the 6th century CE, Sarkar explains how Durgā—and her goddess-clan—had a pride of place at the royal court.[18] Most palpably, political power and goddess-invoking was commemorated annually during Navarātra, the autumnal festival. At this time, the king, Kumāri (living goddess), Taleju (warrior goddess), and Navadurgā mediums became mutually constitutive emblems of state power.[19]

3 Monsoon, Power, and the Goddess-Clan: Banmala Dancer-Mediums during the Ritual Cycle

In Bhaktapur, all dancer-mediums associated with Navadurgā performances are members of the Banmala caste. Their temple (Newa: *dyo-cheṇ*) is located on the edge of Bhaktapur in *Gacchen twā*, also known as Kamālvināyak. Each dancer-medium is allocated a deity and a mask which he will embody at the beginning of each yearly cycle. Determining which deity is delegated to which medium—these mantles rotate annually—was a question I frequently asked Banmala members: When does this occur? From which source—human or literary or astrological—is this procedure governed?

As is conventional among Newars, disclosing any esoteric matters to a foreigner (*videshi*) is eschewed; from their perspective—as keepers of formidable Tantric techniques—such knowledge being broadcast so liberally could be to the ritual's detriment. However, I knew of one literary source they consulted: in the temple's first-floor sanctum—an area prohibited to foreigners—a

18 Sarkar, *Heroic Shāktism*.

19 Ibid.

book described as *vamśāwali* ('chronicles') was stored there; it was supposedly a medieval text, though which century remains unknown. The book was said to contain astronomical, liturgical, and genealogical content which was used to discern which medium would embody which deity. Usually this deity-assignment ceremony had to be processed some weeks before *Gotamangal*, that is, Bhaktapur's first ritual after the monsoon hiatus. Nineteen roles are redistributed, and for purposes of accessibility, I tabulate them below, from eldest to youngest. As Toffin demonstrates, relations between deities, people and territories are postulated in kin or clan terms,[20] a social norm which I noticed during my own fieldwork:

Member of Gaṇa	Role within Navadurgā Gaṇa
Nāyo	He is the elder (Nepa: *tharkāri*) of the Banmala clan—his extensive knowledge of the ritual means he is responsible for the general functioning and logistics of each cycle.
Nakiṅ	She is the female priestess and caretaker of the Navadurgā temple. Each day, she conducts *nitya puja* (daily worship and ablution of temple shrines) at the *dyo-chen* and ensures all preliminary rites are completed before each Navadurgā performance.
Khiṇ Baja	One of three Baja (or musicians) that perform at each Navadurgā ritual—sometimes they are equated with the power of Tripurasundari. The Khin Baja is a drummer.
Taa Baja	Cymbal player
Khaa Baja	Drummer and chanter
Bhairav (Newa: *Bhailah Dyo*)	Deemed the most powerful of all goddess-clan, he is the deity who commences each dance and performs the sacrifice of the *muḥbanaṅ* (pig slaughter), severing the jugular vein of the piglet with his thumbnail. Ujesh outlined the role of Bhairab: "Bhairab distributes *prāsād* to all [*dhāū baji*—a mixture of beaten rice and buffalo curd] and *pāsuka* [a blessed thread of five colours worn around the neck] and so on. During the dance of Bhairab, daily activities [bathing, making *tikā/shila* etc.], everything is expressed through his dance. It helps people to remember how to be hygienic, and general lessons to the people"

20 Toffin, *Newar Society*, p. 210.

(*cont.*)

Member of Gaṇa	Role within Navadurgā Gaṇa
Seto Bhairav (Newa: *Siti Bhailah*)	Seto Bhairav—with his white-face, black moustache and large circular eyes—is the antithesis of Bhairav, he is a benign or "angelic" (as Ujesh called him) form of Bhirav. In his dance with Mahākāli, he acts in passive, submissive fear of her power, thereby inverting nominal gender roles by Newar standards. He is also, quite interestingly, a god worshipped for reasons of fertility; during a performance at Panauti, I spoke with a married couple who requested a personal *puja* with Seto Bhairav. The wife was pregnant; they hoped for a son.
Mahākāli	She is the fiercest of all the goddesses, and during her dance, she searches for the demon *Mahiśaṣura*, and destroys him with her sword (*khaḍga*). In every ritual, she is given two chickens for sacrifice by Seto Bhairav, which she does by severing their necks with her teeth, as testament to her strength.
Varāhi	One of the goddesses—consort of Varāha—viewed and respected as a *buhāri* (daughter-in-law) to her mother, a dynamic shown in her dance. *Bel-biba:a* (the Newar rite of passage, where young girls are married to the *bel* fruit) is also displayed in her dances.
Kumāri	Goddess viewed as the daughter (*bahini*) of the pantheon—who distributes food offerings (*prāsād*)—on a *lapte*—to other members of the troupe. She is known for her anger and ferociousness, which is overcome during her performance. In a section of her dance, she bows her head to the ground, which displays her pacification.
Gaṇeśa	As 'remover of obstacles', he is the deity who places a *mohani sila* (a black line on the forehead, made from charcoal burned during the festival of Mohanī) on each dancer-medium's forehead before any ritual. His dance is the first to inaugurate the performances.
Dhatimā pomi (Newa)	He is the member who carries the silver repoussé plate (New: *kha: cha*) that represents the goddess Mahālakṣmi (Newa: *sipha dyo*). Unlike the other deities, Mahālakṣmi does not have an embodied mask or dancer-medium—she represents the combined power of all goddesses. This is evident from the goddess' representation on the repoussé plate—according to Ujesh, her face has no distinguishable facial features; in this form, she is said to embody the whole pantheon. Indeed, she is always the first to leave the temple during a performance.

(*cont.*)

Member of Gaṇa	Role within Navadurgā Gaṇa
Dhoma pomi (Newa)/ Guje Kali (Nepa)	This member collects the offerings of money (*paisa*) given by devotees
Chimā Pomi	This member watches over the smaller mask of Mahādev (Śiva) that rests upon the plate of Mahālakṣmi. Śiva is carried by the dancer of Gaṇeśa and placed on the *kha: cha* of Mahālakṣmi. According to Teilhet's informant: "Siva must be carried because he is blind with anger and fury [...] Ganesa carries Siva because he is very smart. He knows how to control the anger of his father; he carries Siva to keep him from doing more damage and destruction".[21] During my fieldwork, the Banmalas suggested his mask is smaller because he is not as "tantric" as the goddesses: during ritual, he is the passive god, while the goddesses are the active polarity. This is exemplified in the dance of Mahākāli and Seto Bhairav; in her presence, he adopts the submissive role.
Brahmāyani	The goddess of creation—she is the first of the goddesses (after Mahālakṣmi) to be offered gifts by devotees. At her temple on the peripheries of Bhaktapur city—close to the banks of the Hanumante river—the god-masks are activated at the beginning of the cycle, and 'pass away' at its end in June. One historian I spoke with named her the *ādiśakti* ('primordial power') that sparks the power of all deities (not like Mahālakṣmi, who collectively represents the goddesses—the eight mothers (*aṣṭamātrīkā*)).
Maheśvāri	She is one deity who does not receive sacrifice—she is a pure goddess, often associated with Gaṅgā Mā, whose temperament is peaceful.
Bhadrakālī	Linked with fertility and agriculture, her specific dance recalls the process of planting crops (rice, maize etc.). Her green-faced complexion displays her relationship to nature and agricultural cycles.
Indrāyani	Wife of Seto Bhairab, she is the goddess who oversees moral behaviour. Her instincts are maternal by nature.
Sīma and Dūma	Described as *vahana* (vehicles) of the pantheon, they are sons of Seto Bhairab. They collect money from passers-by during *nya lakegu* (fish-catching dance) of Seto Bhairab. This relation to fish may be linked to

21 Teilhet, 'The Tradition', p. 83.

(*cont.*)

Member of Gaṇa	Role within Navadurgā Gaṇa
	Matsyendranāth and Nāth Siddhi, a linkage I discuss in § 4.3.3.2. They create the "family element of Navadurga".

By way of clarification, the next section will interweave these roles into a description of the Navadurgā cycle's prominent phases.

3.1 *Stage (1): Gotamangal, Navadurgā God-Masks, and the Buffalo*

The first phase commences with the festival of Gotamangal. Briefly, *gotamangal's* (Nepa: *ghantā karṇa*) rationale is exorcistic; it is a celebration that purifies the city's precincts from demonic forces. To assure this purification, each neighbourhood parades a giant effigy of demonic figure, *ghantāsur*—made of straw, wood, and auspicious fruits—around the vicinity. The effigy functions as a conduit that absorbs the negative forces which may have infiltrated Bhaktapur in the absence of the goddess—it is then set alight to signal the expelling of malignant beings (*daitya*). I was told the destructive energies of Śiva and Bhairava are harnessed during *Gotamangal* to allow this cleansing; it is they who are summoned initially because the goddess-clan is dormant until its re-enlivening at Mohani in October.

While Bhaktapurians are celebrating *Gotamangal*, the Navadurgā mediums have other preparatory duties; instead, they perform ancillary duties for Mohani, where the goddess-clan—the deities they embody for the rest of the year—will return after the monsoon. For *Gotamangal*, the Banmala mediums are bedecked in white clothes (*jammā*), and as they leave their temple, three members carry a large painted terracotta vessel (*khoṇcā*) containing soil and rice grains. During *Gotamangal*, the *khoṇcā* becomes highly sacred paraphernalia, which is used to revive Bhairav's power, since his mask, at that point, is still being constructed by the mask-makers (Citrakār). The power of Bhairav—contained in the terracotta vessel—is summoned in a *puja* enacted by their clan's female priestess (*nakiṅ*). Ujesh illustrated how "[before the masks are made at Mohani] the *khoṇcā* keeps and conserves the *śakti*".

Afterward, the dancer-mediums—with the terracotta vessel—visit the house of the mask-makers, the Citrākar family, who have spent the monsoon months crafting god-masks (*khwōpa*) of clay collected from a local riverbed. Prior to this visit, every medium is purified by the *nakiṅ* outside the temple doorway in a rite of ablution called *lāsa kūsa*; their hands are doused in water

FIGURE 7 Navadurgā Performance
PHOTOGRAPH BY AUTHOR

poured from a sanctified water jar (*sija tapho*). At the Citrākar residence, the soil contained in the *khoṇcā* is added to the paints in finalizing the god-masks. This gesture instills the masks with additional divine energy, which was conjured by the *nakiṅ*. During this ceremony, I was told the masks were imbued with "life": according to Tantric tradition, object and bodies are imbued with "life-breath" (*prāṇprothesthān*), which is invoked from divine energy (*śakti*) innate in the territory's body politic. To illustrate this point, a Bhaktapurian historian told me: "the people are the ones who create the gods and the ones who can destroy the gods".[22]

A substantial feast (*bhoj*) concludes *Gotamangal*, which is organized at the Navadurgā temple (*dyo-cheṇ*). For Banmala mediums, dining outside the temple is prohibited before Mohani. After *Gotamangal*, a healthy male black buffalo (*khamei*)—devoid of physical imperfections—is presented to the Navadurgā clan. The animal will remain at the temple for two months until Mohani commences. Here, it will be prepared—nutritionally and ritualistically—for

22 Purusthottam L. Shrestha develops on this notion in *Bhaktapur ko Navadurgā gana*.

its inevitable sacrifice during Mohani. At the festival, *Khamei* are significant, since their sacrifice constitutes the buffalo-demon's destruction (*Mahiśaṣura*); in fact, the translation of *Mahiśa* is precisely that, "buffalo".

For several weeks before the autumnal season, each member rehearses in the Navadurgā temple under the auspices of a *guru*; he is a senior dancer-medium whose knowledge he bequeathed from the Nāyo. During Gaṇeśa Caturthi (Newa: *Chotta puja*), the Navadurgā mediums pay homage at the shrine of Nasādyo[23]—the Newar god of music, dance and tantric knowledge—to assure the ritual's success. He is a deity who transmits tantric knowledge (*vidyā*), and so, to gratify him, the mediums sacrifice a ram at his shrine. At first, I was unsure of Nasādyo's precise origins, for he is unheard of beyond Newar communities. Whilst inadvertently ambling near Nasādyo's shrine with Ujesh, he gestured at the shrine and clarified: "If we want to learn the music, the aesthetics [that are necessary], first we go and worship Nasādyo [...] All Newars know his importance".

4 Blood Sacrifice, Mohani, and the Navadurgā Cycle

4.1 *Stage (2): Autumnal Festival of Mohani and Goddess-Clan Reanimation*

In October, Bhaktapurians welcome the Newari festival of *Mohani*, greeting the goddess in her supreme emanation as *bhagavati*. Held on the first day of waxing fortnight (*Kaulathwa*), it is celebrated for ten days and, on each day, a different goddess is commemorated at differing shrines throughout Bhaktapur.[24] Mohani is, simultaneously, a domestic and public festival that honours the regional goddess-clan through public readings of the Devī Māhātmya myth in Bhaktapur's public squares. In addition to these recitations, a series of ritual libations of rice and barley are offered. Also, Bhaktapurians sojourn for collective river-bathing near the temple of Brahmāyani, Bhaktapur's creator goddess. From her temple, a path extends into the city; this route was designated specifically for festival usage—which became known as Bhaktapur's *jātrā* route.[25]

The first day begins, *ipso facto*, at the monsoon season's end, a period of harvest cultivation.[26] More detailed analyses of the Mohani festival will be

---

23 In Hindu tradition, Nasadyo is a manifestation of Śiva in his 'cosmic dancer' form or Natarājā.

24 Levy, *Mesocosm*, p. 523.

25 Levy, *Mesocosm*, pp. 524–527.

26 Ibid., p. 523.

explored in chapter 3, but for now, I will focus on Mohani's focal point: the first, ninth (*mahānauomi*), and tenth (*mahādasami*) days. All these days directly influence the Navadurgā cycle, for the goddess-clan's power is passed to the Banmala mediums, who are their custodians.

4.2 *Mohani: First Day*

The first day of Mohani rises with the sun at dawn, when local devotees—alongside musicians who accompany them—follow one another to the *pīṭha* (seat) of the goddess revered that day—Brahmāyani.[27] After *puja* at the feet of Brahmāyani, the group makes their way to the local riverbank (*tirtha*), where they bathe in its sacred waters. Levy summarizes how "[…] on this first day it is the god-house, tirtha and pitha of Brahmani to which the townspeople go".[28] For the successive seven days, each member of the goddess-clan is worshipped individually at each of her *śakti-pīṭha*.

4.3 *Mohani: Ninth Day*

The ninth day is particularly salient for the Navadurgā troupe; the buffalo (*khamei*)—tamed at the Navadurgā temple for three months—is to be sacrificed at Brahmāyani's shrine on Bhaktapur's farthest margin. Before being escorted there, the buffalo is prepared by a butcher (*sahī*) in a ceremony called *khamei bwāgegu*: he ties a thread to the buffalo's head (*dhoile bhatccha*), and vermillion powder is smeared on its abdomen. The buffalo is also fed rice wine (*aila*), which Ujesh said "makes him [the buffalo] very wild [*dherai jangali*]". On his journey, crowds torment the *khamei*; of course, the animal symbolizes a demon which the goddess will slay. Adjacent to Brahmāyani's shrine, the buffalo is immersed in the Hanumante river before it is led to the sacrificial altar. In the shrine, the Navadurgā mediums—with their deities' thirteen masks—are welcomed by a Karmācārya priest, and a series of ritual actions follow.

Within the temple's central sanctum (*mulchok*), all the Navadurgā clan's masks, clothes and *ghoṅgala* [anklets] are laid out, whilst the Nakiṅ conducts a *lāsa kūsa* and distributes an array of food offerings to mediums there present. Afterwards, the repoussé plate of goddess Mahālakṣmi—who, after the Mohani festival, will encompass the goddess-clan's power *in toto*—is circumambulated around the shrine; a consecrated necklace (*tisa*) is wrapped around the plate,

27 Ibid., p. 524.
28 Ibid., p. 527.

which consigns Brahmāyani's creative energy to the Navadurgā clan. The buffalo is sacrificed at the altar, and each dancer-medium—in the order tabulated in § 2.3—drinks blood directly from the buffalo's severed neck. I was told this sacrificial act enlivens the deity-mediums; by consuming the demon's essence, they too become fiercely powerful. Devotees gather around the shrine: they praise the deity-mediums by providing offerings to the god-masks. Meanwhile, the Karmācārya priest—with a terracotta jar containing rice (*akhe*)—showers all mediums and god-masks with raw rice-grains and beaten rice (*baji*). According to the Banmalas, rice "contains life ... after we are sprinkled with rice at Nauomi, we become the deities ... the masks are worn and the [transformation] is done. We are prepared for the rest of the year". Rice is powerful for Newars, since it is the product of their land, which is charged with the goddess-clan's essence.

At the festival's penultimate day—also *nauomi*—the Navadurgā mediums participate in a rite overseen by four Karmācārya priests at Taleju's royal temple in the city's central square. Twenty-four buffalo are slaughtered in her honour: all buffalo for this ceremony are brought by a breeder in an area outside Bhaktapur known as *niku thu*. From this point onwards, the Navadurgā cycle officially begins: at the outset, the medium troupe perform in Kathmandu—at Paśupatinath, then in Jaybagiswori—before it returns to Bhaktapur's Suryamadhi precinct for its inaugural performance there. Brahmayani's intra-city temple is located in Suryamadhi; as such, this neighbourhood is linked to Bhaktapur's creator goddess and is, thus, a befitting location for the cycle's initial performance.

4.4 *Stage (3): The Navadurgā Ritual Cycle (October–June)*

The complex liturgies of Navadurgā performances are too convoluted to outline here in their entirety; therefore, a detailed description will be provided in Part 2. To summarize: during the nine months after Mohani, the dancer-medium troupe visit twenty-one areas in Bhaktapur city and eight settlements that border Bhaktapur's vicinity.[29] Sometimes, through a messenger, the mediums are invited by a household to conduct these dances at their quarters (*dyo bokegu*). However, these *dyo bokegu* are more infrequent since, as Levy rightly claims:

> The dance drama, or pyakha(n), which the Nine Durgas troupe performs throughout the city, comes to each of the neighbourhoods in which it

29 Levy, *Mesocosm*, p. 565.

FIGURE 8 Portable shrine of goddess Mahālakṣmī
PHOTOGRAPH BY AUTHOR

is performed as a kind of invasion. The troupe appears in each neighbourhood in an order determined by a traditional annual sacrifice. Local people must prepare for a visit that is beyond their control.[30]

30 Ibid., p. 563.

In all, twenty-six regions welcome Navadurgā performance to their precincts, and I list them here in chronological order:

Cycle of Navadurgā	Places (*twa/tol* of Bhaktapur and other settlements)
1	Pashupatināth, Jaybagiswori, Kathmandu
2	Suryamadhi, Bhaktapur
3	Dattatrāya, Tachapal, Bhaktapur
4	Kwathandou, Bhaktapur
5	Gachhen, Bhaktapur
6	Dastocha, Bhaktapur
7	Inacho, Bhaktapur
8	Golmadhi, Bhaktapur
9	Yachhen, Bhaktapur
10	Sanga, Kavre District
11	Taumadhi, Bhaktapur
12	Talako, Bhaktapur
13	Bangsagopal, Bhaktapur Municipality (Nhesatow)
14	Gahiti, Bhaktapur
15	Kwachhen, Bhaktapur
16	Durupo Dyo (Sukul Dhoka)
17	Nāla, Kavre District
18	Dhulikel, Kavre District
19	Kharpu, Kavre District
20	Balalchu, Durbar Marg, Bhaktapur
21	Tulachhen, Tripurasundari, Bhaktapur
22	Chochhen, Bhaktapur
23	Banepa, Kavre District
24	Panauti, Kavre District
25	Ichhu, Bhaktapur
26	Taleju lāyaku (royal temple), Durbar *lāyaku*, Bhaktapur

On their way to each area or neighbourhood (*twa*), the mediums tread a route (*two: mukhegu*) that halts at each god-shrine on its path. When they reach the neighbourhood, the troupe settle on straw mats placed around the area's public shrine, where a pig (Nepa: *sungur bali*; Newa: *muḥbanaṅ*) is slaughtered in its public courtyard. According to Levy, a pig signifies the 'strategic pig of the Nine Durgas' legend', sacrificed to appease the wild goddesses' hunger; in fact, a pig is also the most pollutive animal in Newar culture.[31] Ujesh avoided meals that contained pork, though, occasionally, he ate pork momos in restaurants. The pig sacrifice is conducted by the medium embodying Bhairava, and similarly, a cockerel is killed by Mahākāli.[32] After sacrificing the pig, Bhairava—his hands defiled by sacrificial blood—offers morsels of curds and beaten rice (*dhāũ baji*) to surrounding devotees as a blessing. It is claimed that the ingestion of *dhāũ baji* apotropaically shields the neighbourhoods' families from local diseases.[33]

All these sacrificial gestures crescendo into the trance-dance itself. In this space, a ritual performance communicates macro-clan values to the people of Bhaktapur; there, supportive ritual kinship, or *affective kin intentionality*, is ceremonially accentuated.[34] This sequence is repeated throughout the season, until May/June, when the monsoon season begins. During the monsoon, symbols of purity and immersion are hallmarks of quotidian life—unlike the impurity of the nine-month ritual season (also, the medieval king's military season)—where, as Levy interestingly states,

> This day [Sithi Nakha] also marks the beginning period during which rice seeds are to be planted to produce rice paddy plants that will be transplanted in the next stage of the rice production. For farmers, this day anticipates the beginning of a long period of hard work and anxiety and traditionally was the (the *only*, it is sometimes said) day in the year when farmers bathed their bodies completely, as a kind of purifying preparation for the period to come.[35]

Bridging the gap between the last cycle's finale (June/July) and the regeneration of the next (October) is a three-month period of cultural inactivity, where religious rites are suspended; although funeral attendance is still obligatory. Public music and processions are also prohibited; such silence conveys the city's collective mourning for the Navadurgā clan, whose masks were cremated to mark the ritual cycle's end (*khwōpa-auyegu*). The moment their masks are burned, the Navadurgā clan's agency is adjourned, until the next cycle comes around. Ujesh explained how: 'in Newar communities, if family members pass away, we don't go to the temple or celebrate festivals [*jātra manaundaina*] … we treat Navadurgā as if our own mother has died between Bagasti and Gota-

31 Levy, *Mesocosm*, p. 564.
32 Ibid., pp. 564–565.
33 Ibid., p. 564.
34 Ibid.
35 Ibid., p. 512.

mangal'. The Navadurgā deities are rendered inactive after the previous cycle's end, which is why all religious life[36] ceases, for all festivals depend on the goddess-clan's defensive capacities to sanctify them. At this point, rice cultivation replaces the stagnation of ritual practice before August (and *gotamangal*) recurs again.

5 Cosmology, Tantric Texts, and Newar Hinduism in Bhaktapur

During the early medieval period, Śaiva deities and Tantric forms of religiosity—as documented in Mantramārga literature—were primarily salvation-focused schools across South Asia. As such, they were systems used, mostly, by ascetic or antinomian lineages i.e. Rudra-worshipping Paśupāta ascetics. Gradually, toward the 9th–11th Centuries CE, these various cultic traditions (Mantrāmarga Śaiva schools) began incorporating goddess- and fertility-cults into their Śaiva pantheons.[37] Broadly, this newly-bolstered Tantric religiosity, or *kaula* (Skt: 'family'), was focused on this-worldly energies personified by Bhairava and the goddess-clan in antinomian or transgressive systems of worship. According to Sanderson, such religiosity reached its peak between 11th–13th Centuries, when it was adopted by Indic sovereigns, during a so-called "Śaiva Age".[38] This change from individual to public soteriology was induced once goddess-focused (Śākta) traditions were introduced. In Bhaktapur, a fully-fledged public Tantric religion is celebrated through annual festivities, ancestor worship (Newa: *dugu pūjā*), and Navadurgā rituals. Levy explains:

> Bhaktapur has gone further in the use and transformation of Tantrism than as an exciting and cathartic antistructural fantasy for upper status men […] It has transformed the tantrism of transcendence of Brahmanical order for the purposes of individual salvation and individual power and put it to the use of the civic order; in so doing complexifying that order. Legendary accounts of the capture of Bhaktapur's protective deities, the Nine Durgas [how these feral goddesses were captured in the wilderness and pacified to protect the city by a religious virtuoso] vividly portray this double movement.[39]

---

36 As Ujesh put it, Navadurgā mediums produce 'a rhythm that brings harmony to the *tol*'.
37 Sanderson, 'Śaivism and the Tantric Traditions'.
38 Sanderson, 'Śaiva Age', p. 253.
39 Levy, *Mesocosm*, p. 231.

Tantra pervades Newar religion—along with Vedic and Purāṇic modes, which Gellner rightly distinguishes[40]—and this popularity is linked to its non-dualism: a non-dual (*advaita*) metaphysics creates a relationship between human and divine beings, so that the distribution of divine power (*śakti*) permeates all beings and bodies, not only priests initiated at the social order's highest rungs. Gellner reiterates this theological inclusivism here: "From a Tantric (esoteric) point of view, all deities, indeed all things, are manifestations of the absolute".[41]

When discussing with my host family in Bhaktapur—while watching 'Nepālmaṇḍal TV' or Hindi movies after dinner—Krishna described to me, on several occasions, his experiences of the 'divine-within'. This 'inner god' he recounted yokes with the personas of Navadurgā goddesses—who mapped Bhaktapur's territory—which he invoked during performances. He also claimed one medium was trained to receive textual guidance (*dharmagranth*) from the goddesses. This transfer of esoteric knowledge between ancestral goddess and his 'inner god/goddess' was received unconsciously in his body, which, later, he would write in the text (*vaṃśavali*) stored in the temple's inner sanctum. This dynamic (what I later call 'somatic textuality') highlights the particular ways Tantric divinities—enshrined in temples, or internally-immanent in persons as '*bhagavān bhitramaa*' or '*Navadurgā-manapsahir bas*'—inter-transmit and converge in Newar cosmology. Further, one of my historian interlocutors exalted the body as a nexus that enunciates the material power of enshrined gods.

The visceral flow between deities, bodies, and territory, then, is the mainstay of Tantric religion—and Navadurgā performances—in Bhaktapur. Grieve also noticed how aspects of Bhaktapurian Tantric religion align deities and humans 'horizontally' rather than 'vertically'. He writes:

> Bhaktapur's prosaic religious practice [Tantra] plays a part in constructing the samsaric aspect by treating stone-gods as if they were extraordinary people.[42]

At the level of Navadurgā rituals, dangerous goddesses (and Bhairava, Śiva, Gaṇeśa, and Hanumān) assume an elevated role at these events. As Levy tells

40 David Gellner, *Monk, Householder and Tantric Priest: Newar Buddhism and its Hierarchy of Ritual* (Cambridge: CUP, 1992).

41 David Gellner, 'Newar Buddhism and its Hierarchy of Ritual', (D.Phil. diss., University of Oxford, 1987), p. 99.

42 Gregory Grieve, *Retheorizing Religion in Nepal* (New York: Palgrave Macmillan, 2006), p. 103.

us, this rationale places these "lesser" deities as guardians of the 'this-worldly' sphere (lineage, fertility, and agricultural concerns) "[by] respond[ing] to the problems that moral religion [Brahmanical religion] cannot deal with [they] protect the moral realm".[43] Therefore, the "impure", but powerful divinities uphold social hierarchy precisely by transcending them.

As I argue later, these heterodoxic deities are identified as '*kin*'—mother goddesses—by their devotees, which is echoed in the familial scenarios that play out between deities during the ritual dance (i.e. Seto Bhairava is the spouse of Mahākālī, and Sīma and Dūma are their offspring). Therefore, the divinities-as-mediums are projections of the social body in formations defined by a territorial 'macro-clan' or ritual kinship focused on a foregone Newar king; I argue that some points of a performance deliberately extricate caste structures to band the polity together as a 'Bhaktapurian' collective.

By becoming a Navadurgā clan—the king's terrestrial pantheon—the Banmalas temporarily invert their socially-ascribed status; in their worship, Bhaktapur's macro-clan is re-made.[44] I suggest this ritual kinship—as expressed in Navadurgā performances—becomes reinforced politically, too, in discourses of Bhaktapur's NWPP party. As I explain in § 2.6.2, the Banmala mediums have close ties with NWPP party members.

During the autumnal festival of Mohani—'Dashain' elsewhere in Nepal—a dramatic narrative is told that recounts the power of the goddesses (*devī*). This story is adapted from Newari redactions of the *Devī Māhātmya*. It is believed that the goddess Durgā—Parvātī in her fierce manifestation—accumulated great power (*śakti*) in order to propitiate and smite *Mahiśaṣura*, the anti-divine adversary. During Mohani, Durgā's, also Taleju's power ("Bhaktapur's political goddess",[45] an epithet used by Levy) is transferred in a power ritual to her dangerous clan 'sisters', the Nine Durgās.[46] From a theological perspective—that is, a Tantric worldview—all goddesses and Bhairava, and matter (*prakṛti*) and spirit (*puruṣa*), are non-bifurcated. *Śakti*—material energy—pervades **all** ontologies as internal to the body consciousness. A local social scientist in Bhaktapur expressed this sentiment in an interview; the goddess is the all-encompassing heart of Bhaktapur, or its yantric triangular vulva (*yoni*): "Gods

43 Levy, *Mesocosm*, p. 602.

44 In his article 'Forging Mandalic Space', Grieve also detects this dynamic at work during the carnival-ésque festival of Gai Jātrā. See Gregory Grieve, 'Forging Mandalic Space: Bhaktapur, Nepal's Cow Procession, and the Improvisation of Tradition', *Numen*, 51.4 (2004).

45 Levy, *Mesocosm*, p. 525.

46 Ibid.

and goddesses [...] are nothing more than *us* ... *śakti* resides not only in one aspect or thing, it is rooted deep in [...] bodies—this is the mantric foundation".

By exsanguinating pollutive animals in ritual sacrifice, the dancer-mediums reshuffle dualism; by tapping into socially-immanent power, the mediums can magically (*siddhi*) manipulate worldly ends, even if only provisionally (i.e. through blood sacrifice, they defy Vedic caste hierarchies to re-focus on material and bodily concerns). For nine months after Mohani, it is Navadurgā clan—manifested as thirteen masked mediums—that ensure the goddess-clan's supreme power is distributed to the city and its inhabitants. This distribution of *śakti* keeps the meddling of demon *Mahiśaṣura* at bay, until Mohani re-commences at the cycle's end.

In Levy's book, it seems some minutiae details are omitted, especially in relation to the Navadurgā cycle, which is undoubtedly a convoluted ritual. This is also noted by his critics, who emphasize his limited scope of informants who, on the whole, were members of Bhaktapur's elite, the Rājopādhyāyā Brahmins.[47] For one, Levy's work (and that of his student, Teilhet) presumes that the Navadurgā ritual cycle begins at Mohani; officially, in terms of its calendrical inauguration, they are accurate. However, there are a host of other ritual obligations, undertaken by the Banmalas, which must be observed before Mohani. As already mentioned, during the *Gotamangal* festival in September, the Banmala troupe (*gaṇa*) make obeisance at the home of the mask-makers, who, at that time, are adding the finishing embellishments to the god-masks (*khwōpa*), which will be used throughout the ritual's upcoming cycle.

6 Politics and Caste Structures in Bhaktapur

As with other Kathmandu Valley settlements, caste stratification still holds considerable sway; though, officially speaking, caste rigidity has been vehemently criticized by NWPP rulership but, **culturally**, a caste order remains.[48] Bhaktapur's caste system was instituted in the 14th Century during the social reforms of King Jayastithi Malla. Quigley writes how Levy uses the term 'lineage' (*thar*) rather than caste to avoid the problem of 'sub-caste' (*jāti*) and 'caste' (*varṇa*) relations.[49] As Parish alternatively observes, the strata of Bhaktapurian Newar

47 Lewis, 'Book review of Mesocosm', p. 54.
48 Ian Gibson, 'Suffering and Christianity: Conversion and Ethical Change among the Newars of Bhaktapur', (D.Phil. diss., University of Oxford, 2015), p. 78.
49 Quigley, 'Kingship', p. 567.

castes is perhaps the most sophisticated system in South Asia because it intercalates two separate systems: a Hindu *varṇa* system (as documented in Vedic texts and the Laws of Manu), alongside a Newar counterpart that includes Newar Buddhist castes.[50] I tabulate Bhaktapur's caste system below; the groups are ranked in descending status, from highest to lowest, as socially perceived:[51]

Hindu Newar caste hierarchy (Bhaktapur)		**Buddhist (*Bare*) Newar caste hierarchy (Bhaktapur)**	
Caste group name	**Assigned role**	**Caste group name**	**Assigned role**
Rājopādhyāyā Brahmin	Priests	Vajrācārya/Śākya	Buddhist priests
Chathar	Merchants (also includes Shrethas, Pradhān, Karmācārya priests)	Urāy	Merchants (Tuladhar is included here)
Panchathār	Sellers and Store owners		
Tini	Ritualists		
Tamrakār	Metal workers (specifically, bronze workers)		
Prajāpati	Pottery-makers and brick masons		
Jyāpu	Farmers		
Sikh:ā*mi*	Woodcrafters		
Vaidya	Tantric healers		
Lochan kh: āmi	Stonemasons		
Cyo/Chipi	Funeral ritualists and civil servants		
Dwiṇ	Sweepers and carriers of deity palanquins		
Banmala/Gāthā	Preferably Banmala. The mediums (*ujāju*) and performers of Bhakatpur's Navadurgā ritual		
Nāu	Barbers		
Bha/Kata/Calaṇ	Rite of passage ritualists		
Kau	Blacksmiths		
Chipa	Fabric-dyers		
Citrakār	Artists/painters/ sculptors		
Kusa	Litter collectors		
Sa:mi/ Manandhār	Mustard oil pressers (nowadays most oil is pressed in the settlement of Khokanā and is exported to other regions of the Valley)		
Sāhi/Nay	Butchers		
Jugi	Ritualists		

50 Steven M. Parish, *Hierarchy and its Discontents: Culture and the Politics of Consciousness in Caste Society* (Philadelphia: University of Pennsylvania Press, 1996), pp. 4–5.

51 See also Parish, *Hierarchy*, pp. 4–5 & Levy, *Mesocosm*, pp. 78–85.

(*cont.*)

Hindu Newar caste hierarchy (Bhaktapur)		Buddhist (*Bare*) Newar caste hierarchy (Bhaktapur)	
Caste group name	**Assigned role**	**Caste group name**	**Assigned role**
Doṇ	Musicians		
Kulu	Leather and musical-instrument makers		
Pode	Sweepers (untouchable)		
Halahulu	Non-homeowners (wandering/begging)		
Non-Newar groups			
Gaine	Musicians		
Sarki	Cobblers and shoe makers		
Dhobe/Christian/Mus-lim/Tamang/Tharu etc.	Other religious/ethnic groupings		

Many Bhaktapurians engage in some form of agricultural work—whether they are *jyāpus* or not—as fertile soils encircle the city's hinterlands. With Ujesh and Dinesh, I frequently visited an area beyond Kamālvinayak—a neighbourhood called Livali—that had crops belonging to Bhaktapur's various social groups.

6.1 *Newar Social Structure: Kinship, Caste, and Guṭhi in Bhaktapur*

All inhabitants of a precinct are attached to an association called a *guṭhi*—members of which are called *guṭhiyār*.[52] Usually these extra-social groups are designed to manage religious practices; each *guṭhi* is assigned land tenure to finance these collective religious activities. There are differing types of *guṭhi* all over the Kathmandu Valley, but here, I list three *guṭhi* integral to Bhaktapurian society: (1) *si guṭhi*—an association assembled for the purposes of funeral organization; (2) *digu dyo guṭhi*—a lineage (*phuki*) association for organizing *digu puja*, a ritual where a lineage worships their family deity through goat sacrifice; and (3) *bhājan khala guṭhi*—this *guṭhi* joins together a family's musicians for a *bhājan* (a musical band that play during Newar festivals). *Guṭhis* can be both intra-caste and inter-caste organizations: for instance, *si guthi* are strictly lineage-bound assemblages, while *bhajan khala guṭhis* welcome all lineages. For example, during Bhaktapur's 2017 New Year celebrations—or 'Nepal

52 Prayag R. Sharma, *Land, Lineage and State: A Study of Newar Society in Medieval Nepal* (Kathmandu: Himal Books, 2015), pp. 57–58.

Sambat' (Nepali New Year)—I joined the Banmala's *bhajan khala* and played a traditional Newari drum (*madal*) as one of their musicians.

In recent decades, traditional *guṭhi* committees have started to diminish. A local historian I spoke with said: "When *guṭhi* land is lost, culture is lost". Even so, *guṭhi* organisations remain in Bhaktapur, mainly for purposes of festival organization. One afternoon, whilst roaming the city, Ujesh and I spoke to an elder at Wakupati Narāyān temple near Suryamadhi. He spoke about a particularly traumatic incident that had occurred there: Brahmāyani's image (*mūrti*) and a segment of her temple's *tōrren* (a semicircular metal plate above a temple gateway) had vanished, supposedly stolen. According to this elder, incidents like these were becoming rife across the Kathmandu Valley, which, he said, could bring about a curse from the deity (*'deutako dhos lageko'*). These deities are becoming riled due to the wide-spread exploitation of *guṭhi* land, which members sell for their own profits. He said:

> [Inf.]: After selling the land, bad luck [*āsribād*] followed him [the young man who sold the *guṭhi* land]. Because of this, he was lying in bed sick for six months. Medicine [*āusadhi*] didn't work for him. An astrologer [*joshi*] told him that the gods were angry with him for violating *guṭhi* land by selling it.

In Newar culture, *guṭhi* land is communal since it binds deities and social groups with the land. Traditionally, any profit accrued from *guṭhi* land should be used for collective purposes—e.g. funding religious festivals—which is greatly valorized among Newars. For non-Newars in Bhaktapur, *guṭhi* merely denotes land ownership and division for the purposes of agricultural deployment only.[53] But, for Newars, as outlined by the interlocutor above, a *guṭhi's* significance lies in its encompassing of social bodies, land, religious conduct, and localized deities *in situ*.

In this book, I argue Navadurgā performances create unions between devotees, mediums, and deities akin to inter-caste *guṭhis*, except that Navadurgā performances encompass the whole territory, not just a single clan. Indeed, fictive kin relationships are pervasive in Newar communities: according to Shakya, fictive kinship—among the Newars of Kathmandu—are labelled *twāy thah*.[54] These relationships enable communication and contact across caste

53 Mark Pickett, *Caste and Kingship in a Modern Hindu Society: The Newar City of Lalitpur, Nepal* (Bangkok: Orchid Press, 2013), p. 147.

54 Anil M. Shakya, 'Newar Marriage and Kinship in Kathmandu', (Ph.D. diss., Brunel University, 2000), pp. 224–225.

divides through certain ventures—trading or travel—that would otherwise be prohibited.[55] In Newar society, Gerard Toffin also argues that a contrast is made between the intimate 'kin-bounded communities [...] the world within the caste' and the segregated 'caste system [that] reproduces a hierarchical order'.[56] By worshipping the polity's ancestral goddess-clan, I argue a Navadurgā performance *spirals* Toffin's binary by producing macro-clan bonds of ritual kinship between lineages, just like the goddess-clan.

6.2 *Politics in Bhaktapur: NWPP Communism*

Since as early as the 7th Century CE, multilateral community organizations (*guṭhi*) have been intrinsic to Newar identity. Such *guṭhi*, and the values of social unity they exemplify, are promoted by the city's now-prevailing political party: Nepal's Workers and Peasants Party (NWPP). Broadly, their policies abide by a unique conglomeration of intra-state, Marxist-Communist principles. Influenced deeply by DPRK ideals, the NWPP has applied radical socialist policies into a traditional Newar city: a worldview steeped in socio-religious institutions and calendrical festivals based upon the worship of Tantric gods and goddesses.[57]

The party is popular and predominates amongst the *jyāpu* ('farmers') of Bhaktapur city. According to Gibson, NWPP developed as a Peasant movement which emerged in the 1970s. The party is centered on the personality of its leader, Narayan Man Bijukchhe, who is a writer and activist.[58] Gibson suggests that NWPP's unusual blending of radical caste resistance and traditional Newar Hinduism appeals to Bhaktapurian farmers.[59] In fact, I spoke with several Bhaktapurians who were still very devoted to the worship of their divinities, even if their political loyalties lay with the communist ideology propounded by NWPP: the immanent power of Tantric deities—described as 'culture' (*sanskriti*) in Bhaktapur—is deeply ingrained in Bhaktapur's cultural world. As Gibson explains:

> while [being] a force for radical change with respect to inter-caste relations, the [NWPP] have been a conservative force with respect to traditional religious and ethical norms within the Farmer community, includ-

55 Ibid.

56 Gerard Toffin, *From Kin to Caste: The Role of Guthis in Newar Society and Culture* (Lalitpur: Himal Association, Social Science Baha Paper, 2005), p. 21.

57 Gibson, 'Suffering and Christianity'.

58 Ibid., pp. 84–85.

59 Ibid.

> ing those related to [social] care [which Gibson defines as 'solidarity with others who are in need'].[60]

NWPP ideology is characterized by its repudiation of higher-caste subservience, which upholds caste hierarchy. According to Gibson, NWPP's primary restructuring of social ideals is based upon values of communal care (*sahārā*) and social service.[61] I would add that this change is closer to traditional Newar attitudes which originate in communal *guṭhi*s and kin lineages. Like Bhaktapur's Navadurgā ritual, NWPP ideology advocates, and practices, a form of mono-ethnic nationalism; persons who are Newar by blood—from the ancestral land of Bhaktapur—comprise the party's majority.[62] Though seemingly proto-nationalist, NWPP retains communication with the world's remaining Marxist-influenced states.

In terms of Nepal's political leadership, Hacchettu notes that those from higher castes continue to occupy positions of political power, which is pandemic across Nepal (the same could be argued for Malabari communist parties too). He writes:

> Though the New Civil Code of 1963 legally abolished the system of caste domination and discrimination, the hill high castes have continued to retain their domination over political power structure even today.[63]

NWPP has attempted to counter this political elitism by extending agency to Newar peasants: for sure, NWPP does provide **some** opportunities for farmers, through social mobilization, within Bhaktapur. Generally, however, the leadership is comprised of Bhaktapurian intellectuals and/or educators, who are respected for their attention to and empathy towards the majority peasant population; farmers, in truth, do not constitute its core leadership.

Navadurgā performances also reflect the disintegration, however temporary, of caste-hierarchies that NWPP ideology propounds: subaltern Banmala mediums (whose non-ritual occupation is gardening or flower-selling) are offered ritualistic deference; they are apotheosized through ritual donations. Nava-

---

60 Ibid., p. 82.

61 Ibid., pp. 88–89.

62 The core principles of NWPP, namely mono-ethnic nationalism and social welfare, parallels, to some degree, a *volksgemeinschaft*.

63 Krishna Hacchettu, 'Municipality Leadership and Governance: A Case Study of Bhaktapur', in *Nepal: Local Leadership and Governance*, ed. by L.R. Baral et al., (New Delhi: Adroit Publishers), p. 36.

durgā rituals, therefore, reflects social values of macro-clan coherence that both contains **and** transgresses unilateral caste stratification in spiraling unison. I conversed with many NWPP supporters who stressed the social significance of Navadurgā—as a ritual of Bhaktapurian solidarity—to be its key element. Ujesh, Krishna, and his family often described Navadurgā as a social performance, driven by sacrifices and worldly concerns, that has always, since the medieval period, deliberately contravened Smārta concerns for purity. In this 21st Century context, Navadurgā ritual cycles (referred to as 'cultural', and not 'religious' by party supporters) have meshed with NWPP communism, which is reflected in the troupe's strong links with the party.

PART 2

Themes

CHAPTER 3

Dancer-Medium Communities and Ritual Kinship

1 Introduction

Following on from Part 1, this chapter will bring us to modernity by providing a window into contemporary Folk Śākta performances. Without a doubt, any analysis of ritual performance must address the communities that propels it. This chapter will take the form of an ethnographic account, which details deity-medium communities, together with their initiation practices. It will also describe the ritual procedures that facilitate ancestral embodiment, and the way such deity incarnation accords extrasensory abilities upon mediums for bestowing prosperity.

In what follows, I argue Folk Śākta performances rearrange the social order by establishing ritual ties between deities and their worshippers. During a performance, this ritual kinship is achieved via exchanges of gifts among goddess-clan, mediums, and partisans. In their ritual, I suggest dancer-medium evoke ancestors of the past for those gathered there. By doing so, deity-mediums strengthen their devotees by re-deploying divine power (*śakti*) for a multitude of worldly needs, which include: (a) distributing blessings that shield a family's cultivated land; (b) healing individuals afflicted by spiritual attacks; and (c) providing solace from social anguish i.e. societal oppression or natural disasters.

2 Dancer-Medium Communities: Teyyāṭṭam and Navadurgā

For centuries, generations of Folk Śākta mediums—in Kerala and Bhaktapur—have forged unbroken lineages since medieval times; most often, these bonds were formed by conventions of consanguineal kinship. In Kerala, Teyyam mediums must belong to sub-lineages (*illam*) of certain *avarṇa* castes, and in Bhaktapur, mediums are confined to one clan—the Banmalas. Having been conferred as a troupe-member, many years of spiritual discipline ensues for that initiand. Each year, this training occurs some three months before the inaugural ritual begins: in Kerala, this preparation occurs within gymnasia (*kalari*)[1]

1 *Kalari* are gymnasia where *Kalaripayāṭṭu* martial art is practiced. Also, martial artists worship the goddess, Bhadrākālī, within these gymnasia.

 DOI:10.1163/9789004439023_005

or in courtyard spaces owned by the troupe. And in Bhaktapur, the training of Banmala mediums—with all their initiations and rituals—take place in the Navadurgā temple (*dyo-cheṇ*).

Conferral into any troupe requires consummate dedication, a fact that engenders a sense of admiration from their worshippers. In Bourdieu's terms, the positive repercussions generated from these rituals grant 'symbolic capital' to the mediums.[2] Still, in the society's higher echelons, this sentiment is not shared, above all among pro-BJP citizens in Kerala. Though, in recent times, dancer-mediums ponder how their traditions can adapt to ongoing processes of modernity, be it capital culture or international employment in the Gulf. For those who have emigrated to the Gulf, as Gabriel indicates, a popular Teyyam god, Mūttappan, has settled among a community of Keralan migrants, who worship him there.[3]

In Bhaktapur, an eminent healer (*Vaidya*)—whose reputation was well-regarded in the city—visited the home of Ujesh's close relatives in Inācho *tol* to heal my unforeseen bout of stomach pains. My host family recommended the Vaidya's medicine for the ailment, which cured it effectively. After this consultation, the Vaidya turned to Ujesh, and his cousin, and urged them to reconsider their modern (*adhunik*) lifestyles. He exhorted that they conserve the traditions (*paramparā*) of Navadurgā, as their progenitors had managed before them.

Despite rapid globalization, these ritual performances still retain an important place, precisely because they reconnect the populace's relations with the land. At the time of my fieldwork, a dancer-medium's power was most sought after, especially in Bhaktapur, where an earthquake had recently occurred. On all accounts, dancer-mediums are viewed as effective conduits that reanimate the tellurian power of ancestral gods and goddess-clans for worldly ends.

In the context of Uttarkhānd, Sax discusses local rituals of mediumship: during these rites, an oracle channels Bhairava to resolve disputes.[4] In those moments, the cultural history and terrain of Bhairava's devout collective become co-integrative. Sax writes: '[…] the experience of the cult of Bhairav is inseparable from local understandings of place and landscape, especially the way that landscape embodies history, memory, and notions of the person'.[5] In Folk Śākta societies, however, a performance marks **and** transcends caste via ritual kinship that re-connects the whole polity; Navadurgā and Teyyāṭṭam

2 Pierre Bourdieu, *Distinction: A social critique of the judgement of taste* (London: Routledge, 2010 [1984]), p. 291.
3 Gabriel, *Playing God*.
4 Sax, *God of Justice*.
5 Ibid., p. 51.

performances, thereby, spiral caste and kinship to form new ritually symbiotic bonds—instantiated by the goddess-clan—through offerings of impurity (animal blood, gifts of food etc.). Such associations resonate with Marx's ideal of 'tribal community', or what Sahlins envisions as 'land, [deities] and ... people as alive and akin'.[6] The dancer-medium troupe—embodying a ritual network that synchronizes territory, medieval ancestors, and citizens—recalibrates the group as a macro-clan, emblazoned by sovereign power, to initiate social metamorphosis.

Embodied mediums, then, have special roles to play in ritual performance; they are access-points to the ambient presence of a territory's deity-circuits, which is diffused to their worshippers. In this chapter, I will sketch the lives, careers, and communities of performers I met—the Banmala mediums of Bhaktapur, and Kerala's *kōlakkaran*.

3 Teyyāṭṭam

3.1 *Communities in North Kerala*

In what follows, I present patterns of kinship—both matrilineality (*morūmakkathīyam*) and patrilineality (*makkathīyam*)—that ground widespread Teyyāṭṭam groves across Kerala. As early as the Cēra dynasty, the region has supported a system of matrilineality that spanned centuries; even today, remnants of matrilineal structures still survive in traditional Teyyāṭṭam culture. Likewise, Kerala's Māppilya-Muslim lineages also adhered to conventions of *morūmakkathīyam*. Although, with the arrival of British colonialism in the 18th Century, such traditional systems of belonging underwent dramatic change. Indigenous principles of enatic inheritance were remolded to fit Western patrilineal patterns instituted by the conquering administration.

Throughout Kerala, matrilineal marriage (*sambandam*) granted limited domestic liberties to women, which was not replicated in other Indian states. *Sambandam* is a matrilineal system of marriage defined by female succession, which unites lineages through matrilineal polygyny. In this system, a woman could own familial property and retain her maiden name. After *sambandam* ceremonies, couples return to the wife's matrilocal residence (that is, **her** ancestral residency) not the husband's, as is conventional elsewhere in India.

In 1896, the Malabar Marriage Act—passed by the Government of Madras—was formed to preserve matrilineal marriages, to the dismay of British colo-

6 Sahlins, *What kinship is*, p. 7.

nialists who decried *sambandam* as tantamount to concubine 'cicisbeism', or 'polyandry'.[7] Certainly, every matrilineal marriage joined lineages in polyandrous unions, forming clans of multi-lineage descendants linked, genealogically, to a common ancestress. In 1976, however, matrilineality was abolished by new legislation, the Kerala Joint Family (Abolition) Act: under this jurisdiction, *sambandam* marriages could no longer be sanctioned by any state in Independent India.

For purposes of definition, then, a matrilineal family (*taravād*) is a family unit whose line of succession and inheritance is bequeathed through the female bloodline, and is governed by a male representative, a *Kārṇavan*, who is married to an exogamous female. Property (*taravād*) owned by a matrilineal family is collectively shared and is presided over by female members. Fuller calls this arrangement, 'family property':

> Family property is that property inherited by a *woman from any matrilineal relative* [...] Family property is for the maintenance not only of the woman in whose name it is held, but also for all her matrilineal descendants.[8]

It is the duty of the male *Kārṇavan* to provide money for the maintenance of 'family property'. This money is accrued through profits collected from cultivating familial holdings or any other job; nowadays, many *Kārṇavan* work in the Gulf. But, as Abraham indicates, a *Kārṇavan* collects the household's earnings, while the females re-distribute them:

> This public face was evident when I was doing the household survey. In the course of a conversation with a couple Vimla and Mukundan, both in their seventies, I said that only one (currently married) woman in the neighbourhood had said that she was the head of the household. [She said], "The men bring in the money but I manage it." Vimala was quick to respond, although half swallowing her words so her husband could not hear, "Oh that is because we don't want the man to feel bad."[9]

As a household's sole economic provider, the *Kārṇavan* holds much authority in family life. In Fuller's account of Nāyar clans, he describes how exploitative

7 Chris Fuller, *The Nayars Today* (Cambridge: CUP, 1976), p. 109.
8 Fuller, *Nayars Today*, p. 65.
9 Janaki Abraham, 'Why did you send me like this?' Marriage, Matriliny and the 'Providing Husband', *Asian Journal of Women's Studies*, 7.2 (2011), p. 42.

Kārṇavan were sometimes usurped by younger members of the family; corrupt elders **can** undoubtably misuse familial resources for their own ends.[10] *Kārṇavan* are also mindful of displeasing their ancestors, and many feared their return as chastising ghosts (*piśācụ*) metamorphized in a crow's body: connected distantly to Śraddhā, the feeding of crows is synonymous with ancestral appeasement. Freeman's informant explains how:

> The rice-feeding in the new moon or cāttam rite is for the offering to the crow. And the crow has that person's spirit (*jīvụ*); it has a human spirit (*manuṣya-jīvụ*). The crow has gone out of that dead person's body.[11]

As I highlight below, ancestor interventions are common occurrences in Kerala. During her ethnographic fieldwork in Central Kerala, Gough spoke with many *Kārṇavan* elders who were wary of their family deity's (*kula daivam*) wrath; sometimes, their ancestor was believed to punish them with misfortune or illness to rectify any violations caused by their unscrupulous actions.[12] In Teyyam performance, ancestors are given human form, such that mediums emerge as the macro-clan's *Kārṇavan*.

3.1.1 Kōlakkaran: Dancer-Medium Communities in Kerala

Generally, Teyyam temple-groves are presided over by several lineages (*illam*) and households within a region's vicinity. In Malayalam, this extra-caste arrangement—of different lineages in a macro-clan—is termed *avakaśikaḷ*. In this order, clan- and household-delegation is conventional, as it reproduces the social structure of Kerala's medieval polities.[13]

Malayali scholar Rajesh Komash discusses the running of his native Teyyam grove—Patakkathi Bhagavati Kāvu—in the town of Paẕangādi: in this grove, an administrative committee deputizes members from fourteen parochial families. These families are responsible for arranging Teyyāṭṭam performances, which are conducted annually during the month of Vricikam (November–December).[14] A Teyyam festival held at a specific grove—either annually, bian-

10 Fuller, *Nayars Today*, p. 59.

11 Freeman, 'Purity and Violence', p. 114.

12 Kathleen Gough, 'Cults of the Dead among the Nayars', *Journal of American Folklore*, 71.3 (1959), pp. 245–246.

13 Freeman, 'Purity and Violence', pp. 170–171.

14 Rajesh Komash, 'Political Economy of the Theyyam: A Study of time space homology', (Ph.D. diss, Mahatma Gandhi University, Kerala, 2013).

nually, or up to a decade apart—is funded by wealthier patrons or senior members of local families who, together, form the grove's administration. At each Teyyāṭṭam, the administrative committee gathers in a designated building or temporary hut constructed especially for the ritual. Here, a nominated committee chairman (*ūrāḷan*) collects monetary donations which he will redistribute to the dancer-mediums performing at the festival.

Throughout the off-season period (May–October), dancer-mediums must undergo training to embody either one or, at the most, two ancestral deities. This training is demanding, for it entails spiritual instruction and ritual ablution (*vṛata*)—in seclusion—for all mediums. At Muṇḍeyād—a precinct in Kannur—a deity-medium extolled seclusion as conducive to the 'meditative' focus required; in this state, he would muse the songs (*tōṟṟam*) and narratives of his god/goddess. One day, whilst visiting a larger grove (22nd November 2015), I asked one devotee to describe these preparations, which he articulated as follows:

> Before the performance, the Teyyam dancers recite the Ślokas [Skt: 'verses'] and Tōṭham [Maly: 'songs'] for hours, even days before. This prepares them by creating a state of mind for the upcoming Kaliyāṭṭam [main segment of the Teyyam performance, where the mediums are fully adorned as the god/goddess].

Dancer-mediums must also be conferred to perform; their status is transmitted, hereditarily, from maternal uncle to nephew, as in a matrilineal clan. As Freeman suggests, the conferral of mediums is staged during an investiture rite superintended by a committee, or in medieval times, the polity's local chieftain.[15] Having prepared to perform as his specific deity, a medium's services are sought by grove committees across Malabar. A medium may be selected by several grove committees at the time their Teyyam festival comes about. In practical terms, dancer-mediums must become peripatetic performers; each medium has a schedule of groves where his deit(ies) is enshrined. A dancer-medium's strenuous schedule means he is paid slightly more than an accompanying drummer or priest; of course, mediums are at the epicentre of any Teyyāṭṭam. Still, some grove committees do not seek itinerant Teyyam performers, instead deciding to select performers from their own parochial troupes. Freeman writes: '[…] the shrine authorities, in consultation with the priests, gather and designate which performers among the troupe will play which par-

15 Freeman, 'Purity and Violence', p. 177.

ticular gods'.[16] Such arrangements must be planned some weeks, or months, before any Teyyam performance is set in motion.

During my visit to Pariyāram kāvu (27th November 2015), Vaṇṇān performers were predominantly recruited by the grove's committee: some ten gods, including Gulikkan, were worshipped there. In the crowd, a devotee was eager to speak to me about this grove. He belonged to the Vaṇṇān community himself, and I—keen to understand further—asked him about his lineage. I reproduce a part of that conversation below:

> [MM:] Who is the Teyyam deity performing now? What is his role?
> [Inf.] It is Gulikkan. Gulikkan is the god of security and time. People go to him to get blessed to ensure their families, communities, and money [issues] are safe.
> [MM:] He is on stilts. Why is that?
> [Inf.] It represents the stretch of time and history. He's also related to Śiva—so he has enormous strength, and by standing on stilts he shows how strong he is. Not everyone can perform like this, you must be historically selected.
> [MM:] What do you mean by 'historically selected'?
> [Inf.] It is a specific caste—a family within the community—I am also a member of that caste but never trained. You're trained from a very young age … [It is the Vaṇṇān caste]
> [MM:] So why do people go to Teyyam performances? It is very busy here today!
> [Inf.] It is a community performance, but it is also a chance for people to see the gods in form, to see the god manifest … Teyyam is not a science, it is based on belief. People believe the power of the Teyyams, that's why they come here.
> [MM:] I've noticed that rice grains are thrown in the air and showered on people and objects. Why is rice used like this?
> [Inf.] It is a custom—just as someone plants one seed to produce many grains, so too do people offer rice to each other. It makes us prosperous—a big family, wealth, and so on. That's why the Teyyam dancer touches the top of our heads with rice during Teyyāṭṭam—it makes our families and our groves prosper.

In this conversation, I was able to draw profound details vis-à-vis Teyyam organisation, which I list here: (a) a medium's status is transmitted hereditarily

16 Ibid., p. 183.

FIGURE 9 *Māviliya Gandharvan Kāvu*, (Kannur, Kerala), 17th November 2015
PHOTOGRAPH BY AUTHOR

through males of the lineage; (b) a Teyyam performance coheres local lineages in *web-like ritual networks*; (c) the deity, Gulikkan Teyyam—installed in most groves—embodies time itself, in such a way that he resurrects ancestors into the present. And, finally, (d) the throwing of rice in Teyyāṭṭam facilitates family prosperity.

Teyyam divinities, too, are enshrined within committee- or household-owned land. In the Kannur district, a local goddess—known as *Rayāṟụ Manulaṭhụ Bhagavati*—gained her name from the micro-region from whence she originated—Rayāru̥ Manulaṭhu̥. All Teyyam deities, thus, have *fons et origio* that are enmeshed within a territory, household, and grove. Subsequently, a mythological narrative is built around each deity, distilled from the deity's presence there. In fact, some, but not all, Teyyam groves are constructed as subsidiary annexes to ancestral households (*taravād*).

One such ancestral grove was named Māviliya Gandharvan Kāvu (lit. 'the grove in Gandharvan's ('uncle's') place'), where the eponymous ancestor deity, a Gulikkan, and a goddess were enshrined. In Kerala, Gandharvan or 'uncle' deities are equated with martyred ancestors, many of whom were proficient warriors or practitioners of Kalaripayyāṭṭu̥. Zarrilli writes how Kalaripayyāṭṭu̥ is 'associated with subgroups of Hindu Nayars whose duty it was to serve as soldiers and healers at the behest of the village head, district ruler, or local rājā, having vowed to serve him to death'.[17] It is said warriors attain apotheosis by dying in the name of the land they served. These figures are commemorated as warrior divinities enshrined in *samādhi*—a resting place of remembrance for the deceased—within their clan's ancestral plot. Throughout Kerala, these gods are also called *kula daivam*, and each unique deity is worshipped by his or her corresponding lineages (*illam*).

At Māviliya Gandharvan Kāvu, I witnessed a Teyyāṭṭam ritual. Before its inauguration, mediums were preparing (via recitation of songs etc.) in the make-up room (*pati*) next to the main shrine. Suddenly, fireworks (*katina*) were ignited, which, at first, startled me somewhat. I was told the act of releasing fireworks kindles collective exultation in the group, especially in smaller groves. These resounding explosions also serve another purpose; they announce to households in the vicinity that a ritual is about to begin.

At one juncture during the performance, Gandharvan—the clan's 'uncle'—walked from his shrine (*palliyāṟā*) to the house's doorway, where he blessed each member of the clan. These blessings were given in the form of turmeric powder (*mañjal-kuṟi*) mixed with puffed rice (*malar*), rice grains, and jaggery. In equal measure, the substance was extended to non-clan individuals sojourned there, too—relative, neighbour, and visitor alike. Finally, the women were blessed outside the veranda of the house: though matrilineality accords more domestic rights for women, this is not the case publicly, for males are always prioritized

Turmeric powder is a widely used blessing (*praśādam*) in Kerala, and it is known for its Āyurvedic properties; according to Arafath, turmeric powder is a 'panaceas for all fertility-related matters', an apposite gift for relaying an ances-

17 Zarrilli, *When the body*, p. ix.

FIGURE 10 Female priestess, 17th November 2015
PHOTOGRAPH BY AUTHOR

tor's power.[18] With the distribution of turmeric powder, a Teyyam ancestor—in embodied form—proclaims loudly to the group: *guṇam varuttaṇe* ("may blessings happen"). The dancer-medium's body, literally, re-animates the ancestor, so that his power can be offered as blessings to his devotees, which protects the receiver's clan. In this way, then, *affective kin intentionality* is rendered between non-consanguineal participants in substantive exchanges of turmeric powder between members, who all worship an ancestor that binds them. The worldly energy—evoked by ancestral deities—derives from the surplus of *śakti* they secured in death; their martyrdom is usually a valiant one which enhances their ancestral might.

It is also customary for visiting worshippers to offer monetary donations to a temple grove's organisation committee. All these fiscal gifts—money and food stuffs—are collected by the committee and are administered to Teyyam dancers and priests in a display of redistribution. To accommodate this, Teyyam mediums have rights (*cerujanman*) to additional food resources supplied by their respective administrative committees. These rights are upheld through a committee's connections with local pastoralists (Maly: *pulaṃ*, 'agricultural field'). In medieval Kerala, this traditional right of fair distribution exempted dancer-mediums from paying taxes. Nevertheless, contemporary Teyyam dancers are not wholly exempt from land taxation. Nowadays, performers' rights are largely symbolic. Yet *cerujanman* rights allow the clan access to food supplies, mainly rice, provided as a donation by local farmers. It is the *Kārṇavan* who is responsible for dispensing food or money to Teyyam performers, in an act of distribution known, in local parlance, as *adalaya paṇam*.

In style, liturgy, and format, all Teyyam performances are standardized; Teyyam groves adhere to a prevailing mode of worship that is characteristically 'Keralan'. However, administratively, groves vary considerably; every grove is managed differently depending on who its patrons are, and how its committee is structured. Similarly, *cerujanman* rights may be implemented in one grove, and laxed in another. To illustrate this diversity, I will explore three distinctive castes for consideration: (1) *Pulayar* (agricultural labourers); (2) *Malayān* (exorcists); and (3) *Vāṇṇan* (washers). These three groups will be summarized in the next section.

18 Yasser Arafath, 'Saints, Goddesses, and Serpents: Fertility Cults of the Malabar Coast (c1500–1800)', in *Histories of Medicine and Healing in the Indian Ocean World*, ed. by Anna Winterbottom & Facil Tesfaye, (New York: Palgrave Macmillan, 2016), p. 106.

3.2 *Kōlakkaran among Three Communities*

3.2.1 Community 1: Pulayars

Throughout Kerala, the Pulayar caste are tiller labourers that work state-owned land. In all, ten lineages (*illam*) are integrated under the designation, 'Pulayar', and most of them are agriculturalists who worked lands for their feudal lords.[19] During Kerala's medieval period, the King was the sole landlord (*janmi*) and divided lands among chieftains in a code of feudal tenure. The *kula* deity of the Pulayar is Pōṭṭan: according to myth, Pōṭṭan was an untouchable drunkard—guised as Śiva—who always challenged his superiors, mainly landlords (*janmi*), but also Śaṅkara, the Vedantic sage himself.

Compared with their male counterparts, female Pulayar engage in significantly less strenuous labour—fishing or field cultivation (Maly: *thappal*)—to succour the household's income. Pulayar can also become employed as priests or *pūjārī* in only **one** of the region's Tantric temples—Mādāyi Kāvu—dedicated to the Kōlattiri rājā. There, a Pulayar priest holds a hereditary position as a para-priest (*polla*). At Mādāyi Kāvu, a *polla* is required to bring the fruits of the new harvest during the festival of *Puterī Kalaśam*.[20] In addition, the *polla* must hold an umbrella made of coconut leaves at a pivotal rite described as *Avil Nivedyam* (Maly: 'beaten rice giving').[21] Teyyam dancer-mediums also take on secondary vocations not typically associated with their caste e.g. rolling cigarettes (bīḍis/pan) or selling items at a market.[22]

3.2.2 Community 2: Malayān

For dancer-mediums, a common secondary occupation among them is ritual healing. Within Malayān castes, however, healing is their primary occupation. As expounded by Komath—himself a Malayān—their expertise in traditional medicine is sought after by many local families. In general, male Malayān administer exorcistic rites for afflicted clientele, while female Malayān become midwives. Komath writes:

> *Kuttiyedukkal*, (midwifery) Theyyam dancing, *vedanpaattu*, *kothamuri* are ritual services rendered by the *Malayan* by virtue of his customary *cherujanmam* rights. In return for this they are given rice and other food items as a matter of gift as a social function, something in return for the service rendered by the *Malayan*. For this very reason when there rose an occa-

---

19 Komath, 'Political Economy'.
20 Ibid.
21 Ibid.
22 Freeman, 'Purity and Violence', p. 176.

> sion when we needed support and help it was always forthcoming from the village homes. This was recognized and accepted as a social commitment by the locals. Today, this practice of a quid pro quo or reciprocity happens only between my family and the Muslim community. They continued to give my mother clothes and other goodies that are made in their homes on special occasions. Now my mother does not visit their homes yet they continue to send her her share for festivals and other celebrations.[23]

In 21st Century Kerala, services of ritual healing are increasingly under threat. Across India and Nepal, biomedicine and Āyurveda has the upper hand. It seems biomedicine surpasses traditional healing in terms of immediate efficiency and 'scientific accuracy'. However, the healing services of Malayān families are still in demand, especially for cases that cannot be tended efficiently by any other means, namely certain psychosomatic conditions. Across South Asia, such psychosomatic afflictions—epilepsy or convulsions—are understood as spiritual incursions. Komath notes:

> Endowed with the skills to perform *kuttiyedupu* or midwifery and treating children, my grandmother's family was known for it. My father's eldest brother, *Kunhambutty Panikkar*, whom we called *'Moothappan'* was an expert in treating epilepsy. Even today when one participates in the Theyyam conducted in the areas around *Kaitheri* we can hear people talk about the expertise of this elder in treating epilepsy.[24]

Because their occupation is seemingly in decline, Malayan lineages are reliant on *cerujanman* for their livelihoods. Traditionally, in medieval Kerala, Malayān groups had no official rights to own land. But, with the election of CPI(M) in the 20th century, land division laws changed for the better; most families, whatever their caste status, were entitled to own land in a system of social welfare. In India's current neoliberal economy, however, Malayān are dependent on *cerumjanman* more than ever, so donations are welcomed, especially from local landlords or wealthier families. These local landlords (*jamni*) provide Malayāns with gifts of food, which include seven bags of rice, all of which was received by Komath's family. Komath describes how any discussion about *cerujanman* donations in these Malayān communities would result in quar-

23 Komath, 'Political Economy', p. 70.
24 Ibid., p. 65.

relling among its members.[25] Malayān *cerujanman* rights are also hereditary, and unlike a matrilineal system, the right is passed from father to son, or in the absence of a son, it is passed to his brother or nephew. Once a Malayān couple are conjugally related—in the manner of patrilineal non-*sambandam*—the wife receives her husband's name and resides in his family home.

3.2.3 Community 3: Vaṇṇān

Unlike the other communities explored here, the *Vaṇṇān*, or washer caste, are numerically predominant throughout Malabar's Teyyam communities. In fact, the supposed founder of Teyyam can be traced to a Vaṇṇān—Manakkaṭan Gurukkaḷ—who was recruited by the royal court (This mythology I describe in § 4.2.1.1). When the time comes for a Vaṇṇān dancer to be conferred, he receives the title 'Peruvaṇṇān'—once a royal epithet—in a rite of investiture planned by a local chieftain.[26] In this conferral rite, a Teyyam neophyte receives a white cloth and a gold bracelet (*paṭṭum vaḷayum*) from a patron; they must keep these gifts throughout their lifetime.[27]

During my first trip to Kannur, I managed to speak with several Vaṇṇān dancer-mediums in Muṇḍeyād and elsewhere in the district. With Akash, I conducted an hour-long interview—with the help of an interpreter—on the porch of his ancestral home. Akash was affiliated with Nambram Muchioṭṭū kāvu, a grove across the Vallapattanam river. He was an experienced dancer-medium, and this was reflected in his minutiae responses. I produce a transcription of that conversation here:

> [MM:] How do you train to become a Teyyam dancer-medium?
> [Inf:] It is a process of continual learning. Together, as a troupe, we watch each other prepare. An elder from the troupe guides us on what to do [because he has the most experience]. Whatever he says and does, we observe and try to replicate through our own bodies. […]
> [MM:] How are Teyyam performers selected?
> [Inf:] Actually anyone who is interested can learn the movements of Teyyam [from Kalaripayyāṭṭu martial arts]. But to be able to perform in an official Teyyam performance, you must be a part of a lineage [*illam*] or community. [He is a Vaṇṇān].
> [MM:] Why is Teyyāṭṭam important to people?

25 Komath, 'Political Economy', p. 74.
26 Nambiar, 'Tai Paradevata', p. 145.
27 Ibid.

[Inf:] It is a ritualistic festival [*utsavam*], every time you see the performance, you get attached to the emotion in the crowd. The more times you watch the Teyyam performance, the layers of meaning slowly unravel and people start to understand the history [of the culture]. This makes it more interesting for people. [...]

When I look in the mirror, I see myself and the god in one self [...] During one performance, a cindered piece of coal got stuck in my anklet [*kaitaṇṭa*], but I had to continue because the performance was not complete, and the devotees would think that I was not a Teyyam god and that the ritual had failed. Because I could not remove the ember, it burned into my flesh, see [he gestures towards a scar on his ankle]. But I tolerated this because I could ... The power of the god gives you strength ... [he is a medium who incarnates the deity Mūttappan].

[MM:] Who designed all your equipment and adornments?

[Inf:] All of these are traditional equipment, and they are passed down the lineage over many years. If any alterations are required [because they do wear over the years], I go to a man near Chirakkaḷ, who can make these corrections. [He demonstrates how anklets are placed on the feet of a medium, and he begins dancing].

[MM:] Are less people going to Teyyam these days?

[Inf:] No it is increasing—many groves and temples are being built and more people are going—not only for devotion to their gods and ancestors, but also for its cultural value [...] It is a social gathering of people from local lineages who visit.

[MM:] What about people who identify with different religious groups? Can they go to Teyyam?

[Inf:] Anyone can go into a grove or Tantric temple—it is just a matter of removing your shoes. [it is as if you are visiting someone's home]. But in a Brahmin temple [*kṣetram*], only Nambutiri and some other castes are allowed.

[MM:] Is there power [*śakti*] in the grove? Can Teyyams only be performed in groves? [Because I have seen Teyyams wandering around Kannur town too]

[Inf:] There is something in the space of the Kavu—shrines [*tāṟā*] of the gods and the priests who activate them. [Deities are also believed to be linked to the area attached to the grove]. If a Teyyam is performed on the stage, it is not as effective.

[MM:] What is the meaning of rice in Teyyam?

[Inf:] Rice is considered very important in Kerala, it is a way of respecting each others' bodies. It is an offering [*nivedyam*]. Same with the

> sword, you shower it with rice—to show it respect and then the medium takes it.

As a performer, Akash had endured many physical injuries and burns. Every dancer-medium's career is paved with many tests of strength: at each ritual, they must perform awesome physical feats which prove their calibre. Depending on the deity incarnated, they may be required to walk on coal, climb coconut trees without equipment, or leap over pyres to prove they are, in fact, channeling the deity. In the case of goddess Cāmuṇḍi, Arafath describes how walking on coals pacifies her anger; her unrestrained fury is so great that it can afflict onlookers with diseases. He writes: 'Theyyam performances contained her [Cāmuṇḍi's] occasional rage by walking on big heaps of burning charcoal, a practice that subsequently became the curative ritual shield against many such issues'.[28]

On 21st February 2016, I travelled early morning to a Teyyam performance where Bappiriyan, a manifestation of Hanumān, climbs a coconut tree to display his transfiguration. Unfortunately, as the medium was descending the tree at the performance's finale, he tragically slipped and fell from a considerable height. The devotees' initial excitement lapsed into ululation as the medium was carried into a car on his way to the hospital. Afterwards, I heard that the medium had sustained some severe injuries, including a fractured leg, but he was in a stable condition; by all accounts, this incident was shockingly unusual, such that it was documented in the Times of India newspaper.[29]

Teyyam performances, then, involve considerable risks, which induce trepidation in those closest to the mediums. As Komath puts it:

> While the Theyyam is closer to god presence/godlike for the believer, for members of the dancer's family and blood relatives the feeling was one that was a mix of devotion and anxiety. Your father, your son, they are the Theyyams, the only prayer is that no harm comes to them in this fire play.[30]

To avoid such risks, stringent preparations are enforced by the troupe's elder. As already discussed, mediums 'meditate' on their deities in solitude, and, for one dancer-medium—who evokes Wayanād Kuḷivan—such solitude focused

---

28 Arafath, 'Saints', p. 104.
29 'Bedridden Gods: A Tale of Suresh Peruvannan', *The Times of India*. 13th March 2017.
30 Komath, 'Political Economy', p. 81.

his mental acuity. My interlocutors also claimed that a lack of focus was the main factor that caused performative blunders.

One afternoon, I watched Teyyam preparations near Kannur town. In the courtyard of his home, a *Kārṇavan*—from a Vaṇṇān clan—was instructing his great nephew; at the time, they were practicing Teyyam choreography. Stood next to me, another troupe member became impatient and criticized the initiand's technique. In response, the novice turned to the *Kārṇavan* to inquire for further guidance. In a moment of wisdom, the *Kārṇavan's* counsel was a philosophical reply: 'These days, the youth always ask too many questions: 'is this correct?', 'why this way?', 'should I move in this way?' … the only way you will know anything is if you *do*'. With the *Kārṇavan's* sagacious advice in mind, we will now proceed to the ritualized actions of Teyyāṭṭam embodiment, and the logic that underscores their shift from human to deity.

3.3 *Processes of Teyyam Embodiment: Rites, Narratives, and Power*

Each Teyyāṭṭam festival begins with the priests (*kōmamram*) who tend to the grove's shrines (*tāṟā*). It is the task of a priest to act as an intermediary between shrined deity and human medium; he must draw out the deity's essence from shrine and into a body. This happens by means of substantive markings and ritual transactions from priest to medium. At the shrine, the priest prepares a coconut leaf parcel—containing a betel leaf, rice grains, and a coconut—lit with a flame at its folded tip (*nākkila*) and sets this aside for a later rite. The god's weapons, shield (*cēdagam*), and toddy pots (*kalaśa-kiṇḍi*) are also prepared. The first rite—a *tōṟṟam*—ensues: here, a Teyyam medium, dressed in a simple red and white cloth, bows to the deity's shrine, narrating that deity's songs (*tōṟṟam*), during which a priest places some rice grains and vermillion powder in his palm. According to one informant, red is a prominent colour in Teyyam since its connotations are associated with Tantrism. All at once, red symbolizes sacrificial blood, the flame of the sacrificial fire (*hōmam*), **and** the goddess-clan's menstrual synchrony.

Sometime later, a Vellāṭṭam rite is coordinated: at this stage, a dancer-medium—donning a deity's smaller headdress—receives a flame from the deity's shrine. In the case of Gulikkan, the priest holds a bronze oil-wicks in one hand and a bell (*duwakwi*) in the other to guide the medium's movements. Gradually, the priests' movements quicken, until the medium (as Gulikkan) is fully energized. As the pace reaches its climax, Gulikkan becomes fully embodied within that medium, while the priest, who guided him, collapses. This loss of consciousness signals that Gulikkan's life-breath (*prāṇa*) has been displaced from the flame, into the priest, before being passed to the medium. In Teyyam

FIGURE 11 Shrine of Gulikkan (god of time)
PHOTOGRAPH BY AUTHOR

liturgies, this transfer of 'life-breath' (*prāṇa*) is a salient component, so much so that this motif has also permeated Malayalam literary works too: my informant once quoted the poet, ONV Kurup, who draws on a metaphor of 'breeze dancing in a courtyard' to portray this cultural notion. In any event, Gulikkan's presence, in Teyyam groves, ensures the resurrection of ancestral 'life-breath' in the world; as we know, he is the god of time itself.

A movement of life-breath (or terrestrial energy) from inanimate objects and into bodies—via substance exchanges onto bodies—is recurrent in Teyyam practice, which finds its doctrinal corollary in Kashmir Śaiva texts as *Śakti-pātha.* Briefly, this doctrine outlines the shifting of power from master to disciple. In Tantric traditions, these bio-physical exchanges are entwined in symbols of power and fertility (rice, turmeric powder, swords etc.). Once deployed, the fully-fledged god becomes embodied: the medium sits on the deity's stool, receiving all his accoutrement with the showering of rice, before staring into a mirror to verify his transformation. At this point, all paraphernalia are brought from the shrine to the stool (*pītham*) where an embellished dancer-medium is perched. The priests activate the deity's weaponry by passing an oil-lamp or torch (*cōtta*)—lit from the shrine's flame—over the instrument (*āyudam-pūjā*,

FIGURE 12 Tripartite oil-wicks holder
PHOTOGRAPH BY AUTHOR

lit. 'weapon worship'). Handfuls of rice are also thrown on the weapon to activate its ancestor's essence.

All the while, a coconut leaf parcel—prepared at the ritual's commencement—is opened by the medium; the coconut inside it is tossed in the air, and the betel leaves thrown before his feet. In Teyyam, these gestures are Keralan methods of divinization: the way the betel leaves fall foretells what the ritual's outcome will be; whether a performance will be propitious, or not, depends on these divinizing rites. As I mention in § 3.3.2.2, Teyyam mediums are highly proficient in methods of divinization and exorcism, even beyond ritual performance. Freeman writes:

> [...] teyyam performers are routinely engaged in sorcery [...] many rites of individual exorcisms, done on an as-needs basis, employ costuming which is morphologically identical to that used in teyyam worship.[31]

With divinization completed, a deity's weaponry—wafted with the sacred flame—is handed to the medium; at that moment, the deity's entire presence becomes embodied. Certainly, this process demonstrates that any weapon (via *āyudam-pūjā*) is said to be animate; as Freeman indicates, it is not uncommon to hear of weaponry jumping or jolting in a medium's hands.[32] This rationale of empowering weapons with flames is verbalized at a performance's later stage, when the deity-medium distributes blessings. To his congregation, a medium declares: "Like the flame of a lamp of a thousand burning wicks is my splendour. And with that splendour, which even a cyclonic enemy-wind cannot extinguish, shall I protect you."[33] Correspondingly, a dancer-medium's eyes are also enounced as 'glowing like embers' (Maly: *Eriyum kanalkaṇṇil*).

All Teyyam paraphernalia, or in this case, the grove's sacred flames are presided over by the priests, most of whom are Thiyyas (or toddy tappers). During periods of grove inactivity—throughout the summer months—priests visit local groves to relight their sacred flames, which ensures their gods' presence remain. To rekindle the lamps, flames are brought from regional Tantric temples; a temple flame relights oil-wick holders (*velākkụ*) deployed in Teyyam performance. Furthermore, these *velākkụ*, too, are inscribed with cultural meaning. Each *velākkụ* is crafted with three lamp holders, symbolizing the goddess-clan's tripartite nature: in Tantric thought, these elements are: (1) *Parā*, or the

31 Freeman, 'Purity and Violence', p. 175.

32 John R. Freeman, 'Formalized Possession among the Tantris and Teyyams of Malabar', *South Asia Research*, 18.1 (1998), p. 85.

33 Freeman, 'Purity and Violence', p. 278.

goddess-clan in a manifested form; (2) *Parāparā*, or the goddess-clan's collective body (i.e. the macro-clan); and (3) *Āparā*, the medium's subtle body.[34]

When a deity's full embodiment is attained within a medium, his movements become increasingly energetic. Those mediums who channel fierce goddesses—i.e. Muchilōṭṭu Bhagavati—proceed by running into the crowd, curved swords in hand; devotees react by backing away, while some onlookers taunt them further to induce a stronger reaction. This effervescence-in-overdrive was claimed to be a result of a divinity's power and the ritual kinship her appearance creates; the wild goddess is an icon of parental ambivalence—the territorial mother—who can be both benevolent and punishing, ferocious and protective. In Durkheimian terms, the dancer-medium comes to personify the ambivalent polarization of society, the *liminal* figure who occupies that threshold amid the sacred and profane. In her discussions of 'mad saints' in Tantric Buddhism, Louise Child describes how:

> this power [communitas or the 'sacred'] is attained by a participation in a broader social tension between structure and communitas. While the individual may utilize this tension, they may come to symbolize it. Appearing to distance themselves from society, [they] incarnate its polarities, and thereby provide an important function.[35]

Spiraling between societal oppositions, a medium's ambivalence must be controlled through rites of blood pacification, which pour from sacrificial chickens. As I mention in Chapter 1, rice is stuffed in the victim's beak before it is slaughtered. This understanding of sacrifice is linked to terrestrial energy, which that goddess (and her clan) emblemizes. The ritual's transference of power (and life-breath) betwixt land, shrines, regalia, and bodies is actuated through blood sacrifice and rice-throwing, which draws out the land's power. Indeed, this notion of sacrifice has resonances with Bloch's concept of 'rebounding violence', in which 'native vitality' (i.e. an initand or a shaman) is subjected to violence—literal or symbolic—so that this ritual specialist can access 'transcendence' or, here, a polity's power incarnated in terrestrial deities.[36] This logic is also expressed in a song sung during the sacrifice: "May a great blessing come to

34 For more about this Tantric worldview, see also Flood, *Body and Cosmology*.

35 Louise Child, *Tantric Buddhism and Altered States of Consciousness: Durkheim, Emotional Energy, and Visions of the Consort* (Aldershot: Ashagte, 2007), p. 35.

36 Maurice Bloch, *Prey into Hunter: The Politics of Religious Experience* (Cambridge: CUP, 1992).

the sacrificer, his patron, his cattle, children, his crops and produce"[37] and the deity replies, "I am happy—very happy'".[38] From that point onwards, the goddess' power—now subjugated—can be distributed as turmeric powder to her partisans.

As with Mauss' notion of '*total prestations*', streams of life-affirming power between the macro-clan and their land are effectuated through exchanges of gifts linked to the earth or blood sacrifice: devotees offer rice, food, and sacrifice, whilst the deities, in return, yield agrarian protection. By embodying symbolic markers linked with agriculture and medieval kings, the devotees become ritual kin on turf they coinhabit. From a Tibetan Buddhist perspective, Huber shows how shamanic yogic practice can also extract this territorial energy. He says:

> where microcosm and macrocosm are equated and integrated [Tantric nondualism] ... [the] powers active in them are represented not only in the geography of the external world but also [...] around an internal network within the psychic body of the yogin.[39]

4 Navadurgā

4.1 *Bhaktapur's Navadurgā Troupe: A Family of* ujāju

After meeting Ujesh's family, I spent much time in their company, mainly at their home. In so doing, I learned some basic Newar customs, especially domestic ones. For example, I was told to avoid ascending a stairwell while someone was descending it (a very inauspicious faux pas!) and to eat only with my right hand, which prevented bodily contamination (*jūto*).

In the months that followed, I established a camaraderie with Ujesh and his immediate family. I was routinely invited to eat food at their home; as is customary, we gathered on a straw mat (*sukul*) in their third-floor kitchen. The family had recently moved to a new house since their previous residence—adjacent to the Navadurgā temple—had suffered severe damage by the earthquake. Ujesh show me his home and it was, indeed, uninhabitable. Just next door, the temple remained unaffected; I was told the temple had been shielded by the goddess-

37 Freeman, 'Purity and Violence', p. 284.

38 Ibid.

39 Toni Huber, 'When what you see is not what you get: Remarks on the Traditional Tibetan Presentation of Sacred Geography' in *Tantra and Popular Religion in Tibet*, ed. by Geoffrey Samuel et al., (Manohar: South Asian Books, 1994), p. 41.

clan's good will. I met with the family on a regular basis—at their new home, in the Navadurgā temple, and at every ritual performance thereafter.

Ujesh's father, Krishna Banmala, was an accomplished dancer-medium who had been initiated into the troupe during his adolescence; throughout this period, he trained interchangeably as demi-deities Sīma and Dūma. These divinities—and atypically Bāl Kumārī—are commended to the troupe's younger members to accustom them with the performance's elaborate regulations. Once they perform as Sīma and Dūma, mediums become fully initiated and can be called upon to perform as any other deity in future cycles.

These roles demand commitment on the mediums' part, and many Banmala mediums had set aside their education to fulfil their spiritual duty. Ujesh and his younger brother, Dinesh, had performed as Sīma and Dūma as troupe initiands, but Krishna encouraged them to pursue other vocations instead; he also encouraged their sister, Babita, who became a fully qualified nurse. Krishna worked additional hours as a labourer to fund their education. This is common among Newari communities; such economic distribution occurs within families, whilst outside the family, exploitative profit-seekers are rife (Nepal has no legislation that polices tort partnerships). In the town of Sankhu, Rankin interviewed a Newar merchant who explained the ways a household head should redistribute his household's earnings:

> Because Bhakta Krisna [household head] is the one who manages the household wealth … he also has the responsibility to take care of the whole family, including each of the brother's children … According to our custom, after collecting the brothers' earnings, he has also to give it out, for clothes, school fees, and different investments.[40]

Such standards of selfless social care (as cited in § 2.6.2), versus individual greed, was an idiom I heard often in Bhaktapur. Krishna always seemed to prioritize his family's financial needs, which he saw as a moral necessity. He said that ritual donations alone could not sustain his family, which is why he worked secondary jobs. This ethos is echoed in Steven Parish's study of morality in Bhaktapur: in the spirit of Meyer Fortes' *The Web of Kinship*,[41] he argues that Newars are nurtured within endogamous 'webs of relatedness' that may instill selflessness

40 Katharine Rankin, 'Newar Representation of Finance: Towards an Anthropology of Profit' in *The Cultural Politics of Markets: Economic Liberation and Social Change in Nepal*, ed. by Katharine Rankin, (London: Pluto Press, 2004), p. 117.

41 Meyer Fortes, *The Web of Kinship among the Tallensi* (London: Routledge, 2018 [1949]).

within them.[42] Here, I would add that *guṭhis*—or extra-caste associations—may also shape ideals of Newar sociality, too.

As mentioned in § 2.6.1, there are generally three main *guṭhis* in Bhaktapur: some are intra-caste (endogamous) groups that re-establish a caste hierarchy, while others are inter-caste (exogamous) formations. In Newar society, social complexity means caste hierarchy is not the prevailing structure which defines their identity. Newars do not view the caste system as determinant of all social relations. To illustrate, Toffin differentiates two social structures in Newar society i.e. caste-based or kin-based groups:

> The first one is linked to the caste system [...] it reproduces a hierarchical order derived from classical India, and is centered on a sovereign [...] and an intimate part of personal tutelary goddesses. The second form of guthi has to do with the world within the caste; it enhances other social functions [...] kin-bounded communities, economic cooperation, and territorial bonds. It stands in sharp contrast to the first one.[43]

Unlike Parish's and Toffin's renderings above, I argue Navadurgā rituals *spiral* both structures—a moiety—to synthesize them as a ritually confined macro-clan. Through blood sacrifice, ritual ties—that are non-consanguineal—are established to re-network denizens in a uniquely ritual community.

4.1.1 Donating to the Banmala Mediums

In Newar culture, every ritual specialist—whether Navadurgā medium or Rājopadhyāyā Brahmin—must accumulate financial income somehow. For the most part, ritual donations provide some income. However, Ujesh often lamented the financial predicaments that face Banmala troupes in modernity, which he sometimes attributed to 'Western' culture. Evidently aggrieved by the system, Ujesh exclaimed that 'there is no longer central government help' [*Sarkar ko sahayog chhaina*]. I realized the Banmalas were always very critical of the central government, which highlighted their resistant attitude towards hegemony. Though, funnily enough, they praised NWPP's municipality, who, they said, supported their cause. Part of that conversation I note here:

> [Ujesh]: If there is a death in the family, members [*gaṇata*] cannot tend to or worship the deities for 14 days like other Newars do when mourn-

42 Steven Parish, *Moral Knowing in a Hindu Sacred City: An Exploration of Mind, Emotion, and Self* (New York: Columbia University Press, 1994), p. 126.

43 Toffin, *From Kin*, p. 21.

> ing. They must still perform, dedication is a must. Now, the Navadurgā are fighting to preserve their performance [*pyakhāṇ*] in light of social changes in the Kathmandu Valley. Bhaktapur Municipality and the administrative committee [*guṭhi songstan*] try to continue festivals and cultural monuments. There is a limited budget and funding. Nothing can be done with this limited budget.

The sentiment of securing public donations is also enunciated in Navadurgā performance. In this case, Navadurgā mediums request funds in exchange for their ritual services. In his discussion of capital, Bourdieu notes that any money received from clientele (i.e. devotees) to a service provider (i.e. mediums) can mobilize the provider's reputation:

> [...] for those who, like the professionals, live on the sale of cultural services to clientele, the accumulation of economic capital merges with the accumulation of symbolic capital, that is, with the acquisition of a reputation for competence and an image of respectability and honourability that are easily converted into political position.[44]

However, the troupe always declared that any money they received would not be savoured for their personal use. Annually, the Banmalas pronounce this promise publicly during the ritual cycle's final ritual (Newa: *gusuṇtanegu*). By doing so, the Banmalas assure that monetary donations are reinvested to fund rituals for the common good.

Managing these donations is entrusted to a committee of Banmala trustees—a Navadurgā *devgan guṭhi*—who superintend funds received on an annual basis; they also maintain land owned by the troupe. This land is located near the hinterland of Livālī, some 2 km from the Navadurgā temple. As in Malabar, trustees must attest that the donations accrued, from Navadurgā rituals, are not-for-profit, insofar as this money conserves their tradition's continuation.

If, for example, a settlement—visited by the Navadurgā troupe—does not provide adequate hospitality when the Banmala visits their temple, then, in response, the ritual will cease performing there.[45] Ujesh listed five regions where the troupe now refuse to perform: (1) Hadigaun, Kathmandu; (2) Tokha,

44 Bourdieu, *Distinction*, p. 291.

45 This is not the case for precincts within Bhaktapur City, for Navadurgā performances are mandatory in the city. These sanctions are only applied to non-Bhaktapur towns, like Banepa, where a performance is not obligatory.

Kathmandu; (3) Chaprigaun, Kathmandu; (4) Tupya; (5) Gokarna. I inquired further, "Why have they [the troupe] stopped going to these areas?", to which Ujesh responded:

> There are three reasons why they have stopped performing in these areas ... there is a lack of facilities by the local municipalities ... the central government don't give us any funding ... And also the ignorance of the people [*mancheharūle appaman gauko*]—they don't believe in our power anymore.

Here, I interpret the 'ignorance of the people' to mean the influence of secular culture in these five regions—three of them are situated in Nepal's globalized capital, Kathmandu. These areas, Ujesh continued, did not understand the diligent hard work Banmala mediums heed to keep their traditions alive. Such financial backing ensures that paraphernalia necessary for the performance is maintained; if faith in Tantric mediumship dwindles within a population, then further struggles could afflict the Banmalas. In the next section I will provide an account of these ritual paraphernalia, traditions, and the dancer-mediums' progression on their path as Navadurgā performers.

4.2 *Preparing To Be a Banmala Medium: The Career of a Troupe Member*

In Bhaktapur, identifying the Navadurgā performers (*ujāju*) is quite straightforward, in that their bodies are marked to reflect this allegiance. In his youth, a male member must pierce his upper helix—as do Nāth yogīs[46]—with a circular metallic earring, which is feathered at its apex with a five-coloured fabric (*pāsuka*). This piercing is a typically Newari mark of passage (Newa: *nhātu chhaḥ*) done in their infancy: the piercing's function is, essentially, eschatological; the piercing induces pain which grounds that initiand in this world (*lokā*), as, in Newari thinking, a newborn's essence may still be attached to his previous existence **qua** reincarnation.[47]

In an initiand's formative years, he will be required to complete years of choreographic instruction (each deity has unique movements or *mūdras*) in advance of each cycle under a *guru's* mentorship. Before these dances are per-

46 Nāth yogis also pierce the cartilage of their ears as a marker of their identity, see Mallinson, 'Nāth'.

47 Sushila Manandhar, 'Supernatural Power of Body Adornment: Beliefs and Practices among the Newars of Kathmandu Valley (Nepal)', *Contributions to Nepalese Studies*, 36.2 (2009), pp. 265–266.

formed in ritual, the *gaṇa* must seclude themselves in a state of purification known in Hindu traditions as *vṛata*. According to Krishna, the *vṛata* is an onerous time for a dancer-medium; not only should they be disciplined, but they must abstain from any 'contaminating' activities—i.e. eating with members of his/her own family or celebrating other festivals (*jātrā*)—which are prohibited. This ritualized seclusion culminates at *Gotamangaḷ*, where the group's efforts are blessed at the shrine of Nasādyo.

The commitment of the Navadurgā troupe became most apparent when they travelled to settlements outside the city (e.g. Banepa, Nala, Dhulikel, and Sanga); the members would walk many kilometers completely barefoot. Over their shoulders, male mediums would carry heavy baskets (*khola*), each containing a Navadurgā mask; some of these, like Barāhī's mask, weighed approximately 30 kg! I accompanied the procession to Nāla, and I asked Ujesh why the troupe did not journey in a truck to hasten the trek. He explained that any path traversed by Banmala mediums would become clear of possible misfortune; the mere presence of mediums and their masks in a locale can rid entire environments of unwanted spirits. On the road to Nala—between a Bhaktapurian hinterland called Chhemasinga and the forest[48] abutting Nala—we rested at a farmer's house whose crops encircled the trail. He summoned the troupe inside his home and provided them with *samye baji* (a dish of beaten rice, buffalo meat, and vegetables). He also offered *prasād* to the deity-masks, which were placed outside on straw mats. The farmer stated that the troupe's annual procession across his lands ensured his crops' fertility. He stated that: "When I invite the Navadurgā to my house each year, I feel a sense of inner peace [*ānanda lagyo*]".

The arduous procedures that the Banmalas' go through literally **reconfigures** their bodies. Becoming the goddess-clan emboldens them, such that any land they tread becomes cleared of adverse energies lingering there. In Tantric cosmology, bodily praxis realigns physical space: bodies and territory are co-constitutive, as indicated by an informant, who claimed the ritual organically interlaces bodies, territories, and society. This concept is reflected in the offerings given, all of which equate with the five elements of space (*bhuta*) and five elements of the body: water (*jāl*), a tika mark (*śila*), rice (*acetta*), flowers (*swāṅ*), and light (*bati*) (or, in Navadurgā, five items of meat and alcohol known as *pañcamṛtya*). In Bhaktapur, the Navadurgā dance is said to mobilize these elements in its performance; I was told the Navadurgā-clan aligns with

48 I was told timber from this forest was used for the colossal wooden poles (*liṅga*) for Bisket Jātrā and Indra Jātrā festivals.

the nine planets (*Navagraha*), who move together with the earth's agricultural cycles, which, ultimately, modify corporeal bodies.

In fact, many informants conveyed Navadurgā ritual as a rite that merges territory, time, bodies, divinities, and royal power in unison, thereby co-creating Bhaktapur's lifeworld. During performance, Navadurgā mediums embody all these confluences at once, the territory's energy incarnate. Below, I provide an excerpt from a Newari historian, who explained this worldview:

> [Me:] Why is the Navadurgā important for the people of Bhaktapur? What is the link with agriculture?
>
> [Inf.] The Navadurgā is presented in a living form/body to show people that there are gods/goddesses, who spread positive messages. The Mother goddesses are always protecting [*mana rakṣa*] us. Our Newar clothes [*daura suruwal*], which we wear every day, have eight knots on the outside and one knot on the inside, that represent the goddesses. Our body has the nine goddesses [mapped] on us, because we have nine orifices [...] The medieval Malla kings also had nine different gods [...] Our whole body is protected by these mother goddesses. Navadurgā flows like blood through the people [*ragat samma*] of Bhaktapur and the *land* itself. In all daily ceremonies, the Navadurgā are present in some form.[49]

To boot, the Banmalas' garments and clothing (Newa: *jammā*)—like their bodies and masks—are also powerfully effectual; devotees often huddled aside and held their garments, while gesturing toward their foreheads in a signal of auspicious transference (*āsribād*). In Newar religion, the cranial crown (*sahaśasara*) is a vital Tantric portal which permeates the body's source of *śakti*. The draping gowns—red, white, black, and green in colour—are embroidered with a crescent moon (*canda*), a regalia that symbolizes Śiva and Śakti's spiraling as *ādiśakti*, which the troupe personifies.

In the intervening months between ritual cycles, all these fabrics—meticulously designed—are crafted by Ujesh's maternal aunt. She is the only individual skilled enough to weave these garments to the required standard. Once worn at a ritual, the items (Newa: *ghajinung*- 'clothes') cannot be washed; cleaning the fabric renders them ineffective. In recent years, the clothing's material is either donated by others or supplied by the Banmalas from their own funds. If donated, the garments are presented in a ritual (*prāsād pūjā*) at the Navadurgā temple.

---

49 Historian from Lalitpur, 2nd December 2016.

Ornamental foot instruments (*ghoṅgālā*)—that chime during the ritual dance—also receive ceremonial consecration too. On the eighth day (*mahāṣṭamī*) of Mohani, at the shrine dedicated to Nasādyo, Karmācārya priests smear cow dung on the ground, before tracing a rice-flour maṇḍala crowned with rice cakes (Newa: *ghoja*). On each cake, a metallic foot chime is placed. Before offering the *ghoṅgālā* to the initiated members, the Karmācārya draws a criss-crossed diagram on the receivers' hands, and proceeds by presenting a *ghoṅgālā* to each member. In Newari language, Mohani's eighth day is known as *ghoṅgālā si-la-lhayegu* (lit. 'the giving of the foot-bangle'). On the ninth day, Mahākālī's sword (*khadga*) is given to the troupe from the Karmācārya priests. Zotter highlights the importance of royal swords in Newar Tantra: swords are insignia which symbolize the absent king, but, at another level, they also signify royal power uniting the goddess-clan with her citizens:

> [...] the [royal] sword is not only an attribute of the king's tutelary deity in her different forms, it is the goddess herself, both on esoteric and exoteric levels.[50]

Ujesh once recalled how Mahākālī's characteristic ferocity is inflamed after the sword-receiving rite at the royal palace (*lāyaku*). He stated that pedestrians are warned to stay away from the palace because, in previous years, she had scythed many civilians blocking her path.

The Banmalas also manufacture apotropaic talisman, which are given to worshippers. When a devotee offers 10 rupees to the gods, these talisman—threads of five-colours (or *pāsuka*, lit. 'boundary threads')—are given out to protect them. Every year, rolls of cotton thread are blessed by the Nāyo's 'tantra-mantra', before being weaved into necklets by the troupe, who do so in the temple's courtyard. Again, these five colours signify the five elements of body-space, as aforementioned above. In brief, Banmala regalia are objects suffused with politico-divine vigour, that impart *śakti* to those who wear them.

As for managing the troupe, the Nāyo ('leader') and Nakiṅ ('female leader') are responsible for deputizing the ritual's rites and activities. They also communicate with other castes on behalf of the clan. When a ritual is due to perform in a new precinct or settlement, it must be announced by the Nāyo some eight days in precedence. At that settlement, the Nāyo informs the area's various households, and dispatches apotropaic *pāsuka* to those individuals.

50 Zotter, 'State Rituals', pp. 269–270.

For many years in succession, Ujesh's maternal grandmother and grandfather were entrusted the roles of Nakiṅ and Nāyo. Both were born in separate Banmala blood-lineages (*phuki*); marrying a spouse outside Banmala lineages would mean that the family, although Banmala in name, could not legitimately participate in the ritual. A Nāyo's life-experience grants him an authoritative position—he is the first port of call for any member requiring counsel on any aspect of the performance. It is he who transmits Tantric instructions to the *guru* or *Naya*, who is his apprentice. The *guru*'s responsibility lies in instructing dancer-mediums.

Likewise, the Nakiṅ is the Nāyo's female coequal; she is a priestess who presides over the Navadurgā temple. Daily, she convenes a *puja* at *Siphā dyo's* shrine on the first-floor sanctum of the temple, which is forbidden for foreigners. Unlike Smārta Hindu tradition—where female priests are forbidden—the Nakiṅ has an otherwise central role: she liaises daily shrine-activation (*nitya pūjā*) that awaken the divinities and oversees the maintenance of the godmasks (*khwōpa*). In doing these tasks, she secures the success of the ritual cycle. In addition, she must perform a ceremony of ablution as the performers leave the temple to perform; in Bhaktapur, this ablution is called *lāsa kūsa* ('welcoming the god'). As mediums descend from the temple stairwell on their way to a precinct, the Nakiṅ scatters water from a bronze jar (*sija tapha*) onto the masks and into the mediums' hands. The water collected for this ablution pours from a public waterspout (*hiti*) situated in Kamalvināyak's precinct, near the Navadurgā temple. Krishna assured me this water was safe enough to drink without boiling it beforehand; its source was high in the mountains above Bhaktapur, in Nagarkot. He said, 'the best water in the entire Kathmandu Valley flows from this tap'.

As keepers of Tantric knowledge—exoteric **and** esoteric, embodied **and** textual—the Nāyo and Nakiṅ were very knowledgeable. I spoke with them quite often and I respected their thoroughgoing commitment to Navadurgā and the burden this duty brings. When I tried to redivert the conversation to discuss liturgical details (considered 'secret'), they courteously declined and remained reticent about discussing these with me—the intrigued foreigner. On occasions, Ujesh successfully mediated between the Nāyo, Nakiṅ, and myself; these gleanings inform much of my data on Tantric matters.

The Nāyo had some interesting narratives to tell about his own experiences as a Navadurgā medium, and he spoke about how Nasādyo's intervention—in the form of a dog—manifested throughout his career:

> [Ujesh:] 'When *baje* [grandfather] was learning the Navadurgā *pyākhaṇ*, he went, one morning, to the local rice mill to purchase some rice for the

> *gaṇa*. On his way back to the temple, a dog followed him, and tried to steal the bag of rice that *baje* was carrying. *Baje* pushed the dog aside, and the dog ran in the opposite direction. Later that evening, when *baje* was practising *mūdra* in the presence of the *guru*, he made many errors (despite having learned each dance proficiently beforehand). Unbeknownst to *baje* at the time, he had insulted the *vahana* ('vehicle') of Nasādyo—the dog he fended away was Nasādyo who, in his anger, had placed a curse on him [*deutako dhos lāgeko*]'.

In retelling their life-episodes, the mediums seemed to talk about confrontations with divine beings they had met, guised as animals or possessed humans. One such case occurred some three days before the April 2015 earthquake: according to Ujesh, a woman in Bhaktapur started warning her neighbours of imminent danger, which became a topic of widespread gossip; it was said she was possessed by Brahmāyani herself.

Specially gifted Banmala mediums (but not all) were sensitive to the surfacing of other-than-human beings in the world (*loka*), which include: (1) the appearance of gods and goddesses as possessed individuals or as incarnations of their respective 'vehicles' (*vahana*); (2) the prophetic 'reading' of bodies (for character assessments, ailments, divination etc.); and (3) astrological constellations (*ākaśa*). Ujesh was fascinated with palmistry, a skill he had cultivated by observing the Nāyo, who was his maternal grandfather. On a bus returning to Bhaktapur from Kathmandu one evening, Ujesh suddenly grabbed my wrist and began reading my palm to deduce my idiosyncratic personality traits; I must admit, his reading was rather accurate. In what ways a Banmala medium's prophetic abilities were nurtured will be discussed in the next section.

4.3 *Banmala Bodies: Masks, Ritual Cycles, and Tantric Power*

Over many years, the Banmala mediums have become proficient as foreseers of prophecies and readers of Bhaktapur's intra-cosmic world. These extra-sensory abilities were capacitated through prolonged exposure to divine power, transferred from Taleju to Siphā dyo, at the autumnal equinox of Mohanī. To guarantee the goddess-clan's reinvigoration within them, a rite of power-rejuvenation, conducted monthly, is administered by the mediums. This ritual is called *choree pūjā*.

In the temple courtyard (*mulchowk*), under the Nakiṅ's direction, all masks are hung on pillars that encircle the space. As expected, the temple is built in traditional Newar style: constructed with terracotta bricks, its architecture is structured in a 'post and lintel' plan, with a joist architrave conjoining the pillars that support its foundations.[51] Engraved on this wooden beam is the *argala stotra*[52]—a mantra from the Devī Māhātmya dedicated to Mahākālī—which also includes salutations to the Navadurgā clan.

Close to the entranceway, Siphā dyo's silver repoussé plate is positioned there, and proceeding clockwise, the masks of Bhairava, Sima, Ganeśa, and the nine Durgās are fastened on hooks to each pillar. At the centre, a *maṇḍala* in the shape of a *siphā* flower (*Nerium Oleander*)—in ode to the Banmalas' gardener origins—is drawn with four lit oil-wicks and a bronze water container (*sija tapho*) surrounding it. It is incumbent upon the Nakiṅ to officiate the proceedings: she provides plates (*lapte*) of food and flowers at the base of each god-masks, and the dancer-mediums follow suit.

Next, a medium who incarnates Bhairava slits the throat of a chicken and smears its bleeding neck on Siphā dyo's image to pacify her. Then, the sacrificial blood is offered to two other divinities: Ganeśa and Kumārī. At first, I wondered why only these deities are offered blood, after which a member explained: "In our culture, Gaṇeś and Kumārī are always worshipped first [*pahila devata bali dinē*]—they are given the sacrifice for this reason—they must be appeased [*phayegu*]"; after all, Gaṇeśa is the 'remover of obstacles'. With handfuls of beaten rice (*baji*), all initiated members shower each other with the grains (even non-performing members were showered with grains). I was told this symbolic deed was a crucial one: *baji*-scattering in *choree pūjā* signifies the consubstantive flow of Navadurgā's power from the shrine, or mask, into temple space, before being re-absorbed into their bodies. From this point, each medium is empowered for every successive ritual.

The *choree pūjā* I had witnessed that evening (6th April 2016) also coincided with the 'night of *bwakṣi* (witches)', a time of great uncertainty for Bhaktapurian citizens. Quite unlike any other time, this night is notorious for the presence of *bwakṣi*, who can imprecate death upon unsuspecting victims. After the *pūjā*, a dancer-medium advised that I stay indoors because: "the *bwakṣi* will be on street corners, with small flames from their thumbs, and they will put malfortune on you". Intrigued, I asked, "Why only tonight should I be worried about *bwakṣi*? Can they attack any other evening?", and he replied, "Tonight is

51 Niels Gutschow, *Architecture of the Newars: A History of Buliding Typologies and Details in Nepal* (Chicago: Serindia Publications, 2011), p. 253.

52 Oṃ Jayanti maṅgala kālī bhadrakālī kapālani | durgachema śivatharī svaha sodha namastute || sarvamaṅgala śiva sarvasatike śarthye trambhake gauri navadurge namastute || Oṃ viśvekhari jagadātrī stitisauār kārīṇmaḥ namaste astunavadurge | bhagavantī raksāṃ me sarvataḥ || namo devye mahādevye śivāya satataṅ namaḥ | namaḥ prakṛti bhadraye niyetāḥ praṇātaḥ sma tām ||

the night of *bwakṣi*. It is said that someone in Bhaktapur will be struck with an illness or die of a curse. They use Tantric techniques negatively to cast a curse, and not to help people [like Navadurgā do]". It seems, that evening, the *spiraling* ambivalence of Tantric culture—creative **and** destructive—manifested most clearly to me: Navadurgā's capacity for *healing* on the one hand, and a witch's *curse* on the other.

4.3.1 The Mask-Makers: Citrakār

The thirteen masks of Navadurgā are intricately designated apparatus, which must be crafted by a community of sculptors, the Citrakār. Having spent most of my time with the Banmalas up to that point, I had not spoken with any Citrakār artists. However, Ujesh was in contact with one Citrakār family, that household which creates the Navadurgā masks—and he arranged a meeting with them in their household-come-workshop. I conducted an interview with a long-serving Citrakār sculptor, and he spoke at length about his (and his family's) craftmanship. Particularly, he outlined the process of making masks—to exacting aesthetic criteria—within a narrow timeframe; some comments I quote here:

> [Inf]: There are many Citrakār families in Bhaktapur—some of these families only make commercial masks for selling in stores. But only here [in our home] are the actual Navadurgā masks [used in the *pyākhaṇ*] made. It takes about three months to sculpt these masks—the whole family engages in the process; it is not a one-person operation [*ek janā kām hundaina*]. The clay is pulverised with cotton and then it is shaped around a mold (made of *mah*—boiled rice-flour water). For three months we work tirelessly, because every mask must be completed before Mohani. If there is a lot of rainfall during this time, then it can cause problems; they must be completed whatever the conditions [...] The clay is brought from the riverbanks near the Brahmāyani temple [she is the goddess of creation]. However, due to the pollution of the river, this can be a problem. Sometimes we ask Prajāpati [potters] to bring soil from their stores [...] Once we begin the process of making the mask, no one apart from our closest family members can enter our home. At first, the clay receives *pūjā* to give it powerful [*śaktisali*] properties, and this is done on the day of Gotamangaḷ. As Śiva [the smallest mask of the whole set] is re-established in Bhaktapur on Gotamangaḷ, we worship at the Śiva-liṅga [a shrine near their house] and Śiva becomes the first mask which we sculpt [...] When masks are near completion, Banmala gaṇa arrive at our house to fix ties on the back of the masks and for [head-circumference] measurements At this stage, if there is a problem with measurements, then we can adjust

> these ties. The ujāju visit every day after these measurements are done to perform pūjā. Every mask's painted pattern must be exact; If these are not done properly, then this would make them ineffective. They are painted by hand, and every god-mask has a different symbol. On the mask of Bhairava, a *Chandra* moon is drawn ... the power and sign of Śiva is painted on the bottom. We continue to use traditional paints [which are filtered to ensure all poisons are extracted], even though artificial paints are popular with other Citrakār [in the Kathmandu Valley].

Though generally harmonious, the partnership between Citrakār and Banmala mediums was not always congenial. For example, a year prior to my visit, a disagreement arose between some senior Banmala and Citrakār artisans; the Banmala were unhappy with one mask's painted exterior (though this was settled, and the issue was corrected for the next Navadurgā season). For apotheosized dancer-mediums, exacting standards must be heeded; these masks are divine, or rather, material equivalents of the gods they represent. A god-mask must be shown the utmost respect; of course, Bhaktapurian people offer obeisance to them as if they were *śakti-pītha* ('seats of [god] power'). On one occasion, a Bhaktapurian social scientist claimed that the masks' power is instilled during a rite in the Navadurgā's temple shrine (*pūjākoṭha*): a flame is passed over the new masks, which charges them with the god's *śakti.* (A comparable rite is used in Kerala: there, Teyyam priests empower Teyyam weapons with flames, lit, instead, from coconut leaf torches (*chōtta*)).

4.3.2 Dyo Bokegu: Offerings to the Goddess-Clan

After the autumnal equinox, offerings to the Navadurgā clan become routinized, and any group wishing to receive their grace can do so. Many times, I witnessed such offerings outside the Navadurgā temple: donors would prepare a cornucopia of plates (*lapte*) for the mediums, each mounded with fruits, sweets, curd (*jū-jū dhāū̃*), syrup pastries (*jalebi*), and rice wine (*aila*). They also provided *kisali* (small terracotta bowls of rice topped with a betel nut (*supari*)) and a pig for sacrifice. These communal ritual offerings (*dyo bokegu*) take place outside the Navadurgā temple's doorway and are conducted a week before the ritual visits that donor's precinct. Certainly, this is not the only time *dyo bokegu* can be arranged; groups may invite the troupe to grant good fortune for new business ventures or to bless a new family. According to one medium (7th April 2016):

> [Inf.]: *dyo bokegu* [literally 'god invitation'] is someone or a household from Taumādhi ... who wants to give an offering to the goddess. They go to

> the Navadurgā temple and invite the god/goddesses to his house. When people get a new business, or get married, they invite the *gaṇa* to perform at the temple to bless them [and they [the troupe] go to their home or *twā* to dance].

A *dyo bokegu* is spaced outside the temple's entrance according to a specific arrangement, and figure 13 is a not-to-scale drawing of that arrangement.

To sum up, then: during *dyo bokegu*, the Navadurgā's capacity for re-creating ritual kinship became most visible; devotees and mediums alike interchanged offerings, blessings, and emotions with one another, which is the ceremony's *sine qua non*. In Bhaktapur, this ritual bonding takes the form of beaten rice and curd (*dhāũ-baji*), which is handed out to the congregation. By all accounts, *dhāũ-baji* is a powerful gift of commensality that amalgamates deities and donors in renewed ritual kin relations. In that way, *dhāũ-baji* could also increase a couple's fertility and protect their offspring. For instance, in Banepa, a group of males surrounded the deity, Seto Bhairava, who, at the time, was apportioning chunks of rice-curd to them. Altogether, the men drew breath, consumed the morsel, then exhaled a baritone grunt, 'Huuss!'. One of the men turned to me and said: "Say it with us *bhāi* (brother), 'Huuss!' ... By doing this we will be powerful". Toffin also notes that certain raw food establishes enhanced ritual ties among Newars. He writes: 'By the sharing of consecrated food that has first been offered to the deities, a sacred bond is created among the members'.[53] For Ujesh, the dancer-mediums were filial 'middle-men' for Bhaktapurians, which, he claimed, was key to their popularity.

Arguably, deity-mediums induce transformative effects, affects and fears in their devotees since they harness deities who constitute the land's *kin* (Nepa: *thākuri*). Ujesh once described Bhairava as the 'father [Newa: *bābā*] of the Navadurgā', which is why he is the ritual's principal sacrificer. When I spoke to devotees during the performances, they would habitually call their goddesses Āma ('mother') or Āji ('grandmother'); indeed, in ritual, they are considered the city's mothers and grandmothers. Furthermore, concerns of familial life are part and parcel of the goddess-clan's life-stories, which are portrayed choreographically. For example, during a segment of the ritual known as *nyalakegu* (Newa: 'fish-catching'), the deity Seto Bhairava contracts gastral pain from *mikhā wanegu* (a curse associated with food). It transpires that his affliction was caused by his reluctance to share a meal of fish with his offspring, Sima

53 Toffin, *From Kin*, p. 25.

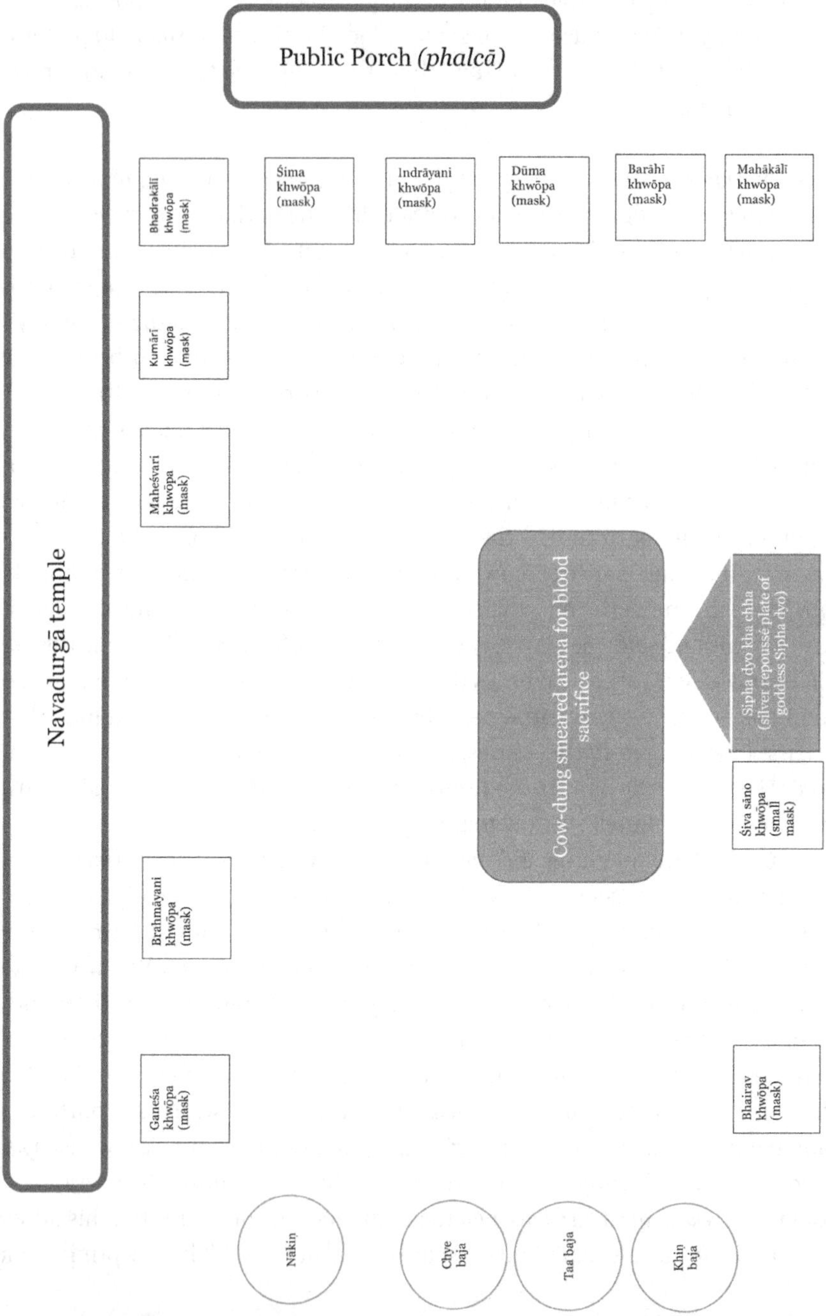

FIGURE 13 Annotated floor plan of *dyo bokegu*, Navadurgā Temple (outside entranceway), (Gacchen Twā, Bhaktapur)
ILLUSTRATION BY AUTHOR

FIGURE 14 Offerings (*dyo bokegu*) to the Navadurgā, (Dhulikel, Nepal)
PHOTOGRAPH BY AUTHOR

and Dūma, who unconsciously foisted a curse upon him. His wife, Indrayāni, is called upon to cure his sickness.

The performance, therefore, rekindles the goddess-clan's collective agency to engender cultural standards of inter-individual concern. As a case in point, Ujesh recalled how devotees—in the wake of the earthquake—visited the mediums for consolation:

> [Inf.]: Navadurgā are the gods of wishes; when people make a wish, their wish [*raja bhane*] comes true […] After the earthquake [*būkampa pacchi*], a very elderly woman—whose house was destroyed—held one of the dancer-mediums and started crying: 'What is going to happen? Where do I stay? Why has this happened?' […] If Navadurgā were no longer in existence, what would happen to our city?

After any societal plight, the dancer-mediums are always their worshippers' first point of call. As representatives of the goddess-clan, Banmala mediums are authoritative figures, who can tap into and navigate Bhaktapur's ancestors, divinities, soil, and medieval (Malla) power, all in unison. As indicated earlier, their bodies are predisposed—psychically and somatically—to the goddess-clan's lifeforce, whose shrines delineate the city's geographical boundary. Given this, a medium rediverts Bhaktapur's flow of material energy—dating back to the medieval kingdom—into the now to activate its life-affirming, defensive capabilities.

In times of need, the Banmala troupe provide a source of solace for their fellow Bhaktapurians. The troupe instigates goddess intervention in the city's urban spaces (and those settlements that were once part of the Malla kingdom): as a result, they pioneer divine reparation, either to mitigate social oppression or to counteract negative forces—curses **and** demons—which infiltrate Newar groups.

To fulfill these ends, deity-mediums must make precarious crossings into the city's subterranean layers, which is typified by the dangerous, yet vigorous, temperament of the goddess-clan they manifest. Admittedly, people feared the Banmala mediums, which was evident when I watched a performance in Banepa, a bustling town east of Nala. Perturbed by the mere sight of the masks, one woman conceded: 'we are frightened of them [*hamile navadurga gana lai dar lagcchaũ*], because they have so much power'. If insulted, these deities can apply expedient, or sometimes extremely terrifying, punishment, which can intimidate their followers. Simply, Tantric worlds are volatile: capricious gods can, in one moment, accord fertility and fortune to the righteous worshipper and, in another, punish those anti-social culprits who defy them.

Despite the ritual's seemingly darker aspects, Banmala mediums always glossed over them to underscore its sanguine character. They said only immoral 'demonic' persons should be agitated by a goddess' fury. Navadurgā is, after all, a time of beneficial somatic connection, however alarming its sacrificial practices may seem. A dancer-medium (in his mid-twenties) once imparted insightful renderings of Navadurgā. He said: "Navadurgā teaches us about how to be civilized, how to be social ... To me, it [Navadurgā] is the beginning of civilization". For their devout followers, embodied deity-mediums epitomize Newari social life.

A Navadurgā performance, like Teyyāṭṭam, binds its participants in a space where ritual kinship is re-established between partisans and their ancestral deities. Informally, at Navadurgā dances, I often overheard Newar men greeting one another as '*pāsa*' (Newa. 'brother'), a form of address which, in Sanskrit, derives from the term '*pāśa*' or 'bond'. Navadurgā rituals, thereby, stand in opposition to caste stratification because Bhaktapur's goddess-clan personifies all her inhabitants' ancestors. The dancer-mediums achieve this macro-clan union by enacting tales of the Navadurgā-clan's domestic life, which maneuvers medieval deities, and their power, to aid their devotees' social concerns.

As with Mauss' understanding of *The Gift*, any gift offered from one party to another within a Navadurgā ritual is not a commodity; gifts constitute the giver's very essence which is relayed to the receiver and vice versa. Specifically, a gift of raw rice or blood is, rather, a mutual interchange of power relations between two exchanging parties. Marcel Mauss famously documents this concept as follows:

> [T]his bond created by things is in fact a bond between persons, since the thing itself is a person or pertains to a person. Hence it follows that to give something is to give a part of oneself [...] It follows clearly from what we have seen that in this system of ideas one gives away what is in reality a part of one's nature and substance, while to receive something is to receive a part of someone's spiritual essence. To keep this thing is dangerous, not only because it is illicit to do so, but also because it comes morally, physically and spiritually from a person. Whatever it is, food, possessions, women, children or ritual, it retains a magical and religious hold over the recipient. The thing given is not inert. It is alive and often personified, and strives to bring to its original clan and homeland some equivalent to take its place.[54]

To re-route this analysis back to our context, I will reiterate my informant, Krishna, here: in performance, Navadurgā deities, and their devotees, merge as ritual kin, which, in effect, means their **concern** for one another intensifies. By offering gifts to Navadurgā dancers, they return the favour by bestowing power, fertility, longevity, and worldly protection to the giver(s). In a Tantric worldview, life is fluctuating between states of suffering and reparation, which is intrinsic to the *Kālī yuga* or 'life-age' in which we live. By forming kin-like bonds in traditional rituals, Navadurgā mediums shepherd their citizens—in this period of uncertainty—by reviving ancestral goddesses of old.

5 Conclusion

In the introduction to this chapter, I suggested that dancer-mediums are conduits that recreate a society's order as a macro-clan of ritual kin unity. They do so by attuning a polity's ancestral lifeforce (*śakti*) into a network that is re-made in Teyyāṭṭam and Navadurgā ritual. To bring forth ancestor divinities into their bodies, dancer-mediums must navigate the territory's inherent ener-

54 Marcel Mauss, *The Gift: Forms and Functions of Exchange in Archaic Societies* (London: Cohen & West, 1967).

gies to release the medieval goddess-clan into a contemporary performance. Blood sacrifice and rice-scattering placates this power—from which divinities re-emanate—into the flesh of those mediums who personify them. Once embodied, the deity's power can be reshaped as blessings via exchanges of commensal gifts between citizen and medium. In doing so, new ritual bonds are generated between ancestral deities, mediums, and the polity's community. In the face of worldly anxieties, it comes as no surprise that dancer-mediums become figures of devotion for Bhaktapurian and Malayali civilians: mediums, thus, are outlets of support for social angst or unjust oppression—arising from caste hierarchies—that can afflict their partisans, in the hope that ancestral connection can assuage these problems.

In setting out their worldview, I would routinely hear Bhaktapurians stating phrases like, '*devata ra samāja ustai chhan*', 'god and society are synonymous', which could well be a Durkheimian rendering of religion; Parish also shows how Bhaktapurians would describe god in terms of society.[55] The biographies of Teyyam deities in Kerala, too, are also related to collective groups. Freeman writes:

> Even among those [teyyam] beings who began their mythical careers as gods, however, it is almost always possible to detect strong associations with particular human groups [...] with whom they originated.[56]

In line with this Tantric logic, if a goddess-clan is inextricably linked to society, then mediums who become 'goddess-clan-in-human-form' also recast those attending their ritual in a similar manner i.e. as a macro-clan. In cognitive science of religion, Whitehouse and Lanman show how rituals fuse an individual's self with a group self; in other words, persons feel a part of a family in ritual, however transgressive, mutinous, or dysfunctional that family may be.[57] In Folk Śākta performances, I would argue that a capacity for creating an alternative family—or macro-clan—is **most** germane: their cosmological contouring is based on deliberate fluidity and a focus on *kula* ('family') connections, which, in Folk Śākta ritual, extend across bodies congregated there.

55 Parish, *Moral Knowing*.

56 Freeman, 'Purity and Violence', p. 67.

57 Harvey Whitehouse & Jonathan Lanman, 'The Ties that Bind Us: Ritual, Fusion, and Identification', *Current Anthropology*, 55.6 (2014), p. 676.

CHAPTER 4

History and Assimilation in Tantric Cosmology

1 Introduction

In this chapter, I will explore the metaphysical foundations that underpin, and therefore re-make, Folk Śākta worldviews. In 21st century Folk Śākta rituals, I advance the idea that textual manuals (*paddhati*)—used in medieval Tantric traditions—were gradually reconceived as *somatic textuality* through performance. By 'somatic textuality', I mean a ritualized process of mapping Tantric concepts—verbalized in songs or inscribed as symbols—onto deity-mediums' bodies, which reflects an emic vision of a goddess-clan enlivened by *mantras*. This move from text to textually inscribed bodies combined Tantra with the vernacular in collective ritual; certainly, in Kerala and the Kathmandu Valley, indigenous fertility cults merged into the clans (*kula*) of translocal Śākta goddesses. Set within *bricolage webs of ritual knowledge*, Navadurgā and Teyyāṭṭam rituals—like bodies integrated in genealogical order—adhered indigenous tenets and gods with their transregional counterparts across South Asia.

This chapter will reconstruct the ways metaphysical ideas were injected into, and meshed with, Folk Śākta performances circa the medieval period. In other words, I seek to establish how far itinerant textual transmissions (of Śaiva-Śākta schools via movements of Tantric specialists) reformulated the metaphysical underlay of Folk Śākta rituals over time. As a result, this chapter will gauge how textual sources, autochthonous worldviews, and embodied knowledge were negotiated on the ground.

Regarding the use of ritual manuals, Sarkar shows how Śākta communities—as early as the 9th century CE—used ritual manuals (*paddhati*) during their ceremonies. For Sarkar, an epigraphic source 'from South-east Asia' corroborates this.[1] Even today, Tantric temples in Kerala use *paddhati*-like texts to organize their collective rituals.[2]

Textual liturgies were also read by the Newars: during a Newar rite of passage I observed in Bhaktapur, a Tantric priest was performing a *hōma* rite guided by a detailed manual with handwritten instructions. (Although, during Navadurgā performances, texts were not publicly read, but were utilized in

1 Sarkar, *Heroic Shāktism*, p. 213.

2 In India, Kerala has the highest literacy rate across social strata.

 | DOI:10.1163/9789004439023_006

esoteric praxes). These occasions were isolated examples, for Teyyāṭṭam and Navadurgā ritualists tend to access and express cultural knowledge onto and through a virtuoso's body. Even from the textual perspective, goddesses are frequently envisaged as *mantric* embodiments (see Biernacki's discussion of the Bṛhannīlatantra, which describes Māyā's 'great feminine speech' bringing about worldly creation).[3]

In Kerala and Bhaktapur, this notion of *somatic textuality* was elicited from dancer-mediums themselves. For them, divine knowledge is retrieved **through** a medium's body due to his attunement with the goddess-clan, which is made visible by symbols embellished **on** his body. Afterwards, this knowledge is written down, and sung by other mediums in preparation for future rituals. In this way, I agree with Flood, who argues Tantric traditions are centred on the body, and whose cosmologies always incorporate 'body-based' metaphors. He states:

> [the body is a] structuring topos [...] closely connected to Tantric revelation and the body's divinisation is closely linked to the text and the ritual construction of the body based on textual models. The body is central as a foundational metaphor in the history of Tantric civilisation.[4]

To trace the development from medieval 'text' to *somatic textuality*, I will unearth the textual flows that occurred between Kerala and Nepal from the middle ages to the present day.

Normally, discussions of Tantric texts are side-lined in ethnographic accounts of Tantric religion. Surmising **which** Tantric thought plays out in **particular** Tantric rituals is an important investigation. In response, this chapter will argue that medieval Tantric texts obliquely influenced Folk Śākta performances. With the passage of time, these texts became recast as 'somatic' ones through ritual performance; by spiralling 'text' and 'body', these performances formed *bricolage webs of ritual knowledge*—from folk and Tantric thought—which grounded their rationale. This theoretical metaphor—a web—I adopt from a translation of 'Tantra' itself, that is, a 'web' of 'woven' streams of transmission (*āmnāya*). In this chapter, § 4.2 examines the context of Teyyāṭṭam, before moving to Navadurgā in § 4.3.

---

3 Loriliai Biernacki, 'The Absent Mother and Bodied Speech: Psychology and Gender in late Medieval Tantra', in *Transformations and Transfer of Tantra in Asia and Beyond* (Berlin: DeGruyter, 2012), p. 221.

4 Gavin Flood, *The Tantric Body: The Secret Tradition of Hindu Religion* (London: I.B. Taurus, 2005), p. 95.

2 Teyyāṭṭam

2.1 *Tantric Texts, Temples, and Kingship in Northern Kerala*

Generally speaking, a Teyyāṭṭam performance combines Sanskritic, Tantric, and 'Dravidian' (or folk) concepts, which forms its worldview and liturgical core. By 'Dravidian' I mean an indigenous worldview—and principles about the human condition—derived from Northern Malabar, which also includes South Indian culture—especially from Karnataka and Tamilnadu—in its widest sense. In Northern Malabar, Tantra exuded an incontestable presence in the region's temples, which continues into the present. Outside Kerala (and arguably, the Kathmandu Valley) Tantric religion—broadly conceived—is defined as a set of peripheral cults shunned by the Brahmanical elite. But, in Kerala, Tantric religiosity is culturally ubiquitous as a public mode of ritual life; even Nambūtiri Brahmans adopted Tantra, but they reconceived it to abide by their ideals of ritual purity. This watered-down version of Tantra still characterizes Nambūtiri Brahman worship today. Keralan Tantra, then, is uniquely multifaceted, and can be classified into two separate systems: (1) as already described, a form of Tantra utilized by Nambūtiri Brahmins, known as 'Keralan dualism' or right-handed Tantra (*dakṣinācārya*). In this style of Tantric worship, animal sacrifice was substituted for vegetative offerings, which are presented to a deity. And (2) a mode of Kashmiri Tantric nondualism that characterized the religiosity of Teyyam groves and royal temples. Here, the use of blood sacrifice and alcohol to appease fierce or ancestral deities were frequent.

Across medieval Kerala (11th–14th Century CE), three distinguishable temple sites were operative, and each espoused a differing model of Tantric practice, which I list here: (1) The temples of Nambūtiri Brahmans (*kṣetram*), which were restricted to members of the Brahman castes. At these sites, a style of Tantric religiosity—known as 'Keralan dualism' or right-hand Tantra (*dakṣinācārya*)—was used in order to avert bodily defilement, which assured the site's ritual purity. As such, any offerings of meat or alcohol (*pañcamṛtya*) were prohibited there. By contrast, (2) royal goddess temples were focused on 'Kashmiri nondualist' or Śākta (goddess-worshipping) rites, which sanctioned blood sacrifices during communal worship. In these temples, devotees from various backgrounds could gather there, regardless of their caste grouping. These sites were superintended by Pidārar priests, who were subordinate to Nambūtiri Brahmins, for they were nondual tantric specialists who sacrificed animals under regal edict. To this day, royal temples throughout Kerala contain shrines to nine Śākta divinities; interestingly, the same deities are venerated at the Navadurgā temple in Bhaktapur too. For instance, at Mādāyi kāvu—a famous royal temple in Kerala—the Seven Mothers,[5] Gaṇeśa, and Bhairava are enshrined at the site's southern end.[6] And (3) Teyyam *kāvu* or 'sacred groves', which house shrines to indigenous ancestors and Śākta deities (as listed above) who become embodied in lower-caste dancer-mediums, and whose liturgies are convened by their own priests (*kōmaram*). Generally, temples (2) and (3) dovetail in terms of their allegiance to the king through sacrificial rites, whilst Brahmanical temples—concerned with upholding ritual purity—were set apart from them, spatially *and* conceptually.

Unlike other medieval Indic kingdoms (like the Bhaktapurian Newars), there was not a harmonious alliance between kingship and the Nambūtiri Brahmans. Frequently, Brahmans would revolt against sovereign jurisdiction, especially in relation to the regulation and taxation of their temples' land. Here, Dumont's theoretical bifurcation between Brahmin and state power validates the purity-over-power hierarchization, when he states '[…] the Nambudiri Brahmans [had an internal organization that] transcended political frontiers'.[7] During these revolts, it seems Teyyam kāvu became reservoirs of religious power for the state. All Teyyam groves were patronized by a regal lineage (11th Century CE), which was relayed via the installation of the king's patron goddess (*tampurāṭṭi*) at each *kāvu*. In this regard, Freeman notes how King Kōlattiri—disgruntled by Brahmin uprisings in his realm—recruited Tantric-educated Brahmins from Karnataka (and Tuḷu-speaking territories) to manage his royal cultus.[8] Alongside Pidārar priests, these Tuḷu priesthoods—known as Embrāntiri—were entrusted to oversee the priests of Teyyāṭṭam too.[9]

2.1.1 Teyyāṭṭam's Beginnings

The origins of Teyyāṭṭam performances—as we know them today—can be traced, mythologically, to the figure of Manākkadan Gurukkaḷ. As a washerman (*Vāṇṇan*), his origins were humble, yet he was an adept practitioner of *mantravādam*. Even today, he is honored as the founding father of Teyyāṭṭam.[10] Below, I present the myth ascribed to him:

> In the realm of Kōlattunātu [now the Kannur, Payyanur, Nileśvaram, and Kasaragod districts of contemporary Kerala], there resided an Untouch-

5 Brahmāyani, Maheśvari, Kumārī, Vaiṣṇavi, Varāhi, Indrāyani, and Cāmuṇḍi.
6 Nambiar, 'Tai Paradevata', p. 143.
7 Dumont, *Homo Hierarchicus*, p. 154.
8 Freeman, 'Purity and Violence', p. 484.
9 Ibid.
10 An interlocutor explained that Teyyāṭṭam—before the reign of the Kōlattiri dynasty—was akin to 'animistic-like' worship.

> able [*avarṇa*] washer-man [Vaṇṇān] who, with the aid of a *suvarṇa* [*Nayār*] companion, became highly literate and, as a result, was proficient in methods of sorcery and healing [mantravādam]. Having received renown across the kingdom for his sorcery-conjuring abilities he—along with his associate—was summoned to the Palace of Kōlattiri rājā to perform a series of miracles in the presence of the king. Many obstacles faced the washer-man on his journey as a deliberate test by the King, including the absence of a suitable vessel to cross two river confluences. In response, he plucked a betel leaf from nearby and, with the vocalization of certain *mantric* formulae, crossed the first standing upon it [with his Nayār companion]. Standing by the next riverbank, he tamed a crocodile with mantra, and proceeded to the palace. Once in the presence of the King, he was ordered to fashion and embody thirty-nine local custodial deities [*teyyam*], with all equipment and ornamentations that would require many different specialists [dancer-mediums and performers]. Having successfully and effectively incarnated *each* deity in turn, he was praised by the King, who dubbed the lowly-washerman, *Manakkadan Gurukkaḷ*, stating that all his Vaṇṇān progenies would be ratified performers of teyyam in Kōlattunādu, and that his rendition should be replicated across the kingdom.[11]

Whether or not this 'mytho-history' is historical fact is beside the point. Myth and history interlace in South Asian histories, as is well documented. As such, it is difficult to ascertain precisely when this narrative emerged, but an approximation can be made; to be sure, this tale has medieval resonances. In sum, Manākkadan Gurukkaḷ's narrative is a medieval account which describes a lower-caste denizen's mobilization, by the king, into the ranks of his royal cult. In my view, the tale conveys, in myth, the hierarchical dismantlement espoused during Teyyāṭṭam rituals on the ground. On that point, Freeman elaborates:

> [...] among teyyams, there is an explicit alternative basis of hierarchy posed against the Brahmanical notions of purity and pollution, and that is one of royal sovereignty.[12]

---

11 Adapted from two informants' retellings during my field-studies in Malabar.

12 Freeman, 'Purity and Violence', p. 147.

2.1.2 How Malabar Became a Tantric Theocracy

2.1.2.1 *From Cera Polity to Kōlattiri Dynasty: Teyyam, Śākta Tantra, and Nambutiri Brahmins*

In medieval Kerala, Teyyāṭṭam developed as a ritual tradition coterminous with state power, in counterpoint to the autonomy of the Nambutiri Brahmans. At that time, sovereign power perfused into temple environments, throughout the realm, via the installation of subaltern-led Teyyam shrines: put another way, the immanent power precipitated via Teyyam groves—like *śakti*-reflecting satellites—directed their power back toward the king (*peẓumal*) and his devolved provinces. In this way, the non-dual cosmology of Śākta Tantra intermingled with Dravidian notions of immanent power (*kalivụ*) as constitutive of state authority: the heterodox nature of Śākta-Dravidian divinities transgressed caste affiliations; these gods, then, were conjurable by all individuals of the body politic.

When I attempted to understand how royal Tantric religiosity suffused Teyyāṭṭam from the historical standpoint, one interlocutor instructed me:

> [Inf.]: The *teyyam, Mūttappan* [martial deity], for example, is beginning to take on the role of pan-Hindu gods—most say he is the same as Śiva. This [link between the Temple and Teyyam] is because of the binding element of Tantra; it allows different systems and ideas to fuse in Kerala. Goddess narratives [or local folklores in the Aithyamala] also shows changes with Tantra; local goddess incorporated with Tantric goddess [like patron goddess Bhadrakali] that mirrors this cultic incorporation. The Tantric element shows within all [religious expressions in Malabar].

In this account, references to processes of *Tantricization* are being articulated (Michael Carrithers' term *polytropy*[13] is also applicable here). Broadly speaking, between the 8th–11th Centuries CE, the dominant ideological landscape was reshaping across the subcontinent, spurred by several converging socio-political factors: firstly, a process of wide-spread cosmopolitanization dispersed Brahmins and Nāth siddhas from the Gangetic plains after the collapse of the Gupta Empire; in doing so, continual power structure fluctuations ensued. Politically, around 8th–11th century CE, South India's three central polities—*Cōla, Cēra*, and *Pandya*—disintegrated into smaller petty or *poli-*

---

13 Michael Carrithers, 'On polytropy: Or the Natural Condition of Spiritual Cosmopolitanism in India: The Digambar Jain Case', *Modern Asian Studies*, 34.4 (2000), pp. 834–835.

gar kingdoms. These smaller kingdoms (*nādu*)—divided into chieftain-led principalities—rose to power across these areas: in what is now Northern Malabar, one of these realms—the Muśaka dynasty—emerged following a hundred-year war led by *Cēra* monarch, Kūlasekhara. These disintegrated polities—which previously encompassed the Muśaka kingdoms[14]—collectively merged around the 14th Century CE under the Kōlattiri dynasty; the territories of northern Malabar became known as Kōlattanādu. At this time, the Kōlattiri kings adopted Nāth Siddha-influenced Śākta Tantric and Teyyam dances as the religion of their royal courts (*kovilakam*); Kashmiri Tantra, then, became popularized across the kingdom (*swarūpam*) as dominant state religion. In addition, social organization also changed: the patrilineal patterns of Muśaka society were recast into a matrilineal social order under the new Kōlattiri dynasty.

2.1.2.2 *How Did Śākta Tantra Reach the Malabar Coast? Nāth Siddha Migrations*

As I argue later in this section, Kashmir Śākta influences—via movements of travelling Tantric (Nāth) yogis after the Gupta empire's collapse—were brought to Kerala, and, as a result, they melded with Kerala's autochthonous ideologies. On the other hand, the Tantric system of elite Nambutiri Brahmans (also *dakṣināčārya*) was not affected by migrating ascetics; Nambutiri Tantra is a product **only** of Nambutiri Brahmin creation. Though considered indigenous to Malabar, Nambūtiri Brahmins are sometimes espoused, in religious textbooks, as having been mythologically incorporated—as sixty-four families—into Keralan polities from contiguous kingdoms brought by Paraśurāma,[15] the supposed sage of Malabari culture who administered elite temple life.[16] This narrative, however, is rhetorical, for it claims that the Nambutiri Brahmins' elite status was mythically pre-ordained by Paraśurāma himself. Alternatively, Menon suggests that Mayura Sarman (345–375 CE)—an early medieval Kadamba sovereign—summoned Brahmin groups to settle in Tuḷuva and Keralan regions: for instance, groups of Raśtrakauta (proto-Śaivite) and Cālukya Brahmans (proto-Vaiṣṇava) established roots in these provinces. Later, in Northern

14 Details of the Muśaka kingdom—whose regal and administrative centre was Ez̲himala, in today's Kasaragod district—is summarized in a 10th-century Sanskrit poem, called the *Muśakavaṃśam* ('The Chronicles of Mushaka').

15 Across South Asia's Hindu traditions, Paraśurāma is considered one of Viṣṇu's avatars, which might also hint at Vaiṣṇava influences in Malabar. Arguably, many Teyyam divinities, like Viṣṇumūrti, have Vaiṣṇava pedigrees.

16 Gabriel, *Playing God*, p. 14.

Kerala (known, at that time, as Ezhimala), these various Brahman groups unified under the rubric of one order—the Nambūtiri Brahmin.[17]

But how about royal religion? How did distant Kaśmiri Śaiva-Śākta thought circulate to the Malabar coast in the first place? This impasse is contentiously debated among scholars of Śaiva traditions. Sanderson theorizes that Southern and Northern communities (i.e. Kerala's in the South and Newars in the North) may have adopted Kaśmir Śaivism by '[…] participating in a more widespread system, which may have included even the Tamil-speaking regions'.[18] In this connection, Freeman argues that excerpts from Abhinavagupta's oeuvre (Vijñanabhairava verses) are evident in specifically Malayalam commentaries. These commentaries belong to a South Indian priest, Varadarāja, who was a student of Madhurāja, a Madurai-based teacher of Abhinavagupta's teachings.[19] This textual attestation, Freeman says, verifies that Kashmir Śaiva ideas were '[…] in fact found in Kerala in Malayalam script, strongly suggesting the presence and activity of this lineage there'.[20] There is clear evidence that Nāth techniques were appropriated by royal Tantric temples and, thence, by Teyyam rituals. In brief, the Nāth Sampradāya was a tradition of wandering ascetics who abided by a nondual Tantric cosmology that may have stemmed from the Southern Deccan plains (though this is uncertain). Later, these groups and their ideas extended to the North eastern Gangetic plains, including Nepal.

Lorenzen adds how Nāth traditions were borne from pre-existing Śaiva Kāpālika sects.[21] In specific *tōṟṟam* songs (i.e. Bhairavan's song), Freeman detects many references to Nāth Siddhas engaging with royal religion: Bhairavan's tale recounts how Nāth virtousi settled in Northern Kerala through conjugal relationships with local Nāyar women,[22] which in turn instituted the formation of a new caste group in the region's social system, the *cōyi* ('householder yogīs').[23] Overall, some five hundred *cōyi* families were dispersed in the districts of Kannur and Kasaragod, many of whom are connected to the Teyyam groves as members of their administrative committees.[24] Nāth mendicants settled regionally, yet they still formed decentralized networks across the

---

17 Sreedhara A. Menon, *A Survey of Kerala History* (Kerala: DC Books, 1995).

18 Sanderson, 'Śaivism and the Tantric Traditions', p. 663.

19 Freeman, 'Untouchable Bodies', p. 160.

20 Ibid.

21 Lorenzen, *Kāpālikas*.

22 This conjugal pattern of marrying a female above a male's caste designation is characteristic of Kerala's matrilineal system, known as *sambandham*.

23 Freeman, 'Śāktism', p. 195.

24 Nambiar, 'Tai Paradevata', p. 142, ff2.

subcontinent. By practicing modes of Tantric healing during pilgrimage cycles, Nāths engaged with differing populations in Śākta temples that extended to the Kathmandu Valley via pilgrimage sites like Śrīsailam[25] from as far as Malabar's coast. From Pinch's perspective, yogis—from various groups (*ākhāṛas*), including the Nāth—were not solitary or apolitical; instead, yogis were active within a polity, either as warriors or religious advisors for a local king.[26] In this light, I argue politically-active Nāth communities, spread over a pan-Indic network, embraced Śaiva, Kāpālika and Śākta elements in spiraling hybridity. This influence, I presume, must have seeped into Newar and Keralan manifestations of Tantra, which also combine Śaiva-Śākta elements as inseparable.

2.1.2.3 *Tantric Goddesses and Fertility Cults in Kerala*

The influx of Tantric ideas into Kerala had inevitable repercussions on the region's temple customs: the political shift from macro-kingdom to poligar polities integrated Tantra with folk phenomena, like Teyyāṭṭam, which bolstered these systems' authoritative legitimacy as royally aligned religion.[27] Also, pre-Śākta fertility cults—associated with the worship of snake deities (*nāgas*) and nature spirits (*yakṣis*)—were being absorbed into royal religion: many sacred groves were built near *nāga* shrines (*pambinkōṭṭa*) to ensure fertile rainfalls. In *Saints, Goddesses and Serpents*, Arafath stresses that fertility cults had been absorbed into Teyyam performances, with songs describing fertility-enhancing practices, which were based on a 'nontextual, moral, and ritual hygiene concept[ual framework]'.[28] In agreement with Geoffrey Samuel, I argue *nāgas* and *yakṣis*—also prevalent in the Kathmandu Valley—were incorporated into migrating Tantric cosmologies that emerged out of post-Gupta South Asia: goddesses and yoginīs replaced fertility deities, who became their demi-gods. Samuel states:

> [...] the deities known to us as yakṣas, nāgas and the like were replaced as protectors of cities and states by deities we now generally find in these roles: fierce goddesses and gods, often explicitly regarded as transforms of Durgā, Kālī, or Śiva, and with close affinities to the central deities of both

---

25 Prabhavati Reddy, *Hindu Pilgrimage: shifting patterns of worldview of Sirsailam in South India* (London: Routledge, 2014) refers to the presence of Nāth yogis at Srilsailam.

26 Pinch, *Warrior Ascetics*.

27 Freeman also argues that it was a reciprocal borrowing of traditions: Tantric high castes also adopted Dravidian logics of 'formalized possession' and vice versa, see Freeman, 'Performing Possession'.

28 Arafath, 'Saints', p. 104.

> Śaiva Tantra and Vajrayāna. This is particularly true in relation to those deities closely associated with the power of the state.[29]

Samuel's hypothesis is highly convincing: this process of integrating local and transregional ideologies—in the guise of goddesses—seems to have operated on the Malabar coast **and** the Kathmandu Valley.

In this association, Menon states that Tamil goddess Kōttavai, alongside the matrilineal kinship patterns (*morūmakkathīyam*) ascribed to her, assumed three appearances throughout her history in Kerala. These incarnations can be listed as: (1) Durgā—the fierce manifestation of goddess Parvātī, consort of Śiva; (2) Tāi Paradēvata—an indigenous Teyyam goddess; and lastly (3) Bhadrakālī—a goddess encompassing Durgā **and** Tāi Paradēvata, who would later become Kerala's patron goddess of warfare.[30] In time, indigenous fertility cults (*pambinkōṭṭa*) were reconciled with goddess worship, and gradually, this mélange absorbed more Śaiva-Śākta divinities into 'lineages'; in this way, trans-local gods became allied with Kerala's ancestor deities as their clan-kin. I argue this process makes sense, since it is consistent with the Śaiva-Śākta idea that deities form clans. While considered heterogenous *prima facie*, Kerala culture and transregional Tantra were, in fact, recapitulated as related phenomena. In Śākta Tantric texts, i.e. the Brahmayāmala (see § 4.2.2), clan (*kula*) and lineage (*gotra*) links between deities—whether snake-spirits, ancestors, or Tantric goddesses—are common, for they are depicted, iconographically, as kin groups. Sanderson states:

> All yoginīs belong to the family (kula) or lineage (gotra) of one or other of a member of higher 'maternal' powers, and in any instance this parentage is ascribed on the evidence of certain physical and behavioural characteristics.[31]

The idea that Tantric and local deities formed kin-like alliances may appear mythological, but these dynamics also had a tangible cultural reality in temple life. In Malabar, the late-medieval goddess Bhadrakālī—including her many manifestation in Keralan Teyyam—was central as the slayer of Dāruka–known as Mahiśaṣura elsewhere in the subcontinent—at his fort (*kōṭṭa*) near the royal temple. This rendition of Bhadrakālī killing Dāruka (indicated by

29 Geoffrey Samuel, *Tantric Revisionings: New Understandings of Tibetan Buddhism and Tantric Religion* (New Delhi: Motilal Banarsidass, 2005), pp. 96–97.

30 Menon, *Kerala History*, p. 92.

31 Sanderson, 'Śaivism and the Tantric Traditions', p. 671.

Gabriel below) constitutes a vernacular retelling of the Devī-Mahātmya popular across Hindu traditions; in this version, Bhadrakālī is a local form of Durgā:

> [...] the goddess was an object of worship by the residents of Kunnatturpadi even prior to Muttappan's arrival, and when the Muttappan came the Devi accepted him as her son. Her tōṟṟam (songs of praise) suggests she is a manifestation of Kali in her benevolent form (Bhadrakali). She was created by Shiva to end the reign of terror of a fierce demon called Dāruka. A small peak of the Sahyadri mountains near Kunnatturpadi is called Dārikan's kōṭṭa (Darikan's fort).[32]

Here, we can see the way elements of vernacular folklore have *spiralled* into a pan-Indic myth, thereby recreating it as a local one. Historically, I claim this point occurred when Kashmiri Śākta thought was advocated, throughout the land, by Kerala's regal cult. By the 12th Century, I argue Kashmiri Śākta Tantric thought was transmitted to and from Malabar and Northern South Asia, including the Kathmandu Valley, by itinerant movements of ascetic groups, especially the Nāth Siddhas. With Freeman's evidence notwithstanding, another Keralan source describes how wandering ascetics conversed with other religious thinkers on their travels. For instance, a certain Trivandrum manuscript, the *Tantrarājavyākhyā-Manoramā* (18th Century), documents how Śrīkaṇtheśa—a Kerala-trained Brahman, who later renounced as a wandering ascetic—was granted an authoritative position by the King of Kaśī to write a commentary on the Nityāṣoḍaśikārṇava. In short, the Nityāṣoḍaśikārṇava is a text of Kashmir Śaiva and Śrīvidyā[33] provenance, and remnants of these schools survive in Kerala today.[34]

In her recent book, *Hindu Pluralism*, Elaine Fisher describes a similar custom of 'public theology' among Śaiva groups, whereby thinkers exchanged theologies with one another, which enabled the mobilization of thought between differing sects.[35] Thus, this historical interchange of Śaiva-Śākta ideas—across different regions—is relevant for our study: it is clear these dialogues were conducive to the development of Folk Śākta performances as we know them today.

32 Gabriel, *Playing God*, p. 63.

33 Śrīvidyā is a Śākta school of Tantric nondualism that focuses on the benign aspect of goddess Tripurasundarī.

34 N.P. Unni, *Tantric Literature of Kerala* (New Delhi: Bharatiya Books, 2006), p. 304.

35 Elaine Fisher, *Hindu Pluralism: Religion and the Public Sphere in Early Modern South India* (Berkeley: University of California Press, 2017).

2.2 *Interactions between Tantric Texts, Teyyāṭṭam Rituals, and Sacerdotal Communities in Kerala*

In Kerala, Nambūtiri Brahmans, Tantric temples and Teyyam groves were three spatially segregated sacerdotal groups, though *sometimes*, Nāyar worshippers could mediate between them. Put differently: Tantric, Brahmanical, and Teyyam temples—unlike other sites in India—often opened their doors for exoteric Tantric-styled worship, though in a Brahmanical site, only twice-borns were welcomed. It is also true that Teyyam groves and Tantric temple culture overlapped on a regular basis, particularly during temple festivals (*perumkaliyāṭṭam*), which blurred this divide. These festivals were opportunities where priests could communicate in circumstances that were otherwise constrained. In Nileśvaram and Payyanur districts, Teyyam priests established a strong rapport with Tantric specialists, most notably *Pidārar* priests, who made extensive blood and alcohol libations under the auspices of Nambūtiri Brahmans. According to Freeman, this relationship was accentuated at temple festivals, during which *Pidārar* and *kōmamram* collaborated at the festival's sacrificial rites.[36] During my second field-trip to Malabar in 2017, I visited an annual temple festival at Śrī Andalur Kāvu, Thalassery, where such interactivity was perceivable: blood sacrifices were practiced at the site's Northern altars (*vatakkan vatil*), which was cordoned off as an enclosed space between the outer walls of a Tantric Temple, but adjacent to a Teyyam grove.[37]

Such interactions at festivals were not the only times priests could communicate. Tantric, Nambūtiri, and Teyyam specialists also interfaced, indirectly, through engagements with middle-class Nāyar worshippers. Nāyars often installed Teyyam shrines to their family homes (*taravād*), while also being socially elevated enough to worship in Brahmanical temples too. For example, the Nāyar community's patron goddess is Bhadrākālī, who they worship as Bhadrākālī in Tantric temples and Tāi Paradēvata at a Teyyam grove.[38] The Nāyars, then, served as intermediaries between Brahmins, Tantric shrines, and Teyyam priests.

As Freeman notices, such interplay between sacerdotal communities is due to Tantra's popularity in Kerala.[39] Keralan Tantra functioned differently to

---

36 John R. Freeman, 'Formalised Possession among the Tantris and Teyyams of Malabar', *South Asia Research*, 18.1 (1998), p. 92.

37 This is customary in Malabar, see also Freeman, 'Formalized Possession'.

38 Nambiar, 'Tai Paradevata', p. 145.

39 John R. Freeman, 'Texts, Temples, and the Teaching of Tantra in Kerala', in *The Resources of History: Tradition, Narration, and Nation in South Asia: 63–79*, (Paris-Pondichéry: Études thématiques 8, 1999c).

FIGURE 15 Śri Andalur Kāvu, Thalassery, Kerala
PHOTOGRAPH BY AUTHOR

Tantra elsewhere; it is not esoteric or gnostic. Instead, Tantra in Kerala was reformulated as collective, during which priests would manage shrine-worship (*ācāram*) in plain view of their worshippers.[40] And yet, generally, Tantra's accreditation in Kerala is automatically attributed to Sanskrit-trained Nambūtiri Brahmans, who are keepers of the region's Sanskrit manuals.

At any rate, in whatever form, Tantra—with its methods of invoking deities through collective worship—also made a foray (via Tantric temple priests) into Teyyāṭṭam rationale: in this formulation, a deity's power (*śakti*) is roused from its essence (*avahāna*) in the subtle body through visualization (*dhyānā*) and verbalization practices (*śloka* or *tōṟṟam*). This divine essence—once awakened in the body—can be transferred or fixed (*uṟanyuka*) into a prescribed deity's shrine image (*palliyaṟa*) or harnessed by a dancer-medium.

In Paẕangādi, I visited a temple where such practices—officiated by tantric priests—were enacted daily. Like Bhaktapur's Navadurgā temple, the royal site of Mādāyi *kāvu* housed many Tantric divinities i.e. Bhadrākāli, Saptamātṛkas,

40 Ibid., p. 64.

Gaṇeśa, Bhairava, Śiva, and Kṣetrapālan; in all respects, my visit to this temple was an illuminating experience. When I arrived at the temple gate, a mid-day rite (*ucca-pūjā*) was under way; devotees formed orderly queues at the temple's four main shrines to offer obeisance inspected by the Pidārar. Luckily, on that occasion, I was granted permission to join the shrine's collective worship, provided I donned a *lungi* (Maly: *mundu*).

According to Cox, these public forms of Tantric worship were initially derived from textual manuals which, in the medieval period, characterized South Indian culture writ large. He remarks how:

> [...] the middle-period Indic civilizations was pronouncedly a civilization of the book, and that—in their widest possible definition—the Tantric religions especially were fundamentally dependent on written texts.[41]

Cox's observation here could apply to medieval Kerala. Freeman's analysis of Mādāyi *kāvu*[42] shows how consecration practices performed there are traceable to specific codices. For Freeman, Mādāyi *kāvu's* liturgies can be found in two ritual texts: *Tantrasamuccaya* [TS] and *Śeṣasamuccaya* [SA]. These texts are condensed digests,[43] which detail precise measurements for temple layouts and detailed liturgies associated with seven[44] deities. The TS was composed circa 15th Century CE by a Brahmin priest called Cenna Narāyāṇa Nambūtiri. As its addendum, the *Śeṣasamuccaya* provides additional liturgies that encompassed twelve rather than nine deities. The SA also contains ritual instructions for rites of subjugating spirit beings (*adṛśya-mūrtikaḷ*). These spirit beings also feature widely in Teyyam narratives; as we know, spiritual beings—of all kinds—are memorialized in Keralan culture.[45]

Later, Freeman explains how the Tantrasamuccaya—initially composed in Sanskrit—was reprinted in a later Malayalam edition (*Kuḻikkāṭṭu Pacca*) and was in expansive circulation.[46] Once published into Malayalam, Sarma notes that these texts soon superseded any other ritual manuals as liturgical templates for Tantric temple practice. Even today, the manuals remain pre-eminent as textual didactics for Tantric religion.

---

41 Whitney M. Cox, 'Making a Tantra in Medieval South India', (Ph.D. diss., University of Chicago, 2006), p. 28.

42 A more detailed description of Mādāyi Kāvu is provided (in much greater detail) by Freeman, 'Śāktism', pp. 194–195.

43 Unni, *Tantric Literature*, p. 230.

44 These deities are: *Śiva, Viṣṇu, Śaṇkaranarāyāṇa, Durgā, Subrahmaṇya, Gaṇeśa, and Śāstā.*

45 Freeman, 'Texts', pp. 66–67.

46 Ibid., p. 68.

Yet, both TS and SA are partly modelled upon an earlier redaction of the *Brahmayāmala* (7th–8th Century CE—a Bhairava Tantra text (from Kashmir) which systematized nascent Yoginī/goddess cults into later forms of Śākta non-dualism). Generally, the *Brahmayāmala* is a ritual text centred on the cult of Yoginīs, which also itemizes Tantric liturgies i.e. a consecration (*abhiṣeka*), an initiation (*vrata*), and a deity-installment rite (*nyāsa*).[47] In all likelihood, this text was, once, a blueprint for the TS and SA written centuries later. Furthermore, the Brahmayāmala's influence may also have funneled into later renditions of Teyyāṭṭam rituals or, at least, percolated its liturgies to some extent.

2.2.1 Dancer-Mediums and Textual Manuals

As Cox has shown us, a text—or even more so, a liturgical manual—was front and centre of South Indian religious culture during the middle ages,[48] and, for that reason, asking whether textual usage continues into the present is a significant inquiry. If so, a text is a unit—not a nugget of knowledge—that contributes to the making and remaking of living culture. As I emphasized earlier on, texts and bodies spiral in Folk Śākta ritual traditions; retold through performance, texts can assume a multitude of possible forms, from orally mandated myths to detailed liturgies. Though written separately, these oral texts are themselves epistemic parts that punctuate ritual action, to whatever degree. With Derrida's *différance* in mind,[49] an embodied ritual performance must refer to a corresponding myth or narrative to complete its meaning, thereby spiraling ritual with its myths. This hermeneutic observation vis-à-vis *somatic textuality* in ritual aligns with the emic worldview: for Śāktas, bodies are vehicles that can be inscribed, re-shaped, and empowered with cosmic knowledge (gnōsis), or as Flood puts it, 'entextualized'.[50] Bodies, thereby, are imbued with transformative, yet inherent, cosmic meaning, which in Teyyāṭṭam, deifies the medium. This is a central Tantric hermeneutic. This same logic was relayed to me by dancer-mediums and worshippers, too.

When speaking with dancer-mediums about their transformation into deities, they often used phrases like 'elevated bodily (*vigraham*) acuity' to convey this visceral process. They also explained how this somatic transformation—from human to deity—was facilitated by the songs they sung or the symbolic make-up they wore. The human-to-deity transformation, then, synthesizes three internal components within the medium's body, which I label (1)

47 Hatley, 'Brahmayāmalatantra', p. 192.

48 Cox, 'Making a Tantra'.

49 Jacques Derrida, *Limited Inc.*, (Illinois: Northwestern University Press, 1988), pp. 7–8.

50 Flood, *The Tantric Body*.

epistemic, (2) somatic, and (3) spatial. The way these symbolic layers intercalate—through ritual observance—within a medium is what spurs his ontological transfiguration from human to deity. Just as a goddess may embody her *mantric* formulae to bring about creation in Śākta texts,[51] a Teyyam dancer-medium will embody the goddess-clan's mantra and terrestrial power to bring back an ancestor deity within him. For instance, a medium must have his face painted for every ritual. Each line and dot has a symbolic meaning, and for each medium, I was told that five circles drawn on his face conveys three layers of symbolism—(1) epistemic, (2) somatic, and (3) spatial—which, together, engender his divine transformation. I list them here: (1) Mantramūrti, or five deities[52] associated with *mantravādam* or sorcery; (2) *prāṇa* or five 'breaths' of the subtle body; and (3) *bhūtam* or five 'elements' of physical space. Freeman also noticed how bodies, symbols, and space are co-constitutive in Teyyam rites, which is arguably a Tantric notion, and true for Navadurgā rituals, too:

> [use of] heat, light, smoke, fluids, substances, insignia, and weapons ... symbolically ratify and intensify this cognitive and physical transformation [...] the subtle body, the sense, the subtle elements etc. [are] mapped into agriculture, herding, and other images [...] The portent of all these [is] that there is an esoteric knowledge, clearly more-than-the-body, whose access point is the mundane body and mind we all possess, and which has been transmitted as a specifically Untouchable gnosis.[53]

Moreover, the vocabulary used to describe deity transformation in Malayalam—*mukhameẕultụ* and *uṟanyuka*,[54] literally 'face-writing' and 'to join'—resonates with clear allusions to writing. But this is not writing in the conventional sense; *somatic textuality* is not a procedure that embosses a *tabula rasa* with scriptural episteme. It is, instead, a process of marking-out—with symbolic signifiers—what is already immanent, that is, the power of *śakti*. This understanding is also key to other facets of Keralan culture e.g. Kalaripayyāṭṭụ. In that regard, Zarrilli claims that any symbolic embellishment empowers a martial artist's physical strength. Zarrilli continues:

---

51 Biernacki, 'Absent Mother'.

52 The Mantramūrti deities are Ghaṇṭakarṇan, Bhairavan, Kuṭṭiccāttan, Ucciṭṭa, and Rakta Cāmuṇḍi.

53 Freeman, 'Untouchable Bodies', pp. 135–165.

54 Freeman translates 'uṟanyuka' as 'to fix' or 'to abide', both of which reinforce my point that the divine essence is brought to the surface, rather than superimposed. See Freeman, 'Purity and Violence', p. 131. Sometimes 'prātiṣṭha' is said, which also means to 'fix in place'.

> By doing *meiabhyasa* (body art) it is not just an external form, but internal as well, affecting the body's inner channels, and all parts physically. If you do these mental repetitions it will have the same effect as doing it physically [...] it will produce energy.[55]

But how is ritual knowledge recorded and transmitted to find its culmination as ritually embodied? If mythological discourse in ritual is grounded in relation to other metaphysical referents (i.e. embodied or textual), then why are texts largely absent during ritual? Apparently, texts or liturgies are not read during ritual because they are consulted before a performance begins. However, this does not mean that ritual texts were always absent: in Bhaktapur, Ujesh stated that some *paddhatis* he had seen were stained with sacrificial blood.

During my interview with Akash in Kannur, he said his family had numerous texts which they continue to consult. From a cabinet, he produced one from this collection, and it was a delicate palm-leaf manuscript. He told me that this was a family heirloom, and its contents contained advice for healing snake bites or *sarpaviṣa* (Maly: 'snake poison'). On closer inspection, I realized it was an *Oothu* manual: according to Cerulli, *Oothu* are early-medieval medical texts, composed in Maṇipravāḷam, which instruct ritual healers in curative methods for expunging snake venom.[56]

More specifically, these Oothu manuals are ubiquitously Keralan and are related to local *nāga* cults. In time, however, these manuals would acquire a Tantric character as *gāruḍika* texts, also extant in North Kerala. In these manuals, the use of a Gāruḍa mantra ('kṣi pa oṃ svā hā') supplemented the traditional methods (*ooṭhu viṣavaidya*) as set out in the Oothu texts.[57] Apart from verifying that dancer-mediums were proficient healers,[58] he presented the manuscript to corroborate that Teyyam songs were conserved in a similar scriptural format. For Akash, a text like this was read by dancer-mediums across Malabar. Textual manuals, therefore, was **one** way deity-mediums inculcated their songs and liturgies.

55 Zarrilli, *When the body*, p. 142.

56 Anthony Cerulli, 'Unpuzzling and Aporia: Theorizing Acts of Ritual and Medicine in South India', *Journal of Ritual Studies*, 29.2 (2015), p. 33.

57 Michael Slouber, *Early Tantric Medicine: Snakebites, Mantras, and Healing in the Garuda Tantra* (Oxford: OUP, 2016).

58 Freeman, 'Dynamics'.

FIGURE 16 Maṇipravālam manual
PHOTOGRAPH BY AUTHOR

2.3 *Multivalence in the Cosmology of Teyyāṭṭam*

The business of producing a paradigm that encapsulates Teyyāṭṭam's metaphysical complexity is a difficult one. The diverse religious communities that have been instrumental to Teyyāṭṭam over the centuries are varied. As an informant once explained to me: "Teyyam is neither Hindu nor [any] other religion. There are Teyyam deities that were once Muslim, Buddhist, and Jain ancestors that became gods. We shouldn't forget the place of these other traditions in the [development of] Teyyam rituals". Sax problematizes this same issue during the pilgrimage of Nandadevī in Uttarakhānd:

> [...] the tradition was being contested, negotiated, and altered, just as the preceding pilgrimage nineteen years earlier ... I hope thereby to suggest that in dynamic social and cultural contexts, "traditions" and interpretations of them are always changing. But they do not change randomly [...] they are constrained by a worldview—that is, a culture's assumptions about what is real, desirable, and possible—and by politics.[59]

By reducing Teyyāṭṭam to a univocal interpretation (say, Hindu or folk), one compresses the worldview such that other religious worlds are dislodged. To be sure, in any local context, one worldview always supersedes as more ubiquitous; for Teyyam, indigenous or 'Dravidian' elements command the arena. In Kerala, an indigenous cosmology considers deities as non-hierarchical ances-

59 Sax, *Mountain Goddess*, p. 162.

tral persons (*āḷukaḷ*) conditioned by royal power and agricultural fertility. In Dravidian thinking, divine luminosity (*kaḷivu/śakti*) is bound within all human beings and blurs the demarcations of the 'human' and the 'divine'; **any** human is potentially divine. 'Dravidian' culture, therefore, encompasses the world of hero-ancestor apotheosis (*kuḷivīran*), demonic beings, and sovereign goddesses.

2.3.1 Dravidian Ideas: Apotropaism, Ancestors, and Goddesses

Throughout Kerala, Dravidian or folk praxes take the form of apotropaic mantravādam, or rites which strive to eradicate *kanneṛu* (loosely translated as the 'evil eye'). Conducted mostly by Malayan castes, these practices consist mainly of mantra-blowing (*jāppichūṭṭaḷ*) techniques and exorcistic rites. If a household is afflicted with *kanneṛu*, a healer is invited to draw a colour-powder diagram of the goddess, Bhadrakālī, on the floor which absorbs any negative forces. (Collectively, these evil-eye ridding praxes are called *kanneṛupāṭṭu*). Any apotropaic powers can also be transferred to objects like sacred threads (*cāradu-japikaḷ*) or oil which can be scattered in households afflicted with misfortune. As with any Tantric-oriented society, it is possible to maneuver such powers to curse (*kanneru*) or cure (*mantravādam*). These customs are also evident in Arabic-Malayalam healing manuals; among Kerala's Sufi practitioners, a manual called *'Fee Shaifau-n-Nas: Ithu Orunmichu Kootappetta Pazhaya Upakaram Tarjam Kitab'* is used in these communities. Arafath observes that notion of spirits (*naf*) and the evil eye (*ayn*) are compatible with indigenous ideas of *kanneṛu*.[60]

2.3.2 Teyyāṭṭam as a Bricolage Web of Ritual Knowledge

In many Teyyam performances I attended, autochthonous ancestors and goddess-clans, together with Sanskritic deities, inhabited mutually correlative positions. At Pariyāram kāvu, near Thrissur, Kannur (27th November 2015), royal goddess *Thirūvarkkāṭṭu Bhagavati*, was invoked alongside Sanskritic deities *Viṣṇumūrti* (or Narasiṃhā) and *Cāmundi*. Freeman also describes how the Teyyāṭṭam complex integrates polyvalent deities: '[certain teyyams become bestowed on certain groups] mean[ing] that a shrine which has all three of these gods established will employ all three castes on the occasion of celebrating its teyyams'.[61]

Nonetheless, as Freeman explicates, these deities can still be subject to stratification according to *guṇa* or three qualities of existence, i.e. (1) 'San-

60 Arafath, 'Saints', p. 104.
61 Freeman, 'Purity and Violence', p. 177.

skritic'/'Brahmanical' constitutes the highest *sattvic*, or luminous, quality; (2) 'Warrior or ancestral deities', and their link with martial warfare in Medieval Malabar, represent the *rajas*, or matter level of existence; and (3) 'sorcerer or lower caste apotheosized beings' are *tamas*, or dark, in nature.[62] Clearly, the ranking of practices in this manner may have derived from Śaṅkara's Vedantic ideas circa the 8th Century.[63] As is well known, Śaṅkara was native to Kerala, and founded a monastery in the Deccan plains—Sr̥ṉgeri, now Southern Karnataka—some one-hundred miles from the Malabar border.

A tripartite model of Brahmanical hierarchy (viz. *guṇa*), then, can be imposed to rank Teyyam divinities. On the other hand, most interlocutors stressed that such ranks dissolve momentarily in ritual, a process which is advocated in *teyyam* songs too. For sure, the performance's link with kingship means every social body is a citizen and is welcomed there. As already noted, royal religion was influenced by Śākta Tantric precepts of non-exclusivist worship e.g. Sanderson cites a verse from Mālinīvijayavārtika 1.196–197 that shows how Śākta Tantric lineages "may initiate even untouchables".[64] This combination of Śākta Tantric inclusivism with Teyyāṭṭam is further exemplified through tales of local women functioning as priests in ritual, though these cases were very rare.

Mythologically speaking, this inclusivism is also expressed in folkloric tales: the sage Paraśurāma is said to have molded the goddess Mariāmma when he conjoined his Brahmin mother's dismembered head with the body of an untouchable woman.[65] This goddess creation-narrative adheres to Freeman's cultural-linguistic model, which he uses to explain Teyyāṭṭam's metaphysics, namely as a 'pidginization' of 'Sanskritic' and 'Dravidian' typologies.

Pidginization, or creolization, refers to the gradual process where transregional elements are assimilated into a region's cultural-linguistic system. In this model, Dravidian and Sanskritic typologies are neither hermetically sealed nor hybridized, rather:

> [...] these complexes were [not] internally homogenous, nor static, nor independently defined; rather they stood in a reciprocally defining and shifting of identity vis-à-vis each other.[66]

---

62 Ibid., pp. 142–143.
63 Freeman, 'Untouchable Bodies', p. 147.
64 Sanderson, 'Śaiva Age', p. 295.
65 Grahn, *Are goddesses metaformic*, p. 100.
66 Freeman, 'Purity and Violence', pp. 12–13.

Though an intricate theory, Freeman admits that pidginization cannot fully capture the system's complexity, because it assumes a **conflation** of Sanskritic and Dravidian systems. Any 'pidginization' model is dyadic, thereby it does not acknowledge other systems beyond a 'Sanskritic' and 'Dravidian' typology. For instance, some *tōṟṟam* songs address Māppiyla (Muslim) Teyyams, who praise Muslim worshippers with the benediction, '*enṭe Māṭāyi nagarame*' (Maly: "Oh, my community of Mādāyi").[67] Hence, I maintain that religious systems in Kerala organically spiral between 'Sanskritic' and 'Dravidian', 'body' and 'text', to create a *bricolage web of ritual knowledge* which subsume other regional thought-streams. In addition, the influences of Nāth Siddha migrations may also have contributed to Muslim inclusivism in Keralan. Bouillier claims how Nāth hagiographies contain references to Muslim practitioners who had been inducted into Tantric lineages. In the final section of the Śrī Nāth Rahasya (13th–14th Centuries CE), Nāth-Hindu-Muslim integration is described as follows:

> Muslim is also Nath [...] In the puppet made of the five elements [*panc-tattva kā pūtlī*], the Invisible One plays [...] We are born neither Hindu nor Muslim. Follow the six *darśana*, Rahmān. We are intoxicated with God.[68]

Teyyāṭṭam cosmologies, too, are constructed as inclusive web-networks; they are mélanges that condense several metaphysical lines from various Malabari communities. Differing communities have attended Teyyam for many centuries, and their influence has permeated the myths and narratives of Teyyam deities. This plural metaphysical concert—or *bricolage web of ritual knowledge*—allows certain culturally available thought-streams to become pronounced during Teyyam performance. And which specific thought-stream is adduced in each ritual depends on the divinity enshrined and the lineage and location of a grove. This allows several permissible interpretations to be filtered from a bricolage of metaphysical possibilities, which fits the Teyyāṭṭam ritual being enacted.

Within the *bricolage web of ritual knowledge*, the various local and transregional thought-streams constitute, but are not limited to, the following: (1) Brahmayāmala; (2) TA and SA; (3) Kubjikā/Kaula (Western Transmission

67 Sreekanth A. Trikaripur, *Mooring Mirror: A Mooring Mirror between Man and God* (Kerala Folklore Akademi, 2014), p. 201.

68 Véronique Bouillier, 'Nāth Yogīs' Encounters with Islam', *South Asia Multidisciplinary Academic Journal*, [Online] 2015, Source: http://samaj.revues.org/3878, p. 6.

(*āmnāya*)) and Śrīvidya Śākta (Southern Transmission) texts, like NSA, derived from nondual Kaśmir Śaivism; (4) Dravidian mantravādam; (5) Markaṇḍeya-Purāṇa (Devī-Mahātmya); (6) Īśānagurudevapaddhati; (7) Vadakkan Pāttukaḷ (Northern Ballads, Malayalam folk tales, 17th–18th Centuries); (8) A selection of Manipravāḷam healing manuals; and (9) Māppilya (Muslim) lineages. Each manuscript or intellectual tradition mentioned can be found in Kerala—not only in the collections of the Trivandrum Manuscript Archives—but operative within Tantric and Teyyāṭṭam communities themselves.

The idea that multivalent doctrinal stances can be contained within a ritual frame is hardly unfeasible in South Asia: 'plural perspective' is central to Jaina tradition as the notion of *anekantavāda*, or accorded to the Hindu-Buddhism of the Newars, a context which we will re-visit in the remaining sections of this chapter.

3 Navadurgā

3.1 *Newar Tantra, Texts, and Local Deities in Bhaktapur*

In Nepal, Newar religiosity is characterized by the polyvalence of its belief systems, which include Śiva-margi (Śaiva-Śākta), Purāṇic (Smārta), Vedic, and Tantric Buddhist tenets. The term 'Newar' is also intricate: whether 'Newar' constitutes an ethnic designation, a socio-religious category, or some combination of both, is unclear. The only historical mention of 'Newar' available to us is an epigraph on Hanumān Dhoka in Kathmandu.

In this book, my use of the category, 'Newar', adheres to the definition posited by Prayag Raj Sharma, which also complements many ethnographic descriptions I collected in Bhaktapur. 'Newar', then, denotes a (1) urbanized, (2) Indic-influenced, and (3) caste-oriented society, that comprised, (4) three kingdoms of the Nepal Valley. Sharma adds:

> Newar society is another regional variant of a pan-South Asian culture and civilisation nursed in the deep sub-Himalayan valley of Nepal [...] The society of the Nepal Valley was a stratified caste society even before the mediaeval period. Their religions, consisting of the two great traditions of Hinduism and Buddhism, both of Indic origin, tell much the same story historically as anthropological observations have found them to be.[69]

69 Sharma, *Land, Lineage, and State*, p. 53.

Historically speaking, the introduction of 'pan-South Asian culture', as Regmi describes it, came to Newar kingdoms during the Lichhavi period (5th–8th Century CE), where the Kathmandu Valley—politically independent from Gupta imperialism—experienced an influx of Gangetic culture:

> [Nepal experienced] the impact of cultural movements from the south since quite a long time in the past[70]

Linguistically, a Newar's mother-tongue is Nepāḷa-bhāṣa—a language that, in its medieval configuration, evolved from encounters with 'proto-Bengali [and] proto-Maithili scripts'[71] intersecting with a Tibeto-Burmese vernacular. Once localized, the language mutated into three regional dialects: Bhaktapurian Newari, Lalitpurian Newari, and Kathmandu Newari. On the other hand, Newar religious life—with 'Hinduism' and 'Buddhism' at its nucleus—should not, I suggest, be reduced as syncretic. Conversely, Hindu and Buddhist perspectives shift in mutually constitutive relationality, since Buddhism and Hinduism are Tantric in Newar society, which unites them culturally. The same is true for Tantric religiosity in Lalitpur, as Gellner writes:

> Newars do not usually stop to consider which of these [Tantric] views they hold, though most of them will be aware, even if only vaguely, of them all. The peaceful coexistence of these various theories permits all Newars, of whatever background, to participate in the same traditions and religious culture.[72]

In Bhaktapur, Folk Śāktism assumes precedence in the articulation of 'Tantric' practice, although this does not impede Buddhist ones from possible enunciation. For Bhaktapurians, Tantra is characterized by rites of blood sacrifice that placate a ferocious goddess-clan enshrined in scattered *śakti-pīṭhs* around the city.

When I spoke with Newar interlocutors in Bhaktapur, the 'Tantra' they practiced was evoked as an autonomous 'Bhaktapurian Tantric' pastiche. As Gellner reminds us above, any mention of Tantric thought-streams with Newar informants is absent since this knowledge is not known by all. A Bhaktapurian histo-

---

70 D.R. Regmi, *Ancient Nepal* (Kolkata: Rupa & Co, 1965a), p. 81.

71 Sharma, *Land, Lineage, and State*, p. 15.

72 David Gellner, 'Hinduism and Buddhism in the Nepal Valley', in *The World's Religions*, ed. by Stewart Sutherland et al., (London: Routledge, 1988), p. 754.

rian told me that each Newar kingdom—Bhaktapur, Kathmandu, and Patan—established their own style of Tantric religiosity; Patan is more aligned with Buddhist or Vajrayāna Tantra, while Bhaktapur is heavily Hinduized. Hence, in Bhaktapur, it is believed Newar Tantra was shaped by Karmācārya and Rājopadhyāyā Brahmins, who gathered texts and traditions from differing Tantras. When I asked about Bhaktapurian Tantric texts, the historian admitted: "Nowadays we are unsure what texts they use [in practice]". In the Kathmandu Valley, any surviving textual collection is stored in Kathmandu's National Archives; I visited there twice to read their catalogues, in order to glean which texts were locally extant.

3.1.1 Esoteric Tantric Texts in Newar Society: Problems of Access

From an ethnographic stance, if one's task is to ascertain which Tantric texts are used in whichever Indic region, you face an inevitable stalemate. Dyczkowski notices this same caveat in his own expanded article;[73] for him, many ethnographies of Newar society tend to overlook textual materials. Dyczkowski highlights, quite accurately, that none of these ethnographies mention ritual manuals (*paddhati*) in relation to Tantric practice.

Understandably, gaining access to ritual texts used by ongoing religious communities—particularly those texts considered powerful—is not a simple proceeding. I experienced such hindrances during my own field-study, where the texts of the Navadurgā troupe were categorically off-limits for non-Banmala members. Among Newars, Tantric manuals are esoterically shielded from the eyes of the uninitiated—foreigners (*videshihāru*) are principally excluded. Such covertness, I was told, is requisite, insofar as mere awareness of secret tantric knowledge (*vidyā*) by a non-specialist can detrimentally affect a ritual's efficacy. Not only that, Ujesh said that anyone who reads an esoteric text may be cursed with blindness or driven mad by the goddess-clan. For instance, whilst in conversation with a *Vaidya* one afternoon, Ujesh cautioned: "he has many powerful Tantric books [*dherai śaktisali kitabharu*] … if we were to read them, we'd go mad! [*yadi hamile kibabharu padhaichhaũ bhane pāgal jaane chhaũ!*]". Even so, the Banmalas still spoke about texts, including the manuscripts they consulted (*vamśawoli*), and esoteric knowledge they received internally from the deity-within (*bhagavān bhitramaa*). For Newars, a ritual text is esoteric for a reason; in Bhaktapur, that which is esoteric (*jyū*) has formidable power. Therefore, textual esotericism is upheld to guard the uninitiated from the text's unpredictable effects.

73 Dyczkowski, *The Cult of the Goddess*.

Though primarily exoteric (*majyū*), some Navadurgā rites were forbidden. At the Navadurgā temple, I was denied entry to the Navadurgā's *vṛata pūjā*[74] (or troupe initiation ceremonies). I was always told these Tantric rites were too powerful (*śaktisali*) for non-initiates to witness. Outside the Kathmandu Valley, Tantric initiation involves blood sacrifice, though in Bhaktapur, sacrifice is celebrated as a public display. Among Bhaktapurians, worshipping deities with sacrifice is thoroughly mainstream as Bhaktapur's 'religion of power' (as Levy puts it). These rites are linked to Bhaktapur's 'dangerous' divinities—Bhairava and the Nine Durgās—whose allegiance to the king and his militia, 'both threaten and sustain the moral realm'.[75] This moral realm constitutes Bhaktapur's 'religion of moral order', and is concerned with Brahmanical norms of ritual purity (led by Rājopādhyāyā Brahmins). Because of its defensiveness, Bhaktapur's 'religion of power'—blood sacrifice, Tantric divinities, and impurity—is culturally dominant, as Levy elaborates:

> [The 'religion of power'] is systematically *higher* [because] it protect[s] the moral order, [as] the religion of power is the proper religion of kings, *kṣatriyas*, merchants, farmers, and craftsmen.[76]

3.1.2 The Beginning of Navadurgā Performances: Taleju, the Goddess-Clan, and the Festival of Mohani

In positing a dichotomy between Bhaktapur's religions of power and purity, Levy's model conforms with Dumont's famous rendering. Though theoretically sound, I am not entirely convinced by his dyad, which, on the ground, is not a stark opposition. During an interview, a Karmācārya priest claimed that Navadurgā's power (*śakti*) is delegated by Taleju's Rājopādhyāyā priests at her royal temple during the festival of Mohani/Dashain. The *guṭhiyār* who form Taleju's association committee (*guṭhi*) are also amassed from a range of Bhaktapurian caste groups.[77] Unlike Panauti—where a religious division of labour is starker—in Bhaktapur, the king celebrates both 'religions of power' (Tantric religion) and 'religion of the moral order' during a unified ceremony at the royal palace (*lāyaku*).

The Dumontian dialectic between civic power and Brahmanical purity, I suggest, is not applicable in Bhaktapur, for multiplex castes, including Rājopād-

---

74 Refers to collective meditative isolation that all *gaṇa* mediums must observe before invoking the deities they each embody in ritual.

75 Levy, *Mesocosm*, p. 602.

76 Ibid., pp. 602–603.

77 Toffin, *Newar Society*, p. 295.

hyāyā Brahmans, were subject to the Malla's monarchical patronage, which was spotlighted during Bhaktapur's festivals. Drawing on royal diaries, D.R. Regmi describes how Malla kings reigned in a somewhat utilitarian manner:

> Royal powers were absolute in general but these were exercised seldom arbitrarily. The king had to be responsive to the pressure of public opinion ... He had to feel the pulse of the nation at every step and conduct himself respecting popular wishes as otherwise he ran the risk of being overthrown.[78]

During festivals, a kingdom-wide macro-clan disrupts vertical caste relations (though they are still included, to some extent), which the king advocated to hinder protest by theoretically-superior Brahmins, who could supplant his authoritative position.[79] Indeed, under the Malla regime, the nine-month Navadurgā cycle aligns with the realm's military consignment period. The other four months are the monsoon season (see § 2.4.4), which renders festival life—including Navadurgā—*in absentia* as military deployment halts and agricultural processes cease. In this light, Navadurgā performances were rituals that assured agricultural and martial defense for Bhaktapur and its allies, by appealing to, eulogizing, and making bodily-manifest the goddesses whose shrines map the territory. A local historian eloquently sketched his own construal of Navadurgā and Tantric cosmology as follows:

> [Inf.]: You cannot divide Navadurgā from Bhaktapurians—cultural life [*sanskriti*] and Navadurgā are two parts of the same coin. If Navadurgā is the body, then its soul is Taleju [political goddess of the Malla kingship]. The Navadurgā receive this soul by tantric *siddhi* on the tenth day of Mohani. The purpose [of Navadurgā performance] was agricultural and political protection, so in Bhaktapur it had a dual role. This relates to the divine essence [*praṇprothesthān*]. The main principle is the body—if divinity is transferred to clay or stone [*sila*], then why can't divine essence be transferred into the human body? The *vidhi* [techniques] of mantra, yantra, mudra makes this happen. Masks of the Navadurga can be bought and sold anywhere, but they are not proper, ritualized ones, because they are not activated by *vidhi*.

78 Regmi, *Medieval Nepal*, p. 399.

79 Ibid.

The masked dances of Navadurgā rituals—that mobilize divine essence (*prāṇprothesthān*) between Bhaktapurian bodies, spaces, and gods—reassert the togetherness of Bhaktapur's macro-clan. To illustrate further, when the Navadurgā troupe reached Banepa (2nd May 2016), a man proclaimed to me: "Through Navadurgā ... we are worshipping our own inner sense".

Officially, Navadurgā rituals are inaugurated at Mohani—the autumnal festival—during which Durgā destroys demonic beings (*daitya*) represented by *Mahiśaṣura*, the buffalo-demon. In Bhaktapur, Durgā is known as *Bhagavati* or *Siddhi-Lakṣmī*, and during Mohani, she is at her most powerful. At this point, Durgā's supreme power (*parāśakti*) re-connects Bhaktapur's goddesses into a goddess-clan: Taleju, Tripurasundarī, the Eight Mothers and the Nine Durgās.

At Mohani, all caste groups in Bhaktapur offer blood libations to the goddess-clan. By doing so, Bhaktapur's worshippers rejuvenate the polity's militia with the land's agrarian fecundity, all at once: like the goddess-clan, Mohani reconfigures Bhaktapur society in a ritualized macro-clan that transgresses stratified relations. As Amazonne argues, Durgā's ambivalent aesthetics—as a warrior goddess—places her outside societal norms of femininity, just as, during the Mohani festival, the contours of Bhaktapur's social groups have also shifted. Amazzone writes:

> I contend that Durgā's battle is not a literally violent one. She intervenes to stop the endless bloodshed and man-made violence. Durgā engages in battle because she has come to liberate us from a system of oppression, hierarchy, and dominant values. Perhaps she has come to remind us of the passionate [...] and egalitarian values of Śākta Tantric traditions.[80]

Mohani, which loosely translates as 'illusion', impels Bhaktapurian worshippers to see their circadian worlds as temporal structures—epistemologically fluctuating and socially constructed—down to the mercurial deities they venerate. Tantric tenets maintain that such instability releases earthly energies—life-altering and preservative—which, in the past, was harnessed by the king through Durgā, his goddess, but today, Banmala mediums emblemize the crown. During Mohani, the goddess perfuses the city's cosmos, the *maṇḍala*,[81] throughout which she is omnipotent. When the festival of Mohani ends, Dur-

80 Laura Amazzonne, *Goddess Durga and Sacred Female Power* (Lanham: Hamilton Books, 2010).

81 Levy, *Mesocosm*, pp. 242–243.

gā's apotropaic power—now personified by Banmala mediums, the goddess-clan incarnate—is piecemeal protracted to Bhaktapur's citizen at each Navadurgā performance, coordinated by the Banmalas. Navadurgā performances, thereby, re-circulate the agency of the goddess-clan for nine months across Bhaktapur's settlements.

But what about male deities, like Bhairava, in this equation? At other festivals, Bhairava is honoured instead i.e. during Bisket jātrā, he is venerated in the form of a chariot alongside his female consort. Why, then, does the goddess slay the demon, and not the ferociously masculine Bhairava? Indeed, when I interviewed a Citrakār painter (14th April 2016), he unrolled a maṇḍalic depiction of Bhaktapur he himself had painted—it was a beautifully intricate diagram. Gesturing at the centre, he described the goddess Tripurasundari, depicted in union with Śiva. She is surrounded by three edges that form a triangular *yonī*. He also noted how: 'Tripurasundari represents the three elements of place (*thāũ*), but also Brahma, Viṣṇu, and Śiva—creation, maintenance, and destruction. It is nature'.

If a bigendered polarity (*sadāśiva*) creates the goddess-clan's nature, then why is Śiva peripheralized when Mohani convenes? On my second visit to Nepal, a historian from Lalitpur explained further: 'Demons [*daityahāru*] are attracted by the feminine form, and so what does Bhagavati incarnate to kill all demons? She becomes nine beautiful women. Ghatasthāpana [nine demons] are drawn to the eyes of the goddesses, and they become easier to kill. The goddess[-clan] draw the demons with their gaze, and the demons are then destroyed'. The goddess-clan's ambivalent nature—as female sword-brandishing warriors—is a necessity; to secure their victory, the king and male gods must heed and exert feminine energy, a power that solely masculine fighters cannot bring into play. The next section will delve more deeply into the historical arrangement of the goddess-clan in Bhaktapur, and where the Navadurgā fit in this interwoven circuit between the King and the territory's array of feminine divinities—transactions re-formed at Mohani.

3.2 *The Autumnal Festival of Mohani: Transactions between Navadurgā, Taleju, and Kingship in Bhaktapur*

While the Eight Mothers (*āṣṭamātṛka*) and Bhaktapur's boundary deities were installed in the 12th Century under Ānanda Malla's rule, Taleju—the patron goddess of the Malla dynasties as Tulāja-Bhavānī—was not primordially founded in Nepal. Taleju was brought to the Valley because Harisiṃhadeva—a 14th Century Maithila King—was incorporated into the Malla lineage; Taleju was Harisiṃhadeva's enclave goddess. This change naturally reshaped Bhaktapur's divine pantheon for Malla rulers who succeeded Harisiṃhadeva's throne.

According to historical fragments, Harisiṃhadeva came to Bhaktapur after he was deposed at Simraungadh by an imperial Mughal invasion. His administration—along with his dynastic goddess, Taleju—was uprooted from Simraungadh and resettled in Bhaktapur's royal temple (*lāyaku*).[82] The goddess was replanted in a cavity of a temple house; the house belonged to an Agnihotra Brahmin—today, an Agnihotra is a Rājopādhyāyā Brahman—who became the goddess' sacerdotal attendants.[83] Many historians debunk the story of Harisiṃhadeva and Taleju, attesting, as a counterargument, that the story shows that goddess Taleju came to Nepal with migratory flows of Tantric practitioners from Kashmir and the Maithili plains to the Valley, as Mughal clashes in these areas intensified.[84]

Taleju incorporated into the pre-existing Tantric culture; this private system, made public in Bhaktapur, is based on the Śrīvidyā traditions used by Malla kings before 1400 CE. It was, at first, an individualised, yogic prescription detailed in texts, like the Yoginīhṛdaya, for initiates to draw the supreme power of Tripurasundari into the subtle body for attainment of superhuman power. The addition of warrior goddess Taleju to the royal pantheon (Sarvāmnaya or Śrīvidyā) remodelled Tantra as a means of allaying military *political*, as well as cosmic, enmity. Jeffrey Lidke's precis states that this integration—of public Taleju with private Tripurasundari ritual—reformed Bhaktapur's religio-political system as we know it today. Lidke writes:

> Śrī Vidyā Tantra interweaves individuals within a fabric of the Godhead through the complex system of ritual and yogic practices that constitute Tantric Sādhana, while it interweaves individuals within the fabric of society through a variety of social, cultural, and political structures, such as rituals of state, national festivals, city layouts, and royal patronage of temples. Through these esoteric and exoteric systems of practice, the discourse of power is inscribed on the bodies of Tantric practitioners as well as on the bodies of the broader Nepalese populace who have internalized the Tantra-suffused sociocultural taxonomies of Nepāla-Maṇḍala.[85]

82 Regmi, *Medieval Nepal*.

83 Levy, *Mesocosm*, p. 236.

84 Ibid., p. 238.

85 Jeffrey S. Lidke, 'The Goddess Within and Beyond the Three Cities: Śākta Tantra and the Paradox of Power in Nepālamaṇḍala', (Ph.D. diss., University of California, Santa Barbara, 2000), p. 4.

When the armies of Prithivinarāyan Shah conquered Newar kingdoms in the 18th Century CE, Malla sovereignty was annexed altogether. However, the dynasty's legacy was symbolically reclaimed by Newars—once the Shah dynasty took hold—in the continued esoteric worship of the Malla's goddess-clan.[86] These praxes, therefore, salvaged the lost authority of the Mallas in Tantric festivals to revive their agency in Bhaktapur.

The relations between the goddesses—as a sisterhood in Bhaktapur—are at their most heightened during the Mohani festival; the nine-nights (*navarātri*) revering the goddess, in all her incarnations. This festival finds its literary beginnings in the Devī-Mahātmya[87] (Markaṇḍeya-Purāṇa). The narrative recounts the victory of Durgā (also Taleju) over her buffalo-demon adversary, that is also recited at the goddess' shrines throughout the festival. When Mohani begins, she is said to emanate from male divinities as a 'light' (*prakāśa*) that divides into eight goddesses when the demon-king (Mahiśasura) arrives: from Brahmā (god of creation) birthed Brahmāyani, from Indra came goddess Indrayani, and so forth. To nourish the warrior goddesses, each goddess is offered flowers (*swāṃtaki wanegu*) and blood at their shrines on each day of the festival: at Brahmayāni's temple—on the first day of Mohani—she is offered coconuts and a buffalo, tied down and slaughtered at her feet.[88] Each goddess is worshipped in the same way on each day; this circumambulation is called *cāḥdankā wanegu* in Newari.

In domestic settings, the goddesses' diffusion into the home is represented by a soil-filled vessel (*khoṇcā*), that, like a shrine, is offered beaten rice (*baji*) and vegetative items. The goddess-clan's sword (*khadga*) is also worshipped in the household. Parish cites a simile used by Bhaktapurians to highlight the festival's dual focus on warriorhood and agriculture: the 'barley shoots are sword-

---

86 David G. White, 'Introduction' in *Tantra in Practice*, ed. by David G. White, (Princeton: Princeton University Press, 2000), p. 34.

87 I had arranged a visit to search the National Archives in Kathmandu during my second trip to Nepal, and discovered two differing redactions of the *Devī Māhātmya* whilst scouring their archival materials on religion: one version in Sanskrit (no doubt imported from elsewhere in the Indian subcontinent) and another in Newari. Dating this literature proved difficult, but to place their origins approximately 8th–10th Centuries CE seemed most logical (in line with approximations based on other versions of the text elsewhere in South Asia). I list them here:

(1) *Devī Māhātmya A333/19* (*Skanda Purāṇa*; *Devībhāgata Māhātmya*; Manuscript name: *Māhātmya 102*) [Sanskrit—Devānāgari Script]

(2) *Devī Māhātmya A333/29* (*Durgāmāhātmya*: Manuscript name: *Māhātmya 102*) [Newāri—Devānāgari Script].

88 Toffin, *Newar Society*, p. 322.

like'.[89] The Devī-Mahātmya 89:12 also condenses the festival's effects on civilians who partake in the Goddess' grace:

> [Durgā spoke:] And at the great annual worship that is performed in autumn time, the man, who listens filled with faith to this poem of my majesty, shall assuredly through my favour be delivered from every trouble, and be blessed with riches, grain and children.[90]

To guarantee the goddess-clan's concordance on the eight day, twenty-four buffaloes led by a larger unmarked animal (*niku thū*)—all bred in the hinterland area of Byāsi—are brought to Taleju's temple via a processional route called *mei tale*. They are decorated with red vermillion powder and fed rice-wine (*aila*), which makes them wild (*jangali*), as demons should be. A Rājopādhyāyā Brahmin—carrying the Malla dynasty's sword (*khadga*)—and a butcher stand at the gate to greet the procession.[91] At the Taleju shrine, buffaloes (and goats) are sacrificed and their blood is splattered on her image.

At their temple, the Navadurgā troupe sacrifice a sheep to the leading goddess of the Navadurgā-clan, Mahālakṣmi—their main clan goddess—in a ceremony called *āgaṅ pūjā*, where dancer-mediums drink blood from the sheep's jugular vein. This act prepares the performers for the receival of Taleju and Tripurasundari, which will occur at the Brahmayāni temple on the festival's ninth and tenth days (outlined in § 2.4). As is reinforced in Levy's ethnographic survey: 'These sacrifices, like the previous ones, represent the strengthening of the Goddess in preparation for her battles, and thus Taleju is here conjoined with Bhagavatī'.[92]

3.2.1 Goddess-Clans as a Ritual Sisterhood

At Mohani, Bhagavati is aggrandized in her supreme form, in which she demands buffalo sacrifice at each of her sisters' shrines in return for her command over life, death, and the malignant demons. For that reason, many goddesses—Taleju, Navadurgā, *āṣṭamātṛka*, Kumārī—receive sacrifice and are worshipped consecutively on each day of the ten-day festival. I would often ask Ujesh as to the relationship between these goddesses and the legions of

89 Parish, *Moral Knowing*, p. 30.

90 Devī-Māhātmya 89:12, trans. by F.E. Pargiter in *The Mārkaṇḍeya-Purāṇam: Sanskrit Text, English Translation with Notes*, by Shastri, Joshi, (Delhi: Parimal Publications, 2004).

91 Levy, *Mesocosm*, p. 535.

92 Ibid., p. 536.

shrines she occupied in the city. I was continually reminded that Bhagavati—as accessed during Mohani—is the active **whole** that infuses all Bhaktapur's goddesses as ritual kin, whom Newars worship as individuated vehicles, each with their unique functions and dispositions. When I conversed with Ujesh's paternal uncle, he clarified the relationship between Taleju and Navadurgā as comparable to two sisters:

> [MM]: Are the Navadurgā goddesses related to Taleju? How?
> [Inf.]: It is a relation like that of a sister [*bahinī*]—Taleju is an elder sister. Both are from the same family [*ustai pariwaar*]. Taleju looks after the Navadurgā ... On the ninth and tenth day of Dashain, Navadurgā and Taleju [both sisters] meet.

On reflection, three categories of distinct, but intersecting, kin-related (*gotra*) goddesses reside in the civic space of Bhaktapur. Like our *spiraling web-like ritual network*, this tripartite divide also parallels the vision of Śākta power as a tripartite trident: Parā (cosmic body in a manifested form), Parāparā (collective body) and Āparā (individual body). Each Bhaktapurian goddess was introduced by a differing Malla king incrementally over three centuries. I list them here: (1) Tripurasundarī and eight *āṣṭamātṛka*—boundary goddesses that prevent cosmic attacks by invisible malevolent beings (12th Century CE, under the rule of Ānanda Malla); (2) Taleju and living goddess Kumārī—political goddesses that enabled military fortification (14th Century CE); and (3) Mahālakṣmi or *Sipha dyo*—a goddess who receives her energies from (1) and (2) for the amelioration of agricultural maintenance, the militia, and Newari apotropaism (*mikhā wanegu* (evil eye)). Mahālakṣmi is a personification of the entire Navadurgā-clan and is, therefore, the Banmala clan's deity.

Like the connectedness created in Navadurgā performance, the power of these goddess 'families', together, form a macro-clan, to such an extent that Bhaktapurians saw *āṣṭamātṛka* and Navadurgā as inextricably related (which exacerbated my initial misunderstanding about the two goddess-clans in Bhaktapur). As described in § 2.4.1, Taleju's power is passed to Navadurgā dancer-mediums at the point between ninth- (*nauomi*) and tenth days (*dasami*) in an esoteric elevation rite (*thā puja*). At the annual cycle's end, this power is extracted by a Karmācārya priest during Bhagasti; this pivotal power exchange, I argue, is key to the Navadurgā's duplex power. Through this transaction, Navadurgā becomes a 'military' and an 'agricultural' system. In traversing the territorial limits of the Bhaktapurian kingdoms, Navadurgā ritual emerged as a technology for the monarchy to purvey cosmic-oriented energy (Tripurasundari) and state power (Taleju)—through *quid pro quo* blessing-exchanges—

to lineages connected in a binding matrix, that was, in the medieval period, presided over by the king himself.

3.3 *Navadurgā Performances, Banmala Mediums, and Somatic Texts*

Apart from some historical approximations that place the Navadurgā performance's formation circa 1500 CE, its beginnings remain an oral tale, still told by Banmala members. It is said the Navadurgā performance was inaugurated by Suvarna Malla as a denouement that brought rains to quell a drought which destroyed the kingdom's crops. Only one other known source directly cites the Navadurgā performance, and that is a monarchical diary (Thyāsapu F): in an entry dated Āśvin 827VS, the king describes a 'Gāthu pyākhaṇ or Ikhuanala pyākhaṇ',[93] which was, at that time, a term for Navadurgā dances. For now, I will recount the origin story of Navadurgā as told and set forth by Banmala interlocutors (Another version of this origin story can be found in Levy's book):

> [The narrative is set during the sovereignty of Malla king Guṇa Kamanā Deva]. Hidden among the Jwāla woods, on the way to Nala towards the Northeast of Bhaktapur city, lived nine ferocious goddesses. Frequently they would catch unsuspecting humans on the path, kill them, and drink their blood, as sacrificial libations to maintain their powers. On the road one day was a teacher named Sunandā, and he was seized by the goddesses. They said to him: 'what is your final wish?', and he replied cleverly: 'I wish that all of you be shrinked from your full forms'. Granting his wish, they began diminishing into a smaller form (unaware of his Tantric mastery). Sunandā—using a series of *vidyā* gestures and *mantra*—began tying them together and trapped them. In despair, they apologized profusely, swearing they would not kill him, if only he let them go. Disbelieving their promises, he placed them in a basket and brought them to a locked room within his house in Bhaktapur.
>
> Following some attempts at placating them, he sought the aid of his *guru*, who was a skilled Rājopādhyāya priest called Somarā. He moved them to a room in his house, and began secretly sacrificing to them, and teaching them mudra and mantra (that would form the basis of the Navadurgā performance). He had two wives: one of higher and one of lower caste, and he warned them not to enter the locked room where the goddesses was stored. One wife—acting on her suspicion and jealousy—opened the door. They escaped filled with rage; this ferocity meant that

93 Regmi, *Medieval Nepal*.

> they slaughtered a pig [*sungur*] on their way back to the forest, so that the Brahmin could not catch them again and return them to his house [as a pig is 'polluting' for Brahmins]. Having found them again, the Brahmin pleaded with them to return, and the Navadurga stressed that they could continue to be worship, but only in the form of embodied dancer-mediums. The Brahmin chose the gardener caste [*Gāthā/Banmala*], to which the Banmala representative replied ecstatically: "Yes, we can handle these goddesses, we are very happy as these gods will help us by bringing us good luck" Following this, the Banmala were trained by the Sunandā [Karmācārya] and Somarā [Brahmin], and so began the *pyākhaṇ* of Bhaktapur.[94]

In this mythological account, the Navadurgā is described as a clan of wild goddesses, in the forests, who required pig sacrifice to placate them. In social terms, the Navadurgā's feral nature were deemed too antinomian for the likes of Karmācārya priests to control. To conduct their awesome power, the Banmala gardeners—familiar with the dangers of the woodlands—were selected by King Suvarna Malla to cultivate and transform their transgressive energies for instrumental purposes. A Bhaktapurian historian I interviewed said the term for a Banmala dancer-medium, *ujāju*, derives from the Bengali term *ojhā*, which means 'sorcery'. Though not directly explicated in the narrative above, a medium's use of Tantric sorcery (*tantra-mantra*) and terrestrial power (*śakti*) in Navadurgā ritual can assist a Bhaktapurian with social issues. As a matter of course, Banmala dancer-mediums are consulted to heal maladies; bring rainfall; ensure crop success; grant fertility to couples; and pacify demonic forces.

Through Tantric tutelage, these techniques were transmitted between Banmala troupes and Karmācārya priests. As scholars of Newar Tantra are aware, these Tantric practices derive from traditions of Kashmir Śaivism (and remnants of Kāpālīkā praxes) fused with the Śrīvidyā systems brought to Nepal by householder ascetics (*Nāth Sampradāya*). As Regmi mentions, references to Bhaktapur's Tantric practices are found in *Yāmala* literature cited by Kashmir Śaiva scholar, Abhinavagupta. The demon-effigy rite (*ghantāsur*) at Bhaktapur's *Gotamangal* festival is a case in point, since its origins are embedded within the Rudrayāmala.[95] Furthermore, Hatley shows how, in Brahmayāmala 54, Tantric adepts use the 'eight mother mudras' (*mudrāpīṭhādhikāra*) in ritual, which was emulated by Navadurgā mediums during their dance sequences.[96]

94 Adapted from Banmala retellings, and Levy, *Mesocosm*, pp. 503–504.

95 Regmi, *Medieval Nepal*, p. 662.

96 Hatley, 'Brahmayāmalatantra'.

Many times, I asked Navadurgā ritualists if they ever consulted Yāmala texts as a part of their performative training. I was told that one text in particular—known in local parlance as *vaṃśavāli*—was read by the Nāyo to annually determine the distribution of deities to dancer-mediums each year; this process changed with each new cycle. Puzzled, I inquired how one written document—dated to the medieval period—could calculate future deity-to-medium delegation. At first, the mediums remained tactiturned on this matter; this was certainly an esoteric process, and it remained that way until Krishna agreed that I had accrued enough knowledge to understand the process. In discussion with Krishna, he explained how one troupe-member intuitively receives these annual role changes each year—as if by shamanic means—from the 'deity-within-his-body' (*bhagavān bhitramā*). It was this unconscious correspondence between the internal divinity and a dancer-medium which determined the cyclic delegation of each deity-to-medium, which would later be annotated in the temple's text (*vaṃśavāli*). Krishna stated:

> *bhagavān bhitrābata abhilekh dharmagranth raamro bicar ra śakti aaune. Ani tyaspacchi wahāle lekhne hunchha sabai guṇa mancheharulai ko lagi* [From the divine within, he receives the religious writings, good thoughts, and power. Afterwards, he will write these down for all the troupe members].

Somatic experiences and internal visions of the goddess are not uncommon in nondual Śākta Tantra: the Brahmayāmala 157: 25–56—vast recensions of which were catalogued in the National Archives—brings to our attention the goddess' ontological presence within her initiates' bodies; she is sometimes imagined as an additional limb (*āṃśa*):

> Through this yoga [...] the clans of the groups of Mothers and Yoginis, [and] of Sakinis bestow Siddhi on the Sādhaka [initiate]; and they speak the true essence—the highest scriptural wisdom arising from the clans[97]

In these descriptions, a transference of 'scriptural wisdom' is generated between internal divine self (*bhagavān bhitramā*) and enshrined gods/goddesses they invoke. Among Newars, civic goddesses are independent entities that can intercept the *bhagavān*—like radio-wave frequencies—to become active within them through 'divine play' (*līla*). For example, one morning,

97 Brahmayāmala 157: 25–56, trans. by Hatley, 'Brahmayāmalatantra', p. 16 f. 47.

Ujesh's cousin suddenly announced to the group: 'I have seen god [*dyo*]'. Because Navadurgā troupes are frequently enmeshed in ritual kin bonds, the dividing lines separating human and divine, from their perspective, seems to interlace, overlap, and attune ceaselessly. Theoretically, in Durkheimian terms, the sacred and profane are negotiated within the body of a virtuoso through non-linguistic forces that transcend language. Telepathic emotional transference, therefore, characterizes collective consciousness, as Louise Child indicates:

> [...] because collective consciousness is based upon an intensity of energy, I suggest that both Turner and Durkheim refer to a level of communication between beings which is beyond language and therefore, to some degree, unconscious and almost telepathic in nature.[98]

3.3.1 Newari Concepts: Witchcraft

The essential fibre of an 'internal god-within' (*bhagavān*)—like their clan goddess, Mahālakṣmī/Sīpha dyo—is a conglomeration of Śākta Tantra with native Newari concepts of apotropaism. These are: (1) *atma wanegu*, an unconscious spiritual attack, in which an individual envies the food consumption of another, resulting in the contamination of his/her food, inflicting them with illness (*pet dukhyo*); (2) *mikhā wanegu*, another version of spiritual misfortune focused on non-food related jealousies and disputes; and (3) *waheli wanegu*, a curse foisted by a deity, usually if you have displeased the god/goddesses in some way. These folk logics are associated with witchcraft (*bwāksi*), the malefic accompaniment to Tantric techniques (*siddhi*). In addition, *bhagavān* can be applied as witchcraft's antithesis—a moral compass that guides the behavior of Bhaktapurian citizens, which brings about the materialization of 'good thoughts' (*raamro bicar*) within them. In this way, the *bhagavān* is a porous nexus in human bodies that acclimatizes mediums with a web-network of divinities and powers that pulsate as the circulatory lifeblood of Bhaktapur.

3.3.2 Navadurgā Performers and Nāth Ascetics

According to the royal diary entry (Thysāpu B) that mentions Navadurgā explicitly, Navadurgā dances were performed to bring rains during a drought, which it did, as later diary-entries also support. The oral origin story—of earlier provenance—however, makes no detail of this. Following Geoffrey Samuel's

98 Child, *Tantric Buddhism*, p. 32.

hypothesis in § 4.2.1.2.3, this discontinuity, I suggest, may be linked to the later assimilation of snake-spirit worship (nāga)—who were bringers of rainfall—and the role of harvest god, *Bungah dyo* (Matsyendranāth) into Bhaktapur's Navadurgā performances. In this connection, Ujesh often described the Kathmandu Valley as a basin which was once a mythical lake. He recounted how, with his sword, bodhisattva *Manjuśri* drained the water to tame the lake's fierce demigods (*yakṣas*) and snake-spirits (*nāgas*), known collectively as *chephah* in Newari. These meteorological deities became consecrated in temples to ensure harvest rainfalls in the Valley.

Additionally, McCoy Owens stresses that the festival of Rato Machindranāth in Patan reveres Matsyendranāth, a deity who was brought in the form of a bee to restore the rains during a severe drought. (It is said that Matsyendranāth was originally destined for Bhaktapur but was re-diverted to Patan at the last minute).[99] Matsyendranāth is known as the leader of the Nāth Sampradāya, a group of predominately householder *yogis* who worship goddess Tripurasundarī. Nāth hagiographies narrate how *yogis* could induce miraculous feats through their extreme bodily praxis; Mallinson writes how Nāth yogis: '[…] use of the *siddhis*, [for] the ability to fly or to break droughts'.[100] Competent Nāth householder yogis were, in Newar accounts, respected by the Valley's Malla kingdoms. Nāth siddhas administered many aspects of royal religion and, even today, Nāth practitioners reside at Paśupathināth's temple complex.

From my own fieldwork insights, I noticed clear confluences between Matsyendranāth, Nāth ideas, and Navadurgā dances, which I list here: (1) the Navadurgā performers pay their respect to the goddess Karuṇāmāyā, also Matsyendranāth, during a performance in Nala (a Newar town which was historically allied with the Malla kings of Bhaktapur); (2) the Navadurgā rite of *nya-lakegu* (fish-catching) can be linked to the figure of Matsyendranāth, whose name translates as 'Lord of fishes'; (3) the Navadurgā cycle's first performance after Mohani is conducted at Paśupathināth (they could have potentially communicated with Nāth yogis there); (4) Navadurgā mediums describe their healing powers as *siddhi* (as do Nāth practitioners); and (5) the Śrīcakra ritual of the Nāth—as prescribed in the Nityāṣodaśikarnava 2.32—was used for the prevention of disease, which is cognate vis-à-vis Navadurgā temple rites.

With all this evidence considered, we could surmise that, at some point in the 16th Century CE, Nāth weather-controlling abilities **may** have flowed into

99 Bruce M. Owens, 'Accounting for Ritual in the Kathmandu Valley', in *Sucāruvādadeśika: A Festschrift Honoring Professor Theodore Riccardi Jr.*, ed. by Todd Lewis & Bruce M. Owens, (Kathmandu: Himal Books), p. 105.

100 Mallinson, 'Nāth', p. 18.

Bhaktapur's Navadurgā performances. I attest that the Navadurgā ritual is a Newar corollary to Nāth practice. Milan Ratna Shakya also notices the Nāth influences of Navadurgā dances:

> The offbeat aesthetic stance of Nāth is fervently represented by the […] assembly [of] nineteen-members as *gaṇa*. In this cluster of masked images depicting the spiritual spectrum of the three spiritual spectrum of three spiritual qualities of sattva, rajo, and Tamasa […] Bhairava is also considered as Kabandha, one of the redeemers from the shackles of saṃsāra.[101]

I do not, however, present Navadurgā performances and Nāth ideas as mutually exclusive; on the contrary, I claim that the metaphysical notions of the latter could have added to the interpretations of the former. Like Teyyāṭṭam, Navadurgā's metaphysical tapestry is constructed in several lines of Tantric thought and practice, that include: Śaiva Kāpālika tradition, Śākta streams, and Newari apotropaism in combination. Levy makes this clear in his description of Bhaktapurian religious life:

> Experience in Bhaktapur is greatly more complex; multiple points of view are not only possible but forced upon people. Living systematically in shifting and contrasting worlds, many citizens of Bhaktapur are forced into an epistemological crisis, forced to the understanding that external reality, as well as self is constructed, and in some sense illusory, or in the Hindu philosophical expression, Māyā.[102]

Like the clan goddesses themselves, it seems multiple metaphysical tenets—as somatic texts—dance among and through the city's macro-clan.

4 Conclusion

In retrospect, the metaphysical ideas of both ritual performances—from the mid-medieval period to the 21st Century—are varied and numerous. The regional cosmologies of Newars and Malayalis are connected as an osmo-

101 Milan R. Shakya, *The Cult of Bhairava in Nepal* (Kolkata: Rupa & Co), pp. 23–24.

102 Levy, *Mesocosm*, p. 31.

sis of folk praxes, textual flows, Śaiva Kāpālika, and Śākta Tantric thought—circulated by emigrating priests and Nāth siddhas—which were popularized in Indic kingdoms from 9th Century CE. These flows of Tantric ideas precipitated this union, for they were adopted by various sovereign rulers across post-Gupta South Asia (Mallas in Bhaktapur, or the Kōlattiris in Northern Malabar). This environment of assimilation created inclusive *bricolage webs of ritual knowledge* in these realms, which would subsequently shape the cosmological underlays of Teyyāṭṭam and Navadurgā rituals in later centuries.

As mentioned in the Introduction to this chapter, textual manuals (*paddhati*) were, initially, used to carry out royal Tantric rites; to this day, the Devī-Māhātmya is still read during the festival of Mohani in Bhaktapur. However, in the context of Teyyāṭṭam and Navadurgā, textual manuals have become subsidiary, for the medium's body has become the text. By spiraling 'body' and 'text' in ritual—be it through singing stories or using symbols—dancer-mediums channel their *territoire* ancestors, which transforms their bodies into texts. And this shift to *somatic textuality* in Folk Śākta ritual means that deity-mediums—incarnating the past in the present, or text in the body—can remember, and resurrect, the land with all the many metaphysical ideas it accrued with the passage of time.

CHAPTER 5

Sacrifice, Earth Cycles, and Self-Reflexive Affect

1 Introduction

Interlaced at varying points throughout this book, I have raised the import of blood sacrifice. Sacrificial rites are omnipresent in the Kathmandu Valley and, to a lesser extent, in Northern Malabar as effective practices that catalyze specific social functions. Therefore, the *raison d'être* of sacrifice is closely associated with group matters. In these locales, blood sacrifice is actuated either on an animal victim or substituted by a vegetative symbol at a deity's shrine.

This chapter will explore customs of blood sacrifice in Bhaktapur and Northern Kerala. Throughout South Asia, sacrificial practices have been denounced by a range of groups, especially renewal movements (ISKCON, Theravāda Buddhism etc.) and bourgeois activists, who condemn sacrifice as animal cruelty. From their perspective, sacrifice is an outdated shibboleth that inflicts unnecessary suffering on an innocent scapegoat. However, Folk Śākta practitioners continue to defend sacrifice, and persistently offer blood to their divinities with some regularity. This defense, I claim, may be bound up in the view that sacrifice has social value for Bhaktapurian and Malabari denizens. My informants stressed that meat from a sacrificial animal is always gifted to a dancer-medium troupe. In this fashion, a sacrificial rite procures many power-inducing functions which cannot be tended effectively by any other means, thereby rendering the practice justifiable. In Nepal, even strict vegetarians consider sacrifice a highly efficacious act; according to Adhikari and Gellner, one Vaiṣṇava adherent was 'convinced that blood sacrifice was the only way to avoid a dire astrological conjunction for his family'.[1]

In parallel with Folk Śākta's *ritual network*, I suggest blood sacrifice—in Malabar and Bhaktapur—also operates on three levels. Here, Hubert and Mauss' theory on sacrifice may resonate, when they assert that sacrifice has three designated, but separated functions:

1 Krishna Adhikari & David Gellner, 'Ancestor Worship and Sacrifice: Debates over Bahun-Chhetri Clan Rituals (kul puja) in Nepal', in *Religion, Secularism, and Ethnicity in Contemporary Nepal*, ed. by David Gellner et al., (Oxford: OUP), 2016, p. 257.

 | DOI:10.1163/9789004439023_007

> In this festival, three actions must be distinguished: (i) the death of the victim, (ii) communion, (iii) the victim's resurrection.[2]

Yet, during Folk Śākta sacrifice, these three actions tend to *intertwine*; as already explained, everything in Folk Śākta performances converge in mutually constitutive web-networks.

In our context, then, a sacrificial victim—integrated in a network of coordinated agents—is slain in such a way that its dismembered body unleashes the terrestrial power (*śakti*) that co-substantially binds all locally-contained phenomena. By that means, Tantric sacrifice is communion with the body (and *śakti*) of an ancestral goddess-clan, whose presence courses through the veins of the polity. By ingesting sacrificial meat, the person absorbs divine power for reasons of apotropaic security; in other words, a transubstantiation of blessed *śakti*—as an edible gift—produces ritual kinship. Thence, the victim must be an animal or vegetative surrogate, whose body becomes an edible benefaction—offered to the goddess-clan—that **regenerates** tellurian power for communion across the ritual network.

At a deeper level, sacrificial rituals in Kerala were viewed as *self-reflexive practices*, where a devotee, on an existential level, identifies with the victim's untimely fate. The act of identifying a sacrifice with the 'self' provokes a cognitive reflection; for my informants, sacrifice revealed the fragility of our own worldly existence and, particularly in Bhaktapur, the fragility of the society at large. Bhaktapurians certainly viewed sacrificial animals—pigs, goats, chickens, and buffaloes—as representations of societal flaws (*phohor ko samāj*), be that hierarchical stratification, or malevolent forces (*daitya*). With the victim's death, both society and fierce deity are appeased; the problem has, thus, been eradicated. Taken together, I argue that blood sacrifice (a) represents and, therefore, regenerates ritual kin relations, which, resultantly, (b) spurs cognitive self-identification with the victim, so that (c) the group experiences effervescent emotions of shared alarm, fascination, and strength. In Bhaktapur, this collective response—what I henceforth label *self-reflexive affect*—was evoked by Grieve's Newar informants as 'the shivers' (Newa: *jhinjan minjan*).[3] As per Folk Śākta logic, then, a bleeding victim exteriorizes several somatic processes all at once, namely those intrinsic to territory and bodies, i.e. birth, menstruation, hunting, warfare, and death. Put simply: sacrificial rituals, at the centre of these rites, **spiral** sacrificial victims with the sacrificers' selves. This chapter

2 Henri Hubert & Marcel Mauss, *Sacrifice: Its Nature and Functions* (Chicago: University of Chicago Press, 1964 [1898]), p. 68.

3 Grieve, *Retheorizing Religion*, p. 105.

will also consider the activism of those who oppose sacrifice altogether (e.g. ISKCON), and the ways Teyyāṭṭam have responded to their criticisms by use of blood substitutes, thereby lessening the number of victims.

2 Teyyāṭṭam

2.1 *Chicken Sacrifice at the Northern Altars: Terrestrial Goddesses, Warfare, and Communion*

For all Teyyam performances, a specific juncture is reserved purely for the giving and receiving of offerings. Within a ritual's timeframe, this stage succeeds the rite through which the medium becomes that deity (*Veḷḷāṭṭam*). At this stage, a donor can offer a blood libation to the dancer-medium: whether this offering is a chicken sacrifice (Maly: *kōḻi*) or a vegetative substitute (coconut) is determinant on the divinity's nature. As we shall see, not every deity in a Teyyam pantheon requires sacrifice; only goddesses of the royal clan or heroic warriors (*kuḻīvīran*) are dynamized by blood. These deities—once embodied—are offered sacrifice at a crucial point in the rite, a point where a medium has transformed into the named deity.

During each Teyyāṭṭam performance, it is the priest (*kōmamram*) who enacts sacrificial rites. In ritual, he selects a chicken, waves its body in all cardinal directions, and stuffs some rice grains into its beak. Before the chicken is sacrificed, the priest plucks a few feathers from its neck, and casts them upon the altar of the Northern shrine (where the Teyyam medium is perched on his stool).[4] Its jugular vein is cut over a bowl of blood substitute (*guruti*), in order that droplets of its blood splash into the substitute liquid. This action transubstantiates the red-water into an entire bowl of chicken blood, which, I was told, quenches the deity's thirst.[5] The 'blood'-filled cauldron is emptied at the feet of the medium, and a benedictory phrase is uttered: '[...] May a great blessing come to the sacrificer, his patron, his cattle, children, his crops and produce',[6] to which the *teyyam* replies, '[...] I am happy—very happy'.[7] Cosmologically, interactions between divinities, persons, and their territories are consubstantial in Tantric societies, that is to say, a sacrificial animal—as a blood libation—revitalizes the shared essence (*śakti*) of the body politic as a menstrually synchronized macro-clan. For Hubert and Mauss, these rites are

4 Freeman, 'Purity and Violence', pp. 266–267.
5 Ibid., p. 267.
6 Ibid., p. 284.
7 Ibid., p. 284.

'agrarian sacrifices', where the victim—fed with 'firstfruits' or 'rice-grains' of the new harvest—regulates the social group's relationship with its territorial environs and paddy-fields:

> It [victim] has embodied the divine spirit immanent in the firstfruits it has eaten. It becomes that spirit, so much so that its slaughter is a sacrilege. The victim of the agrarian sacrifice always represents symbolically the fields and their products. Thus it is brought into contact with them before the final conservation. In the present instance the bullock eats the cake made of the firstfruits, in others it is led through the fields or he victim is killed with agricultural implements.[8]

In recent times, the use of a blood substitute indicates that Teyyam traditions have undergone conservative shifts towards Brahamanical or high-caste temple culture (*kṣetram*). Some Teyyam goddesses are vegetarian, accepting only coconuts: when severed, a coconut, like a bleeding body, exudes organic liquid. Normatively, these goddesses—e.g. Nilmaṅgallāṭṭū Bhagavati—belong to the Nāyar community, who adhere to Brahmanical ideals of purity.[9]

In my view, this explanation, however, undercuts the historical use of blood substitution in Kerala; blood-water (*guruti*) has always been a part of Teyyam liturgies. I was told a large bowl of *guruti* is obligatory, because the goddess' thirst can be so great that even multiple chickens would be insufficient. Some informants said only a human sacrifice could maximally appease her. At one grove, a large stone, known in Malayalam as *teṇṇākaḷḷu*, was installed on the periphery of the grove. People were purchasing coconuts at a stall outside the grove's gates to smash them against the *teṇṇākaḷḷu* stone, with some force I might add! Over a loudspeaker, a committee member exclaimed: 'Come and smash a coconut! Come and join our group!'. One informant stated that smashing coconuts (*teṅṅā*) 'remov[ed] obstacles in a person's life', which I interpret here to mean sacrifice's role in readjusting imbalances of the goddess-clan's (that is, a polity's) grace. A sacrificer's problems stem from an exiguity of material balance (*śakti*), which is rectified by re-concentrating a grove's ancestral power in the offeror's direction.

8 Hubert & Mauss, *Sacrifice*, p. 69.

9 John R. Freeman, 'Gods, Groves and the Culture of Nature in Kerala', *Modern South Asia*, 33.2 (1999a).

2.1.1 Sacrifice Re-connects the Groups: Agriculture, Martial Defense, and Material Energy

In every Teyyam grove, blood sacrifices take place on the northern altar (*vadakkan vatiḷ*). It is towards the Northern altar that Teyyam mediums face when fully adorned, usually whilst sitting on a stool (*pītham*). Next to the stool, green tree-stalks are arranged in quadrangular formation with four wicks placed in each corner. Banana leaves also surround this structure, and each leaf is piled with rice-grains, coconuts, and betel leaves. A bowl of *guruti* (or artificial blood, a mix of turmeric powder, lime, and water) is also placed there. In Malayalam, this diagrammatic arrangement is called a *kalaṃ* or *maṇḍalam*, and its role mimics that of a *maṇḍala* in Sanskritic tradition. In this context, a *kalam* depicts multileveled realities, or in this case, those internal relations linking a grove's ritual space, the medium's subtle body, and the body politic. During ritual performance, worshippers construed the *kalaṃ* as a grand *praśādam*—a salubrious offering to the gods—which it certainly is! However, on another occasion, I was told that its connotations are much more complex. As Freeman elucidates, the *kalaṃ* conveys many territorial space-time levels simultaneously: (a) the cultivated land of a lineage; (b) martial battlefields of ancestral warriors; (c) the battlefield of goddess Bhadrakālī slaying buffalo-demon Dāruka; (d) a dancer-medium's subtle body; and (e) the entire universe.[10] He writes:

> The significance of this word [kalaṃ] is that while it refers primarily to a granary yard or any open space or area used for similar purposes of conclave, it also has a cluster of secondary meanings ... What I believe is operative here is a rich interplay of significations on the theme of battle, sacrifice, and fertility which is fundamental to the archaic Dravidian ethos and the sacralization of a martial polity.[11]

Hence, in Folk Śākta traditions, the *kalaṃ*—body, blood, and land in tune—is symbolically constitutive of terrestrial web-like power (*śakti*). As shown in Figure 17, a bowl of *guruti* is emptied on the ground adjacent to the *kalaṃ* structure, which foregrounds blood sacrifice as a mode of reconnecting cosmic realities, through blood, whereby all bodies—divinities, denizens, and ancestors—are reattuned once more with the earth. In Keralan culture, primarily, death is not equated with decay or defilement *per se*, but a process conducive to new

10 Freeman, 'Purity and Violence', p. 261.
11 Ibid.

FIGURE 17 *Kaḷam*
PHOTOGRAPH BY AUTHOR

life, inspired by Kerala's agricultural (re)cycles; after all, as per Kerala custom, ancestral cremains are buried in a lineage's land-tract, so as to revitalize their crops.[12]

The location of the sacrificial altar—at a grove's northern end—is also meaningful: Freeman explains how, in local mythology, the North is a cardinal direction where, each autumn, Bhadrakālī and the goddess-clan defeat an army of demonic beings—led by buffalo-demon, Dāruka—to protect her kingdom's territory.[13] Blood sacrifice offered to these warrior goddesses calm their ferociousness, a fact they pronounce to their worshippers; they thank them for

12 Osella, 'Vital Exchanges', p. 222.
13 Freeman, 'Purity and Violence', pp. 260–261.

having brought them happiness. We can deduce, therefore, that sacrificing to the goddess enhances a polity's territorial bonds (macro-clan), with the aim of eliminating spiritual adversaries or foreign militia.

2.1.2 Sacrifice as a Demon: Purging and Exorcism

When I visited Mattyoor Kāvu (near Payyanur) for a Teyyam performance, a devotee joined me as I stood adjacent to the grove's *teṉṉākaḷḷu* stone. In our conversation, he divulged some interesting insights about the history of sacrifice in Kerala:

> [Inf.:] This is a shrine where they break coconuts. At many Teyyams, people are not allowed to sacrifice goats, so instead they break coconuts on a stone like this—it [replaces] the sacrifice. It is even said that, in the past, some Teyyam needed human for sacrifice.

At the conceptual level, a sacrificial offering—in whatever form—is considered a demonic being. For the most part, the sacrifice is emblematic of Dāruka, the 'buffalo-demon', who is defeated by a warrior goddess. Literally, the sacrifice *is* the demon, the scapegoat of social ills; in Newari festivals, too, a buffalo manifests a demon, known there as Mahiśaṣura. From a historical vantage point, Freeman shows how chicken sacrifices and exorcising demons are coterminous, and I quote him here:

> [the] kōḻi-stōtram, [a text] which reveals the history of sacrificial chicken [...] originated as Dāruka [demon] who fled the goddess by taking various forms as he was successively slain as a warrior, and finally as a chicken:
>
> "Previously, I devotedly hacked a man and gave you his blood. Then when a man could not be happily gotten, I slaughtered an elephant for you [...] Now getting not a single elephant, nor man, nor goat, by cutting a chicken I am giving you blood today".[14]

He suggests this local 'kōḻi-stōtram' text—which details the myth of the sacrificed demon—is paralleled in the Brahmayāmala 522: 90–92 (a translocal Śākta text), which may explain the related logic among the Newars of Bhaktapur, who also view sacrificial victims as 'demons'.[15] Though I tend to dismiss Girard's notion of sacrifice as a 'collective catharsis of mimetic or competitive violence'

---

14 Freeman, 'Śāktism', p. 165.
15 Ibid.

in this context, his description of sacrificial victims as 'indifferent' and 'sacrificeable' is applicable to Teyyam's view, i.e. that sacrificial victims are demons. In sacrifice, Girard claims, '[…] there is no question of "expiation". Rather, society is seeking to deflect upon a relatively indifferent victim, a "sacrificeable" victim, the violence that would otherwise be vented on its own members, the people it most desires to protect'.[16]

Indeed, sacrificial chickens and *guruti* are also incorporated in rites of exorcism, which are regulated by Mayalān caste groups in Malabar. As Freeman notes, exorcism is sought by individuals afflicted by demonic incursions in their bodies, who are tended by Teyyam deity-mediums (of Malayān castes). A Malayān medium throws rice grains at the patient's body to draw out the demon, and with the spilling of *guruti*, the demon is annihilated: '[…] the beings are conducted into this [guruti] through the medium of rice grains passed over the victim's body that are thrown into the cauldron of guruti'.[17] According to Freeman, this reference to *guruti* can also be found in the Īśānagurudevapaddhati (a 12th Century CE Keralan liturgical manual) which frequently mentions an exorcistic rite involving 'blood-water' (Skt: *raktodaka*).[18] In a sense, for folk Śākta performances, the sacrifice is a demon who must be killed to ensure that human beings are shielded from their own inner 'demons' (or violated by invisible ones). In Teyyāṭṭam, dancer-mediums, and those individuals afflicted by demonic forces, must clear their body to allocate space for divine agency to heal their bodies, which extends to those bodies present in the ritual too. Every medium must undertake a ritualized purification (*śuddhi*) in preparation for this. Many of these rites can be traced to medieval warrior rituals (*tēvāram kuṟi*), where bodies and swords were smeared with sandalwood paste, which prepared them for battle. Freeman writes: '[…] the dance is a battle and the weapons and the body are therefore in need of purification after the killing'.[19]

2.1.3 Sacrifice and Warrior Culture

In Teyyam, all deities associated with warfare or death almost always receive a blood sacrifice, and these divinities include Kerala's deified hunters. My interlocutors often said these deities were brave hunters lionized in tales of Kerala's mythic past. One of these deities is Mūttappan, a martial deity who, in

16 Rene Girard, *Violence and the Sacred* (Baltimore: The John Hopkins University Press, 1972), p. 4.
17 Freeman, 'Dynamics of the Person', p. 165.
18 Freeman, 'Śāktism', pp. 165–166.
19 Freeman, 'Purity and Violence', p. 259.

his Teyyam form, carries a bow and arrow. Across Malabar, Mūttappan is a noticeably popular deity, and he is famed both as a hunter and swidden agriculturalist. Freeman shows that Mūttappan's prevalence among Keralans may be related to his image as a resistant fighter; in medieval Kerala, many of these forest hunters—like Mūttappan—may have formed militant groups. For instance, Mūttappan is said to have led hunter rebellions in the highlands, whose lineages felt oppressed by their landlords.[20] As I argue in Chapter 6, such instances of subaltern resistance, mainly against landlords, seem to pervade Teyyam liturgies; influenced by Weber, I suggest such discourses became inbuilt within the region's cultural memory which, perhaps, has continuity with Marxist ideology in 20th Century Kerala.

Another god connected to traditions of highland hunters is Wayanād Kuḻīvan. He was the son of two hunters who, according to the myth, were Śiva and Parvāti in disguise. During his adolescence, the boy became afflicted with blindness—a curse foisted by his lineage deity—for having drank toddy that was meant as a divine offering.[21] Having begged for the deity's forgiveness, he was granted a pair of *poy kunnu* (silver, false eyes). But, in another unfortunate turn of events, he was grievously immolated in a forest fire while swiddening his land and was reborn a deity.

As Figure 18 shows, Wayanād Kuḻīvan's weapon is a burning torch (*cōtta*), which was used by hunters in medieval Kerala to swidden land. Wayanād Kuḻīvan's aptitude as a hunter is also enacted ceremonially: the dancer-mediums—who embody him in ritual—must pluck feathers from a chicken as a display of the 'hunt'. Further, Freeman adds that Waynād Kuḻīvan is the 'god of the hunt *par excellence*',[22] who, it is said, later mobilized to the status of a military official.

As already highlighted, various weaponry is used during Teyyāṭṭam; each deity wields a different weapon. Apart from characterizing one deity from another, these accoutrements also serve as ritual markers of the region's traditional practices—hunting, land cultivation, and warrior recruitment—to the group. In Kerala's mytho-history, all these practices are associated with the tribal hunters of the region's northern hills. According to Freeman:

> [...] traditionally hunts themselves were explicitly declared as a form of warfare against the animals who were mythically and ritually assimilated

20 Ibid., p. 281.

21 Trikaripur, *Mooring Mirror*, pp. 150–151.

22 Freeman, 'Gods', p. 285.

FIGURE 18 Wayanād Kuḻīvan
PHOTOGRAPH BY AUTHOR

to the status of human or demonic enemies. Each village ideally had special shrines where these hunts were organised and ritually dedicated [...] There is evidence that this assimilation of warfare and hunt to a divinely-mandated sacrifice was once more common and widespread amongst the higher castes.[23]

23 Ibid., p. 278.

Furthermore, many of my informants regarded Teyyam paraphernalia and chicken sacrifices as aesthetic homage to medieval mores of swiddening and hunting. Some Teyyam deities are also therianthropic by nature, e.g. Puliyoor Kālī—a tiger goddess who lived in the forest lowlands—who memorialize traditional hunting. A sacrifice, then, can also represent, to the group, a mythic battle, a hunt, and a martyr who perished in the region's folkloric myths.

As described in Waynād Kuḻīvan's narrative above, the drinking of liquor from toddy pots (*kalaśa-kiṇḍi*) is part and parcel of the hunt because drinking enhanced their inner divine strength (*kalivụ*). Close to the *kalam maṇḍalam*, all warrior divinities drink toddy, and share it with the congregation, alongside sacrifice, to prepare their bodies for this surge of divine power. Durkheim brilliantly encapsulates the power of alcohol in ritual settings; for him, it is a way of exciting the body, so that it can acclimatize to the **sacred**:

> It is quite true that religious life cannot attain any degree of intensity and not carry with it a psychic exaltation that is connected to delirium. It is for this reason that men of extraordinarily sensitive religious consciousness—prophets, founders of religion, great saints—often show symptoms of an excitability that is extreme [...] These physiological defects predispose them to great religious roles. The ritual use of intoxicating liquors is to be understood in the same way [...] a very intense social life always does a sort of violence to the individual's body and mind and disrupts their normal functioning. This is why it can last only a limited time.[24]

This concept of 'disrupting' the mundane body is also observed by Freeman vis-à-vis Teyyāṭṭam. Any sacrificial slaughter near the *kalam maṇḍalam* (which, on one level, constitutes the individual's subtle body) is said to purify the medium's body in order to instill the deity's strength within him:

> There is almost certainly some such idea in teyyattam as to why the breaths or elements of the mundane body are laid out as an offering where blood-sacrifices are performed; they must be destroyed before being replaced with their divine counterparts.[25]

24 Emile Durkheim, *The Elementary Forms of Religious Life*, trans. By Karen Fields, (New York: The Free Press, 1995 [1912]), p. 228.

25 Freeman, 'Performing Possession'.

Once sacrificed, chicken carcasses are not disposed as impure—on the contrary, I once saw six dead chickens hanging in the mediums' preparatory hut; they were being kept for a meal, prepared for the troupe after the ritual. In line with Durkheimian theory, all sacrificial rituals not only mark a movement from individual to collective forces within the virtuoso's body, but also prepare these respective formations; the individual (via sacrifice) must be prepared for *entrée* to the ritual's *collective effervescence*. In emic terms, this *effervescence*—coterminous with the deity's charismatic authority—is the revitalizing source of *śakti/kalivu* (i.e. that ontologically immanent energy binding humans, animals, deities, and sacred objects *in terris*). Durkheim states:

> The individual soul is regenerated by immersing itself once more in the wellspring of its life; subsequently, it feels stronger, more in control of itself, [and] less dependent on physical necessities.[26]

For Durkheim, this rejuvenation takes effect in *Intichiuma* sacrifice after sacrificers eat that sacrifice, ingesting the 'sacred' within. This same idea is inherent in Teyyāṭṭam's sacrificial meals, which finds its corollary within texts of medieval Yoginī cults. Sanderson summarises that interpretation here:

> It [sacrifice] is a privilege means of access to the blissful expansion of consciousness in which the deities of the kula permeate and obliterate the [individual] ego of the worshipper. The consumption of meat and alcohol is interpreted along the same lines. Their purpose, like that of everything in the liturgy, is to intensify experience, to gratify the goddesses of the senses.[27]

As I describe in this chapter's introduction, sacrifice has three correlated functions in South Asian folk Śākta traditions. The first—sacrifice as a way of subduing demons for the successful renewal of the goddess-clan's 'web'—has been outlined in this sub-section. We will now move to the second function, self-reflexivity. In general, among my interlocutors, it seems sacrificial acts spurred worshippers to reflect on their own worldly existence as ephemeral ones. Before I present these descriptions in the next section, I close here with an apposite aphorism from Durkheim's classic, The *Elementary Forms*:

26 Durkheim, *Elementary Forms*, p. 259.

27 Sanderson, 'Śaivism and the Tantric Traditions', p. 680.

> [...] what the worshipper really gives his god is not his food he places on the altar, or the blood he spills from his veins, but his thought.[28]

2.2 *Sacrifice as Self-Reflexive Affect: Narratives on Sacrifice and Emotion in Malabar*

In Kerala culture, the idea that chicken (or vegetative) sacrifices symbolize martial hunts of demonic forces, I argue, consigns the victim not as an object, but as a life-empowering subject. The surrogate subject must be annihilated to redress generative life-forces within that society. Freeman reinforces this point; for him, Teyyam sacrifice is 'modelled on the human sacrifice of the battle',[29] such that sacrifice exposes those struggles that arise from battle: death, disease, and fragility.

With that in mind, one of my closest informants detailed his subjective response witnessing sacrifice: he saw sacrifice as a way of reflecting on his own existence in-the-world, what is described, in Sanskrit, as *saṃsāra*. He described how Tantric tradition presents a mirror to our fragile existence, which is enacted ritually when dancer-mediums stare in a mirror to confirm their divine transformation. Sacrifice, he said, unconsciously relates to natural processes that are intrinsic to the human condition, such as birth, bleeding and death, which are personified by the maternal and menstrual nature of the mother goddesses. Such sacrificial displays spur unconscious reminders of birth and death, through bleeding, within the collective; it is a self-reflexive combination of human nature's own capacity for transformation, and its simultaneous fragility. A sacrifice (*bali*) is not an object, but a tangible reflection of the group's own nature, their battles, and every individual's opportunity to feel empowered. Sarah Caldwell argued that *guruti* in Kerala culture is constitutive of a goddess' menstrual blood, inasmuch as a symbolic dead fetus—birth, death, and cyclicality—is offered to the ancestors to menstrually synchronize human cycles, the land, and cosmic relations.[30]

Such a symbiosis of sacrifice with human life-cycle experience is also posited by Hubert and Mauss, who famously note that the sacrifice is the 'religious act ... that modifies the condition of the moral person'.[31] They continue:

---

28 Durkheim, *Elementary Forms*, p. 257.

29 Freeman, 'Purity and Violence', p. 606.

30 Caldwell, 'Oh Terrifying Mother', p. 336.

31 Hubert & Mauss, *Sacrifice*.

> Indeed it is not enough to say that it [sacrifice] represents him [sacrificer]: it is merged in him. The two personalities are fused together.[32]

From this standpoint, sacrifice is an act of cosmological proportions. The act lays bare a Keralan worldview to its social *conscious collective*. In Malabar, this worldview is enmeshed in warrior culture, hunting, agriculture, and swiddening, all of which are intertwined within the overarching perpetuity of *saṃsāric existence*, the cyclical regeneration of worldly births and rebirths. This is also apparent in textual discourse, when Sarkar explains how Nidrā-kālarātri's sacrifice to save her brother became emulated by her warrior-devotees in religious practices of self-mutilation. Sarkar writes:

> Such warrior-practices are connected to Nidrā's self-sacrifice in the myth of the Harivaṃśa. She offered her own body, to be violently smashed against a rock, in order to save the life of her brother. In this respect, Nidrā's sacrifice is the highest form of heroism that a warrior can demonstrate.[33]

Sacrifice, then, is about surrendering one's own life to protect the life of one's kin (which enhances feelings of *affective kin-like intentionality* in that group). Kimberley Patton maintains this same point in the context of Nuer society: a sacrifice directed towards god ('kwoth') interconnects two simultaneous movements of cosmological power: (1) a return of the animal's life-force to its divine source, and (2) a surrender of one's own self to the deity. She writes: 'Sacrifice is therefore nothing less than a visible ratification of the existential symbiosis of Nuer theology'.[34] This notion of sacrifice as spiraling between individual and collective forces is also adduced in the South Asian context.

From Marriott's stance, South Asian persons are 'dividuals' nested in interactive flows of fluid power that compose a larger whole. In Tantric society, particularly, the material world, deities, and animals are co-constitutive in dynamic networks of blood relations. The sacrificed animal, too, is nested in this dynamic network of agency, and its blood releases the ties that connect the web. For Appadurai:

---

32 Ibid., p. 32.

33 Sarkar, *Heroic Shāktism*, p. 66.

34 Kimberley Patton, 'Animal Sacrifice: Metaphysics of the Sublimated Victim', in *A Communion of Subjects: Animals in Religion, Science, and Ethics*, ed. by Kimberley Patton & Paul Wandau, (New York: Columbia University Press, 2006), p. 395.

> Sacrifice can only work when what is offered, or given up, usually to a God or ancestor, is a dynamic part of some apparent whole. In other words, the parts that are given up by one actor to another, in the world of precapitalist sacrifice, are dynamic parts, which also carry their own energies, vitalities, and strivings (in the sense that Spinoza used the term *conatus*).[35]

Moreover, as an entity in this web-network, the sacrificial animal is not treated inhumanely. In Teyyāṭṭam sacrifice, my informant detailed how the animal's body is greeted, purified, and respected in the same way human participants greet one another, that is, with handfuls of rice grains. Before any chicken is slaughtered in a Teyyam rite, it must be fed raw rice grains; its body is also sprinkled with water from a water pot (*kiṇḍi*). The gesture of rice-feeding (discussed in Chapter 3) confers prosperity upon the chicken, who, once deceased, is reborn as a high-ranking human; Nambiar claims that the rice-feeding '[…] symbolises that the sacrifice is not done as a punishment to the cock'.[36] Such acts give thanks to the chicken, who will enjoy an opulent existence in the next life.

The eschatological fate of the sacrifice was also asserted in the Kathmandu Valley, an observation I elicited during a blood-lineage deity rite (*dugu puja*) in Bhaktapur. I suggest acknowledging the animal's eschatological destination in ritual eases the sacrificer's guilt, which Kimberely Patton also notes is significant among Nepali priests in Kathmandu:

> [in Kathmandu] Eric Mortensen told me he observed a domestic sacrifice of multiple goats to Kali in front of a home near Bodhanath in Nepal. The priest whispered something in the ear of each goat that he slaughtered […] the priest […] divulged what he was saying: 'Next life you kill me'.[37]

The sacrificial substitution is not, I would argue, *mimetic violence*—a rivalry between group members which must be expulsed via a sacrificial victim. Sacrifice is rather a tangible reminder of existential concerns of the world. Here, I am influenced by Flood's interpretation of sacrifice as a 'refusal' (of subjective self for universal subjectivity), which is apt in the Teyyam context: 'sacrifice is about suffering and the relinquishing of a *self-focused* subjectivity in favour of

35 Arjun Appadurai, 'The Wealth of Dividuals' in *Derivative and the Wealth in Societies*, ed. by Benjamin Lee & Randy Martin, (Chicago: University of Chicago Press, 2016), p. 26.

36 Nambiar, 'Tai Paradevata', p. 155.

37 Patton, 'Animal Sacrifice', p. 402.

a *shared* subjectivity in which that which is most precious, a life itself, is given up to affirm that very life'.[38] As previously outlined, Flood's hypothesis could be accurately applied in Teyyāṭṭam qua the individual's immersion in an immanent web-network. This is further reflected in connotations of blood—a symbol of the society's life-force—a sacred liquid that can become a collective representation.[39] As such, sacrifice sustains both individual and collective poles equally, in the Durkheimian sense. Durkheim states: '[...] the life of the group must "enter into" individuals and become "organized within" them'.[40] Embodied *śakti* within the individual is harnessed during sacrifice and is returned to its divine source, the Teyyam divinity—the cradle of the macro-clan's power.

Sacrificial substitutes also enable the same self-reflexive process within the collective. Coconut-smashing is a substitute for the victim in Nāyar Teyyam groves. Returning to my point in § 5.2.1, the coconut, like blood sacrifice, is a symbol of carnal power that represents the society's web-networks and flows of power (terrestrial, ancestral, martial etc.). Enacting blood sacrifice sparks a cosmological self-reflexivity among individuals, where they somatically commune with a sacred grove's immanent *śakti*. As Mary Douglas reminds us, natural symbols—blood and sacrificial death—are metaphysical portrayals of cosmological worldviews, which in Kerala, are populated by an array of deities, humans, spirits, and demons. During Teyyāṭṭam, blood sacrifice's dénouement is threefold: macro-clan regeneration, self-reflexivity, and emotion. Sacrificial death is paradoxically concerned with worldly life, an act which always consigns back to the underlying *maṇḍalic* network (read, macro-clan) of the body politics' lifeworld(s).[41]

3 Navadurgā

3.1 *Sacrifice in Newar Bhaktapur: Lineage Deities, Goats, and Buffaloes*

In Bhaktapur city, every aspect of religio-cultural life is centred around blood sacrifice. At the most basic level, families in Bhaktapur offer animal sacrifice to ferocious deities—enshrined or embodied in a masked medium—in order to appease them. Of these, Navadurgā divinities must be propitiated first and foremost to ensure their power protects the civic environs. For the most part,

38 Gavin Flood, 'Sacrifice as Refusal', in *Sacrifice and Modern Thought*, ed. by Julia Meszaros & Johannes Zachhuber, (Oxford: OUP, 2013), p. 123.

39 See also Shilling, 'Embodiment', p. 214.

40 Durkheim, *Elementary Forms*, p. 211.

41 Mary Douglas, *Natural Symbols: Studies in Cosmology* (London: Routledge, 1970).

iconographic representations of Newar deities—in myths—contain some portrayal of sacrificial slaughter: deities are depicted smiting demons, fighting in warfare, or exsanguinating animals.

During festivals (*jātrā*) in Bhaktapur, I would frequently see families preparing chickens, buffaloes, pigs, or goats for sacrifice at god-shrines that chart the city's streets. Conventionally, an animal's blood is spilt at the base of a god-stone (*pikaliki*), before its intestines are draped around the stone, and its head is offered to the deity on a platter. The gesture of daubing a victim's innards and blood on the image (*mūrti*) is volitional; the sacrificial body is revived with the divinity's presence, which is later ingested by worshippers as a meal. At one Navadurgā performance in Dhulikel town, Krishna's neighbour mixed beaten rice with raw goat-meat cut from a newly sacrificed animal. He handed me a portion and gestured goadingly: 'You should eat this meat. We are eating Navadurgā's power. Eat this and you will be strong like them'.

Michaels claims that such practices of animal sacrifice in Bhaktapur are so deep-seated that one interlocutor told him: 'we don't know why [we sacrifice], but it has to be'.[42] From my own ethnographic perspective, sacrifice was always explained to me in terms of social transformation or conferring well-being on a lineage (*phuki*). Through sacrifice, the deity's power (*śakti*) is placated, regulated, and transmitted to ensure a lineage's affluence is preserved.

On the third day of Vaisakh (April–May), Bhaktapurian blood lineages (*phuki*) visit the shrine of their lineage deities (Newa: *dugu dyo*) to offer them a goat sacrifice. These lineage shrines are numerous in the city, and several of them surround Bhaktapur's ponds and lakes; Siddhapokharī and Kamālpokharī are two such lakes where lineage shrines had been constructed. At Kamālpokharī, Ujesh and I observed a lineage worshipping their ancestors (*dugu pūjā*): at that time, at least a dozen families were gathered around the lake, each had sacrificed a goat to their lineage deity-stone. Goats were garlanded with flower festoons and rubbed with vermillion powder, before being walked to their impending immolation at a god-stone. The animals were showered with rice, their throat slit, and their blood splattered on the stone. Afterwards, families lit small fires to cook their goats in preparation for a communal meal.

As with buffalo sacrifice at Mohani—the autumnal festival—all animals must be unsullied he-goats who are asked permission to die in a rite managed by the sacrificing priest. This is a crucial aspect of sacrifice; if left unappeased,

42 Axel Michaels, 'Blood Sacrifice in Nepal: Transformations and Criticism', in *Religion, Secularism, and Ethnicity in Contemporary Nepal*, ed. by David Gellner et al., (Oxford: OUP, 2016), p. 216.

FIGURE 19 Goat sacrifice, (Kamalpokharī, Bhaktapur)
PHOTOGRAPH BY AUTHOR

it is believed the animal may return as a vengeful spirit who can curse a lineage by wreaking havoc on its members. This rite of victim approval is a requirement in any sacrificial ritual, as Patton highlights:

> [sacrificial animals are] glorified mediators between realms, whose cooperation is essential to the efficacy of the ritual, whose forgiveness is often sought from kinship groups to avert vengeance [...] Often [...] a luminous fate in the afterlife for the victim is guaranteed by their immolation on earth.[43]

Ujesh claimed any animal who grants his approval as a sacrificial offering is guaranteed a felicitous rebirth. The animal's rebirth will be a prosperous one, i.e. as a high-ranking human, or a divine being who resides in the heavenly realms. This eschatological assurance is also expressed ritually: the animal's head is placed near the stone, where several lamps are lit in its honour. This rite is known as *mukhti paunśa*, and it ensures the animal's auspicious rebirth. As I outline in § 5.2.2, Newar priests express this eschatological oath verbally, too: in the next life, the roles will reverse so that the reincarnated animal will sacrifice the priest. Therefore, the cycles of *saṃsāra* and *karma* underlie sacrificial rationale; a sacrificial victim is granted an opportunity for retribution in the next life.

Without a doubt, Navadurgā dancer-mediums are continually subjected to animal sacrifice—one could argue that sacrifice dynamizes these performances. Among their many sacrifices during Navadurgā ritual is the chicken sacrifice enacted by Mahākālī. The goddess—with Seto Bhairava, her consort—is handed two chickens to calm her ferocity. During performance, the dancer-medium takes both chickens, and, with his teeth, he draws blood from the chickens' jugular veins until they exsanguinate. Here, sacrifice calms the goddess' wrath; her overwhelming power (*śakti*) is pacified during sacrifice, which protects her shrines and Bhaktapurian citizens from inauspicious influences. In a sense, the animal's blood releases the goddess-clan's unrestrained power. According to Michaels:

> The life of the animal is given primarily for a new and better life as well as for the prosperity and power of the individual sacrifice and his family or clan or *guthi*.[44]

43 Patton, 'Animal Sacrifice', p. 393.
44 Michaels, 'Blood Sacrifice', p. 201.

3.1.1 Buffalo Sacrifice at Mohani: From Navadurgā's Perspective

At Mohani, buffaloes are traditionally offered to the goddess-clan. Among Navadurgā lineages, an unblemished buffalo—nurtured by breeders from *niku thu* (an area in Bhaktapur)—is venerated at the Navadurga temple for three months, before it is sacrificed at Brahmayāni's temple on the banks of the Hanumante river. The buffalo is a manifestation of demon Mahiśaṣura, and with his death, the goddesses' *śakti* can flow forth into the city and its many clans and associations (*guṭhi*). The Navadurgā mediums are pivotal in this process; they even eat directly from the buffalo's neck after its immolation. From the animal's charred bones, the dancers produce a black paste called *Mohani tikā*, which is painted as a line on a worshipper's forehead (for prosperity) throughout the Navadurgā cycle. These processes, I suggest, show that, in Bhaktapur, sacrifice is an act enmeshed in life cycles and lineage life. When I asked Ujesh about the role of sacrifices in Newari culture, he said:

> [Inf:] Navadurga shows the process of life to death ... it is a way of teaching the people [about life-cycles]. People think that death is not the end. At the end of Navadurga performances [in May], people cry a lot and they miss the gods.

As with Teyyam sacrifices, Navadurgā performances also induce thoughts of existential self-reflexivity among those participating in them. But how can devotees reflect upon life cycles when this sacrifice is a 'demon'? A Bhaktapurian historian I interviewed drew my attention to this conundrum: for him, most deities (*dyo*) and demons (*daityaharu*) are depicted in anthropomorphic form; as such, they reflect our own fluctuating emotions and personalities. He explicated as follows:

> [Inf:] I am the god, you are the god [...] sometimes I am like a god, sometimes I am like a demon [...] God is inside us: I am a god, man, animal, and demon; how you react depends upon your thought [*bicar*].

For those lineages who cannot afford buffaloes or castrated goats (*khasi*) to sacrifice in ritual, an egg (Newa: *khae*) or a pumpkin (Newa: *kuṣmāṇḍa*) can also be offered. According to Levy, the ways an animal's meat is divided up for the distribution reflects lineage (*phuki*) life. (Paradoxically, a sacrifice can also express an anti-caste sentiment—see § 5.3.1.2). Levy articulates this hierarchy here:

> These hierarchically arranged portions are called *siu* (in Kathmandu Newari, *si*). The particular parts of the head made use of and their hierar-

> chical value varies in various communities and groups [...] In Bhaktapur the *siu* is presented in order to the eight highest members of the *phuki* group that is holding the feast. For upper-level and middle-level *thar*s, at least, the system of ranking among the *phuki* as symbolized by the *siu* division is arranged by age within a generation, rather than only by relative age. In other words, even if a member of an older generation is younger than a male in a descending generation, he has more status in the *siu* distribution system.[45]

Sacrifice—as I argue for Teyyāṭṭam—is a natural symbol that exhibits the society's *web-like ritual network* as a unified territory to itself; not just to human beings, I might add, but to all 'persons' populating that society's lifeworld, whether tangible or intangible.

To expand upon this point in greater detail, I will now return to our description of *dyo bokegu* introduced in Chapter 3.4.3.2. Whenever a Navadurgā troupe is due to perform in a new precinct or lineage household, they are offered two pigs for sacrifice (slaughtered by the medium embodying Bhairava). Before its slaughter, the pig is walked around the precinct of the donor's territory in a ceremony known, in Nepali, as *sungur lakatne*. Bhairava grabs the pig by its hind legs with a crowd of devotees following them on their circumambulation. On 11th March 2016, during a *sungur lakatne* in Kaumā twā—near the palace square—I asked Ujesh why this circumambulation rite was necessary before the pig is sacrificed. He explained:

> [Inf:] The pig [*sungur*] is a dirty [*phohor*] animal, and it is sacrificed to get rid of all the dirt and problems in the *tol* (precinct).

In Tantric mythologies linked with Bhairava—as narrated in the Śiva-Purāṇa—he is described as having sacrificed a Brahmin by decapitating him with the nail of his left thumb. Bhairava is said to have killed the Brahmin as a means of gaining supreme authority over the pantheon and, as a result, he was expediently punished by Śiva for his crime. As a punishment, he was ordered to wander the subcontinent for twelve years carrying the Brahmin's head until he adequately repented.[46] In ritual, this mythology is enacted by the Bhairava dancer, who

45 Levy, *Mesocosm*, p. 330.

46 Elizabeth Chalier-Visvulingam, 'Bhairava and the Goddess: Tradition, Gender and Transgression', in *Wild Goddesses in India and Nepal*, ed. by Axel Michaels et al., (Bern: Verlag Peter Lang, 1996), p. 259.

slits the throat of the pig with his thumbnail during *dyo bokegu*. Having done this, Bhairava proceeds by mixing curd with beaten rice, which is distributed to the audience. This symbolic act is crucial; it is, in fact, a societal critique of Brahmanical caste itself. The pig **is** a portrayal of that hierarchy, which is openly defied by worshippers through the distribution of rice-curd that re-renders a ritual kin network between them. An informant in Lalitpur described how this sacrifice defies caste purity:

> [MM]: Do all castes participate in Navadurga?
> [Inf:] In Navadurgā, whether you are Brahmin, Chettri, or Shudra, it doesn't matter. Navadurga sees them the same [...] An example of this is the *dyo bokegu*. A pig is not accepted by Brahmins as a sacrifice, but afterward [the pig is sacrificed] Bhairava mixes the curd and baji with his hand during the offering [*dhāū-baji walegu*] ... but his hands are polluted [*jūto*] with blood [*ragat*]. The rice-curd offering binds the people, it is a time where people's caste and backgrounds are not important.

The pig sacrifice is also recounted in the Navadurgā oral mythology, which I describe in § 4.3.3. The wild (*jangali*) goddesses—before being brought to the city as enshrined protectors of Bhaktapur—hunted animals on their path to assuage their anger. In this way, sacrifice is conducive to the maintenance of Bhaktapur's urban borders and its population. Thus, a sacrificial rite is not always a socio-political critique in Bhaktapur. In recently gentrified areas outside Bhaktapur's traditional borders, Grieve argues that worshippers perform a 'forged sacrifice' (*nākali bali*) at their Gaṇeśa shrine, so that the new settlement was included into Bhaktapur's traditional macro-clan; sacrifice menstrually synchronizes this area with the rest of Bhaktapur. He states:

> [sacrifice] was not a 'dance of symbols' performed out of the unconscious replication of an existing cultural structure. Instead, it was a conscious manipulation of available "traditional" cultural logics that were strategically utilized to solve a contemporary problem [...] To articulate how people use religious agency to forge new traditional lived worlds, I coin the term 'generative cultural matrixes'.[47]

47 Grieve, 'Forging Mandalic Space', pp. 473–474.

Here, sacrifice is a blood-rite that forms new connections that flow into the traditional society's web of territorial togetherness. Sacrifice can therefore reconfigure the territory's network of relations to integrate a newly built territory into its macro-clan.

3.1.2 Blood Sacrifice as a Political Act: NWPP and the Peasant Struggle

I would argue that Folk Śākta traditions—which includes sacrifice, in whatever form—are not only conservative praxes that reproduce and uphold the social system. Conversely, these systems of practice can become potential sites that can re-shape traditional logics for political ends. On many occasions during my stay in Bhaktapur, several informants would narrate their determination to preserve their inherited Newar culture. This narrative was often specified in terms of the Municipality's sacrifice, governed by the city's NWPP party. One informant expressed how Bhaktapurians sacrificed to maintain their heritage:

> The central government is reluctant to give aid to the Navadurga and other significant cultural activities [...] In Bhaktapur, the municipality is a self-reliant and local decentralized body which has protected these activities. These are [maintained] with sacrifice and a volunteering spirit of Bhaktapurian citizens.

As I elucidate in §6.4, Bhaktapurian 'communism' has recast the traditional understanding of sacrifice to account for the peasant struggle in the city: the festival of Mohani, for instance, is framed as the victory over 'injustice' (Nepa: *ānyāya*) which, NWPP claims, represents the victory over caste stratification and global capitalism. Interestingly, they stated that Nepal's government—and their officials—lack 'emotion' or 'feeling' toward Newar culture, especially Navadurgā. Certainly, Baltutis suggests how Newars vocalize this injustice by evoking their 'indigenous' rights as *janjātis* ('indigenous people') peripheralized in a Parbatiyā-dominated Nepal.[48] In this regard, Newars often retell the mythology of Yalambar: a Kirāti king—identified with Bhairava, who was killed at the hands of a Hindu monarch—whom, Newars farmers believe, is their ancestor. Baltutis explains:

> [...] like other marginalized communities throughout Nepal, Newars are deploying a janjāti ('indigenous people') rhetoric that utilizes the visceral

48 Michael Baltutis, 'Sacrificing (to) Bhairav: The Death, Resurrection, and Apotheosis of a Local Himalayan King', *Journal of Hindu Studies*, 9 (2016), p. 207.

> image of Yalambar's sacrificial bleeding to further contextualize their lower hierarchical place vis-à-vis a dominant Hindu monarchy.[49]

In the next section, I will consider sacrifice as a mode of producing social affect in rituals spaces, something described in Navadurgā performances as *jhinjan minjan*, 'the shivers'.

3.2 *Sacrifice to Navadurgā Dancer-Mediums: Five-Animal Sacrifice (pañcābali), the 'Shivers' (jhinjhan minjan) and Self-reflexive Affect*

On 28th April 2016, I was informed that a rather prodigious sacrifice was being organized for the Navadurgā troupe by the elders of Bayeshi twā, a precinct in Bhaktapur that had been hit severely by the 2015 earthquake. Ujesh notified me that some forty people died in this area after the earthquake had struck; in one family, he said, only a single member had survived. In response to this destruction—which had devasted properties—local lineages began offering regularly to the dancer-mediums, and now they had enough resources to offer five animals for sacrifice (*pañcabali*)—a buffalo, sheep, goat, duck, and chicken. These animals were being prepared by the farmer community in Bayeshi for the occasion of the Navadurgā performance. Below I provide a section from my field-notes that relays this special event:

> 28th April 2016—Pañcabali of Navadurgā mediums—beginning in the Navadurgā temple, Kamalvinayak, and ending in Bayeshi twā:
>
> All the members are donning their new dress (jammā) that was gifted to them by the community in the town of Banepa. On the day of the pañcabali, the Navadurgā troupe initiate a procession (with all masks and equipment) to Bayeshi twā, and once there, they lay their straw mats and equipment in an area just beyond the Ganesha shrine near Tripurasundari twā. The Ganesha medium leads a mudra dance with Kumari, Bhadrakali, Indrayani etc. in front of the repousse plate of goddess Sipha dyo. The household who invited the troupe offer some 15 plates of food offerings to each medium who is sat on their straw mates.
>
> One of the women from the household offers a pile of beaten rice (baji) to the goddess Sipha dyo, and from there, every member of the locality begin offering prashad to the repousse plate and each Navadurgā mask [...] Then a bhajan kahala (marching band) follow a procession led by five men carrying a duck, chicken, goat, sheep, and a buffalo. The Bhairav

49 Ibid.

> dancer-medium washes his hands with a khorwaa (bronze jug), throws beaten rice at the shrine of Sipha dyo (khaa chha) three times, and offers several eggs and kisali (terracotta pots of rice) to the goddess. Then the animals are prepared. Each animal is sprinkled with water from the khorwaa, and the medium draws a crescent moon with a knife on the ground adjacent to the goddess' shrine. Each animal is then daubed with turmeric powder, and adorned with flower garlands and wafted with incense. Rice is thrown at each victim, The duck is the first to be sacrificed. The Bhairav medium decapitates the duck and rubs its blood on the goddess' repousse plate. The chicken is killed by medium Mahakali in the same way. The goat and sheep are sacrificed together by the Bhairav medium and their blood is sprayed on the repousse plate. The sheep's throat is slit, before each dancer-medium drinks the blood from its jugular vein, before it is eventually decapitated, and its head offered to the goddess' portable shrine.
>
> The buffalo (kha mei) is the last to be sacrificed. A sahi (butcher) sacrifices the buffalo. The buffalo is tied down, and a white ribbon is tied on the head of the sacrificer. The knife is blessed with rice and vermillion paste, and its throat slit. Each of the dancer-mediums then proceed to drink from the neck of the buffalo, apart from goddess Mahesvari. Ujesh said that Mahesvari never receives sacrifice because she is a pure manifestation of the river Ganga. [Like in Teyyam] one of these goddesses is vegetarian. The head of the buffalo is severed and is placed beside the other animal heads by the goddess shrine. A grand feast for each member of the troupe is laid out on the straw mats near the shrine. Grand plates (lapte) piled with ginger, lentils, soya bean, gundruk root, pumpkin, potatoes, rice-wine, rice-beer etc. are placed on the floor in front of each member […]

Some fifty to hundred local people—native to the area—were present at the sacrifice, and everyone gathered, quite energetically, around the shrine with their camera-phones, eager to see these sacrifices in action.

In Bhaktapur, the rise of ISKCON and Christian converts has produced some resistance against such sacrificial rites. As Gibson mentions, ISKCON's focus on Krishna, a vegetarian diet, and empathetic love for all beings makes sacrifice a highly aggressive act that is the antithesis of ISKCON ideals.[50] But, for Tantric Newars, the *pañcabali* was an occasion electrified with social emotion, a feeling derived from the group's collective energy, which Bhaktapurian Newars call 'jhinjan minjan', or the shivers.

50 Gibson, 'Suffering and Christianity', p. 60.

According to Grieve, 'jhinjan minjan'[51] is enounced as a somatic reaction to ritualized death that the entire social group experiences, something akin to anxious fascination or the 'heebie-jeebies'. It is not a feeling induced by transcendence, but one inscribed and encoded in worldly power—Grieve suggests *jhinjan minjan* is a 'social, even legal, matter tied up with material local concerns'.[52] This may explain why Bhaktapurians claimed central government officials did not understand Tantric rites in Bhaktapur, in that they failed to 'feel' them. Grieve elaborates in further detail:

> When I talked with people about how they felt during sacrifices they tended to describe them as "horrifying" (*jhinjan minjan danigu*). The adjectival phrase jhinjan minjan is used to describe a feeling possessed by the home of a deceased person (a "haunted house"), walking alone in the jungle etc. In Bhaktapur, animal sacrifice is a technique for producing jhinjan minjan. Such horrifying animal sacrifices are performed for two reasons: first, they produce a tantric form of shakti, which here can be understood as an emotional discourse that draws people into relationships with inanimate objects.[53]

I would argue that a Durkheimian rendering of social effervescence is theoretically applicable here: the sacrifice is an ambivalent action located in a web of ritual relations that spurs emotional intensity among them. This idea of 'self-reflexive shivers' can be doctrinally located in the doctrine of Kashmiri Śaiva-Śākta *Spanda* ('vibration'): in these texts, sacrifice conjures a subjective response of *vimarśa* ('Reflective awareness') and *spanda* ('vibration') grounded in an intersubjective reality (in our context, a *web-like ritual network*). Dyczkowski writes:

> Spanda (a creative-cum-destructive activity of Reality) [...] is a pulse [...] which he [philosopher, Rājānaka Rāma] equates with the 'principle of power' (*śāktatattva*) [that] is none other than the Supreme Goddess (*parameśvari*), who manifests Herself as all the principles (*tattva*) constituting the one reality—including Śiva himself. Therefore, according to Rājānaka Rāma, Spanda [qua a *web-like ritual network*] is the Goddess Who is the highest principle[54]

51 Grieve, *Retheorizing Religion*, p. 112.

52 Ibid.

53 Ibid., p. 105.

54 Dyczkowski, *Doctrine of Vibration*, p. 29.

Visions of death, blood, power, and subjugation all generate self-reflexive sentiments in a collective; seeing death spurs one to reflect upon death as an existential reality. On the ground, however, subjective experiences of 'self-reflexivity' during blood sacrifice did not prompt vegetarianism among the Banmalas; eating sacrificial meat fortifies a dancer-medium's efficacy. The only vegetarian in the family was Ujesh's mother who explained that she no longer needed nor liked meat.

The sacrificial victim—as a mirror-image of the inevitable demise that befalls all beings (in Heidegger's taxonomy, we are 'beings-towards-death'[55])—is self-reflexive, in such a way that sacrifice was adopted socio-politically in Bhaktapur as a metaphor that exteriorized their struggle against centralized hegemonic oppression. (In another context, Axel Michaels also shows how: 'blood cults and visualizations [are] found in posters and videos in two instances of martyrdom: the Tamil Tigers and the Maoist movement in Nepal'.[56]).

4 Conclusion

Sacrificial animals, in Folk Śākta traditions, are agents encoded within fluid sets of power relations—entangling bodies, terrestrial energy (*śakti*), and divine agents—which comprise that society's macro-clan. Through sacrifice, worshippers commune in bonds of ritual kinship that bind them, i.e. a sacrificial ceremony can bind new localities to a pre-existing macro-clan, as we have seen in Bhaktapur. With Bloch's concept of 'rebounding violence' in mind, I suggest sacrifice is a violent act that placates this-worldly power to transform or readjust power-streams flowing through the land to heal, or to appease the gods. On another level, the sacrificial victim is also an actor in this web-network, and its death produces self-reflexive emotion in the group. Such emotions were, later, appropriated by peasant-oriented political parties to convey their struggles. And finally, it is this combination of blood, death, transformation, self-reflexivity, and placation that creates emotional reactions in the social group. For that reason, blood sacrifice persists in Folk Śākta rituals; for their devotees, sacrifice seems a wholly natural, even socially edifying, praxis. In the next chapter, I will consider the relationship between political parties and Folk Śākta rituals in Kerala and Bhaktapur.

---

55 Martin Heidegger, *Being and Time: A Translation of Sein und Ziet*, trans. by Joan Stambaugh, (Albany: SUNY Press, 1996 [1953]).

56 Michaels, 'Blood Sacrifice', p. 194.

CHAPTER 6

Politics, Ritual Performance, and Caste

1 Introduction

In South Asia, the state of Kerala, and Bhaktapur City, are known for their political associations with communism; both are strongholds of revolutionary peasant movements. Influenced, in part, by political science, I suggest communism is given **some** momentum by the disintegration of a region's indigenous social structures, whether positive (e.g. dissolution of feudalism in Bhaktapur) or negative (e.g. the decline of matrilineal norms in Kerala). From a Durkheimian stance, any native structure of segmental cohesion—be it a kin group, clan, or ties to land—is a society's first phase of development ('mechanical solidarity'), before its second phase ('organic solidarity') emerges to overhaul the former with a stratified division of labour.[1] In Kerala's case, Jeffrey demonstrates how the impact of declining matrilineality (as 'mechanical solidarity') brought about the conditions for communist revolution.[2]

However, any hypothesis of 'social disintegration'—arguably, *post hoc ergo propter hoc* in design—can seem insufficient, since political formation cannot be reduced to a single dimension. Nevertheless, this hypothesis **is** useful, for it has been applied successfully—by South Asianists—to interpret India's postcolonial politics. Put simply, these scholars argue that colonialism sought to eradicate indigenous social orders by setting a caste hierarchy—based on Hindu exclusivism—in its place, which provoked resistance. Dirks famously posits this perspective: colonial India, he writes, was unified under British colonialism who instituted a universal caste system across its territories, which eased bureaucratic reshuffling.[3] Particularly in Kerala, colonial rulers, and later, the Hindu right, suppressed matrilineality, in order to re-establish caste as the dominant social order.

---

1 Emile Durkheim, *The Division of Labour in Society*, trans. by W.D. Halls, (New York: The Free Press, 1997 [1893]).

2 Robin Jeffrey, 'Matriliny, Marxism, and the Birth of the Communist Party of Kerala, 1930–1940', *The Journal of Asian Studies*, 39.1 (1978).

3 Nicholas B. Dirks, *Castes of Mind: Colonialism and the making of modern India* (Princeton: Princeton University Press, 2001).

 DOI:10.1163/9789004439023_008

In multi-ethnic Nepal, meanwhile, several attempts were made, throughout the 20th Century, to restore a Parbatiyā[4]-centred Hindu kingdom.[5] Such plans were opposed by marginalized ethnic groups[6] (*janjāti*), many of whom aligned with the anti-hierarchy Maoists who ousted the Hindu monarchy; in time, pledges for a constitutional assembly eventuated. Clearly, for Nepal's various communities, ethno-religious identity is vital to a group's feelings of belonging. This trend also extended to Maoists insurgents: by recruiting combatants from under-represented ethnicities, identity politics coalesced with the Maoists' radical ideology. De Sales explains how '[…] the practice of Nepalese Maoism [was] hardly a secular affair […] [since they were] willing to follow local traditions'.[7] A similar tendency exists among Keralan Marxists; their anti-religious politics are set in motion by senses of belonging derived from indigenous rituals.

2 Marxist-Influenced Politics and Ritual Performance in Postcolonial South Asia

In hindsight, I claim the hypothesis of 'socio-economic disintegration' cannot wholly account for the rise of South Asia's subaltern politics. As a response, this chapter will ask: can folk rituals—alongside other historical factors i.e. colonialism—explain the development of Marxist-influenced ideology in Kerala and Bhaktapur? On one hand, classical Marxist thought prohibits 'religion' on the grounds that it is conservative and occludes proletarian revolution. For any Marxist thinker, religion reproduces a hegemonic hierarchy by providing a 'transcendental' escape from class-based exploitation. On the other hand, I argue Folk Śākta performances—in postcolonial South Asia—are platforms for Marxist-influenced politics, such that they form inchoate blueprints for group-centred political agency.

In other communist regimes, too, I suggest ritual and politics can also dovetail. For instance, after the Cuban revolution, restrictions on traditional religion (Santería) did not effectuate on the ground. For many Cubans at that

4 Parbatiyā is an Indo-Gorkhali ethnic group from Nepal's Hill regions. Historically, Parbatiyā men have dominated central positions of state governance in Nepal.

5 The official governmental slogan during Hindu-nation restructuring was 'ek desh, ek besh, ek bhasa' (one country, one dress, one language), see Michael Breen, *The Road to Federalism in Nepal, Myanmar, and Sri Lanka: Finding the Middle-Ground* (London: Routledge, 2018), pp. 83–84.

6 These groups include Hindu-Buddhist Newars, tribal Thangmi, Buddhist Tamang, and Tharu.

7 Anne de Sales, 'The Kham Magar country, Nepal: Between ethnic claims and Maoism', trans. by David Gellner, *European Bulletin of Himalayan Research*, 19.2 (2000), pp. 65–66.

time, Fidel Castro's charismatic authority was rationalized in terms of Santería's notion of *oshun* ('divinity'). According to Valdés: "On January 8, 1959, as Fidel spoke to a crowd at the old military headquarters in Havana, several doves landed on his shoulder [...] Especially to Cubans immersed in the country's popular religiosity of Santeria, that was a sign, the confirmation, of the revolutionary leader's uniqueness."[8] Furthermore, in the 1990s, Santería ceremonies were no longer outlawed; as De La Torre tells us, Cuban legislation was changed to encourage Santería religiosity, because it increased tourism.[9]

At a deeper level, I argue a Folk Śākta performance's foregrounding of (1) meat-eating and sacrifice; (2) agrarian-timed ritual kinship; and (3) narratives of peasant injustice were consolidated, piecemeal, into a materialist ideology that coincided with Bhaktapurian and Keralan communist politics. From a different angle, Mannathukkaren notes how Marxism's success in Kerala was due to its continuity with 'traditional forms of consciousness'. He writes: 'the communist movement [in Kerala was not an] alien imposition, extraneous to traditional forms of consciousness [...] Instead, [it] correspond[ed] to [...] pre-existing aspirations to equality'.[10] As a corollary to Mannathukkaren's claim, I suggest any 'pre-existing aspiration' for revolution is drawn, partly, from collective ritual action, e.g. Teyyāṭṭam. I argue the same is true for the Newars of Bhaktapur, whose Navadurgā performances also exhibit socialist predilections.

In agreement with Gellner, I outline how a Weberian model of *elective affinity* can explain the commensurability of Newar religion with their socialist proclivities.[11] Sometimes unconsciously, and at other times deliberately, Folk Śākta performances tend to intersect with Bhaktapurian and Keralan Marxist ideology. By 'deliberately contributed', I mean that these affinities did not always take immediate effect in propounding the revolutionary ethos. At first, in 1930s–1940s, Teyyāṭṭam was dismissed by Marxists as a ritual which memorialized feudalism and caste subservience. In their view, Teyyāṭṭam was a tra-

8 Nelson P. Valdés, 'The Revolutionary and Political Content of Fidel Castro's Charismatic Authority', in *A Contemporary Cuban Reader: Reinventing the Revolution*, ed. by Philip Brenner et al., (Lanham: Rowman & Littlefield, 2008), p. 29.

9 Miguel A. De La Torre, *Santeria: The Beliefs and Rituals of a Growing Religion in America* (Michigan: William B. Eerdsman Publishing, 2004), pp. 175–176.

10 Nissim Mannathukkaren, '*Communism and the appropriation of modernity in Kerala*', (Ph.D. diss., Queen's University Canada, 2006), pp. ii–iii.

11 David Gellner, *The Anthropology of Hinduism and Buddhism: Weberian Themes*, (Oxford: OUP, 2001).

dition restrained by feudal deference, which hindered revolution.[12] Nevertheless, in time, certain Teyyam narratives—in particular, tales of socially ostracized deities, e.g. Pōṭṭan and Muttappan—were rhetorically re-envisioned as archetypes for revolution. Usually, ancestor worship and kingship are understood as products of kinship and religion, which breach Engels' insistence that 'family' is constitutionally capitalist,[13] and Marx's proclamation that religion is the 'opium of the people'.[14]

On the other hand, in Bhaktapur and Kerala, the macro-clan unity formed in Folk Śākta rituals are based on ritual kinship, and not consanguineal kinship *per se*. The ritual's macro-clan is a territorial cohesion that adopts metaphors of bodily proximity, blood, and meat-eating, in contradistinction to the social segregation of elite Brahmanical ideals. Folk Śākta rituals utilize inter-caste meat-eating practices to violate higher-caste dietary purity: in Kerala, beef-eating—the most transgressive act of all for Hindus—is legalized as per state policy.

Spiraling between conservatism and radicalism, the rituals—and, by the same token, local communist parties—fuse a radical attitude toward caste eradication with territorial oneness. As Geertz would put it, folk goddess rituals—by remaking traditional macro-clans—serve as 'models of' and 'models for' their region's communist cadres.[15] In Kerala, Ruchi Chaturvedi shows how CPI(M) ideology perceives its cadres as 'alternative families' led by a *Kārṇavan*; Keralan cadres, then, are as much affectively driven as ideologically-centred. Chaturvedi states: 'These communities in Kerala [are] bound by ties of friendship, camaraderie and fictive kinship cultivated over a lifetime in party-affiliated clubs and organisations or *shakyas*'.[16] Bhaktapur's Nepal Majdur-Kisan [Worker and Peasants'] Party [NWPP] also utilise kin titles in identifying party members; Ian Gibson documents how NWPP comrades call their party leader *dāi* (lit. 'elder brother').[17]

12 Gilles Tarabout, 'Malabar Gods, Nation-building, and World Culture: On Perception of the Local and the Global', in *Globalizing India: Perspectives from Below*, ed. by Jackie Assag & Chris Fuller, (Cambridge: CUP, 2004), p. 194.

13 Fredrich Engels, *The Origin of Family, Private Property, and the State* (Chicago: Charles H. Kerr & Co., 1909 [1884]).

14 Karl Marx, *Critique of Hegel's 'Philosophy of Right'*, trans. by Joseph O'Malley, (Cambridge: CUP, 1977 [1843]), p. 131.

15 Geertz, *Interpretation of Cultures*, p. 95.

16 Rudi Chaturvedi, 'Political violence, community, and its limits in Kannur, Kerala', *Contributions to Indian Sociology*, 49.2 (2015), pp. 167–168.

17 Gibson, 'Suffering and Christianity', p. 90.

In this chapter, I suggest that Folk Śākta performances ally with local styles of Marxist ideology, since both accentuate inter-caste cooperation—*in territoire*—as constitutive of their mechanisms; outside ritual, social relations become immutably hierarchized. Besides, Kerala's medieval kingdoms were themselves based on clan-like coherence: Mailaparambil's study of Kolathanādu (North Kerala) notes how political authority was a 'collective entity' (*swarupam*) that 'fragmented' power through chieftain lineages 'closely resembl[ing] a *tarvadu* [household]'[18] which 'was the main obstacle to the emergence of a powerful king'.[19] Among the peasant population, I argue that Folk Śakta *web-like networks*—as autochthonous ritual structures—were simulated by Marxist cadres to fortify their anti-caste ideology. In South Asian communism, cadres, like Folk Śākta rituals, are ordered as empowered kin-like networks that contravene caste purity through proximate pollution i.e. through practices of meat-eating and sacrifice.

In her work on domestic economies, Katharine Rankin states how, among Newars, familial or inter-caste units—especially festival organizations (*guṭhi*)—are upheld as the society's most secure and collaborative group. She writes: 'A merchant-caste young man put it frankly, 'We Newars work together for feasting and festivals all the time [as *guthi*], but when it comes time for business, well, we don't get along''.[20] More widely, this chapter will show how Folk Śākta performances and Marxist ideology—in confirming ritual kin and popular religion—are mutually co-extensive. Theoretically, in our context, I will evaluate the extent to which Durkheim's **collective** and Marx's **communism** can intertwine; for Kerala and Bhaktapur, traditional religious rituals and modern political ideologies—though ostensibly disconnected in many communist regimes—display inarguable porosity.

3 Teyyāṭṭam

3.1 *Kerala Revolutionaries: The Historical Emergence of CPI(M) Politics*

3.1.1 Kerala: Landowners, Tenancy, and Teyyam Groves

Since medieval times, the land of what is now Kerala was apportioned into 77 *taluk* or administrative micro-regions, which were centrally controlled but locally governed—as settlements and, later, districts. During colonial governance, however, the British homogenized these territories to expedite their

18 Mailaparambil, *Lords of the Sea*, p. 29.
19 Ibid., p. 37.
20 Rankin, 'Newar Representation', p. 117.

authority—77 *taluk* became 3 macro-districts: the southern district of Travancore, the central district of Cochin, and Northern Malabar.[21]

According to Freeman, Northern Malabar's distinctive landscape encompasses three natural 'zones' of habitation: the forest highlands, the agricultural lowlands, and the coast.[22] After the Cēra dynasty's dissolution (8th–10th Centuries CE), the coasts became economic hubs of maritime trade and trawling. Similarly, forest highlands accommodated communities of swiddening hunters and warriors. More generally, the rice-paddy lowlands were densely populous, for they housed much of the overall population.[23]

Accumulated from census documents—from the 17th Century to the 1930s—Nossiter tabulates Malabar's settlement statistics: in all, some 75% of all agrarian workers were tenants on cultivated land.[24] The sovereign divided land amongst regional chieftains and their joint-families: land-owning chieftains were conferred as having gained sovereign favour and were, therefore, noblemen of Nayār heredity.[25] These tenancies were financed by the crown and protected through *janman* laws, which assured the land would be inherited. The temples of Nambutiri Brahmans, however, were exempt from any regal jurisdiction, for their temple estates had legal autonomy.[26]

Ownership of state land was directly divided among chieftain lineages. In this way, their land could be inhabited by lower class tenants, who paid rent to their local chieftain (landlord). On these tracts, rice-paddies and coconut groves were worked by untouchable peasants (*Pulayar*) and toddy tappers (*Tiyya*). Collectively, these groups—landowner, tenants, and workers—formed villages on these land tracts, or at least, within close-proximity of the land they worked. In Malabar, this pattern of village formation meant villages were not atomic but dispersed over a wide area—in what Nossiter calls, a 'ribbon development'.[27] Many households peppered the landscape in a pattern of variable dispersal, contra close-proximity settlements (or 'clusters') that define villages elsewhere in India.[28] Under a chieftain's sponsorship, Teyyam groves were constructed at the village's epicentre; I was told annual Teyyāṭṭam drew families and households of shared land (a 'village') together.

---

21 Freeman, 'Gods, Groves', p. 257.

22 Ibid., p. 258.

23 Menon, 'The Moral Community', p. 191.

24 Nossiter, *Communism*, p. 15.

25 Kathleen Gough, 'Modes of Production in Southern India', *Capital View*, 15.5/7 (1980), p. 349.

26 Ibid.

27 Nossiter, *Communism*.

28 Ibid., p. 14.

For the most part, village land holdings were presided over by matrilineal Hindu Nāyars, and by the 1880s–1900s, their matrilineal system was slowly diminishing; British colonial legislation deplored matrilineality in support of patriarchy and caste hierarchy. (Although, in constitutional law, matrilineality was abolished during India's Independence). Nossiter claims how Mappila-Muslim communities also assimilated matrilineal patterns: most Mappilas occupied professions that were peasant and non-elite, whether agricultural labourers or maritime traders. (Due to the Mappilas history as sea-traders, many Mappila families lived near the coast). During the 1920s, matrilineality's eventual collapse—replaced by the colonists' patriarchal family values—spawned further economic stagnation; in revolt, the peasants coordinated skirmishes and uprisings to resist colonial 'reform'. For Jeffrey, this climate of social disarray quaked Kerala's agriculturalists into revolutionary action:

> With the depression of the 1930s, smaller peasants increasingly had to alienate their land or surrender their tenancies. In the northern part of Malabar district, the majority of those affected were Hindu, already deeply disturbed by the breakdown of the matrilineal joint-family.[29]

Even prior to British rule, Kerala had a caste-based social order already in place: perhaps 'caste' existed there as early as Śaṅkara's dissemination of Vedantic norms across the subcontinent. In that case, Swami Vivekananda's now infamous observation that Kerala was a 'madhouse' of caste is particularly valid:[30] lower-caste agriculturalists were forbidden to walk within a certain distance (some 60–80 meters) of bourgeois Nāyars and Brahmin priests in fear of violent protest or punishment. Jeffrey documents the ways lower-caste individuals were constrained by obligations of 'exaggerated deference' toward the higher castes, to such an extent that their clothing and manner of speaking was constricted to reflect this subservience.[31] These customs of caste partitioning were markedly intensified at the village level. However, as migration to urban areas accelerated into the 20th Century, draconian divides of bodily distance—which defined village life—could no longer hold, as Stokes explains: '[…] at a wider territorial level the solidarities of class make their intermittent appearance'.[32]

---

29 Jeffrey, 'Matriliny', p. 83.

30 See also Gabriel, *Playing God.*

31 Ibid., p. 82.

32 Eric Stokes, 'The return of the peasant to South Asian history', *Journal of South Asian Studies*, 6.1 (1976), p. 109.

In time, increasing access to communist literature in the region catalyzed antagonism toward caste orthodoxy among the populace; under British rule, caste relations had become ever-more reified. For Jeffrey, Malayalam translations of revolutionary literature were being issued for wide readership in colonial Kerala: around 1912, a biography of Karl Marx was published, which was later translated into Malayalam.[33] Malabar had exceptionally higher literary rates, as compared to the rest of India, which Jeffrey claims is related to matrilineal customs of household 'vernacular education', funded by two 'princely rulers [influenced by] the Religions of the Book and the printed word [which] was to facilitate the spread of Marxist ideas in the 1930s'.[34] Fascinatingly, he argues that 'religions of the book' actuated Marxist literacy in Kerala. I disagree with Jeffrey here, considering that communist ideology at that time was popular internationally. In terms of its structure, Nossiter labels Marxism a 'faith' among the religions of Kerala, which is no exaggeration; as we shall see, communist leaders in Kerala are ritually commemorated in a way comparable to Teyyam deification.[35] In Kannur, it is not unusual to find red hammer-and-sickle monuments earmarking majority CPI(M) neighbourhoods. Interestingly, such political monuments are also installed near Teyyam temples: one communist shrine sits near a renowned Muttappan temple at Parasinnikadāvu.

3.1.2 CPI(M): Communism in Kerala

During the summer of 1934, the CPI(M)'s rise to power occurred in earnest: the party—known as the Congress Socialist Party [CSP] at that time—was inaugurated by Jaiprakash Narayan in Kozhikode. The party steadily accrued some 4000 comrades (mostly Nayar) from the Northern Malabar district.[36] Incrementally, the process of unifying the CSP with the CPI(M) began in 1937; this co-option was spearheaded by P. Krishna Pallai, K. Damodaran, N.C. Sekhar, and E.M.S. Namboodiran (these leaders were all bourgeois elite: three Nayars and a Malayali Brahman). In the party's initial activism, middle-class members dominated its leadership. This was conventional in South Asia since educated classes were communism's motivators: the 'educated' were the first to disseminate Marxist ideology to the peasantry as a way of spurring resistant sentiments within them. (The same could be said for Bhaktapurian Marxism—all its party leaders are also elite and connected to intelligentsia in some way). Keralan peasants joined the movement much later in 1940. Between 1938–1941, middle-

33 Jeffrey, 'Matriliny', p. 87.

34 Ibid., pp. 78–79.

35 Nossiter, *Communism*, p. 21.

36 Jeffrey, 'Matriliny', p. 88.

FIGURE 20 Communist monument outside Parasinikkadavu Muttappan temple, (Kannur, Kerala)
PHOTOGRAPH BY AUTHOR

Nāyars formed approximately 45% of all its revolutionary membership.[37] Menon claims that CPI(M)'s recruitment of elite leaders produced a somewhat 'paradoxical programme', in which:

> [elite leaders] were products of the new intellectual climate that rejected caste, but they were able to work and organize cultivators and labourers, not only because they had worked alongside them in cultivation, but also because they commanded respect as members of the rural elite [...] in one sense, as a renegade rural elite organised on the basis of a vestigial deference to their position against the very idea of deference itself.[38]

CPI(M), like NWPP, is not a vanguard party that peddles 'the dictatorship of the proletariat' that Lenin forwarded. No doubt mindful of this, the CPI(M) leadership used strategies of 'peasant empathy' to accrue popularity, and thus, muster subaltern comrades. During the economic depression of the 1930–1940s, the party emphasized, in various publications, the worsening conditions of indigence inflicted upon the workers. This economic crisis hit peasants severely, which was further exacerbated by Malabar's steadfast feudal system. This anti-feudal line was reflected in CPI(M)'s policymaking, and below, I provide a list (from Jeffrey's article) of CPI(M) fiscal policies aimed at actuating social change. Jeffrey writes:

> security of tenure, assignment of half the net produce of the land to the tenant, reduction in land revenue, and, most important, abolition of feudal subservience to landlords.[39]

To dissolve the lower- and higher-caste divide even further, bourgeois leaders would dine with lower-castes, which was welcomed, and in time, peasant converts became devoted to their leaders' subaltern cause.[40] (Bhaktapurian NWPP leaders were also judged as being sympathetic to lower-caste farmers, and this is reflected in the leader's willingness to dine among them). Additionally, in Kerala state legislation, the eating and preparation of beef is legal, which, again, foregrounds Kerala's stance as historically sympathetic to communist values.

---

37 Dilip Menon, 'A Prehistory of Violence? Revolution and Martyrs in the Making of a Political Tradition in Kerala', *South Asia: Journal of South Asian Studies*, 39.3 (2016), p. 669.

38 Ibid., p. 669.

39 Jeffrey, 'Matriliny', p. 90.

40 Ibid., p. 96.

On September 15th, 1940, these revolutionary policies were presented by the CPI(M) at political rallies in various towns across Northern Kerala, which riled gathering supporters into some violent action. Overall, some 108 protestors were detained by police; Menon states that in Tellicherry, armed police opened fire on a group of rowdy protestors, who retaliated by throwing stones at their opponents—two protesters died at the rally.[41] And in 1957, the democratic election was won—substantially—by CPI(M), who held office intermittently until a new Kerala-only Communist Marxist Party (CMP) was formed in 1986 by M.V. Raghavan. CPI(M) was reconceived in 1964 as a splinter party schismatically severed from its previous 1940 CPI(M)-CSP party merger. Since that time, CPI(M) has governed and dominated Kerala's political scene.

In terms of CPI(M)'s structure, inter-member comradeship (*sakhakal*) is modelled on an autochthonous framework of matrilineal clan, wherein a leader is described as a *Kārṇavan*. As described by Jeffrey, early CPI(M) leaders expressed their devotion to the party as akin to a 'deep concern [a *Kārṇavan* has for] the welfare of his family'.[42] Keralan Communism, in these earlier days, absorbed elements of the then-disintegrating relations founded on the matrilineal clan. These bonds of filiation and joint-lineage unity—arguably derived from Teyyam performances—were deployed to prop up empowered connection between bodies as a way of resisting hierarchical class divisions. Chaturvedi's analysis of Keralan political parties demonstrates how bonds of fictive fraternity between members, both in CPI(M) and RSS, were imperative for party formation. She writes:

> We encounter members of the two groups [CPI(M) and RSS] who have organised themselves into masculine fraternities and communities that share forms of commonality imbued with notions of sameness and possibilities of being strangely united with one another; their experience of fraternal commonality goes hand-in-hand with vengeful hostility towards opposing groups.[43]

The convergence of subversive communism with 'fraternal' commonality seems incongruous with classical Marxism, which rejects the family unit as conducive to capitalism: how can fictive kinship be so strongly situated in South Asian Marxist-influenced politics? Naomi Katz, in her entry on 'kinship' in the *Dictionary of Marxist Thought*, argues that fictive kin communities deviate from family-based capitalism: while bourgeois classes integrate fam-

41 Menon, 'A Prehistory of Violence', p. 672.

42 Nottiter, *Communism*, p. 39.

43 Chaturvedi, 'Political violence', p. 165.

ily structures to preserve profit-making capitalism, fictive kin 'fraternities' create horizontal relationships of mutual support.[44] Despite its communist past, Kerala is economically affluent: money from Keralan migrants in the Gulf is transferred to their native families, thereby strengthening the economy. As with Bhaktapur, Kerala's Marxist government reinjects external capital for purposes of redistribution as 'mixed economy' social welfare. Corresponding to Teyyāṭṭam's system of distribution (*cerujanman*), the communist government has built upon this tradition in their policies of capital redistribution.

3.1.3 CPI(M) Propaganda and Teyyam Motifs: Brothers, Blood, and Sacrifice

In Malabar, fictive kinship is central to the way members refer to each other; kin titles and 'comrade' are used interchangeably. Furthermore, one of Chaturvedi's CPI(M) informants went as far as applying **bodily** imagery in recalling his affiliation to the party and its members. He said:

> To tell you the truth, it [the CPI(M) party] is in my blood from early childhood—from the age of thirteen. Even in times of trouble, I would not like to be away from party organization and its different families.[45]

The CPI(M) party evoked organic relations of bodily affinity and fictive kinship to counter bodily segregation compounded at the village level. And yet, ironically, it is within the confines of the village that Marxist parties were active in underground cadre communities. (The dispersed nature of Malabari villages—mentioned at the beginning of § 6.3.1—were ideal for potential 'agitators' to evade state authorities). Menon argues that CPI(M) endorsed affective concepts and imagery of violence, sacrifice, blood-bonds, and familial love (Maly: *sneham*) to provoke radicalism in their followers.[46]

Evidence of these body-based, kin-like sentiments are artistically displayed in CPI(M) propaganda: some murals also depict images of famous Communist leaders; in Kannur, I noticed posters of Che Guevara in many neighbourhoods. One of these propaganda murals—as translated by Menon—perfectly delineates this promotion of communism through language and motifs of emotion, blood, sacrifice, flames, and history (all, I might add, are redolent motifs intrinsic to Teyyam rites, which I recount in Chapter 3.3.3). The mural reads:

44 Naomi Katz, 'Kinship' in *The Dictionary of Marxist Thought*, ed. by Tom Bottomore et al., (Oxford: Blackwell, 1991).

45 Chaturvedi, 'Political violence', p. 175.

46 Menon, 'A Prehistory of Violence', p. 663.

> O flowers of flame, who have sieved the blood from the sacrificial altars and made a tilak of heroism with which you adorn your forehead. Time itself bows its head before the ritual killing fields that you ceaselessly generate.[47]

References to battle, martyrdom, sacrificial altars, emotions, flames, and time have clear resonances with themes of Teyyāṭṭam performances. It seems CPI(M) propaganda has assimilated imagery of indigenous customs to proliferate its political radicalism. Kerala communism, then, has adopted local traditions as a basis for its propaganda, in contradiction to other Communist regimes (apart from NWPP and other Newar communist parties, who uphold religio-cultural traditions in veneration). From the CPI(M)'s vantage point, Teyyam traditions were deemed religious systems that replicated feudal structures the party was attempting to dismantle. The turning point occurred when lower-castes emphasized Teyyam narratives and deity-songs (especially Pōṭṭan's narrative) as tales that recounted caste injustice. It is in this way that CPI(M) *interpellated* Teyyāṭṭam as conforming to their policy of subaltern welfare. By 'interpellation', Althusser coined the ways ideology is interiorized by an individual or group as a subjective reality: here, Teyyam and CPI(M) politics were identified, or rather *interpellated*, as inter-determinant ideologies.[48] One of my informants went as far as to say: 'If Karl Marx could be [deified as] a Teyyam deity, I think that is possible here! [laughs]'. It is toward these areas of convergence between Marxist politics and Teyyāṭṭam that I will now turn.

3.2 *'What Is Pure and What Is Impure, Please Tell Us!': Teyyam Narratives, Lower-Caste Resistance, and Existential Politics*

At first, Teyyam was viewed by Marxist parties as a tradition that commemorated landlord and lower-caste tenant relations. Even so, in medieval Kerala, Teyyam groves were ritual spaces where the entire village could congregate *in toto*, regardless of their caste grouping. It seems Teyyāṭṭam was a double-edged sword for Marxist politics; by valorizing lower-caste oppression via the worship of martyred ancestors, Teyyāṭṭam became a quandary that was paradoxical. But, gradually, tales of oppressed Teyyam divinities were spotlighted by CPI(M) to advocate caste disintegration; Dilip Menon argues how Teyyam songs (*tōṟram*) expressed a sense of 'moral community' which established a 'recognition of mutual space [between caste groups and clans]', as he untangles further:

47 Menon, 'A Prehistory of Violence', p. 666.

48 Louis Althusser, 'Ideology and ideological state apparatus', in *Lenin and Philosophy and Other Essays*, by Louis Althusser, (New York: Monthly Review Press, 1989).

> The performative tradition of the teyyam [...] that deified victims of caste violence and ritually reiterated their stories within annual performances at shrines in Northern Kerala recalled the violence that underlay the law of caste.[49]

In Teyyam folklore, one deity who experienced severe persecution was Pōṭṭan (lit. 'deaf-mute')—an untouchable drunkard who lived near a cremation ground. It is believed he is a manifestation of Śiva, who transforms into an untouchable to loiter on the path of some wealthy Nāyar proprietors or higher-caste Brahmins to test their knowledge and compassion. In several versions of the song—listed by J.R. Freeman—Pōṭṭan appears before the teacher, Śaṅkara, who is performing certain austerities in pursuit of *sarvajña-pīṭham* (lit. 'the seat of omniscience'[50]). Below is Freeman's translation of this narrative:

> [Having encountered the untouchable on his path, Śaṅkara states:]
> You are an Untouchable who should leave the path and withdraw into the distance; [...]
> Ignorant of past, present, or future,
> You are of vile caste, wreckers of social norms.
> Your caste observes none of the rites of purification, ablution, and such.
> Your nature is crude and your regard for deity slight.
> Not only that—the stink of such as fish and flesh never leave your bodies.
> Your trickery intends to wreck my journey—it's astounding!
> Drop this cunning and clear the path, you fool who lacks any discriminating knowledge.
> Of vile race, you chief among the rogues, begone!
> If you dare to oppose me, you will be honoured with a beating.
> So clear the way! Stand aside, you magnificent idiot![51]
> [Pōṭṭan replies:]
> What is the path, and who is it that should stand aside?
> What is pure and what is impure? What is eternal and what is transitory?
> What is truth and what is error? What is purity of mind?
> What is feminine, what masculine, what neuter?
> What things are gross and what subtle?

49 Menon, 'A Prehistory of Violence', pp. 666–667.
50 Freeman, 'Untouchable Bodies', p. 141.
51 Ibid., p. 142.

> What are 'those of the Veda' and what is a debased caste?
> What is the path of rectitude? Point this out for us!
> The basis for distinguishing between you and ourselves,
> Please tell us, if indeed you are the knower of Brahman! [...]
> If the body (*vigraham*) is cut, can you tell any difference from the colour of the blood
> Between a Brahmin and myself?
> How can one have notions of duality? When you don't even know yourself,
> how can you have aversion to me? [...][52]

Having been challenged by Pōṭṭan, Śaṅkara (or, in other versions, a tyrannical landlord) respectfully bows to Pōṭṭan's feet in reverence; some versions state how Śaṅkara recited verses of praise in his honour.[53] I claim these discursive instances of reversed deference are emphasized by CPI(M) to inspire a sense of protest that was not indifferent to their policies.

In Malabar, I would frequently read historical newspaper articles that discussed Teyyāṭṭam's link to Marxist politics: An article, "When the gods come down", *The Hindu* (November 5th, 2011) narrates how beliefs in the deities and Marxism are commensurable for Malayalis: 'Whether one believes in the transcendental powers or not; Theyyam is a big part of social life and cultural ethos in Northern Kerala. Paradoxically many of the people here are followers of communist movements; Marx and Theyyam are inseparable identities of faith for them'.[54] Another article—also published in *The Hindu*—describes the life of Mr. Sasidharan, a Theyyam dancer-medium (and part-time auto rickshaw-driver) who is a CPI(M) campaigner:

> Mr Sasidharan, a third generation Theyyam artiste, has a jam-packed schedule. After two days of campaigning for the polls [...] he has a slew of Theyyam performances lined up in the coming season opening later this month (on Thulam 10 of the Malayalam calendar).
>
> "The first of these is as Muttappan next week at Payyoli. It's a busy season ahead" says Mr Sasidharan, a lead figure in Theyyam [...]
>
> "Theyyam and politics are about faith and I'm dabbling in both in earnest" says the artiste, also a poll veteran.[55]

52 Ibid., p. 143.
53 Ibid., p. 145.
54 'When the gods come down', *The Hindu*, (November 5th, 2011).
55 'Theyyam binds candidates together at Pariyaram', *The Hindu*, (October 2015).

For Malayalis, communism and Teyyāṭṭam contain elements of 'faith', which could be construed as emotional attachment to an ideological cause. For Teyyāṭṭam, as in Kerala's Marxist cadres, collective groups merge in alternative families, a *web-like ritual network*, such that comrades are co-related as ritual kin: in practice, a Teyyāṭṭam's and communism's mechanisms of emotive and political agency are not so far removed. For one, subaltern self-empowerment—practiced in Marxist cadres—finds its provenance in Teyyāṭṭam, in which low-caste mediums become worshipped through offerings that sustain their clans. Unlike capitalist forms of profit, money in ritual kin networks—either cadres or Teyyam groves—are donated to those who require it most, who in Teyyāṭṭam's context, are the deity-mediums.

In South Asia, then, communist politics, religion, and culture converge in intersecting Venn diagrams. I argue these intersections form affective structures stemming from the goddess' webbed network, in addition to pastoralist concerns for land that manifested in a Marxist regime, fashioned as fictive brethren. Within Malabar's Marxist cadres, the apotheosis of dead comrades is common, which was later assimilated by the CPI(M): customarily, Malabaris commemorate swiddening warriors or oppressed women as lineage deities in local *samādhi* memorials. Menon presents this continuity here:

> Both at the shrines as well as on the waysides, the medieval tradition that celebrated heroes who had fallen in battle, and those who had been killed for their transgressions, continued. The Communist Party built upon this tradition by creating a territorial inscription of martyrdom marked by *raktasakshi mandapams* (martyr memorials) dedicated those who had fallen in political struggle.[56]

Red Marxist flags can also fly in or within the vicinity of a Teyyam grove to demonstrate that area's dominant political allegiance (so too can yellow RSS banners or green Muslim party flags). According to one of my interlocutors, the colour red exteriorizes the 'Tantric' power of the goddess in Teyyāṭṭam, whilst also fitting within a broader history of 'red' as an emblem for Communist states—the 'red' army of the Bolsheviks, and in Bhaktapur, 'Rohit' (lit. 'Red') is the NWPP party leader's *nom de guerre*. With this in mind, I will interrogate Newar society similarly: how far was Newari social organization and Tantric festivals conducive to Bhaktapurian socialism?

56 Menon, 'A Prehistory of Violence', p. 668.

4 Navadurgā

4.1 *The Historical Emergence of NWPP in Bhaktapur: 1964 Land Reform, Caste Subservience, and Newar Farmers*

4.1.1 Political Trajectory of 20th Century Nepal: A Broad Sketch

The history of 20th Century Nepali politics is a notoriously tangled one. Nepal's political trajectory has taken many sharp, unexpected, and violent turns over the past few decades, which I broadly outline here in chronological order: First, the country was governed by an autocratic Raṇa regime (1846–1951), which dissolved with the revival of a Hindu monarchy. Next, a partyless Panchyat system (1960–1990) was implemented in the kingdom, which spawned ethnic-based federalism and movements of communalism. From this federalism, Maoist insurgents incited revolution in Nepal—the Civil War (1996–2006)—which ultimately dismantled the monarchy. And since 2008–2009, the country has become a multi-party democratic republic.

In 1990, the first ever attempt at instituting democracy in Nepal (albeit a democratic Hindu kingdom) materialized with the new Constitution of 1990. Before 1990, a Partyless Panchyat system meant multi-party representation was restricted. Throughout the mid-20th century, communist parties were marginalized and could not be elected for central representation. In response, certain factions of the Communist party were spurred into active rebellion by becoming vocally dominant at the local level: for instance, the NWPP of Bhaktapur was formed in 1975 as splinter party of Nepal's Communist Party, which emerged from the peasants' movement (Nep: *kisan andolan*) of Newar farmers in Bhaktapur.[57]

As Malagodi details, the 1990 Constitution welcomed the advent of multi-party representation, and yet, this new constitutional legislation was still received with mass disapproval. Delayed by further opposition into the 2000s, a 'finalized' Constitution was passed in 2015. Each successive constitutional assembly—between 1990–2015—promulgated wide-spread resistance among *janajati* groups, precisely because the amendments remained biased toward Nepali-speaking Parbatiyās.[58] It was this representational disparity at the state-level that sparked a turn toward 'ethnic-based federalism' as a solution. In short, 'ethnic-based federalism' is a system that enables the politicization of under-represented ethnic groups into separate political entities within a united

57 Gibson, 'Suffering and Christianity', p. 84.

58 Mara Malagodi, *Constitutional Nationalism and Legal Exclusion: Equality, Identity Politics, and Democracy in Nepal (1990–2007)*, (Oxford: OUP, 2012), p. 3.

nation-state. All anti-monarchy Communist parties were pro-ethnic federalism, while Bhaktapurian NWPP remained opposed to federalism. In 1996, these Marxist-influenced political movements—unified as the first People's Movement (Nep: *jan andolan I*) in 1996—rebelled against the government during the Civil War (1996–2006). Shneiderman writes how, in 2006, a second People's movement (Nep: *jan andolan II*) peaked shortly afterwards. She notes:

> The 2006 People's movement in Nepal did not emerge overnight. Rather, it was the culmination of decades of political activism dating back at least to 1950, with the civil conflict between the Maoists and state forces that began in 1996 only the most recent turn in an ongoing process of state restructuring [...] Thangmi [tribal ethnic group in Nepal] became involved in party politics, largely via communism, and then ethnic activism, and slowly political power and ritual power began to articulate with each other.[59]

This is an incisive observation by Shneiderman; the ways political shifts are re-articulated in traditional ritual spaces (à la Clifford Geertz) is particularly discernible among South Asian resistance fighters. Indeed, for Newars and Keralans, political influences—geared primarily toward populist threads of class consciousness—can re-enter popular ritual spaces forasmuch as their expression of group-belonging quadrate on multiple levels. (Although, in Malabar, Teyyam can also be interpreted through the lens of the Hindu Right. From the Right's perspective, Teyyāṭṭam is a folkloric dance that brings-to-life or dramatizes Hindu deities for the popular masses who are unable to worship these gods in Brahmanical temples).

4.1.2 1964 Land Reform and NWPP Policies

To understand how NWPP communism was shaped, we must focus on specific political events in Nepal's history that sowed the seeds of change, namely the 1964 Land Act. Before 1964, all state land (*raikar*) was divided among landowners. Their lands were inhabited and worked by peasants, farmers, and worker-tenants, and, throughout the 1950s, the landowner-tenant relationship was inflicted with tensions. Tenants comported themselves as subservient to the landowner, which meant landowners were free to exploit tiller tenants financially; before 1964, landowner exploitation was rife. Rankin's compelling study of Newar merchants describes how asymmetrical landlord-tenant

59 Shneiderman, *Rituals of Ethnicity*, p. 250.

relationships—characterized by excessive deference—was usual in Newari communities. Such imbalances of power were compounded when tenants required a loan from their landlord. Her informant said:

> In addition to paying 25 per cent interest rates per growing season (1 *pāthī* interest per 4 *pāthī* grain borrowed), borrowers had first to supplicate the *sāu* [merchants] with *ghiu khāne*—gifts of fruits, eggs, sweets, clarified butter and such—in order to express deference and win the attention and favour of the lender.[60]

Practices of exaggerated deference dissipated with the institution of the 1964 Lands Reform Act, which gave tillers the right to cultivate the land as they so wished. The Act also introduced some additional legislation—such as a 'receipt-giving' system—that supplied tenants with evidence to challenge landowner decisions in disputes over land.[61] Section 26.1.b ('Rights and obligations of tenant') of the Act highlights how the completion of legal documentation was mandatory for registering land with named tenants. The section declares:

> [26.1.b]: If any landowner lets any peasant till his/her land, such landowner shall give a notice thereof to the prescribed authority within one month; and the prescribed authority shall subpoena and inquire the concerned landowner and the tenant about the matter, if necessary, and register the matter in the Registration Book.[62]

Bhaktapur's Municipality was populated mainly by tiller tenants, and thus, after the publication of the 1964 Lands Act, Bhaktapurian farmers forged a peasants' movement to ensure the Act was instituted there.[63] One of Ian Gibson's informants remembers the prominent changes in Bhaktapur after the implementation of the 1964 Act:

> I can still remember that after the Land Reform of mid-1960s, the local peasants started renovating the roof [sic] of their houses … Likewise, farmers started buying improved seeds, chemical fertilizers, and har-

60 Rankin, 'Newar Representations', p. 108.

61 Gibson, 'Suffering and Christianity', p. 84.

62 The Lands Act 2021 [1964], Published: 1/8/2021 (15 November 1964), source: http://admin.theiguides.org/Media/Documents/LandAct1964.pdf [http://www.lawcommission.gov.np].

63 Gibson, 'Suffering and Christianity', p. 83.

> vested increased production. This eventually increased the purchasing capacity of the ordinary farmers. I think, if communists of Bhaktapur had not launched a peasants' movement at that time, we could not have come out of that [sic] harsh living conditions, instead [we] would have continued the life of *das* [a slave] like earlier.[64]

With the rise of Bhaktapur's Peasant movement, the Nepal Majdur-Kisan party (NWPP) consolidated its political ranks by establishing itself as Bhaktapur's communist party led by Narayan Man Bijukchhe (also Comrade Rohit), a teacher-turned-Communist leader. Gibson describes his biography in detail, including how he—Narayan Man Bijukchhe—gained popularity among Newar farmers by displaying empathetic prioritization for those communities in his policy making.[65] The NWPP holds sway in Bhaktapur Municipality's public services: the party runs local administrative offices; it presides over medical posts and hospital facilities located just outside the main city gate; and the party funds Bhaktapurian colleges. The party leadership are largely intellectuals or educators by profession; as in Malabar, only a small percentage of the party's officials are farmers or pastoralists themselves. In Newar Tantric religion, deference to one's teacher is pertinent, and this is assimilated by contemporary NWPP leadership. Dyczkowski notes how 'the Tantra devote long sections to listing the qualities required of the disciple and those of the teacher [...] Like the teacher, he must be a moral person and not deceitful'.[66]

By using the disintegration of feudalism to their advantage, NWPP utilized this event as a backdrop for their political stance that challenges caste subservience. Indeed, since the 14th Century CE, Newars have been ordered into a rigid caste system that differentiates groups spatially in the Kathmandu Valley. (Though, the spatial zones (*tol*) that divide castes from centre to periphery still exists). However, Marxism's presence in Bhaktapur means hierarchy has become overhauled for inter-caste communication—albeit limited to Bhaktapurian Newaris—across the city's spatial zones.

4.1.3 NWPP Ideology

Many Bhaktapurians describe each other in terms of familial bonds, which emphasizes their close communal affinities as an ethnic group. As such,

64 Gibson, 'Suffering and Christianity', p. 83.
65 Ibid.
66 Dyczkowski, *The Cult of the Goddess*, p. 3.

NWPP—Bhaktapur's most popular political party—has tried to conserve Bhaktapurian solidarity by advocating its religious life: one NWPP member in Bhaktapur described religion to me as 'culture' (*sanskriti*), which, he said:

> is embedded inside the hearts of the people [...] Navadurga performances and traditional religion has a spirit of emotional connection with the people.

Like Gramsci's framework in § 6.5, it seems Bhaktapurian communism cannot dismiss traditional Newar religiosity (especially if that religiosity is set so heavily in idioms of familial ties, and the worship of Hindu deities). Gibson translated a series of NWPP revolutionary songs, which, in the same way, venerates religion-as-equal-with-culture:

> [Song 1]: Art and religion is the property of our nation,
> Everyone must remember to protect this property,
> Religion is also our culture [...]
> It is we who keep religion alive [...]
> There are many religions here, foreigners are also coming to stay here.
>
> [Song 2]: They [foreign imperialists] change our religion by enticing us, showing us our greed,
> They come to our place in the name of religion, and destroy our society.[67]

I will elaborate more on the role of Newar religion in Bhaktapurian communism in § 6.4.2. Structurally, the NWPP is at Bhaktapur's administrative heart and controls its central Municipality offices. They have progressed in reducing cases of political corruption, which, party propaganda claims, is endemic elsewhere in Nepal. NWPP claims that anti-corruption has been achieved in Bhaktapur because any external influences (outside political and/or foreign social factions) have been inhibited in the city's administration. Apart from extirpating foreign influence in Bhaktapur, NWPP launched other anti-corruption initiatives. Kapila Silva lists them here:

> Outsiders, whether they are Newar or non-Newar, are not given management roles in these institutions. [They] are also usually taxed at a

67 Gibson, 'Suffering and Christianity', pp. 87–88.

> higher rate than Bhaktapurians and are discouraged from owning or developing land in town. These policies in turn have facilitated the continued Newar presence in Bhaktapur, leading to the sustenance of its social character irrespective of the morality of such political interference.[68]

In this sense, NWPP's *zeitgeist* advances autonomous 'self-reliance', which, in the spirit of a Stalinist model of 'intra-state communism', exclusivizes the party's administration. This principle of communist autarky—or rather, ethnic nationalism—finds its equivalent in the North Korean ideal of *juche*.[69] Indeed, NWPP propaganda reveres the North Korean system as a germane point of reference for their distinctive form of governance.[70] As in the DPRK, all non-Nepali foreigners are monitored: their passports are inspected at the city gate and a mandatory Tourist payment is issued, which, I was told, finances the city's infrastructures.

The incentive for 'Tourist fees' was likely an outcome of the 'Bhaktapur Development Project' (1974–1985) financed by the German government. According to Grieve, the funding was used to rebuild and preserve damaged temple complexes.[71] Like communist policy in Malabar, NWPP has ambitiously embraced foreign investment for redistribution as communalist social welfare. By drawing on ritual gift distribution as a model, NWPP refashioned profit-making capital—as a mixed economy—to achieve its communist objectives (indeed, high numbers of independent entrepreneurial businesses (local stores, hotels etc.) are run by Bhaktapurian Newars in the city, which justifies this claim). Paradoxically, in communist Bhaktapur, I also realized that many interlocutors divulged irrefutably nationalist beliefs. After the April 2015 earthquake, India enforced an oil-blockade on the India-Nepal border, and its effects were still perceivable when I visited Nepal ten months later. The blockade insti-

68 Kapila D. Silva, 'Bhaktapur, Nepal: Heritage Values and Conservation Practices', in *Cultural Landscapes of South Asia: Studies in Heritage Conservation and Management*, ed. by Kapila D. Silva & Amita Sinha, (London: Routledge, 2017), pp. 185–189.

69 'Bhaktapur's Dear Leader', *The Nepali Times*, (29th April–5th May 2016).

70 The DPRK's Kim dynasty also adopts kinship to expound its parental-style dictatorship according to Korean folk mythologies that exalt 'Mother Korea' (interestingly, North Korean propaganda depicts a Kim leader as the nation's simultaneous mother *and* father). See B.R. Myers, *The Cleanest Race: How North Koreans see themselves* (Brooklyn, N.Y.: Melville House, 2010), which argues that the North Korean regime functions more clearly as a nationalistic, race-oriented state. Myers claims ultra-nationalist ideas were borne from the days of Japanese imperialism (1910–1945) on the Korean peninsula.

71 Grieve, *Retheorizing Religion*, p. 27.

gated nationalist fury in Nepal against India's government. NWPP leaders condemned India's actions on the Nepal border as expansionist.[72] To turn a phrase, NWPP fights fire with fire, or, in political parlance, they fight nationalism with their own style of Newari nationalism.

4.1.4 Newari Politics and Navadurgā Performances

Indications of a 'self-reliance' dogma are also adduced in Navadurgā performances: like extended families, Bhaktapurian citizens are encouraged to strengthen each other, financially and emotionally, by worshipping their filial goddesses. One Navadurgā member told me that performances were important because they conveyed moral lessons of *virtuous* unselfishness. A common phrase used by mediums to describe Navadurgā was 'it is a ritual that shows the beginning of [Newar] civilisation [and ideals of familial bonds]'. Partly enhanced by NWPP ideology, Navadurgā performances have been resketched as cultural phenomena which abate class consciousness through mono-ethnic social cohesion. In this way, Gibson claims NWPP has subverted norms of traditional caste acquiescence in Bhaktapur by 'reconstituting' its ethics towards active 'social service'.[73] As I have noted in the context of Malabar, a kin-like communist cadre—in the face of opposition—can turn defensive. For example, when NWPP actively opposed Panchyat governance in 1988, a series of revolutionary uprisings occurred in Bhaktapur.[74] Similar narrations of political upheaval can be found in Yogesh Raj's *History as Mindscapes*.[75] However, before the Civil War of 1996, agitated tensions and belligerent rebellions were common across Nepal, particularly in Western Nepal, which was a Maoist centre. I claim that this ideological defensiveness is bounded up in a strong sense of communal coherence, derived from Tantric religion, that is at the heart of Bhaktapurian religious life. These web-like relations have also reinforced alliances between Newar farmers (*Jyāpu/Maharjāns*) throughout Nepal with the establishment of a 'Newar Farmer Association' (*Jyāpu Mahāguṭhi*) in the 1990s.[76]

---

72 'NWPP Chair blames India for industry collapse in Nepal', *The Himalayan Times*, (10th March 2016).

73 Gibson, 'Suffering and Christianity'.

74 One of these uprising was led by the NWPP leader in 1988. A group of farmer rebels rioted against a parliamentary member who had embezzled and profited from the city's financial budget for earthquake relief and social aid. See Louise T. Brown, *The Challenge of Democracy in Nepal: A Political History* (London: Routledge, 2002).

75 Yogesh Raj, *History as Mindscapes: A Memory of the Peasants' Movement of Nepal* (Kathmandu: Martin Chautari Publishers, 2010).

76 Toffin, *Newar Society*, pp. 370–371.

Though Newar farmers are distinguished territorially, there is still a sense of proletarian unity that binds them across the Kathmandu Valley. As Baltutis outlines, Newar farmers conglomerate in shared, multi-ethnic cultural festivals—viz. the Indra Jātrā festival in Kathmandu—by politically asserting themselves as a *janajāti* group peripheralized from the Parbatiyā majority. During the festival, Newar farmers claim their descent from Yalambar-Bhairav-Āju (an ancestral deity) and in doing so, they worship him as their king. According to Newar accounts, described by Baltutis, Yalambar-Bhairav-Āju—or Kathmandu's Ākāś Bhairava—was previously embodied as King Yalambar, a king from the region of Kirāt who was beheaded by a hegemonic Gorkhali deity. Yalambar's shrine was later installed in Kathmandu by lower-caste Newar farmers in his honour.[77]

As in Bhaktapur, Newar farmers seemed to reminisce, quite often, about their true historical descent as Newar citizens of a pre-Shah Malla monarchy. Navadurgā performances are also salient sites from which Bhaktapurian Newars can assert this ethnic identity: Navadurgā cycles commemorate key elements of Newar mythology, such as the Malla monarchy. Indeed, a Newar farmer's link to medieval militia in the Nepal Valley is striking and deep-rooted. Toffin suggests that Newars are 'feared because of their association with the highly perilious Bhairava',[78] and that 'some even say that farmers were enrolled as soldiers in the Malla armies during the mediaeval period [...] the word *māhāṃ*, used for soldiers in the Malla period, seems to be related in one way or another to the title, Maharjan'.[79] In the next section, I will discuss to what extent Navadurgā performances—where lower-caste dancer-mediums are honoured in cases of inverted deference—promotes NWPP's peasant rhetoric.

4.2 *Religious-Communism 'Interpellated': Navadurgā, Folk Performance, and "Marxism"*

Although medieval in origin, Bhaktapurian "communists" continue to venerate Navadurgā performances as relevant social phenomena. In their view, Navadurgā performances demonstrate 'caste reversal', that is, a ritual situation where lower-caste dancer-mediums become subjects of social veneration, contrary to higher-class priests nominally considered rightful recipients of such subservience. Before Banmala castes were ordained as Tantric virtuosi (around the 16th Century CE), their official vocation was flower selling; according to the caste hierarchy, a Banmala troupe is not historically perceived as elite or higher caste but, rather, a subaltern priesthood.

77 Baltutis, 'Sacrificing (to) Bhairava', p. 215.
78 Toffin, *Newar Society*, p. 367.
79 Ibid., p. 366 ff5.

According to Ujesh, Dinesh, Krishna, and other interlocutors, Navadurgā performances had numerous interlocking social roles for the Newars of Bhaktapur. At one point during a Navadurgā performance, Ujesh expressed how such events "bind people together to spread positive messages and ideas to them". In Nepal and elsewhere, Navadurgā performances have accrued much negative publicity in relation to their liberal slaughtering of animal sacrifices. (In reality, themes of sacrifice are central to most, if not all, religious traditions[80]). To dispel what Ujesh considered misconceptions about Navadurgā, he continued, throughout the course of my fieldwork, to portray Navadurgā dances as acts of mutual empowerment that dissolve class rankings through reciprocal offerings with gods/goddesses who, essentially, are the group's filial ancestors. Ujesh also added that acts of reciprocity act to confer a deity-mediums' power (*śakti*) or blessings to revitalize a worshipper's family, business, or health in return.

During an interview with another interlocutor, he elaborated on Ujesh's interpretation; for him, a performance's capacity for transferring ancestral strength meant devotion toward Navadurgā mediums intensified after the 2015 earthquake. In response, Bhaktapurians offered gifts—with increased regularity—during the Navadurgā's rotational performances throughout the city. This increased fervour was linked not only to the performance's ability to enhance the population's power (*śakti*), but also to senses of security the dancing mediums—as their ancestral deities—created in the group. I was told that Navadurgā performances distribute power and ancestral guidance which bolstered Bhaktapur's citizens in their attempts at rebuilding the wreckage. In conversation with a NWPP member, we discussed, in further detail, the effect of the earthquake on Navadurgā worship. He amplified how the collective unity created in Navadurgā ritual correlates with NWPP communism: their mutual focus on communal self-reliance and strength, he said, were coterminous. He continued:

> [Inf.] Culture has always been in the hearts of the people, even after the earthquake disaster, and in time, their lives began improving slowly. But there was a clear change in their lives—lost lives and lost households. Culture, like Navadurgā, has a spiritual and emotional connection with people. It continued even during the crisis period because it was a way of reviving the life of the community again. People learn from Navadurgā because it is a social practice with important social messages about life. It is like an integrated teaching, which all people watch. It is also *democratic*,

80 Meszaros & Zacchuber, *Sacrifice in Modern Thought.*

> the neighbourhoods can invite the Navadurgā troupe into their homes to give blessings; it is about offering and contributing ... it is a way of showing honour [*ijjat*] and being hospitable to the troupe.

Throughout the conversation, it became clear that Navadurgā performances had been reclaimed by NWPP supporters as a remnant of pre-1700s religio-cultural life; a life that focused on uniting people in bonds of social solidarity as 'Newari Bhaktapurians'. All Navadurgā members supported NWPP communism, which, they emphasized, was not incompatible with their religious beliefs. Ujesh commended NWPP as an important party that had changed Bhaktapur for the better: NWPP's strategies for cultural and architectural conservation aligned with his own concernments about Bhaktapur's future as a hub of Newar culture. Ujesh was also devoutly religious; whenever we visited a temple in Bhaktapur or elsewhere in the Kathmandu Valley, he always offered *prāsād* to the residing deity. He often claimed that NWPP communism and goddess-worship were not irreconcilable—the social nature of Newar religiosity was congruous with the ideals of collectivity promoted by NWPP Marxism. Throughout Nepal, it seems goddess-worship and Maoist politics tend to converge; in his study of Eastern Nepal, Ghimire noticed how 'substantial numbers of [Maoist] supporters' were goddess-worshippers.[81]

A sense of ideological interpellation (in the Althusserian sense) was indelible in Ujesh's understanding of Newar religion.[82] In Ujesh's case, Newar religion and Marxist-influenced ideology were reconciled or, in Althusser's words, 'hailed' as contingent.[83] Further, it was clear that Ujesh was guided by his family's example, who, like him, were supporters of NWPP: as with Navadurgā performances, adhering to the political loyalties of your kin group is typical among Nepali groups. For Zharkevich, an interlocutor in Thabang village capsulized this tendency as an adage: 'Where the friends and kin are, there we should give our voice'.[84]

To help us untangle this concept of 'ideological interpellation' further—through which communist ideology *interpellates* traditional religiosity and kinship—Zharkevich's ethnographic study of Thabang (a Maoist-occupied village) becomes an invaluable source. During her fieldwork, she witnessed several social practices that were unavowedly religious. On one occasion, during

81 Ghimire, 'Living Goddesses', p. 185.

82 Althusser, 'Ideology'.

83 Ibid.

84 Ina Zharkevich, 'De-mythologizing 'the Village of Resistance': How rebellious were the peasants in the Maoist base area of Nepal?', *Dialectical Anthropology*, 59.4 (2015), p. 375.

a family's Śraddhā ceremony at a home in Thabang, a local woman became 'possessed'—quite spontaneously—by the village divinity, *Jaljala*.[85] Zharkevich describes how, during the Civil war, Maoist villagers were 'trapped between the two worlds',[86] insofar as they continued to practice Kham Magar religiosity irrespective of conflicting Maoist claims that were, in truth, 'anti-Hindu[-state], rather than as anti-religion per se'.[87] From this predicament, the Maoists of Thabang sought to reconstruct the internal meaning of time-honored ancestor religion to comply with a proletarian, anti-Hindu ideology. Zharkevich explains how a *Jaljala* festival in Thabang was acceptable because it was 'primarily local in character, that is, it had nothing to do with [state-]official Hinduism'.[88] Maoist rhetoric transformed a festival into a 'cultural' non-Hindu celebration (despite claims that Kham Magars—as a group—are themselves rooted as Hindu). Above all, the festival's impetus had been politically reframed to abide by an overarching Maoist ideology; a ritual performance—in Zharkevich's interpretation—was no longer about fulfilling the will of distant divine beings. On the contrary, in this communist cadre, a ritual became an opportunity for the group to worship its own collective identity as 'sacred'. Zharkevich tell us: '[…] the performance of animal sacrifice could be a display of one's ethnic identity rather than a genuine propitiation of the gods'.[89]

For folk Śākta performances, however, I argue the transformation of ritual, by politics, into identity worship was *not* asymmetrical, since the source of a divinity—or a goddess-clan—is already distributed in her adherents' bodies as a webbed-network. Historically, I suggest Folk Śākta goddesses in Bhaktapur operated as hitherto autochthonous paradigms for social-group worship that were consonant with the political (that is, NWPP) revisioning. In *Rituals of Ethnicity*, Shneiderman frames her analysis of Thangmi culture on similar ground: she writes that Thangmi society has no detectable or tangible material culture with which to authenticate its cultural mores and, in lieu of this void, '[…] all […] ritualized action […] has a shared sacred referent: Thangmi identity itself'.[90] With all this evidence together, we can see how a ritual centred on shared ancestors, land, and group-identity worship can combine two

85 Ina Zharkevich, ''When Gods return to their Homeland in the Himalayas': Maoism, Religion, and Change in the Model Village of Thabang, Mid-Western Nepal' in *Religion, Secularism, and Ethnicity in Contemporary Nepal*, ed. by David Gellner et al., (Oxford: OUP, 2018), p. 91.

86 Ibid., p. 103.

87 Ibid., p. 80.

88 Ibid., p. 84.

89 Ibid., p. 105.

90 Shneiderman, *Rituals of Ethnicity*, p. 36.

oppositional ideologies in spiraling tandem: put differently, a Folk Śākta performance indirectly resonates with socialism's goal of empowering bodies—in Newar groups—across caste hierarchies.

As per NWPP ideology, the antimony of traditional religion and revolutionary revisionism seems critical to the party's popularity among Newar farmers: many Newars in Bhaktapur actively abide by conservative 'Hindu' cultural values alongside a belief in quasi-anarchistic caste abolition. A clear dichotomization persists in Bhaktapurian socio-political life, which can be articulated as a distinction between 'traditional' Newar religiosity and 'modern' social developments. In what ways can a Marxist-sympathizing party advocate **both** religious conservatism **and** a progressive vision of "communist" ideals? Like the spiraling web-network engendered in Navadurgā performances, NWPP is a complicated political ideology because it *spirals* between two paradoxical polarities: the party has synergized left- **and** right-wing policies such that it incorporates mono-ethnic Newar traditionalism with radical socialism.

This apparently paradoxical policy was also an issue for Gregory Grieve, who noted how his informants saw this paradox as a Western construct. To explain this, Grieve's interlocutor drew a distinction between a Western idea of 'tradition' as the historical past and a Nepali understanding of 'tradition' (*paramparā*). For him, Nepali *paramparā* should be construed as a 'history of the present', that is, a genealogy that can reawaken pragmatism from the past into the present, which, he claims, stands in counterpoint to Western ideas of 'tradition'. Grieve continues:

> Unlike the [Western view of] tradition, [Bhaktapurian] tradition is neither seeking of pure origins, nor the plotting of an evolutionary time-line. Instead, like a "history of the present" a genealogical tradition chronicles the pragmatic use of those past social practices that are currently effective [...] Paramparā ['tradition'] means to use as a model what your father and grandfather did.[91]

Bhaktapurian NWPP have also employed this pragmatic approach to history and tradition: by utilizing effective conventions from the genealogical past, they seek to improve the present. A monograph written by Narayan Man Bijukchhe—*Bhaktapur after a Century* (*Saya Barsha Pachiko Bhaktapur*)—draws

91 Gregory Grieve, 'Histories of Tradition in Bhaktapur, Nepal: Or, how to compile a Contemporary Hindu Medieval City', in *Historicizing Tradition in the Study of Religion*, ed. by Steven Engler & Gregory Grieve, (Berlin: DeGruyter, 2012), p. 271 & p. 278.

our attention to this ideological slant. In it, Bijukchhe writes that an ethos of 'preserving traditional culture' should *not* be rendered irreconcilable with progressive scientific development. He notes:

> Krishna, you raise the question of Nepal's art, culture, language and literature being destroyed or defiled by the attack of foreign cultures. [...] But despite 150 years of attack by imperialism and colonialism, the language, literature and culture of countries like China, India, Korea, Vietnam [etc] could not be wiped out. Foreign cultures will not succeed in destroying Nepali language, literature and culture. Instead, new science and technology will be used to conserve and promote our language, literature and culture.[92]

I posit that this view of history—as a pragmatic tool to promote technological advancement—may find its radix in Folk Śākta performances: an ancestral deity's agency is intentionally embodied in contemporary dancer-mediums to aid social problems that afflict their devotees.

In the same way, genealogical history is focal to Navadurgā worship, too; a *clan* of deity-mediums—selected for their hereditary status as religious specialists—are offered gifts for their power-distributing services. Navadurgā performances, therefore, redistribute resources as fictive kin organisations (*guthi*) may administer them. This has profound resonances with NWPP's abiding political rhetoric, which endorses the dissolution of caste and Western capitalist globalization in exchange for a distributive mixed economy. Rankin also observes the native ideal of social welfare at work in the Newar town of Sankhu:

> Sankhu Newars describe such social investments as a kind of welfare system: the generosity and hospitality that goes along with religious and social duties such as *guthi* membership works to redistribute resources and level economic difference; 'No one goes hungry in Sankhu' is a common refrain, or 'Nothing goes to waste: even leftover food and clothes of the dead get put to good use'. Indeed, obligations to kin, *guthi*, neighbours, priests and other ritual specialists encircle the own in tight webs of interdependence that ensure levels of provisioning for all social citizens who conform to the logic of the honour economy, however much gender-, caste-, and age-based hierarchies may endure.[93]

---

92 Narayana Man Bijukchhe, *Saya Barsha Pachiko Bhaktapur*, VS 2059, translated in Gibson, 'Suffering and Christianity', p. 96.

93 Rankin, 'Newar Representations', p. 127.

I suggest that Navadurgā's use of ritual kinship and re-distribution provided farmers with notions of class consciousness which, in time, reached its political zenith with the advent of NWPP communism. NWPP ideology was another metaphysical strand in the *bricolage web of ritual knowledge* on which Navadurgā's 'spiraling web-network'—between conservatism and radicalism—is constructed.

5 Conclusion

Though nominally anti-religious in ideology, South Asian Marxism, by contrast, draws upon elements of localized religiosity to rampart its ideological popularity. Theoretically, political ideologies are as malleable to local conventions as the population that adopts them. This could be posited for North Korea; their regime fuses socialism, religious zeal (stemming from Korean mythology), and militaristic nationalism that emerged from remnants of Japanese imperialism.[94] In Bhaktapur, NWPP's ideological malleability stems from the interpellation of two seemingly paradoxical claims, which *spiral*—like an indigenous Navadurgā cosmology—between right-wing conservatism and left-wing economic radicalism. In keeping with this, the innovators of Subaltern Studies—led by Italian Marxist, Antonio Gramsci—re-envisioned Communism as a 'philosophy of praxis'.[95] Like Weber's notion of 'elective affinity', Gramsci shows how a community's traditional culture induces subaltern protest, which, he suggests, precedes the political ideology. Mansueto fascinatingly condenses Gramsci's 'Cultural Marxism' hence:

> What Gramsci has done here is to break not only with the Marxist theory of religion, but with the whole classical Marxist understanding of the material and spiritual connections for communism. It is not the development of the productive forces, with its attendant increase in the division of labour and thus in the level of real material interdependence, but rather the traditional communal institutions and popular religious traditions of the masses themselves, which are the fundamental condition for the emergence of mass socialist movements.[96]

---

94 B.R. Myers, *Cleanest Race*.

95 Cf. Fourth Notebook § 38 in Antonio Gramsci, *Prison Notebooks Vol. II*, trans. by Joseph Buttigeg, (New York: Columbia University Press, 2011 [1975]), pp. 176–177.

96 Anthony Mansueto, 'Religion, Solidarity and Class Struggle: Marx, Durkheim, and Gramsci on the Religion question', *Social Compass*, 35.2–3 (1988), p. 274.

Commensurate with this logic, Durkheim's vision of collective effervescence (as 'mechanical solidarity') can be implicated here as a form of group-based, anti-hierarchy revolution: perhaps social effervescence—electrified in popular religious ceremonies—is a domino in the domino effect of socialist formation. In this light, a subaltern kin-focused ritual performance may correspond with the creation of a socialist movement. According to this paradigm, CPI(M) in North Malabar, for example, was predetermined by Teyyāṭṭam's ritual kin assembly which was intensified by an analogous political history—of caste struggle—exacerbated by colonialism. In principle, the idea of a secular state—a Western-derived model that compresses religious expression into private (and exclusivist) spheres to facilitate their intra-state coexistence[97]—does not translate, in practice, in South Asia, for religio-cultural sentiments—even among anti-religious Marxists—are deep-seated as inveterately public **and** private, collective **and** individual, like the spiraling nature of Folk Śākta performances themselves. In this analysis, South Asian political movements are also *web-like networks* where 'religious', 'political', and 'cultural' streams flow inseparably, just as they do in Folk Śākta performances.

---

97 For an in-depth study of secularism in modern Nepal, see Chiara Letizia, 'Ideas of Secularism in Contemporary Nepal', in *Religion, Secularism, and Ethnicity in Contemporary Nepal* (Oxford: OUP, 2016). And, for Western conceptions of secularism, see Charles Taylor, *A Secular Age* (Cambridge, Massachusetts: Harvard University Press, 2007).

Conclusion

At the end of our comparative 'network', it is time we reconnect the book's themes to consolidate its main hypothesis. As has become evident, Folk Śākta performances *spiral* three sets of structural dichotomies into synthetic *web-like ritual networks* at three levels—*societal, metaphysical*, and *political*. Through ritual gatherings, these dichotomies synthesize, such that everything contained in their ritual networks—bodies, regalia, metaphysical systems, liturgical texts, and social orders—realign within the land's macro-clan. Socially, a spiral-like motion from caste hierarchy to folk lineages produces a ritual macro-clan that typifies a Folk Śākta performance: its ritual network, then, valorizes interpersonal connection—across these two social structures—as opposed to caste-based stratification alone.

In ritual, the use of transgressive bodily practices, coordinated by lower class dancer-mediums—i.e. the imbibing of pollutive substances and use of blood—foregrounds them as propelled, primarily, by inter-caste territory-wide proximity. However, as is argued throughout this book, Folk Śākta rituals do not occlude caste *entirely*—caste affiliations are absorbed in this web-network too—but, instead, the tension between structures of verticality and horizontal connection are recast such that they infringe these structures altogether. And in this way, Folk Śākta rituals are latent platforms for radical political sentiments, which were conducive to the development of Marxist-influenced politics in 20th-Century Bhaktapur and Kerala (both of which were defined by their anti-caste, intra-state ideology).

Clearly, the resplendent appeal of Folk Śākta performances—with *leitmotifs* of ritual communion, blood, and consecrated costumes—draw upon the most connate crevice of the human psyche—social emotion—by fostering fictive relations in ritual macro-clans to heal or, indeed, to curse. It is no wonder, then, that local inhabitants feel a connection toward these ritual traditions.

For Folk Śākta rituals, 'webs' emically articulate their complex mechanisms at three levels: their societal workings, metaphysical formation, and political expression. In anthropological theory, 'web' metaphors are also presented by Clifford Geertz who—in Weberian style—construed cultural systems as web-like structures. Geertz tell us, 'man is [...] suspended in webs of significance that he himself has spun, I take culture to be those webs'.[1] But why a web? What

1 Geertz, *Interpretation of Cultures*, p. 5.

 | DOI:10.1163/9789004439023_009

properties do webs demonstrate which are so apposite in exemplifying cultural or, in this book, ritual traditions? Perhaps recent zoological research may assist us in this endeavour.

Mortimer et al. illustrate how webs have 'multifunctional' built-in properties; most magnificently, a web's structure can transmit information and 'vibrational frequencies' (what could be effervescent *spanda* ('vibration') in Tantric thought) to other spiders and prey caught in its structure. This transmission is traceable to its 'spiral' centre, from which the network's inter-connections are built up on three levels. This environment of vibration, spiraling, and structural interlinkages can aid a spider in navigating its world. Mortimer continues:

> Orb webs are multifunctional structures that need to balance mechanical performance and information transfer to ensure that spiders can successfully catch prey, mate and avoid predators. Major ampullate silk is intrinsically multifunctional as it acts to absorb energy during web impace [2,52] and tranmit vibrations [existential *Spanda* in a Tantric worldview] to the spider [3,17]. Our data have showed that the capture spiral also has multiple functions; it not noly acts to retain prey [in this context, blood sacrifice] long enough for the spider to reach it, but is also an aspect of web architecture that directly affects transverse wave propagation. Although transverse waves dispersed to neighbouring radials via the capture spiral, longitudinal waves did not, which suggests they could provide valuable information on the location of a vibration source.[2]

1 Teyyāṭṭam and Navadurgā Compared: Revisited

To summarize this book's core arguments, I tabulate them here in order:

	Teyyāṭṭam (Northern Malabar, Kerala)	**Navadurgā (Bhaktapur, Nepal)**
Dancer-Medium Communities and Ritual Kinship	Indigenous horizontal social formation: **matrilineal joint-families**	Indigenous horizontal social formation: **guṭhi inter-caste association**

2 B. Mortimer et al., 'Tuning the instrument: Sonic properties in the spider's web', *Journal of the Royal Society: Interface*, Vol. 13, 2016, 0341.

(*cont.*)

Hypothesis: A ritual performance *spirals* caste and kinship to synthesize them as a *macro-clan*.	Vertical social formation: **Caste hierarchy (systematized around 8th Century CE)** Dancer-medium community: **Matrilineal and Patrilineal families of certain lower caste groups**	Vertical social formation **Newar Caste hierarchy (introduced during the Lichhavi era, but systematized by Jayasthiti Malla, 14th Century CE)** Dancer-medium community: **Banmala caste and guṭhi**
History and Assimilation in Tantric Cosmology Hypothesis: A ritual performance *spirals* body and text to synthesize metaphysical lines in *bricolage webs of ritual knowledge*.	8th–16th Century CE (Kōlattiri Period) Nondual, *Kaula* (non-Saiddhantika) Tantric cosmology derived from Kaśmir Śaivism fused with local fertility cults. The Tantric cosmology was brought with the diffusion and settlement of itinerant Nāth Siddha communities. Chapter 4 suggests that several commentarial works (i.e. Vijñanabhairava) of Kaśmir Śaiva origins and Śākta Yāmala and Nityāṣoḍaśikārṇava (ritual) texts were translated into Malayalam language and utilised by Tantric practitioners in the region. Sanskritization of local divinities was also in operation (especially as part of BJP's expansionist agenda)	11th–18th Century CE (Malla Period) A conglomeration of nondual and dualist Kaśmir Śaiva (*Kaula* traditions of non-Saiddhantika) Yāmala, and Śākta theological, ritual texts (Nityāṣoḍaśikārṇava) were used by royal priesthoods which permeated the theological worldview of Newar religion.[3] Many of these texts from Kaśmir and beyond were extant in the Kathmandu Valley with the movement of Nāth siddhas and mendicant virtuosi who settled at Paśupathināth (most of this literature is stored in micro-film form at the National Archives, Kathmandu)
Sacrifice, Earth Cycles, and Self-Reflexive Affect	Chicken sacrifice and the use of blood substitutes (*guruti* and/or coconuts)	Most deities accept pig, goat, buffalo, and chicken sacrifices. No substitutes are used.

3 A list of Nepalese *paddhatis* used by Newars is itemized in Alexis Sanderson, 'The Śaiva Religion among the Khmers (Part I)', in *Bulletin de l'École française d'Extrême-Orient*, 90/91 (2003–2004), pp. 366–372.

(*cont.*)

Hypothesis: A ritual performance *spirals* sacrifice and sacrificer, which creates communal feelings of *self-reflexive affect.*	Only ancestral warriors or royal goddesses accept blood libations. Emotional/Tantric communion with the power of a regal ancestral goddess-clan as a webbed network	Emotional/Tantric communion with the power of a regal ancestral goddess-clan as a webbed network
Politics, Ritual Performance, and Caste Hypothesis: Like Folk Śākta performances, a political movement *spirals* conservatism and radicalism, thereby forming a 'territory-conscious Marxist ideology'	In Northern Malabar (especially Kannur), a CPI(M) party was political dominant during the early 20th Century. Although, Teyyam practitioners and devotees have alleigances with both RSS and CPI(M). A tension between state and Brahmanical power	A Newar communist party (NWPP) has governed the political infrastructure of Bhaktapur since the early 20th Century. NWPP is defined as a form of intra-state Marxist-influenced socialism. Less tension (but distinction between) state and Brahmanical power

As a conclusive auxiliary, I shall, in turn, revisit each of these themes below.

2 Dancer-Medium Communities and Ritual Kinship

Since the mid-medieval era, dancer-medium communities have survived due to the transmission of their ritual knowledge from one generation to the next. Not only that, but the mediums' totemic relations to a royal goddess-clan—whose power and knowledge they embody in ritual—is also bequeathed. During their rituals, the dancer-mediums draw the goddess-clan's divine power—territorially enshrined—into their bodies, which renews the land and coheres worshippers with each other, and with their ancestors. When mediums invoke these deities, people from different castes and lineages congregate to worship them. They share this ritual, which establishes connections of ritual kinship or *affective kin-like intentionality* across families and castes; these rituals integrate denizens with their land's divinities, which unites them as citizens (akin to the goddess-clan's *menstrual synchrony*).

This process of invoking medieval energy is invocated by sets of sacrificial and symbolic gestures that distill and incarnate the territory's *śakti*. Dancer-medium spectacles, in this way, are not tantamount to a divine masquerade or artistic performance; for dancer-mediums, the presence of ancestor deities is literally inborn in their hereditary bloodline. Resurrecting ancestral deities muster their devotees' fortitude in the face of social woes, which may afflict them in an ever-changing, capricious world.

3 History and Metaphysical Underlays of Folk Śākta Ritual

Under the patronage of local kings, Folk Śākta performances were instituted in the early medieval period. To protect the king's polity from invasion or drought, the land's ancestor deities and royal goddesses were embodied in mediums to do so. To enable this ability, dancer-mediums read ritual manuals, which they later incarnated during rites of Tantric mediumship. By doing so, many Tantric ideas that were known to them—brought to the regions by migrating Tantric ascetics—were assembled in *bricolage webs of ritual knowledge* that form the phenomenon's metaphysical foundations. Unlike Hindu-Brahmanical religion, which disseminated power and knowledge only to the Brahmins, Tantric religion is diverse, with its influence spiraling across micro-sectarian divides, whether Śaiva and Śākta, or Hindu and Buddhist. It is Śaiva-Śākta Tantra's orientation as a spiraling horizontal network that established connections between such categories. By spiraling ritual action with textual knowledge, Folk Śākta rituals were constructed of multiple metaphysical thought-streams from traditions which, at one time or another, inhabited their soil.

4 Blood Sacrifice and Self-Reflexive Affect

Because Folk Śākta divinities are lodged in the material world (kingship, land etc.), they require a blood offering to placate the capricious forces inherent in that life world. During Folk Śākta rituals, blood sacrifices—of many forms—are common: briefly, a sacrifice represents a demonic or malevolent being, which must be subjugated so that these forces do not erupt into the realm and disrupt what was the king's political power. On another level, the animal victim considered a node in the ritual network, and a part of the macro-clan. The Tantric life world of the macro-clan is one defined by protean fluctuation and mutability, and many informants described how blood sacrifice made them reflect on their own tenuous existence, and the ways it brings to light a human's ever-changing nature and personas. This merging of demon-smiting and self-reflectivity which sacrifice brings about creates accelerated emotions in the group; the exsanguinating sacrifice reminds the *macro-clan* of the blood that runs in their bodies universally.

5 Politics and Caste Structure

Though initially rejected by 20th-century Marxist activists—in Bhaktapur and Kerala—as religious feudalism, I suggest certain aspects of Folk Śākta performances were connate in shaping their revolutionary ideology. Indeed, several affinities exist between Folk Śākta ritual and their Marxist politics, which includes ritual kinship; lower-caste mediumship; agriculture and farmers; motifs of self-reflexive sacrifice; and narratives of landlord defiance. These mutual commonalities were accentuated (or 'interpellated') as consistent with the iconoclastic principles that this territory-conscious Marxist ideology advocated. It is the nature of Folk Śākta performance—*spiraling* between **conservative** caste and **radical** ritual kin, whilst linking religion, culture, politics, and society—means this ritual correlates with the emergence of a revolutionary political party.

Glossary of Key Terms

Unless otherwise indicated as Sanskrit (Skt.) or Nepali (Nepa.), all terms will be listed in their indigenous dialects.

Glossary 1: Teyyāṭṭam, Northern Malabar, Kerala (Malayalam)

Abhiśēkham A Sanskritic term for an image-bathing ceremony in Kerala's Tantric temples

adalaya paṇam The act of distributing resources (money and food) among a dancer-medium lineage

adrśya-murtikaḷ Literally 'invisible beings'. A collective noun that refers to a group of invisible beings in Keralan cosmology, which include malevolent spirits, and serpent deities or *nāgas*

ālukaḷ A category of divine beings in Kerala: god, goddesses, and Teyyam divinities

Aniyara A temporary preparatory hut for dancer-mediums that is erected adjacent to the Teyyam grove

Anjipali A five-circle pattern painted on the face of an adorned Teyyam dancer-medium

antitiriyan Head priest in a Teyyāṭṭam grove

avarṇa Caste groups who are not twice-born, and thus refers to all castes below Nambutiri Brahmans in the caste hierarchy

avatāra Sanskritic term that describes the various mythological manifestations of god Viṣṇu

bhagavati General designation for a 'goddess' in Kerala

caitanyam Literally 'consciousness', which refers to divine consciousness within the subtle body (etheric)

cēdagam Shield used by Teyyāṭṭam dancer-mediums

cenda Traditional drums played in Teyyāṭṭam performances

ceripāṭṭu Malayali folk songs and tales (unlike *tōṟṟam* songs, these are not confined to Teyyāṭṭam)

cerujanman Traditional (medieval) rights of tax exemption and food aid limited to castes who perform as Teyyam dancer-mediums

cōyi Derived from the Sanskrit 'yogi', it describes a group of householder mendicants from Nāth ascetic lineages who settled in Northern Malabar during the early medieval period

cōṭṭa A burning torch. This is sometimes used as a weapon wielded by certain Teyyāṭṭam gods associated with swiddening practices

dakṣinmārga (Skt) A non-transgressive form of Tantric practice used by Nambūtiri Brahmans which maintains rules of purity by forbidding blood sacrifice. It is known as 'Keralan dualism' and is restricted to Brahmanical temples in Kerala

guruṭi Blood substitute (turmeric water) used in sacrificial rites during Teyyāṭṭam

illam Lineage

janmi Landlord

kalaṃ A rectangular structure made of green tree stalks and lanterns that represents the multileveled cosmos in Teyyāṭṭam. Also known as *maṇḍalam*

kalaśa-kiṇḍi Literally 'alcohol vessel'. This is a small bronze drinking vessel with a spout containing *kalaśa* or coconut sap liquor known colloquially as 'toddy'

Kalaśakkaran Official priestly attendant who oversees the distribution of 'toddy' or coconut sap liquor to the Teyyam dancer-mediums

kalivụ Interchangeable with the Sanskrit term *śakti*, it refers to immanent divine power associated with the maternal aspect of divinity viz. multivalent worldly power of the earth, king, and ancestral deities.

kalaripayāṭṭụ Kerala's traditional martial art. Several Teyyāṭṭam divinities were masters of kalaripayāṭṭụ. Many dancer-mediums receive training in this martial art in various gymanasia across Northern Kerala

kannerụ Literally 'eye'. A notion of 'apotropaic misfortune' or the 'evil eye'

kārṇavan A male elder in a matrilineal household

kāvu Term used for the sacred grove in which Teyyāṭṭam performances are conducted

Kōlakkaran Teyyāṭṭam dancer-medium

Kōmamram Priests who guide and assist dancer-mediums in Teyyāṭṭam performances

Kōlattiri rājā Medieval king of Northern Malabar (approx. 11th Century CE) whose dynasty ruled the region following the collapse of the Cēra dynasty. Most Teyyāṭṭam narratives recall this dynastic period.

Kōlattanādu Medieval kingdom of the Northern Malabar region which was ruled by the Kōlattiri dynasty

kōḻi Chicken sacrifice

kṣetram Literally 'field', which refers to a place of worship in its widest possible usage, but is usually used in colloquial parlance to designate a Nambūtiri Brahman temple

kula-daivam Family deity (usually an ancestor)

kuḻivīran An ancestral warrior god

Mādāyi Kāvu A Royal Tantric Temple which was the religious centre of the medieval Kōlattiri dynasty

Manakkāttan Gurukkaḷ Supposed founder of Teyyāṭṭam performances in Malabar, who standardized the tradition during the reign of the medieval Kōlattiri dynasty

mantravādam Traditional modes and techniques of 'sorcery' or power-conjuring abilities

Makkathīyam Patrilineal lineage or household

Māppilla Traditional Muslim community of Malabar

Morūmakkathīyam Matrilineal lineage or household

mukhamezultụ Literally 'face-writing'. Intricate symbolic face-painting drawn on the faces of adorned Teyyāṭṭam dancer-mediums

nāndakam Ritualized curved sword brandished by Teyyam dancer-mediums embodying royal goddesses

nādī (Skt) A Tantric concept of 'body' that denotes five nodes or portals in an individual's subtle or etheric body

nādu A local polity connected to a sovereign central state which is led by a chieftain

Nāyar Caste group who were state warriors in medieval Malabar. They are an avarṇa group between Nambutiri Brahman and the lower castes

palliyāṟā The main shrine of a family deity in a Teyyāṭṭam grove

pambinkōṭṭa Serpent deity (*nāga*) temple groves

perumkaliyāṭṭam A collaborative temple festival that unites a local Tantric Temple with a Teyyāṭṭam performance

peẕumaḷ In medieval Malabar, this term referred to the central administrative state which was governed by a sovereign

Piśācu Ghosts

prāṇa (Skt) A Tantric notion which denotes 'life-breath' that circulates in subtle or etheric bodies

Praśādam Offerings of food or material goods to a specific deity

sakhakal 'Comradeship'. Used in the context of the Communist Party.

Sambandam Matrilineal customs of conjugal union in Kerala

sneham Familial love

śuddhi Ritual purification undertaken by dancer-mediums before a Teyyāṭṭam performance

suvarṇa (Skt) Twice-born caste (Nambūtiri Brahman)

taluk A micro-region or administrative region. There are 77 taluk in Kerala.

Taravād Household

tampurāṭṭi Eulogistic terms for the royal goddess (Bhadrākālī) whose presence in a shrine is required in many Tantric temples and some Teyyam groves

tāṟā A shrine of a Teyyam deity in a Teyyāṭṭam sacred grove

Teyyam From the Sanskrit 'daiva', this refers to the deities worshipped in Teyyāṭṭam. It is also used to denote the ritual performance itself.

teṅṅā Coconut

teṅṅākāḷḷụ Literally 'coconut-stone'. A large rock or stone in a Teyyam grove which is used for smashing coconuts

tōṟṟam A song and biographical narrative unique to each Teyyāṭṭam divinity. This song is sung during the ritualized process when the medium transforms into the deity

ucca-pūjā A mid-day religious obeisance at a Tantric Temple

urāḷān Main representative of an administration committee that organizes a Teyyāṭṭam performance

Urumī Double-edged long swords used in Kalaripayāṭṭu. These are also used by dancer-mediums who embody martial divinities during Teyyāṭṭam performances

vigraham Literally 'physical body'

Glossary 2: Navadurgā, Bhaktapur, Nepal (Bhaktapurian Newari Dialect)

Āsribād A curse or blessing

aṣṭamatṛkā Literally 'the eight mothers'. Eight mother goddesses whose shrines surround the geographical boundary of Bhaktapur city. These mothers are connected to the Nine Durgās, which comprise the Navadurgā clan

ātma punegu This term describes a variation of apotropaic misfortune associated with food

Banmala Caste group who form the Navadurgā troupe. They are also flower sellers or gardeners. Sometimes their group is disparagingly labelled *gāthu*

bali dine (Nepa.) Verb 'to give sacrifice'

betali Cloth headdress worn by Navadurgā dancer-mediums

bhoj Ritualized feasting in Newar society

choree pūjā After the autumnal festival of Mohani, *choree puja* denotes a monthly ceremony conducted in the Navadurgā temple which ensures that the power of the deities remains strong among the dancer-mediums. Only initiated members of the Navadurgā troupe participate in this ceremony

daijo pratha Dowry gifts. In Newar tradition, goddesses are understood as having been mythologically established in an area because they were given as a dowry from a king to his daughter or daughter-in-law

Daitya Literally 'demon', which refers to malevolent spirits or external forces in Newar cosmology

dhaū-baji Literally 'curd-rice'. A mixture of buffalo curd and beaten rice that is distributed by a dancer-medium to devotees after a pig sacrifice. It has many significant properties, which include: temporarily binding caste groups in ritual, protecting people from diseases, and enhancing a couple's fertility

dhin chūwanegu Eight days before a Navadurgā performance in a neighbourhood or household, the Nāyo (male elder of the troupe) visits that neighbourhood or area to announce the specific timings of the performance

dugu dyo Family deity

dugu pūjā Annual worship of a family deity. Also known as '*kul puja*' in Nepali

dyo Deity. Also, *devāta* in Nepali

dyo bokegu A ceremony where people invite the Navadurgā troupe to their neighbourhood or home to present the deities with offerings to secure their blessings

dyo-cheṇ Literally 'god-house', this refers to a temple. In this book, this term is used to denote the temple of the Navadurgā troupe in Bhaktapur

gaṇa 'Troupe'. Used to describe the family of Navadurgā dancer-mediums and priests

goṭamangal First festival after the summer months before the autumnal equinox. It celebrates the re-awakening of deity Śiva/Bhairav and the purging of Bhaktapur city before the festival of goddesses begins in Autumn (Mohani/Dashain). Also known as *ghantākarṇa* in Nepali

gulli Narrow alley in a Newar city

guṭhi A religious association in Newar society, whose role is the organization of certain festivals or death rites. Traditionally, these organizations can be inter-caste (exogamous) or intra-caste (endogamous) formations, and each are attached to certain lineages and a tract of land

Jan andolan (Nepa.) The 1996 (and a reprised 2006) People's movement which fought for multi-party democracy during the partyless Panchyat system

Jātrā Term used to describe all religious festivals generally

Jyāpu Mahāguthi (Nepa.) A Newar farmer association or union, whose members comprise Newar farmers from the Kathmandu Valley and beyond

Karmācārya Newar Priests of Tantric temples (different from higher-caste Rājophadyāyā Brahmans)

kha-chha Bronze shrine that contains the repoussé plate of central goddess Siphā *dyo/Mahālakṣmi* during a Navadurgā performance

Khamei Buffalo who is sacrificed during the autumnal festival of Mohani. The buffalo represents the demon Mahiśaṣura (according to the myth of the Devī Mahātmya)

Khorūwa A spouted water vessel used in Tantric ceremonies and in Newar households

khwōpa Masks of the Navadurgā deities worn by dancer-mediums during a performance. It is also a term for Bhaktapur city itself

kolachhen In Sanskrit '*pātra*', a skull-cup that contains *aila* (rice-wine) which is imbibed by the troupe *lapte* Plate made of leaves that are used in Newar communities for religious offerings

lasa kūsa A rite of 'welcoming the deity', where the Navadurgā priestess splashes water onto the hands of the dancer-mediums as they leave their temple to conduct a procession to a neighbourhood or shrine

Lāyaku Royal temple square or court that was the residence of a Newar king or ruler

makai charne deuta (Nepa.) The notion that offering to the Navadurgā divinities will ensure plentiful rains for planting the seeds of maize

mikhā wanegu A form of apotropaic misfortune in a Newar worldview; literally 'eye going'

Mohani The autumnal festival that celebrates the regal goddess Durgā conquering demonic forces. This festival is the official inauguration of the agricultural cycle and the cycle of Folk Navadurgā performances in Bhaktapur

Mohani Unlike Mohani (the festival), this refers to black paste made from charred buffalo bones that is distributed as a blessing that is painted as a line on the forehead (a *tikā* in Nepali)

mūbahaṅ An auspicious or specific blood sacrifice. In Navadurgā performances, this animal is a pig (*sungur*)

Mulchowk The central sanctum or courtyard of a temple complex

mukhti paunśa (Nepa.) A post-sacrificial rite across Nepali Hindu traditions where the head of the animal placed on a platter before the deity-stone, in the hope that it will achieve a prosperous afterlife

Nākiṅ Female priestess who oversees the shrines and procedures of the Navadurgā temple. She is an elder member of a Banmala lineage

Nāch (Nepa.) Lit. 'Dance'

Nāyo Male elder and priest of the Navadurgā troupe. He oversees the overall organization of the nine-month cycle of performances

Nepāl-maṇḍala Kathmandu Valley basin (which includes Kathmandu, Lalitpur, and Bhaktapur cities and associated towns/villages)

nya lakegu 'Fish-catching rite' in Navadurgā performances, which involves a narrative in which deity Seto Bhairav is catching fish to feed his family

paddhati (Skt.) Liturgical manuals for use in Tantric rites

Pancabali Literally 'five sacrifices'. A five-animal sacrificial offering to a Tantric deity in Newar religion

pāsuka A five-coloured thread given as a blessing by Navadurgā troupe members in exchange for monetary or food offerings to the deities at a performance

pauba This is a Newari term for a *maṇḍala* or a geometrical representation of the cosmos.

Phalcā Public porches. In Nepali, these are called *pati*.

Phuki Blood (consanguineal) lineage in Newar society

pikaliki A deity-stone that serves as a shrine to a specific Tantric god or goddess. *Śila* in Nepali

prāṇprothesthān (Nepa.) A Tantric concept of 'life-breath' or essence of a deity that resides within the subtle body of an individual

prasād Offering to a deity

pyākhaṇ Literally 'dance'. This refers to Navadurgā performances themselves; also *nāch* in Nepali

Śakti This concept refers to immanent divine power associated with the maternal aspect of divinity as multivalent worldly power linked to the earth, king, and ancestral deities. This theological concept is notably Tantric in scope

Sarkāri pūjā Literally 'worship [by] government'. A rite of worship funded by local authorities to the Navadurgā performers

sungur lakhatne (Nepa.) A Navadurgā rite in which a pig is walked throughout a precinct of Bhaktapur or another region, before it is sacrificed at the image of the goddess Siphā dyo/Mahālakṣṃi

thar Newar term for caste

thudal (Nepa.) Carved wooden pillars that support the roof of a traditional Newari temple

tõrren A decorated arch above the door or entranceway of a Newari Temple

twā or *tol* (Nepa.) A neighbourhood or precinct in Bhaktapur city

two: mukhegu Procession by the Navadurgā dancer-mediums around a precinct or neighbourhood before a performance begins

Ujāju Literally 'seers'. A term for Navadurgā dancer-mediums

Vaṃśavali 'Chronicle'. A written text

Vaidya Tantric healer

Vidyā Tantric mastery or techniques

waleli punegu A form of apotropaic misfortune in Newar communities

Yalambar-Bhairava-āju (Nepa.) A Kirāti king who was believed by Newars to be an embodiment of deity Bhairav. He is commemorated as the statue of deity Akaś-Bhairava in Indra Chowk, Kathmandu, and many Newar farmers claim to be descendant from this divine king and the god Bhairav.

Bibliography

Primary Texts (Manuscripts and Accompanying Translations)

Bṛhadāraṇyaka Upaniṣad, in *Upaniṣads*, trans. by Patrick Olivelle, (Oxford World's Classics Series: OUP, 1996)

Devī-Mahātmya, in *The Mārkaṇḍeya-Purāṇa: Sanskrit Text, English translation with Notes and Index of Verses* by Joshi Shastri, trans. by F.E. Pargiter, (Delhi: Parimal Publications, 2004). For details of National Archive (Kathmandu) manuscripts, see § 4.3.2

Kaṭha Upaniṣad, in *Upaniṣads*, trans. by Patrick Olivelle, (Oxford World's Classics Series: OUP, 1996)

Markaṇḍeyā-Purāṇa, in *The Mārkaṇḍeya-Purāṇa: Sanskrit Text, English translation with Notes and Index of Verses* by Joshi Shastri, trans. by F.E. Pargiter, (Delhi: Parimal Publications, 2004)

Mūlamadhyamakakārikā, in *The Fundamental Wisdom of the Middle Way: Nagarjuna's* Mūlamadhyamakakārikā, trans. by Jay L. Garfield, (Oxford: OUP, 1995)

Nityāṣodaśikārṇava [NSA], in *Upodghāta to his edition of the* Nityāṣodaśikārṇava *Tantra*, ed. by V.V. Dviveda, (Varanasi: 1968)

Ṛg Veda, in *The Rig Veda: An Anthology*, trans. by Wendy Doniger, (Penguin Classics, 1981)

Śeṣasamuccaya [SA] in *Śeṣasamuccaya: with Vimarśini of Śaṅkara*, ed. by Narayana Pillai, (Trivandrum: Trivandrum Sanskrit Series at Government Central Press, 1951). Translation in Unni, N.P., *Tantric Literature in Kerala*, (Delhi: Bharatiya Books, 2006)

Tantrasamuccaya [TS] in *The Tantrasamuccaya of Narāyāṇa; reprinted with an English translation of the text*, trans. by N.P. Unni (Delhi: New Bharatiya Books, 2014)

Secondary Sources

Abraham, Janaki, "'Why did you send me like this?' Marriage, Matriliny and the 'Providing Husband' in North Kerala, India", *Asian Journal of Women's Studies*, 7.2 (2011), 73–106

Adhikari, Krishna, & Gellner, David, 'Ancestor Worship and Sacrifice: Debates over Bahun-Chhetri Clan Rituals (kul puja) in Nepal', in *Religion, Secularism, and Ethnicity in Contemporary Nepal*, ed. by David Gellner et al., (Oxford: OUP, 2016)

Althusser, Louis, 'Ideology and ideological state apparatus' in *Lenin and Philosophy and Other Essays*, by Louis Althusser, (New York: Monthly Review Press, 1989)

Amazzone, Laura, *Goddess Durgā and Sacred Female Power*, (Lanham: Hamilton Books, 2010)

Appadurai, Arjun, 'Introduction: Commodities and the Politics of Value' in *The Social Life of Things: Commodities in Cultural Perspective*, by Arjun Appadurai, (Cambridge: CUP, 1986)

Appadurai, Arjun, 'The Wealth of Dividuals' in *Derivative and the Wealth in Societies*, ed. by Benjamin Lee & Randy Martin, (Chicago: University of Chicago Press, 2016)

Appleton, Naomi, *Shared Characters in Jain, Buddhist, and Hindu Narrative: Gods, Kings, and Other Heroes*, (London & New York: Routledge, 2017)

Arafath, Yasser, 'Saints, Goddesses, and Serpents: Fertility Cults of the Malabar Coast (c1500–1800)', in *Histories of Medicine and Healing in the Indian Ocean World*, ed. by Winterbottom & Tesfaye, (New York: Palgrave Series in Indian Ocean World Studies, Palgrave Macmillan, 2016)

Asad, Talal, *Genealogies of Religion: Discipline and Reasons of Power in Christianity and Islam*, (Baltimore: The John Hopkins University Press, 1993)

Ashley, Wayne & Holloman, Regina, 'Teyyam' in *Indian Theatre: Traditions of Performance*, trans. By Farley Richmond et al., (Hawaii: University of Hawaii Press, 1990)

Bakhtin, Mikhail, *Rabelais and his world*, trans. by Helene Iswolsky, (Bloomington: Indiana University Press, 1984 [1965])

Baltutis, Michael, 'Sacrificing (to) Bhairav: The Death, Resurrection, and Apotheosis of a Local Himalayan King', *Journal of Hindu Studies*, 9.2 (2016), 205–225

Bamberg, Michael & Andrews, Molly, eds., *Considering Counter-Narratives: Narrating, Resisting, Making Sense* (Philadelphia: John Benjamins Publishing, 2004)

Bayly, Susan, 'Saints' Cults and Warrior Kingdoms in South India', in *Shamanism, History, and the State*, ed. by Nicholas Thomas & Caroline Humphrey (Michigan: University of Michigan Press, 1996)

Bell, Catherine, *Ritual Theory, Ritual Practice*, (Oxford: Oxford University Press, 1992)

Bhattacharyya, N.N., *History of Śākta Religion*, (New Delhi: Munshiram Manoharial Publishers Pvt. Ltd, 1974)

Biernacki, Loriliai, 'The Absent Mother and Bodied Speech: Psychology and Gender in late Medieval Tantra', in *Transformations and Transfer of Tantra in Asia and Beyond*, ed. by Isvan Keul, (Berlin: DeGruyter, 2012)

Bloch, Maurice, *Prey into Hunter: The Politics of Religious Experience*, (Cambridge: Lewis Henry Morgan Lectures Series, Cambridge University Press, 1992)

Bouillier, Véronique, "Nāth Yogīs' Encounters with Islam", *South Asia Multidisciplinary Academic Journal* [*Online*], 2015, Source: http://samaj.revues.org/3878

Bourdieu, Pierre, *Distinction: A social critique of the judgement of taste*, (London: Routledge, 2010, [1984])

Bottomore, Tom et al., eds., *A Dictionary of Marxist Thought: Second Edition*, (Oxford: Blackwell Publishing, 1991)

Breen, Michael G., *The Road to Federalism in Nepal, Myanmar, and Sri Lanka: Finding the Middle Ground*, (London: Routledge, Politics in Asia Series, 2018)

Brooks, Douglas Renfrew, *The Secret of the Three Cities: An Introduction to Hindu Shakta Tantrism*, (Chicago: University of Chicago Press, 1990)

Brown, Louise T., *The Challenge to Democracy in Nepal: A Political History*, (London: Routledge, 2002)

Caldwell, Sarah, 'Oh Terrifying Mother: The Mudiyettu Ritual Drama of Kerala, South India', (Ph.D diss., University of California, Berkeley, 1995)

Carrithers, Michael, 'On polytropy: Or the Natural Condition of Spiritual Cosmopolitanism in India: The Digambar Jain case', *Modern Asian Studies*, 34.4 (2000), 831–861

Carsten, Janet, *After Kinship*, (Cambridge: CUP, 2004)

Castoriadis, Cornelius, 'Radical Imagination and the Social Instituting Imaginary', in *Rethinking Imagination: Culture and Creativity*, ed. by Gillian Robinson & John Rundell, (London and New York: Routledge, 1994)

Cerulli, Anthony, 'Unpuzzling an Aporia: Theorizing Acts of Ritual and Medicine in South India', *Journal of Ritual Studies*, 29.2 (2015), 25–43

Chalier-Visvulingam, Elizabeth, 'Bhairava and the Goddess: Tradition, Gender and Transgression', in *Wild Goddesses in India and Nepal*, ed. by Axel Michaels et al., (Berlin: Verlag Peter Lang, 1996)

Chandra, T.V., *Ritual as Ideology: Text and Context in Teyyam*, (New Delhi: Indira Gandhi National Centre for the Arts, 2006)

Chaturvedi, Rudi, 'Political violence, community, and its limits in Kannur, Kerala', *Contributions to Indian Sociology*, 49.2 (2015), 162–187

Child, Louise, *Tantric Buddhism and Altered States of Consciousness: Durkheim, Emotional Energy, and Visions of the Consort*, (Aldershot: Ashgate Publishing, 2007)

Courtright, Paul, *Gaṇeśa: Lord of Obstacles, Lord of Beginnings*, (Oxford: OUP, 1985)

Cox, M. Whitney, 'Making a Tantra in Medieval South India', (Ph.D. diss, University of Chicago, 2006)

Davies, Charlotte, *Reflexive Ethnography: A guide to researching selves and others*, (London: Routledge, 1999)

De La Torre, Miguel A., *Santeria: The Beliefs and Rituals of a Growing Religion in America*, (Michigan: William B. Eerdmans Publishing Company, 2004)

Deleuze, Gilles & Guattari, Felix, *A Thousand Plateaus: Capitalism and Schizophrenia*, (London: Continuum, 1988)

De Maaker, Erik, 'Integrating Ethnographic Research and Filmmaking: Video Elicitation for a Performance-Oriented Analysis of the *Teyyam* Ritual', *Visual Anthropology*, 13 (2000), 185–197

Derrida, Jacques, *Limited Inc*, (Evanston, Illinois: Northwestern University Press, 1988)

Dirks, Nicholas B., 'The Structure and Meaning of political relations in South Indian little kingdoms', *Contributions to Indian Sociology*, 13.2 (1979), 169–206

Dirks, Nicholas B., 'The Original Caste: power, history and hierarchy in South India', *Contributions to Indian Sociology*, 23.1 (1989), 59–77

Dirks, Nicholas B., *Castes of Mind: Colonialism and the making of modern India*, (Princeton: Princeton University Press, 2001)

Doniger, Wendy, *The Rig Veda: An Anthology*, (London: Penguin Classics, 1981)

Douglas, Mary, *Natural Symbols: Studies in Cosmology*, (London: Routledge, 1970)

Dumont, Louis, *Homo Hierarchicus: The Caste System and its Implications*, (Chicago: University of Chicago Press, 1966)

Durkheim, Emile, *The Rules of Sociological Method*, trans. by W.D. Halls, (New York: The Free Press, 1982 [1895])

Durkheim, Emile, *The Division of Labour in Society*, trans. by W.D. Halls, (New York: The Free Press, 1997 [1898])

Durkheim, Emile, *The Elementary Forms of Religious Life*, trans. by Karen E. Fields, (New York: The Free Press, 1995 [1912])

Dupuche, John, 'Appropriating the Inappropriate', in *Conceiving the Goddess: Transformation and Appropriation in Indic Religions*, ed. by Jayant Bapal & Ian Mabbett, (Melbourne: Monash University Press, 2017)

Dyczkowski, Mark, *The Doctrine of Vibration: An Analysis of the Doctrine and Practices of Kashmir Shaivism*, (Delhi: Motilal Barnarsidass Publishers, 1987)

Dyczkowski, Mark, *The Cult of the Goddess Kubjika: A Preliminary Comparative Textual and Anthropological Survey of a Secret Newar Goddess*, (Stuttgart: Franz Steiner Werlag, 2001)

Engels, Fredrich, *The Origin of Family, Private Property, and the State*, (Chicago: Charles H. Kerr & Co., 1909 [1884])

Engler, Steven & Grieve, Gregory, eds., *Historicizing Tradition in the Study of Religion*, (Berlin: De Gruyter, 2012)

Fisher, Elaine, *Hindu Pluralism: Religion and the Public Sphere in Early Modern South India*, (California: University of California Press, 2017)

Flood, Gavin, *Body and Cosmology in Kashmir Shaivism*, (San Francisco: Mellen Research University Press, 1993)

Flood, Gavin, *An Introduction to Hinduism*, (Cambridge: CUP, 1996)

Flood, Gavin, 'Ritual Dance in Kerala: Performance, Possession, and the Formation of Culture' in *Indian Insights: Buddhism, Brahmanism and Bhakti, Papers from the Annual Spalding Symposium on Indian Religions*, ed. by Peter Connolly & Sue Hamilton, (London: Luzac Oriental, 1997)

Flood, Gavin, *The Tantric Body: The Secret Tradition of Hindu Religion*, (London: I.B. Taurus, 2006)

Flood, Gavin, 'Sacrifice as Refusal', in *Sacrifice and Modern Thought*, ed. by Julia Meszaros & Johannes Zachhuber, (Oxford: OUP, 2013)

Fortes, Meyer, *The Web of Kinship among the Tallensi*, (London: Routledge, 2018 [1949])

Foucault, Michel, *The Archaeology of Knowledge*, (London: Routledge Classics, 2002 [1969])

Freeman, J.R., 'Purity and Violence: Sacred Power in the Teyyam Worship of Malabar', (Ph.D. diss., University of Pennsylvania, 1991)

Freeman, J.R., 'Performing Possession: Ritual and Consciousness in the Teyyam Complex of Northern Kerala' in *Flags of Fame: Studies in South Asian Folk Culture*, ed. by Heidrum Brückner & Lothar Lutzer, (New Delhi: Manohar Publishing, South Asia Books, 1993)

Freeman, J.R., 'Possession Rites and the Tantric Temple: A Case-Study from Northern Kerala', *Diskus*, 2.2 (1994)

Freeman, J.R., 'Formalised Possession Among the Tantris and Teyyams of Malabar', *South Asia Research*, 18.1 (1998), 73–98

Freeman, J.R., 'Gods, Groves and the Culture of Nature in Kerala', *Modern Asian Studies*, 33.2 (1999a), 257–302

Freeman, J.R., 'Dynamics of the Person in the Worship and Sorcery of Malabar' in *La possession en Asie du Sud: parole, corps, territoire*, ed. by Jackie Assayag & Gilles Tarabout, (Éditions de l'École des hautes études en sciences sociales, 1999b)

Freeman, J.R., 'Texts, Temples, and the Teaching of Tantra in Kerala', in *The Resources of History: Tradition, Narration and Nation in South Asia*: 63–79, ed. by Jackie Assayag, (Études thématiques 8. Paris-Pondichéry, 1999c)

Freeman, J.R., 'The Teyyam Tradition of Kerala' in *The Blackwell Companion to Hinduism*, ed. by Gavin Flood, (London: Blackwell Publishings, 2003)

Freeman, J.R., 'Untouchables Bodies of Knowledge in the Spirit Possession of Malabar', in *The body in India: Ritual, transgression, performativity*, ed. by Axel Michaels & Christophe Wulf, (Paragrana: International Zeitchrift für Historische Anthropologie, Vol. 18, Heft. 1, Akad-Verlag, 2009)

Freeman, J.R., 'Śāktism, polity, and society in Medieval Malabar' in *Goddess Traditions in Tantric Hinduism: History, Practice, and Doctrine*, ed. by Bjarne Wernicke-Olesen, (London: Routledge, 2016)

Fuller, Chris, *The Nayars Today*, (Cambridge: CUP, 1976)

Fuller, Chris, *The Camphor Flame: Popular Hinduism and Society in India*, 2nd edn., (Princeton: Princeton University Press, 2004)

Gabriel, Theodore, *Playing God: Belief and Ritual in the Muttappan Cult of North Malabar*, (London: Equinox, 2010)

Geertz, Clifford, *The Interpretation of Cultures: Selected Essays*, (New York: Basic Books, 1973)

Gellner, David, 'Language, caste, religion, and territory: Newar identity ancient and modern', *Archives Européennes de Sociologie*, 27.1, (1986), 102–148

Gellner, David, 'Newar Buddhism and its Hierarchy of Ritual', (D.Phil. diss., University of Oxford, 1987)

Gellner, David, 'Hinduism and Buddhism in the Nepal Valley', in *The World's Religions*, ed. by Steward Sutherland et al., (London: Routledge, 1988)

Gellner, David, 'A Newar Buddhist Liturgy: Śrāvkayānist Ritual in Kwā Bāhāh, Lalitpur, Nepal', *The Journal of the International Association of Buddhist Studies*, 14.2 (1991), 236–253

Gellner, David, 'Hinduism, Tribalism, and the Position of Women: The Problem of Newar Identity', *Man*, 26.1 (1991), 105–125

Gellner, David, *Monk, Householder, and Tantric Priest: Newar Buddhism and its hierarchy of ritual*, (Cambridge: CUP, 1992)

Gellner, D., Pfaff-Czarnecka, J., & Whelpton, J., eds., *Nationalism and Ethnicity in a Hindu Kingdom*, (Abington: Routledge, 1997)

Gellner, David & Pradhan, Rajendra, 'Urban Peasants: The Maharjans (Jyapu) of Kathmandu and Lalitpur' in *Contested Hierarchies: A Collaborative Ethnography of Caste among the Newars of the Kathmandu Valley, Nepal*, ed. by Declan Quigley & David Gellner, (Oxford: OUP, 1999)

Gellner, David, *The Anthropology of Buddhism and Hinduism: Weberian Themes*, (Oxford: OUP, 2001)

Gellner, David, 'Does Symbolism 'Construct an Urban Mesocosm'? Rebert Levy's *Mesocosm* and the Question of Value Consensus in Bhaktapur' in *The Anthropology of Hinduism and Buddhism: Weberian Themes*, ed. by David Gellner, (Oxford: OUP, 2001)

Gellner, David, 'Initiation as a site of cultural conflict among the Newars' in *Hindu and Buddhist Initiations in India and Nepal*, ed. by Astrid Zotter & Christof Zotter, (Wiesbaden: Harrassowitz Velag, 2010)

Gellner, David et al., eds., *Religion, Secularism, and Ethnicity in Contemporary Nepal*, (Oxford: OUP, 2016)

Ghimire, Pustak, 'Living Goddesses Everywhere? On the possession of women by the goddess Bhagavati in some mountain villages in Eastern Nepal', in *Religion, Secularism, and Ethnicity in Contemporary Nepal*, ed. by David Gellner et al., (Oxford: OUP, 2016)

Gibson, Ian, 'Suffering and Christianity: Conversion and Ethical Change among the Newars of Bhaktapur', (D.Phil. diss, University of Oxford, 2015)

Gibson, Ian, 'Pentecostal Peacefulness: virtue ethics and the reception of theology in Nepal', *JRAI*, 23.4 (2017), 765–782

Girard, Rene, *Violence and the Sacred*, (Baltimore: John Hopkins University Press, 1972)

Gombrich, Richard, *Theravada Buddhism: A Social History from Ancient Benares to Modern Colombo*, (London: Routledge, 1988)

Goudriaan, Teun, & Gupta, Sanjukta, *Hindu Tantric and Śākta Literature*, (Wiesbaden: Otto Harrassowitz, A History of Indian Literature, Vol. II, 1981)

Gough, Kathleen, 'Cults of the Dead among the Nayars', *Journal of American Folklore*, 71.3 (1958), 446–478

Gough, Kathleen, 'Tiyyar: Northern Kerala', in *Matrilineal Kinship*, ed. by David Schneider & Kathleen Gough, (Berkeley & Los Angeles: University of California Press, 1981)

Gough, Kathleen, 'Modes of Production in Southern India', *Capital View [Economic and Political Weekly]*, 15.5/7 (1980), 337–364

Grahn, Judith, 'Are goddesses metaformic constructs? An application of Metaformic theory to menarche celebrations and goddess rituals of Kerala and contiguous states in South India', (Ph.D. diss., California Institute of Integral Studies, 1999)

Gramsci, Antonio, *Prison Notebooks Vol. II*, trans. by Joseph Buttigieg, (New York: Columbia University Press, 2011 [1975])

Greenwold, Stephen, 'Kingship and Caste', *European Journal of Sociology*, 16.1, (1975), 48–75

Grieve, Gregory, 'Forging Mandalic Space: Bhaktapur, Nepal's Cow Procession and the Improvisation of Tradition', *Numen*, 51.4 (2004), 468–510

Grieve, Gregory, *Retheorizing Religion in Nepal*, (New York: Palgrave MacMillan, 2006)

Grieve, Gregory, 'Histories of Tradition in Bhaktapur, Nepal: Or, how to compile a Contemporary Hindu Medieval City' in *Historicizing Tradition in the Study of Religion*, ed. by Steven Engler & Gregory Grieve, (Berlin: Walter de Gruyter, 2012)

Gutschow, Niels, *Architecture of the Newars: A History of Buliding Typologies and Details in Nepal*, (Chicago: Serindia Publications, 2011)

Gutschow, Niels, and Michaels, Axel, *Handling Death: the dynamics of death and ancestor rituals among the Newars of Bhaktapur*, (Wiesbarden: Harrassowitz Berlag, 2005)

Hacchettu, Krishna, 'Municipality Leadership and Governance: A Case Study of Bhaktapur', in *Nepal: Local Leadership and Governance*, ed. by L.R. Baral et al., (Delhi: Adroit Publishers, 2004).

Hacchettu, Krishna, 'Social Change and Leadership: A Case Study of Bhaktapur City', in *Political and Social Transformations in North India and Nepal*, ed. by Hiroshi et al., (New Delhi: Manohar, 2007)

Handelman, Don, *One God, Two Goddesses, Three Studies of South Indian Cosmology*, (Leiden: Brill, 2014)

Hart, George, 'Early Evidence for Caste in South India', in *Dimensions of Social Life: Essays in honor of David B. Mandelbaum*, (Berlin: De Gruyter, 1987)

Hatley, Shaman, 'The Brahmayāmalatantra and Early Śaiva Cults of Yoginīs', (Ph.D. diss, University of Pennsylvania, 2007)

Hausner, Sondra, *Wandering with Sadhus: Ascetics in the Hindu Himalayas*, (Bloomington: Indiana University Press, 2007)

Hausner, Sondra & Gellner, David, 'Category and Practice as Two Aspects of Religion: The Case of Nepalis in Britain', *Journal of the American Academy of Religion*, 80.4 (December 2012), 971–997

Hausner, Sondra, *The Spirits of Crossbones Graveyard: Time, Ritual, and Sexual Commerce in London*, (Bloomington: Indiana University Press, 2016)

Heesterman, J.C., *The Inner Conflict of Tradition: Essays in Indian Ritual, Kingship, and Society*, (Chicago: University of Chicago Press, 1985)

Heesterman, J.C., *The Broken World of Sacrifice: An Essay in Ancient Indian Ritual*, (Chicago: University of Chicago Press, 1993)

Heidegger, Martin, *Being and Time: A Translation of Sein und Zeit*, trans. by Joan Stambaugh, (Albany: SUNY Press, 1996 [1953])

Hertz, Robert, *Death and the Right Hand*, (London: Routledge Reprint, 2013 [1909])

Hocart, Maurice, *Caste: A Comparative Study*, (London: Methuen, 1950)

Hopkins, Thomas, *The Hindu Religious Tradition*, (Belmont: Dickenson, 1971)

Huber, Toni, 'When what you see is not what you get: Remarks on the Traditional Tibetan Presentation of Sacred Geography', in *Tantra and Popular Religion in Tibet*, ed. by Geoffrey Samuel et al., (New Delhi: International Academy of Indian Culture and Aditya Prakashan, 1994)

Hubert, Henri & Mauss, Marcel, *Sacrifice: Its Nature and Functions*, (Chicago: University of Chicago Press, 1964 [1898])

Inden, Ronald B., *Imagining India*, (London: Hurst & Co, 1990).

Jeffrey, Robin, 'Matriliny, Marxism, and the Birth of the Communist Party in Kerala, 1930–1940', *The Journal of Asian Studies*, 39.1, (1978), 77–98

Johnson, William, ed., *Oxford Dictionary of Hinduism*, (Oxford: OUP, 2009)

Keay, John, *India: A History*, (London: Harper Collins Publishers, 2000)

King, Richard, *Orientalism and Religion: Postcolonial Theory, India and the 'Mystic East'*, (London: Routledge, 1999)

Komath, Rajesh, 'Political Economy of the Theyyam: A Study of time space homology', (Ph.D. diss., Mahatma Gandhi University, Kerala, 2013)

Kottakkunnummal, Manaf, 'Indigneous Customs and Colonial Law: Contestations in Religion, Gender, and Family Among Mappila Muslims in Colonial Malabar, Kerala, c.1910–1928', *SAGE Open*, January–March (2014).

Kreinath, J., Snoek, J. & Strausberg, M., eds., *Theorizing Rituals: Issues, Topics, Approaches, Concepts*, (Leiden: Brill, 2008)

LeCompte, Margaret D., & Goetz, Judith Preissle, 'Problems of Reliability and Validity in Ethnographic Research', *Review of Educational Research*, 52.1, (Spring 1982), 31–60

Lee, Benjamin, and Martin, Randy, eds., *Derivative and the Wealth in Societies*, (Chicago: University of Chicago Press, 2016)

Letizia, Chiara, 'Ideas of Secularism in Contemporary Nepal', in *Religion, Secularism, and Ethnicity in Contemporary Nepal*, ed. by David Gellner et al., (Oxford: OUP, 2016)

Lewis, Todd, 'Book Review of *Mesocosm: Hinduism and the Organization of a Traditional Newar City in Bhaktapur* by Robert I. Levy', *Himalayan Research Bulletin* [*Himalaya*], 14.1, (1994), 53–55

Lewis, Todd, 'Tantra: The Diamond Vehicle', in *Buddhism: An Illustrated Guide*, ed. by Kevin Trainor, (London: Duncan Baird Publishers, 2001)

Lewis, I.M., *Ecstatic Religion: A Study of Shamanism and Spirit Possession*, (London: Routledge, 2002 [1971])

Lévi, Sylvain, *Le Népal: étude historique d'un royaume hindou*, (Paris: Ernest Leroux, 1905)

Lévi-Strauss, Claude, *The Savage Mind*, (Hertford: The Garden City Press, 1966 [1962])

Levy, Robert, *Mescocosm: Hinduism and the Organization of a Traditional Newar City in Nepal Vol. I*, (Berkeley: University of California Press, 1990)

Lidke, Jeffrey S., 'The Goddess Within and Beyond the Three Cities: Śākta Tantra and the Paradox of Power in Nepāla-Maṇḍala', (Ph.D. diss, University of California, Santa Barbara, 2000)

Lidke, Jeffrey S., 'The Resounding Field of Visualised Self-Awareness: The Generation of Synthesized Consciousness in the Śrī Yantra Rituals of the Nityāṣodaśikārṇava', *Journal for Hindu Studies*, 4 (2011), 258–257

Lidke, Jeffrey S., *The Goddess Within and Beyond the Three Cities: Śākta Tantra and the Paradox of Power in Nepāla-Maṇḍala*, (New Delhi: DK Printworld, 2017)

Lorenzen, David N., *The Kāpālikas and Kālāmukhas: Two Lost Śaivite Sects*, (Los Angeles: University of California Press, 1972)

Lutgendorf, Philip, 'Monkey in the Middle: The Status of Hanuman in Popular Hinduism', *Religion*, 27.4 (1997), 311–332

Mailaparambil, Binu J., *Lords of the Sea: The Ali Rajas of Cannanore and the Political Economy of Malabar (1663–1723)*, (Leiden: Brill, 2012)

Malagodi, Mara, *Constitutional Nationalism and Legal Exclusion: Equality, Identity Politics, and Democracy in Nepal (1990–2007)*, (Oxford India Series: OUP, 2012)

Malamoud, Charles, *Cooking the World: Ritual and Thought in Ancient India*, (Delhi: OUP, 1996)

Malik, Aditya, 'Is possession really possible? Towards a hermeneutics of transformative embodiment in South Asia' in *Health and Religious Rituals in South Asia: Disease, Possession and Healing*, ed. by Fabrizio Ferrari, (London: Routledge, 2011)

Malik, Aditya, *Tales of Justice and Rituals of Divine Embodiment: Oral Narratives from the Central Himalayas*, (Oxford: OUP, 2016)

Mallinson, James, 'Nāth Sampradaya' in *Brill's Encyclopedia of Hinduism, Vol. III*, ed. by Knut Jamison, (Leiden: Brill, 2012)

Manandhar, Sushila, 'Supernatural Power of Body Adornment: Beliefs and Practices among the Newars of Kathmandu Valley (Nepal)', *Contributions to Nepalese Studies*, 36. 2 (2009), 259–288

Mannathukkaren, Nissim, 'Communism and the appropriation of modernity, Kerala, India: A critique of Subaltern Studies and Postcolonial Theory', (Ph.D. diss, Queen's University, Canada, 2006)

Mansueto, Anthony, 'Religion, Solidarity and Class Struggle: Marx, Durkheim, and Gramsci on the Religion question', *Social Compass*, 35.2–3 (1988), 261–277

Marglin, Frédérique A., *Wives of the God-King: The Rituals of the Devadasis of Puri*, (Delhi: OUP, 1985)

Marglin, Frédérique A., 'Refining the Body: Transformative Emotion in Ritual Dance' in *Divine Passions: The Social Construction of Emotion in India*, ed. by Owen M. Lynch, (Berkeley: University of California Press, 1990)

Marriott, McKim, ed., *India Through Hindu Categories*, (New Delhi: SAGE Publications Pvt., 1990)

Marriott, McKim, 'Constructing an Indian ethnosociology', in *India Through Hindu Categories*, ed. by McKim Marriott, (New Delhi: SAGE Publications Pvt., 1990)

Marriott McKim & Ronald B. Inden, 'Toward an ethnosociology of South Asian caste systems', in *The new wind: Changing identities in South Asia*, ed. by David Kenneth, (The Hague: Moulton, 1977)

Marwaha, Sonali Bhatt, 'Roots of Indian Materialism in Tantra and Pre-Classical Sāṃkhya', *Asian Philosophy*, 23.2 (2013), 180–198

Marx, Karl, *Critique of Hegel's 'Philosophy of Right'*, trans. by Joseph O'Malley, (Cambridge: CUP, 1977)

Mauss, Marcel, *The Gift: Forms and Functions of Exchange in Archaic Societies*, (London: Cohen & West, 1966)

McDaniel, June, *Offering Flowers, Feeding Skulls: Popular Goddess Worship in West Bengal*, (New York: OUP, 2014)

Menon, A. Sreedhara, *A Survey of Kerala History*, (Kerala: DC Books, 1995)

Menon, Dilip, 'The Moral Community of the Teyyattam: Popular Culture in Late Colonial Malabar', *Studies in History*, 9.2, (1993), 187–217

Menon, Dilip, 'A Prehistory of Violence? Revolution and Martyrs in the Making of a Political Tradition in Kerala', *South Asia: Journal of South Asian Studies*, 39.3 (2016), 662–677

Meszaros, Julia & Zachhuber, Johannes, eds., *Sacrifice and Modern Thought*, (Oxford: OUP, 2013)

Michaels, Axel, 'On 12th–13th Century Relations between Nepal and South India', *Journal of the Nepal Research Centre*, 7 (1985), 69–73

Michaels, A., Vogelsanger, C., and Wilke, A., eds., *Wild Goddesses in India and Nepal*, (Bern: Verlag Peter Lang, 1996)

Michaels, Axel, *Hinduism Past and Present*, (Princeton: Princeton University Press, 2004)

Michaels, Axel, 'Blood Sacrifice in Nepal: Transformations and Criticism' in *Religion, Secularism, and Ethnicity in Contemporary Nepal*, ed. by David Gellner et al., (Oxford: OUP, 2016)

Monier-Williams, M.A., *A Sanskrit-English Dictionary*, (Oxford: Clarendon Press, 1872)

Moreno, Manuel, 'God's Forceful Call: Possession as a Divine Strategy' in *Gods of Flesh, Gods of Stone: The Embodiment of Divinity in India*, ed. by Joanne Waghorne & Norman Cutler, (Chambersberg: Anima Books, 1996)

Mortimer, B. et al., 'Tuning the instrument: Sonic properties in the spider's web', *Journal of the Royal Society: Interface*, 13 (2016), 0341

Mullard, Jordan C.R., 'Status, Security, and Change: An ethnographic study of Caste, Class, and Religion in Rural Rajasthan', (Ph.D. diss., London School of Economics, 2010)

Muller-Ortega, Paul E., *The Triadic Heart of Śiva: Kaula Tantricism of Kashmir Shaivism in the Nondual Shaivism of Kashmir*, (New York: SUNY Press, 2010)

Myers, B.R., *The Cleanest Race: How North Koreans See Themselves—and why it matters*, (Brooklyn, N.Y.: Melville House, 2010)

Nambiar, Balan, 'Tai Paradevata: Ritual Impersonation in the Teyyam Tradition of Kerala' in *Flags of Fame: Studies in South Asian Folk Culture*, ed. by Heidrum Brückner & Lothar Lutze, (New Delhi: Manohar Publishing, South Asia Books, 1993)

National Population and Housing Census 2011: Bhaktapur, Government of Nepal, Central Bureau of Statistics, Kathmandu, Nepal (published: March 2014), p. 16. Source: http://cbs.gov.np/wp-content/uploads/2014/04/26%20Bhaktapur_VDCLevelReport.pdf [accessed: 1/4/2015]

Nicholas, Ralph W., 'Śrāddha, Impurity, and the Relations between the Living and the Dead', *Contributions to Indian Sociology*, 15.2 (1981), 367–379

Nossiter, T.J., *Communism in Kerala: A Study in Political Adaptation*, (California: University of California Press, 1982)

Osella, Filippo & Caroline, "'Ayyappan saranam': Masculinity and the Sabarimala pilgrimage in Kerala", *JRAI*, 9.4 (2003), 729–754

Osella, Caroline & Filippo, 'Vital Exchanges: Land and Persons in Kerala', in *Territory, Soil and Society in South Asia*, ed. by Daniela Berti & Giles Tarabout, (New Delhi: Manohar Publishers, 2009)

Owens, Bruce McCoy, 'Accounting for Ritual in the Kathmandu Valley', in *Sucāruvādadeśika: A Festschrift Honoring Professor Theodore Riccardi Jr*, ed. by Todd Lewis & Bruce McCoy Owens, (Kathmandu: Himal Books, 2014)

Padoux, André, *The Hindu Tantric World: An Overview*, (Oxford: OUP, 2017)

Parish, Steven, *Moral Knowing in a Hindu Sacred City: An Exploration of Mind, Emotion, and Self*, (New York: Columbia University Press, 1994)

Parish, Steven M., *Hierarchy and its Discontents: Culture and the Politics of Consciousness in Caste Society*, (Philadelphia: University of Pennsylvania Press, 1996)

Patton, Kimberley and Wandau, Paul (eds.), *A Communion of Subjects: Animals in Religion, Science, and Ethics*, (New York: Columbia University Press, 2006)

Payyanad, Raghavan, 'Religion—native and alien: Interaction, assimilation and annihilation—a study based on worldview' in *Folklore as Discourse*, ed. by M.D. Muthukumarasaswamy, (Chennai: University of Madras, 2006)

Pickett, Mark, *Caste and Kingship in a Modern Hindu Society: The Newar City of Lalitpur, Nepal*, (Bangkok: Orchid Press, 2013)

Pinch, William R., *Warrior Ascetics and Indian Empires*, (Cambridge: CUP, 2006)

Plavoet, Jan, 'Rattray's Request: Spirit Possession among the Bono of West Africa' in

Indigenous Religions: A Companion, ed. by Graham Harvey, (London & New York: Cassell, 2000)

Pradhan, Rajendra, 'Sacrifice, Regeneration and Gifts: Mortuary Rites among Hindu Newars of Kathmandu', *Contributions to Nepalese Studies*, 23.1, (1996), 159–194

Qirko, Hector N., 'Fictive Kinship and Induced Altruism', in *The Oxford Handbook of Evolutionary Family Psychology*, ed. by Todd K. Shackleford & Catherine A. Salmon, (Oxford: OUP, 2011)

Quigley, Declan, *The Interpretation of Caste*, (Oxford: Clarendon Press, 1993)

Quigley, Declan, "Kingship and 'contrapriests'", *International Journal of Hindu Studies*, 1.3, (December 1997), 565–580

Quigley, Declan & Gellner, David, eds., *Contested Hierarchies: A Collaborative Ethnography of Caste among the Newars of the Kathmandu Valley, Nepal*, (Oxford: OUP, 1999)

Raheja, Gloria G., *The Poison in the Gift: Ritual, Prestation, and the Dominant Caste in a North Indian Village*, (Chicago: University of Chicago Press, 1988)

Raj, Yogesh, *History as Mindscapes: A Memory of the Peasants' Movement of Nepal*, (Kathmandu: Martin Chautari Publishers, 2010)

Rankin, Katharine, 'Newar Representations of Finance: Towards an Anthropology of Profit', in *The Cultural Politics of Markets: Economic Liberation and Social Change in Nepal*, ed. by Katharine Rankin, (London: Pluto Press, 2004)

Regmi, D.R., *Medieval Nepal: Vols. I & II*, (New Delhi: Rupa & Co., 2007 [1965])

Reddy, Prabhavati, *Hindu Pilgrimage: shifting patterns of worldview of Srisailam in South India*, (London: Routledge, 2014)

Sahlins, Marshall, *What kinship is-and is not?*, (Chicago: University of Chicago Press, 2013)

Sales, Anne de, 'The Kham Magar country, Nepal: Between ethnic claims and Maoism', trans. by David Gellner, *European Bulletin of Himalayan Research*, 19.2, (2000), 41–71

Salmon, Catherine and Shackleford, Todd (eds.), *Oxford Handbook in Evolutionary Family Psychology*, (Oxford: OUP, 2011)

Samuel, Geoffrey, *Mind, Body and Culture: Anthropology and the Biological Interface*, (Cambridge: CUP, 1990)

Samuel, Geoffrey, 'Paganism and Tibetan Buddhism: Contemporary Western Religions and the Question of Nature' in *Nature Religion Today: Paganism in the Modern World*, ed. by Geoffrey Samuel & R.H. Pearson, (Edinburgh: Edinburgh University Press, 1998)

Samuel, Geoffrey, 'The effectiveness of goddesses, or, how ritual works', *Anthropological Forum*, 11.1 (2001), 73–91

Samuel, Geoffrey, *Tantric Revisionings: New Understandings of Tibetan Buddhism and Tantric Religion*, (Delhi: Motilal Banarsidass, 2005)

Samuel, Geoffrey, *The Origins of Yoga and Tantra: Indic Religions to the Thirteenth Century*, (Cambridge: CUP, 2008)

Sanderson, Alexis, 'Purity and Power among the Brahmins of Kashmir', in *The Category of the Person: Anthropology, Philosophy, History*, ed. by Michael Carrithers et al., (Cambridge: CUP, 1985)

Sanderson, Alexis, 'Śaivism and the Tantric Traditions', in *The World's Religions*, ed. by Stewart Sutherland et al., (London: Routledge, 1988)

Sanderson, Alexis, 'The Doctrine of the Mālinīvijayottaratantra', in *Ritual and Speculation in Early Tantrism: Studies in honor of Andre Padoux*, ed. by T. Goudriaan, (Albany: SUNY Press, 1992)

Sanderson, Alexis, 'The Śaiva Religion among the Khmers (Part I)', *Bulletin de l'École française d'Extrême-Orient*, 90/91 (2003–2004), 349–462

Sanderson, Alexis, 'The Śaiva Age: The Rise and Dominance of Śaivism during the Early Medieval Period', in *The Genesis and Development of Tantrism*, ed. by Shingo Einoo, (University of Tokyo: Institute of Oriental Culture, 2009)

Sarkar, Bihani, *Heroic Shaktism: The Cult of Durga in Ancient Indian Kingship*, (Oxford: OUP, 2017)

Sax, William, *Mountain Goddess: Gender and Politics in a Himalayan Pilgrimage*, (Oxford: OUP, 1991)

Sax, William, *Dancing the Self: Personhood and Performance in the Pandav Lila of Gorwhal*, (New York: OUP, 2002)

Sax, William, 'Agency' in *Theorizing Rituals: Issues, Topics, Approaches, Concepts*, ed. by Jan Kreinath et al., (Leiden: Brill, 2008)

Sax, William, *God of Justice: Ritual Healing and Social Justice in the Central Himalayas*, (Oxford: OUP, 2009)

Schneider, David M. & Gough, Kathleen., eds., *Matrilineal Kinship*, (Berkeley & Los Angeles: University of California Press, 1981)

Schröder, Ulrike, 'Hook-swinging in South India: Negotiating the subaltern space in Colonial society' in *Negotiating Rites*, ed. by Ute Hüske & Frank Neubert, (Oxford: OUP, 2011)

Shakya, Anil M., 'Newar Marriage and Kinship in Kathmandu, Nepal', (Ph.D. diss, Brunel University, 2000)

Shakya, Milan Ratna, *The Cult of Bhairava in Nepal*, (Kolkata: Rupa & Co., 2008)

Sharma, Prayag Raj, *Land, Lineage and State: A Study of Newar Society in Mediaeval Nepal*, (Kathmandu: Himal Books, 2015)

Shaw, Miranda, *Passionate Enlightenment: Women in Tantric Buddhism*, (Princeton: Princeton University Press, 1994)

Shilling, Chris, 'Embodiment, emotions and the foundations of social order: Durkheim's enduring contribution', in *The Cambridge Companion to Durkheim*, ed. by Jeffrey C. Alexander & Philip Smith, (Cambridge: CUP, 2005)

Shneiderman, Sara, *Rituals of Ethnicity: Thangmi Identities between India and Nepal*, (Philadelphia: University of Pennsylvania Press, 2015)

Shrestha, Purusthottam Locan, *Bhaktapur ko Navadurga Gana*, (private copy, VS 2060, [2003])

Silva, Kapila D. & Sinha, Amita, eds., *Cultural Landscapes of South Asia: Studies in Heritage Conservation and Management*, (London: Routledge, 2017)

Slouber, Michael, *Early Tantric Medicine: Snakebite, Mantras, and Healing in the Garuda Tantras*, (New York: OUP, 2017)

Smart, Ninian, *The Phenomenon of Religion*, (London & Basingstoke: Macmillan Press, 1973)

Smith, Brian K. & Doniger, Wendy, 'Sacrifice and Substitution: Ritual Mystification and Mythical Demystification', *Numen*, 36. 2 (1989), 189–224

Smith, Frederick, *The Self Possessed: Deity and Spirit Possession in South Asian Literature and Culture*, (New York: Columbia University Press, 2006)

Srivinas, M.N., 'A Note on Sanskritization and Westernization', *The Far Eastern Quarterly*, 15.4, (1956), 481–496

Staal, Frits, 'The Meaninglessness of Ritual', *Numen*, 26.1 (1979), 2–22

Stokes, Eric, "The return of the peasant to South Asian history", *Journal of South Asian Studies*, 6.1 (1976), 96–111

Swan, Michael & Whitehouse, Harvey et al., 'When Group Membership gets Personal: A Theory of Identity Fusion', *Psychological Review*, 119.3, (2012), 441–456

Tambiah, Stanley, 'The galactic polity in Southeast Asia', *HAU: Journal of Ethnographic Theory* [*HAU Reprints*], 3.3, (2013), 503–534

Tarabout, Gilles, 'Malabar Gods, Nation-building, and World Culture: On Perception of the Local and the Global' in *Globalizing India: Perspectives from Below*, ed. by Jackie Assayag & Chris Fuller (Cambridge: CUP, 2004)

Tarán, Leonardo, *Parmenides: A Text with Translation, Commentary, and Critical Essays*, (Princeton: Princeton University Press, 1964)

Taylor, Charles, *A Secular Age*, (Cambridge, Massachusetts: Harvard University Press, 2007)

Teilhet, Jehanne H., 'The Tradition of Nava Durga in Bhaktapur, Nepal', *Kailash*, 2.6 (1978), 81–98

The Lands Act 2021 [1964], Published: 1/8/2021 (15 November 1964), source: http://admin.theiguides.org/Media/Documents/LandAct1964.pdf [http://www.lawcommission.gov.np]

Toffin, Gerard, *From Kin to Caste: The Role of Guthis in Newar Society and Culture*, (Lalitpur: Himal Association, Social Science Baha Paper, 2005)

Toffin, Gerard, *Newar Society: City, Village and Periphery*, (Nepal: Himal Books, 2007)

Toumela, Raimo, *Social Ontology: Collective Intentionality and Group Agents*, (Oxford: OUP, 2013)

Trautmann, Thomas R., *Dravidian Kinship*, (Cambridge: CUP, 1981)

Trainor, Kevin, ed., *Buddhism: An Illustrated Guide*, (London: Duncan Baird Publishers, 2001)

Trikaripur, Sreekanth A., *Mooring Mirror: A Mooring Mirror between Man and God*, (Kerala: Folklore Akademi, 2014)

Urban, Hugh, *Tantra: Sex, Secrecy, Politics, and Power in the Study of Religion*, (California: University of California Press, 2003)

Urban, Hugh, *The Power of Tantra: Religion, Sexuality, and the Politics of South Asian Studies*, (London: I.B. Taurus, 2010)

Urban, Hugh, 'The Womb of Tantra: Goddesses, Tribals, and Kings in Assam', *Journal of Hindu Studies*, 4.3 (2011), 231–247

Unni, N.P., *Tantric Literature of Kerala*, (Delhi: Bharatiya Books, 2006)

Vadakkiniyil, Dinesan, 'Images of Transgression: *Teyyam* in Malabar', *Social Analysis*, 54.2 (Summer 2010), 130–150

Valdés, Nelson P., 'The Revolutionary and Political Content of Fidel Castro's Charismatic Authority' in *A Contemporary Cuba Reader: Reinventing the Revolution*, ed. by Philip Brenner et al., (Lanham: Rowman & Littlefield Publishers Inc, 2008)

Vergati, Anne, *Gods, men, and territory: Society and Culture in Kathmandu Valley*, (Delhi: Manohar Publishers, 2002)

Visuvalingam, Sunthar, 'Transgressive Sacrality in the Hindu Tradition' in *Antonio de Nicolas: Poet of Eternal Return*, ed. by Christopher Chapple, (Ahmedabad: Sriyogi Publishers, 2017)

Waghorne, Joanne & Cutler, Norman, eds., *Gods of Flesh, Gods of Stone: The Embodiment of Divinity in India*, (Chambersberg: Anima Books, 1996)

Weber, Max, *The Protestant Ethic and the Spirit of Capitalism*, (London & New York: Routledge Classics, 2001 [1930])

Weber, Max, *The Theory of Social and Economic Organization*, (New York: The Free Press, 1947)

Wernicke-Olesen, Bjarne, ed., *Goddess Traditions in Tantric Hinduism: History, Practice, and Doctrine*, (London: Routledge, 2016)

White, David Gordon, *The Alchemical Body: Siddha Traditions in Medieval India*, (Chicago: University of Chicago Press, 1996)

White, David Gordon, ed., *Tantra in Practice*, (Princeton: Princeton University Press, 2000)

Whitehouse, Harvey & Lanham, Jonathan, 'The Ties that Bind Us: Ritual, Fusion, and Identification', *Current Anthropology*, 55.6, (December 2014), 674–695

Wyman, Alex, 'Totemic beliefs in the Buddhist Tantras', *History of Religions*, 1.1 (1961), 81–94

Zarrilli, Phillip, *When the body becomes all eyes: Paradigms, Discourses, and Practices of Power in Kalaripayyattu*, (Delhi: OUP, 1998)

Zaroff, Roman, 'Aśvamedha—A Vedic Horse Sacrifice', *Studia Mythologica Slavica*, 8 (2005), 75–86

Zharkevich, Ina, 'De-mythologizing 'the Village of Resistance': How rebellious were the peasants in the Maoist base area of Nepal?', *Dialectical Anthropology*, 59.4 (December 2015), 353–379

Zharkevich, Ina, "'When Gods Return to their Homeland in the Himalayas': Maoism, Religion, and Change in the Model Village of Thabang, Mid-Western Nepal", in *Religion, Secularism, and Ethnicity in Contemporary Nepal*, ed. by David Gellner et al., (Oxford: OUP, 2016)

Zotter, Astrid, 'State Rituals in a Secular State?' in *Religion, Secularism, and Ethnicity in Contemporary Nepal*, ed. by David Gellner, (Oxford: OUP, 2016)

Newspaper Articles

'When the gods come down', *The Hindu*, (5th November 2011)

'Theyyam binds candidates together at Pariyaram', *The Hindu*, (18th October 2015)

'NWPP Chair blames India for industry collapse in Nepal', *The Himalayan Times*, (10th March 2016), https://thehimalayantimes.com/kathmandu/nwpp-chair-blames-india-industry-collapse-nepal/

'Bhaktapur's Dear Leader', *Nepali Times*, (29th April–5th May 2016) http://archive.nepalitimes.com/article/nation/Bhaktapur-dear-leader,3010

'Bedridden Gods: A Tale of Suresh Peruvannan', *The Times of India*, (13th March 2017) https://timesofindia.indiatimes.com/city/kozhikode/bedridden-gods-a-tale-titled-sumesh/articleshow/57610205.cms

'Sabarimala Case: How the deification of man affected woman', *Qrius*, (28th August 2018), https://qrius.com/deification-of-man-women-sabarimala-case/

'Two women below 50 claim they entered Kerala's Sabarimala temple', *The Times of India*, (2nd January 2019), https://timesofindia.indiatimes.com/india/two-women-below-50-claim-they-entered-keralas-sabarimala-temple/articleshow/67343779.cms

Filmography

Teyyam: The Annual Visit of the God Vishnumurti, dir. by Erik de Maaker, (Department of Visual Ethnography, Leiden University: 57 min, 1998)

Index

Any page number in bold refers to a sub-section of the book which specifically addresses the term or name.

Abraham, Janaki 126
Abhiśēkham (image-bathing ceremony) 70
Adalaya Panam see Donations
Aniyara (preparatory hut) 68–69, 128, 213
Anjipali (five-circle make-up) 178
'Akash' 17, 136–138, 179
Alcohol 2, 26, 33, 67, 76, 149, 165
  rice-wine 105, 156
  toddy 76, 139, 142
Althusser, Louis 241, 254
Amazzone, Laura 189
Ancestors 2, 4, 6, 16–18, 22, 28, 38–39, 46, 50, 59, **60–62**, 65, 71, 76, 81, 86, 91, 123
  as crows 28, 39, 127
  feeding of 28, 127, 216
  power of 4, 63, 68, 205
Anthropology **9–10**
Anthropologically informed religious studies **8–9**, 11
Apotropaic 98, 109, 151, **181**, 190, 194, **198**
Appadurai, Arjun 3n9, 215–216
Arafath, Yasser 131–132, 138, 171, 181
Asad, Talal 8
Ascetics
  Nāth 6, 33, 46–47, 83, 95, 148, **168–171**, 173, 183, 196, **198–200**
  warrior 47
Āsribad see Blessings
Aṣṭamatṛkā see Goddess-clan
Aśvamedha (horse sacrifice) 26–27, 30
Ātma punegu see Curses
Auspiciousness 4–5, 20, 82, 150
Avarṇa see Caste
Ayyappan (god) 42

'Babita' 145
Bali see Sacrifice
Barāhī (goddess) *see* Varāhī
Bayly, Susan 43, 88
Bhadrakālī (goddess) 1n1, 62, 67, 101, 123n1, 168, 172–174, 181, 206–207, 225
Bhagvān bhitramā ('god-within') 54, 111, 186, 197
Bhairava 2, 22, 32, **33–34**, **37–38**, 45, 47, 88, 96, 99, 102, 109–110, 112, 124, 154, 157, 176, 187, 190, 200, **222–223**, 224, 252
Bhaktapur
  city 13, 55, **95–96**, 117, 195–196, 217, 229
  shrines 13–14, 38, 55, **96–98**, 104–105, 107–108, 111, 149, 151–152, 156, 185, 192–194, 218, 225
  peripheries 2, 21, 96, 101
Bhoj (ritual feast) 13–14, 103, 226
Bhuta, rituals of 60n2
Biernacki, Loriliai 164
Bijukchhe, Narayan Man 117, 244, 248, 256–257
BJP (Bharatiya Janata Party) 42, 82, 90–91, 124
Blessings 36, 60, 68, 71, 77–78, 91, 97, 109, 131, 194
Bloch, Maurice 12, 143
Blood 2–4, 13, 19–21, 26, 31, 33, 36–37, 41–42, 43, 54, 60, 63, 67, 71, 75–77, 88, 95, 96–97, **104–106**, 109, 118, 125, 139, 146, 150, 154, 165, 179, 185, 187, 189, 193, 195, **202–228**, 232, 240–241, 243, 260, 264
Bouillier, Véronique 183
Brahmayāmala 54, 172, 177, 183, 196–197, 208 *see also* Texts
Brahmāyānī 1n1, 1n2, 101, 104–106, 116, 153, 155, 166n5, 192–193, 221
Bricolage webs of ritual knowledge 23, 33, 46–47, 49, 56, 84, 95, 163–164, 181, 183, 200–201, 258, 262, 264
Brooks, Douglas 2, 55n181
Buddhism
  festivals of 95
  Newar 23, 55, 94–96, 114, 184–186, 230n6
  Theravāda 34–35, 93, 202
Bwakṣi (witches) *see* Witchcraft

Caldwell, Sarah 41, 214
Caste 4, 18–19, 21–22, 24–25, 35, 43–46, 49, 62, 65–66, 75, 79, 88, **89–90**, 93, 96, 98,

112, **113–115**, 118, 124, 129, 134–136, 146, 160, 184, 221–223, 224, 229–230, 232–233, 235, 241–242, 248, 252, 256, 260, 265
Cēra, dynasty of 125, **168–169**, 234
Cerujanman (Teyyam troupe rights) 133, 135, 239–240
Cerulli, Anthony 179
Chandra, T.V. 79
Charisma 15, 213, 231
Chaturvedi, Rudi 12, 232
Child, Louise 143, 198
Choree puja (Navadurgā's monthly ceremony) 153–154
Citrakār (Mask-making caste in Bhaktapur) 102–103, 114, **155–156**, 190
Clan *see* Caste
Communism
 Bhaktapur **117–119**, 224, **246–254**
 Cuba 230–231
 Kerala 42, 91–92, 135, **232–241**
 North Korea 117, 250, 250n70
Cōṭṭa 140, 210 *see also* Flames
Cōyi 170–171
Cox, Whitney 176–177
CPI(M) (Communist Party of India, Marxist) 42, 91–92, 135, **232–241**
Cremains 65, 71, 207
Crows 28, 39, 127 *see also* Ancestors
Culture, definition of 8
Curses 21, 116, 155, 157, 159, 181, 198, 210, 220, 260

Daitya (demonic being) 39, 96, 102, 189–190, 203, 221
Dākinīs 33–34
Dakṣinācārya (right-handed Tantra) *see* Tantra (Keralan dualism)
Dancer-mediums
 Navadurgā 45, 98–102, 144–160, 195–200, 222–228, 253–254, 263–264
 Teyyāṭṭam 55, 59–60, 62–63, 66–68, 74, 84–85, 90, 127–144, 174–180, 204–214, 240–244, 263–264
Dashain festival *see* Rituals (autumnal)
Davies, Charlotte 9
Deities
 ancestral 1–4, 12, 16–17, 18, 22, 28, 38–39, 46, 50, 59–61, 63, 65, 71, 76–77, 81–82, 86, 91, 110–111, 117, 123–124, 128, 131, 133, 136, 140, 160–161, 165, 182, 203, 252–253, 257, 263, 264
 martial 22, 32, 43–44, 49, 54, 81–82, 85, 98, 131, 182, 189, 191–192, 207–208, 209–210, 212, 215
 goddesses 1–4, 19, 22, 33, 36–38, 41, 54, 59, 71, 77, 91, **96–98**, 102, 104–106, 110, 117, 124–125, 139, 143, 149, 151, 153, 156–157, 159–160, 162, 163–164, 178, 181, 185–186, **187–190**, 192, **193–195**, 203, 205, 207, 213, 220–221, 255, 263
Deleuze, Gilles 23
De Maaker, Erik 77–78
Derrida, Jacques 177
Dharma 25
Dhaū-baji (rice-curd) 157, 223
'Dinesh' 14–15, 115, 145, 253
Dirks, Nicholas B. 44–45, 229
Dogs 39, 152–153
Donations 20, 68, 77, 118, 128, 133, 135, 145, **146–147**
Doniger, Wendy 24, 27
Douglas, Mary 217
Dravidian 65, **80–81**, 91, 165, 168, 180, **181–183**
Dugu dyo (lineage deity) 115, 216, 218
Dugu puja (lineage worship) 110, 216, 218
Dumont, Louis 44–45, 166, 187
Durgā 37–38, 55, 96, 98, 112, 172–173, 176n44
Durkheim, Emile 5, 8, 11–12, 15, 33n97, 74, 76, 143, 162, 198, 212–213, 217, 229, 233, 259
Dupuche, John 48
Dyczkowski, Mark 21, 38, 39n121, 186, 227, 248
Dyo bokegu 106, **156–159**, 222–223
Dyo-chen see Temples

Engels, Fredrich 232
Epilepsy, healing of 135
Ethnography 5, 7, 9–10, 11, 19, 123, 164, 184, 186, 218

Fertility 1, 26, 37, 48, 50, 76, 81, 100–101, 110, 112, 131, 140, 149, 157, 160–161, 163, **171–172**, 181, 196, 262

Festivals 1–3, 9, 13–15, 21, 33, 46, 93, 95, 98, 102, 104–105, 109–110, 113, 115–116, 117, 127–128, 137, 139, 147, 149, **174–175**, 188–189, 192–193, 196, 199, 203, 208, 218, 224, 233, 252, 255
Fieldwork 2, 5, 7, 9, 11, **12–18**, 41, 82, 99, 124, 199, 253
Fisher, Elaine 173
Flames 21, 59–60, 62, 70–71, 86, 139–140, 142, 154, 156, 240–241
Flood, Gavin 2, 29, 41–42, 143n34, 164, 177, 216–217
Food *see Dhaū-baji*; Rice; Sacrifice
Forests 25, 60, 98, 149, 196, 210, 212, 234 *see also* Groves
Fortes, Meyer 145
Foucault, Michel 10
Freeman, John R. 6, 12, 21, 51, 62, 68–69, 73–74, 76–77, 81–83, 128, 142, 162, 166–167, 170, 174, 176, 178, 181–183, 206–207, 209, 210, 212, 214, 234, 242
Fuller, Chris 12, 66, 126

Gabriel, Theodore 12, 68n16, 74, 75, 91, 124, 173
Gaṇa (Navadurgā medium-troupe) *see* Dancer-mediums
Gaṇeśa 2, 37–39, 96, 100–101, 104, 111, 154, 166, 176, 223
Geertz, Clifford 8–9, 12, 232, 246, 260
Gellner, David 12–13, 42n130, 94–95, 111, 185, 202, 231
Ghimire, Pustak 24, 254
Gibson, Ian 12, 93, 117–118, 232, 248–249, 251
Girard, Rene 208–209
God-masks 1, 97, 102–103, 106, 113, 154, **155–156**
Goddess-clan 1–4, 19, 22, 33, 36–38, 41, 54, 59, 71, 77, 91, **96–98**, 102, 104–106, 110, 117, 124–125, 139, 143, 149, 151, 153, 156–157, 159–160, 162, 163–164, 178, 181, 185–186, **187–190**, 192, **193–195**, 203, 205, 207, 213, 220–221, 255, 263
Goṭamangal (Newar festival in Bhaktapur) 99, **102–103**, 110, 113, 149, 155, 196
Gough, Kathleen 12, 127
Grahn, Judith 41
Gramsci, Antonio 249, 258
Greenwold, Stephen 45
Grieve, Gregory 12, 93, 111, 112n44, 203, 223, 227, 250, 256
Groves
Teyyam 17, 39, 55, 59–60, 61–63, 65, 67, 79, 82, 86, 90, 125, 127–129, 130–133, 136–137, 140, 142, 165–166, 168, 171, 174, 183, 205–206, 217, 233–234, 241, 244
Gupta empire **28–29**, 33, 46, 83, 168–169, 185, 201
Gutschow, Niels 154n51
Guṭhi (Newar inter-caste groups) 15, 18, **115–117**, 146–147, 187, 221, 233, 257, 261

Hacchettu, Krishna 12, 118
Handelman, Don 37n113
Hanumān 111, 138
Hart, George 44
Hatley, Shaman 196
Hausner, Sondra 22, 29, 94
Heesterman, J.C. 29–31, 43
Heidegger, Martin 228
Hocart, Maurice 4, 45
Huber, Toni 144
Hubert, Henri 202, 204, 214

Idealism 18, 30, 48
Illam see Lineage
Inden, Ronald B. 25, 74n41
Indra 24, 26, 192
Indra Jātrā (Newar festival) 149n48, 252
Indrayānī (goddess) 101, 159, 192, 225

Jan Andolan (Nepal's People's Movement) 246
Janmi ('landlord') 134
Jātrā ('festival') 13, 93, 95, 109, 149, 190, 218, 252 *see also* Festivals
Jeffrey, Robin 12, 229, 235–236, 238–239

Kaḷam 206–207, 212 *see also Maṇḍala*
Kalaripayāṭṭu (Keralan martial art) 47, 55, 60, 131, 136, 178
Kalivụ 59, 74, 82, 168, 181, 212–213 *see also Śakti*
Kannerụ ('evil eye') 181
Kannur 9, 16–18, 55, 59–60, 66–67, 80, 85–86, 89–90, 128, 130, 136–137, 139, 166, 170, 179, 181, 236, 240, 263

Kārṇavan (household elder) 17, 65, 126–127, 133, 139, 239
Karnataka 60n2, 165–166, 182
Kathmandu 6, 12, 38, 93–94, 96, 106, 108, 115–116, 147–148, 152–153, 156, 184–186, 192n87, 216, 252, 262
Kāvu see Temples
Keay, John 29
Khamei (sacrificial buffalo) 103–105, 192–193, 221
Khwōpa see God-masks
Kinship
  Consanguineal 18, 20, 123
  Endogamy 3n8, 5, 20, 65, 145–146
  Fictive 10, 15, 19–20, 46, 54, 75, 116, 232, 239–240, 244, 257, 260
  Matrilineal *see* Matrilineality
  Patrilineal *see* Patrilineality
  Ritual 3, 15, 19, 41, 65, 74–75, 88, 109, 112, 117, 123, 143, 157, 160, 203, 228, 231–232, 258
King, Richard 9
Kōlatiris, medieval kings of Northern Kerala 36, 43–44, 62, 85, 89, 136, 166–169
Komath, Rajesh 134–135, 138
Kōlakkaran (Teyyam dancer-mediums) *see* Dancer-mediums
Kōmamram (Teyyam priests) *see* Priests
Kōlattanādu (Medieval kingdom of North Kerala) 43, 62, 169
Kottakkunnummal, Manaf 75
'Krishna' 15, 111, 119, 145, 149, 152, 161, 197, 253

Lalitpur 12–13, 94–95, 185, 190, 223
Land Act, 1964 246–247
Land-tracts 65, 207, 234
Landlords 88, 134–135, 210, 234, 238, 241, 243, 247, 265
Lapte (Newari plate) 100, 154, 156, 226
Lāsa kūsa (ablution) 102, 105, 152
Laterite 16–17, 59
Laukika (worldly existence) 26, 30
Lewis, Todd 7n23, 35, 113n47
Lewis, I.M. 52
Lévi, Sylvain 93
Lévi-Strauss, Claude 23
Levy, Robert 12, 93, 105, 108, 111, 112, 113, 187, 200, 221
Lidke, Jeffrey S. 6, 191
Lineage 1–3, 14, 17, 19, 21–22, 28, 31–32, 36, 42, 60, 65–66, 85, 97, 112–113, 115–116, 126, 129–130, 136–137, 166, 170, 172, 183, 190, 206, 210, 216–217, 218, 220–222, 239, 244
Lorenzen, David N. 18n36, 55, 88, 170

Macro-clan 3n8, 4, 20, 22, 24, 38, 40, 41, 66, 80, 109, 117, 119, 125, 127, 143–144, 160–161, 188–189, 200, 204, 208, 217, 223–224, 232, 260, 262, 264
Mādāyi Kāvu 62, 134, 165, 176
Mahākālī (goddess) 1n1, 96, 100, 109, 112, 154, 220, 226
Mahālakṣmī 100, 152, 153–154, 194, 198, 225–226 *see also* Sīphā dyo
Maheśvarī (goddess) 1n1, 101, 226
Mahiśaṣura ('buffalo-demon') 21, 100, 104, 112–113, 172, 189, 192, 208, 221
Mailaparambil, Binu J. 43–44, 80n63
Malagodi, Mara 245
Malamoud, Charles 27
Malik, Aditya 51
Mallas, medieval kings of Newari kingdoms 4, 32, 36, 45, 97, 113, 150, 160, 188, 190–192, 194–196, 199, 252, 262
Malayalam 7, 16–17, 50, 59, 63, 81, 140, 170, 176, 184, 236
Maṇḍala 4, 6, 40–41, 59, 83, 96, 151, 154, 189, 206
  kalam (Kerala) 206–207, 212
  Śrīcakra 6
Mantra 4, 4n14, 7, 32, 68, 84–85, 154, 167, 178–179, 181, 188
Mantramārga 33, 110
Mannathukkaren, Nissim 231
Mansueto, Anthony 258
Māppila-Muslims 80–82, 125, 184, 235 *see also* Sufi
Marglin, Frédérique A. 3–4
Marriott, McKim 25
Marx, Karl 5, 12, 125, 230, 232–233, 236, 241, 243
Materialism 16, 18, 30, 30n84
Matrilineality 18, 65–66, 125–126, 131, 229, 235
Mauss, Marcel 12, 144, 161, 202–203, 204–205, 214–215
McDaniel, June 49–50

Menon, A. Sreedhara 170, 172
Menon, Dilip 12, 238–239, 240–241, 244
Menstrual synchrony 4, 20–21, 139, 263
Michaels, Axel 6, 32, 218, 220, 228
Mohani festival *see* Rituals (autumnal)
Mohani tikā 221
Monier-Williams, M. 1n3
Monsoon 3, 37–38, 54, 60n1, 97, 98–99, 102, 109, 188
Moreno, Manuel 53
Morūmakkathīyam see Matrilineality
Mukhameẓultu ('face-writing') 178
Muller-Ortega, Paul E. 85
Mūdras (ritual hand gestures) 148, 196
Murti (god-image) 54, 116, 218
Mūttappan (god) 16, 124, 137, 168, 173, 209–210, 232, 236, 246
Myers, B.R. 250n70

nāḍī (nodes of subtle body) 32, 52, 70–71
Nākiṅ (female priestess of the Navadurgā troupe) 99, 102–103, 105, 151–152, 153–154
Nambiar, Balan 73n30, 89n82, 216
Nambutiri Brahmins 33, 35, 62, 82, 89, 137, 165–166, 168, 170, 174–175, 234
Nāndakam see Swords
Nāth 6, 33, 46–47, 55, 83, 95, 102, 148, 168–171, 173, 183, 196, 199–200, 262
Nationalism 118, 118n62, 250–251, 258
Navagraha (nine planets) 150
Nāyar 21, 62, 82, 88, 90, 126–127
Nāyo (elder/leader of the Navadurgā troupe) 99, 104, 151–153, 197
Newari language 7, 13–14, 19, 45, 50, 93–94
Nicholas, Ralph W. 28
Nityāṣodśikārṇava 6, 173, 199, 262 *see also* Texts
Non-dualism 34, 55, 81–82, 85, 111, 165
Nossiter, T.J. 234–235, 236
NWPP 15, 22, 112–113, 117–119, 224–225, 232, 245–257
Nya lakegu (fish-catching performance) 14, 101, 157–158, 199

Odisha
  Jagannātha, temple of 3–4
Osella, Filippo & Caroline 12, 63, 65
Owens, Bruce McCoy 199

Paddhati (ritual manual) 85, 163, 179, 184, 186, 201, 209, 262n3 *see also* Texts
Padoux, André 23, 32, 36, 46–47, 49
Parish, Steven 12, 113, 145–146, 162, 192
Parsons, Talcott 15
Pariyāram Kāvụ 129, 181
Paśupatināth temple 6, 108, 199
Patrilineality 125, 136, 169
Patton, Kimberley 215–216, 220
Payyanad, Raghavan 80
Pinch, William R. 47
Pitṛ see Ancestors
Platvoet, Jan 50
Politics
  Revolutionary 24, 229, 231, 235–236, 238–239, 249, 251, 256, 265
Pradhan, Rajendra 19
Prāṇa ('life-breath') 32, 139–140, 178
Priests
  Karmācārya (Tantric priests in Bhaktapur) 15, 96, 105, 106, 114, 151, 186–187, 196
  Nambūtiri Brahmins (Kerala) 33, 35, 62, 82, 89, 137, 165–166, 168, 170, 174–175, 234
  Kōmamram (Teyyāṭṭam priests) 59, 61–63, 70, 75, 77, 139, 174, 204
  Pidarār (sacrificial priests in North Kerala) 165–166, 174, 176
Purāṇas 28
purity-pollution dichotomy 3–4, 5, 22, 82
Pyākhaṇ ('dance') *see* Ritual

Qirko, Hector N. 20
Quigley, Declan 45, 113

Raheja, Gloria G. 20–21, 52
Raj, Yogesh 251
Rankin, Katharine 145, 233
Regmi, D.R. 6, 185, 188, 196
Religion, definition of 8
Rice
  Rice-curd 157, 223
  rice grains 71, 77, 102, 106, 129, 131, 139, 204–205, 206, 209, 216
Ritual
  autumnal 9, 13–14, 98, 104–105, 153, 189, 190–191, 218
  liturgical 4

lineage deity (*dugu puja*) 216
sacrificial 20, 24, 26, 31, 43, 68, 77, 105, 154, 166, 202–228
RSS 239, 244, 263

Sabarimala 42
Sacrifice 20, 24, 26, 31, 43, 68, 77, 105, 154, 166, 202–228
Sahlins, Marshall 19, 125
Śaiva 28, 33–34, 46–47, 48, 55, 83, 110, 140, 170–173, 196, 201, 264
Śiva 6, 32–33, 53, 55, 83, 88, 92, 101–102, 129, 134, 150, 155–156, 168, 172, 176, 190, 210, 242
Śiva-margi 95 *see also Śaiva*
Śakti (life-force) 2–5, 18, 19, 31–32, 34, 37, 51, 52, 54, 70–71, 74, 82–83, 97, 102, 104, 111–113, 123, 133, 137, 150, 156, 161, 168, 175, 181, 189, 196–197, 203, 204, 205, 206, 213, 217, 218, 220, 228, 253, 263
Śakti-pīthā (shrine in Bhaktapur) 13, 38, 96, 105, 156, 185
Sales, Anne de 230
Sambandam (matrilineal marriage) 65, 125–126, 136
Samuel, Geoffrey 32, 33–34, 35, 41, 171
Sanderson, Alexis 18n36, 31, 33–34, 35, 53, 55, 110, 170, 172, 182, 213, 262n3
Śaṇkara 86, 88, 134, 182, 235, 242–243
Sarkar, Bihani 33, 37, 98, 163, 215
Sax, William 2n5, 47, 48, 74, 124, 180
Śeṣasamuccaya 176 *see also* Texts
Schröder, Ulrike 86
Self-reflexive affect 202–228
Shakya, Anil M. 116–117
Shakya, Milan Ratna 200
Sharma, Prayag Raj 184
Shaw, Miranda 34
Shneiderman, Sara 20–21, 246, 255
Shrestha, Purusthottam Locan 97
Siphā dyo (goddess) 100, 152, 153–154, 194, 198, 225–226
Smart, Ninian 8
spiraling
web-like ritual network 18–22, 23, 40, 46, 83, 194, 256, 258, 261–263
Śraddha see Ancestors
Srivinas, M.N. 46, 48
Staal, Frits 26–27
Stokes, Eric 235
Śuddhi (purification rite) 209
Sufi 47–48, 55, 181
Sungur lakhatne (pig sacrifice) 108–109, 222
Suvarṇa 62, 66, 89, 90, 167
Swords 34, 59, 60, 67, 71, 75, 82, 140, 143, 151, 209
Swiddening 75, 210, 212, 215, 234, 244

Tambiah, Stanley 40
Tantra
in Bengal 2, 196
Keralan dualism 33, 165, 169
Kashmir Śaivism 83, 140, 170, 173, 184, 232
Newar Tantra 151, 184–186, 196
Practices 33, 165, 185, 186
Worldview 31–32, 37–39
Tantrasamuccaya 176 *see also* Texts
Tantricization 46
Tarvād (household) 65, 131
Teilhet, Jehanne H. 12, 113
Temples
Navadurgā *dyo-chen* (Bhaktapur) 96, 98, 103, 124, 153–154
Tantric (Kerala) 6, 52, 137, 174–175, 176
Nambutiri Brahmin 173–175
Teyyam 82, 89, 166
Territory 13, 18, 36, 63, 65, 73–74, 97, 111, 116, 125, 131, 150, 203, 222, 224, 260
Texts
somatic textuality 84–85, 111, 163–164, 177, 195–196, 200–201
liturgical manuals 163, 175–176, 177–178, 181, 184, 186, 201, 264
Toffin, Gerard 12, 99, 117, 146, 157, 252
Trautmann, Thomas R. 65–66
Trikaripur, Sreekanth A. 18

'Ujesh' 14–15, 54, 95–97, 99–100, 102, 104–105, 109, 116, 119, 124, 144, 146, 148, 149, 151, 153, 155, 157, 159, 179, 186, 193, 199, 218, 220–221, 225, 253–254
Upanayana (sacred thread ceremony) 24
Upaniṣads 25, 30, 35
Urban, Hugh 45, 54

Vadakkiniyil, Dinesan 91–92
Valdés, Nelson P. 231

Vāmācāra (left-handed Tantra) 33
Varāhī (goddess) 100
Varṇāśramadharma 25, 29
Vedic
  Sacrifice 26–28
  Religion 24–28
  social structure 24–26
Visuvalingam, Sunthar 26
Vṛata (pre-ritual seclusion) 67, 128, 149, 177

Warriors 3, 28, 38, 47, 65–66, 75, 81, 91, 131, 171, 190, 204, 234, 244, 263
Wayanād Kuḻīvan (god) 138, 210–212
Webs 260–261
Weber, Max 12, 22, 210, 231, 260
White, David Gordon 40–41
Witchcraft 154–155, 198–199

Yoginīs 36–37, 53, 171–172, 177, 197

Zarrilli, Phillip 55, 131, 178–179
Zaroff, Roman 27
Zharkevich, Ina 254–255
Zotter, Astrid 151

Printed in the United States
By Bookmasters